The
EARTH
Beneath My Feet

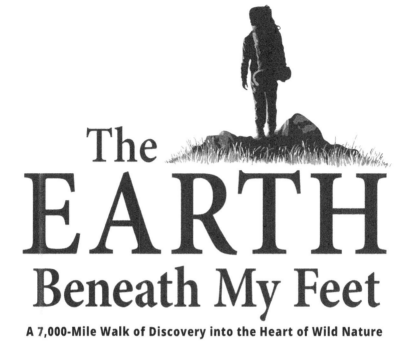

The
EARTH
Beneath My Feet

A 7,000-Mile Walk of Discovery into the Heart of Wild Nature

ANDREW TERRILL

Enchanted
RockPress

Golden, Colorado

DEDICATION

To my parents, Valerie and Ken—Base Camp,
for a lifetime of unwavering support.

And to my wife Joan,
for her patience and love, and for
taking me on the greatest journey of all.

CONTENTS

AUTHOR'S NOTE

The Earth Beneath My Feet is the first of two books that describe a 7,000-mile walk across Europe. The second book, *On Sacred Ground*, concludes this journey.

All the events within this book occurred, but to preserve the privacy of individuals and to improve the clarity of storytelling some names and locations have been changed. A handful of locations are composites and won't be found on any map. However, this remains a true story, written to accurately represent the journey that took place.

Readers should note that this book is written in British English, and also that imperial units of measurement are used: miles for distance, feet for altitude, Fahrenheit for temperature. Metric units are occasionally given, such as within the maps, but for readers who struggle with miles and feet, please take heart: as will hopefully become clear, the 'numbers' aren't the point.

PROLOGUE: AN ALPINE BOUNCE

The Bernese Oberland, Switzerland

ON THE SECOND day of June, 1993, I fell down a mountain. It was a spectacularly unpleasant thing to do. As an experience it isn't something I'd recommend, but for the way it changed my approach to life I remain eternally grateful.

The accident took place in the Bernese Oberland, a mountain range on the northern edge of the Swiss Alps. Rearing 10,000 feet from gentler country, the range forms a startling wall of snow, rock and ice. In the Oberland there are sharp pointed peaks, mighty glaciers, sheer-sided chasms, and soaring rock precipices. There are shadowy forests and sunlit meadows, sparkling rivers and deep blue lakes. The Oberland is a landscape as unlike my suburban home as any place could be, and that was why I went.

At twenty-three, I lived for mountains, and for long journeys on foot through them. Ordinary life didn't compare. How could waking indoors in the same bedroom each morning compare with waking in a tent somewhere new and wild? How could catching the same cattle-truck commuter train each day compare with striding off alone into the wilderness? How could the same view through the same office window compare with a panorama never before seen from a summit never before visited? Ordinary life was predictable, comfortable, limited by rules; mountain life was mysterious, challenging, unshackled. London was where I lived, but the high places were where I went *to live*. In the mountains life could be everything I felt, deep down, it was supposed to be all the time, and so I escaped to them as often as work allowed.

The plan for this escape was to walk for seven days beneath the Oberland's highest peaks, crossing several passes, camping high and wild. In summer thousands of hikers followed the route I'd chosen, but I wasn't going in summer. I wanted to escape my own species and choose my own path. Most of all I wanted adventure—an experience not possible for me following a crowd.

To begin with, the journey was exactly what I wanted: uncluttered, wild and free. For three idyllic days I wandered through wildflower meadows and forests scented with pine, and slept in glorious solitude beneath glacier-capped peaks. But on the third night a storm erupted with idyll-shattering violence: clouds clashed, lightning flashed, and rain pummelled my tiny one-man tent. Sleep was impossible. All I could do was cower and hope for the best. Some mountain nights last longer than others, and that night lasted longer than most.

Weary from it, I slept later than planned the following morning and didn't strike camp until noon. Ahead were the highest miles of the week's route: the lofty Hohtürli Pass, the kind of Big Mountain Pass one shouldn't treat lightly. Its crossing demands a good night's sleep, an early start, a full day's labour, and perfect conditions underfoot. I had none of these things.

I set out beneath a fierce sun and sweat came streaming within minutes. Tatters of cloud hung about the walls and glaciers of surrounding mountains, revealing and then hiding the scenery I'd come so far to see. The summits weren't often in view, but when they appeared they were impossibly white and pristine, more like fantasy peaks than real mountains. Such glaciated giants were clearly beyond my solitary reach, but I still wondered which I could climb. I ached to stand upon them.

Although it was the first day of June, snow still lay deep above 6,000 feet. The snow was why I was here and other hikers weren't. It made progress harder, the high places higher, the wild places wilder, which was how I wanted it. Of course, it might also make the pass impassable, but not knowing the outcome wasn't a bad thing.

Progress above snowline was slow. I wallowed, sunk, gasped. My shirt clung to my back and my legs quivered. Thoughts weren't focused on the banalities and stresses of everyday existence, on bills unpaid, chores not yet

Sunset in the Bernese Oberland, Switzerland, June 1, 1993.

done, on other people and the demands they made. Instead, my thoughts were fixed entirely on the present moment, on the sensations of it: the burning sun on the back of my neck, the sugary taste of snow scooped into my mouth, the heaviness of legs pushed to their limit. This wasn't like my job, repetitive and tedious; or like my home life, easy and bland; this was new, engrossing, difficult, thrilling. I dug a thigh-deep trench-trail upwards through unbroken snow and celebrated every challenging step.

Hours passed. Rising heat gnawed at the snow, softening it horribly. Slowly, pleasure in the climb faded and concerns grew. Each step triggered small snow slides that accelerated towards the valley thousands of feet below. The situation soon seemed precarious: could the entire slope give way? It felt possible, and I paused many times, debating the wisdom of pushing on, but each time—rightly or wrongly—the desire to achieve what I'd set out to achieve kept me climbing. Soon, all I could think about was reaching the pass and descending safely from it. I could only hope the way down was going to be easier than the way up.

My relief at the top felt overwhelming, but it lasted seconds only, vanishing when I looked down the far side. The route fell away with intimidating steepness. It was so steep I couldn't even see the first 500 feet. In summer, wooden steps and a rope handrail eased passage, but they were buried beneath snow. One look down was enough to confirm I wasn't going that way—not with the snow so unstable. But neither could I safely head back the way I'd come.

Fortunately, this was Switzerland, not some vast northern wilderness. Standing a couple of hundred feet above the pass was an Alpine refuge, the Blüemlisalphütte. Although it wasn't yet open for the summer it still offered basic shelter: a small unlocked winter room. I settled upon a new plan: I'd sleep there and tackle the descent the next morning when, hopefully, the snow would have frozen hard. In the meantime, I had my own magical kingdom to enjoy up there at 10,000 feet. By sunset, a fire-tinged cloud sea stretched away to the horizon with mountains breaking through like islands. Later, a full moon washed the glaciers with silver light, and once the clouds had dispersed village lights shone far below, flickering in the dark like distant constellations. It was almost worth what followed, seeing such extraordinary sights, feeling such extraordinary isolation.

I was underway the next morning long before first light hit the highest tops. A hard frost had killed off any avalanche risk, but as I picked my way back to the pass my stomach twisted with anxiety. I wasn't sure I was doing the right thing.

I held an ice axe in one hand but didn't strap on crampons. Although the snow had frozen hard, a line of bucket-sized steps led downwards; reassuring evidence that others had recently accomplished what I was now setting out to attempt. Crampons can be awkward in a tight space. They can catch and trip, and with boot-sized holes for my feet I judged they'd be more hindrance than help. Afterwards, of course, I wondered: if I'd worn them would I have fallen? Would my entire life have been different?

I peered over the crest and began down, facing into the mountain. I moved each foot with great deliberateness, and then each hand, holding the axe firmly, digging it into the snow, loving its bite. At my heels the slope fell away in great leaps and bounds, levelling off briefly 1,500 feet below like an oversized ski-jump before plunging into a void. How I wished my pack weighed less than 60 pounds; I could feel it tugging me backwards. And how I wished I were already down. I'd travelled to the Alps for adventure, but not *this* much adventure.

And then it happened.

From a small crag overhead came the clatter of falling stones. Instinctively, I looked up, but too swiftly; my feet slipped, I lost balance, and never got to see if the stones posed a threat. I landed on my back and momentum flipped me onto my front. Urgently, I stabbed my axe into iron-hard snow, throwing the weight of my shoulder onto it just the way I'd practised many times, but hit a bump at exactly the wrong moment and the axe flew from my hands. I saw it all in fine detail: the axe embedded in ice above me, the tiny scratches on its shaft, the hopeless reach of my fingers. I had time to think *not good*—an understatement—and then I was off.

It is true what they say: in such situations time slows. No, more than that: it stops, becomes irrelevant. I plunged into another time and existence altogether.

I bounced, spun, flew through the air, cast around like a rag doll on the way to oblivion. The ice slope, the sky overhead, the abyss below, the pass behind: the world around me became an incomprehensible blur. I hurtled downwards, towards the void, out of touch with time and reality, moving so impossibly fast, but with time available for a million thoughts. I thought it strange that I had time to think so much.

There was complete disbelief that this was happening, and embarrassment that it was happening to me. *What*, I cringed, *would they say back home? And why haven't I been knocked out?* I could feel my head slamming into ice after every leap through the air, but oddly couldn't feel any pain. *Why is there no pain?*

And I thought—with shock that I was even thinking it—*so this is what it's like to die.*

But NO, I screamed silently, raging inside, I was not going to let myself die. I had no control but could perhaps regain it. It was the pack, I reasoned, weighted with a week's food, that was prolonging my fall. In desperation I tried to remove it, but my body was beyond my control, my fingers couldn't reach the straps. And so I found optimism in the failure, positives even in the midst of the fall. The pack contained a metal frame, perhaps saving me from a broken back, although I couldn't understand why my arms and legs hadn't snapped long ago.

Onwards I skimmed, skipping down the ice-slope like a rock tossed from above. *If I am about to die*, I thought, *shouldn't my life be flashing before my eyes?* But instead I saw rocks, evil black teeth, jagged and sharp, directly in my path. Pain approaching. But somehow I missed them, hit a bump and cartwheeled on, and then bounced again, and flew through the air for thirty, forty, maybe fifty feet. *Will this never end? Do I even want to reach the end?* But the questions were academic: the fall was now everything. There was no past anymore, no future. My life consisted of nothing but this mad, unstoppable fall.

But then suddenly, unexpectedly, incredibly, I found myself on my front, with my head higher than my feet, and for once not bouncing.

Instinctively, I spread myself like a star, feet up to stop myself flipping over again. In desperation I dug my fingers into the ice, tearing at the surface, shredding it, shredding flesh too, plucking several fingernails clean off, and slowly, wonderfully, miraculously I ground to a halt.

And there I was: stopped.

What a feeling!

I yelled at the top of my voice; an exultant, adrenaline-charged scream of sheer relief and raw emotion. It echoed about the valley, across the mountains. I was alive, ALIVE! I was living, breathing, moving, feeling. I could hardly believe my luck.

I sat for a minute, savouring my existence. My fingers were a bloody mess. My limbs were battered, grazed, bruised. One eye was swollen half shut, my clothes were torn, and my left ankle was fractured, although I didn't then know it. But I felt no pain, just euphoria. Everything I experienced now was a bonus.

Soon it was time to move on. I wasn't safe yet and couldn't stay where I was. Days might pass before anyone chanced by, and I wouldn't be missed for a week. I was entirely responsible for myself—a choice I'd consciously made, with consequences I now had to accept. Already I could feel my body stiffening. I had to move right away before I became incapable of moving at all.

In a few brief seconds I'd lost 1,000 feet of altitude, but another 2,000 still lay between me and easier ground. Much of it was exposed and treacherous, and I had no axe to steady myself or catch another fall. For a moment I succumbed to the idiotic idea of climbing back to retrieve the lost axe, but after taking a few steps up the slope I came to my senses and stopped. At least I still had crampons. I tried strapping them on, but my bleeding fingers couldn't manage it. So I began the descent as I was. I kicked my way down frozen snow in slow motion, bringing more care and attention to the task than I'd brought to any task before. My legs quaked from imagining another fall, from the intense effort of avoiding it. At the steepest and most precarious section I eased off my unbalancing pack and pushed it down the slope ahead of me. It slid away, gathering speed, bouncing violently, and I shuddered at the sight. I wondered if I had looked like that.

It took five hours—a lifetime—to descend to safe ground, and the intensity remains etched in my mind. The mountains I'd travelled so far to see passed by entirely unseen. I left a trail of blood in the snow, and when I finally reached help I really had endured enough. An elderly man stood outside the first building I came to, a remote mountain restaurant. Tanned and heavily lined, with a wise-looking gaze accustomed to distant horizons, the man watched me calmly as I stumbled closer. Bloody and ragged, I finally stood before him. Suddenly, I couldn't hold it together any longer. I burst into tears, and surrendered responsibility for myself to someone else. Speaking gentle words in German, the man clasped my elbow and guided me indoors. He gave me water to sip and a place to sit, then brought out a basin of warm saltwater for my torn hands. And then, avoiding every jarring pothole in the mountain road, he drove me carefully to hospital.

Later that night, while lying between clean hospital sheets, the euphoria returned. And what euphoria it was! It didn't match the sterile hospital environment, the dimmed lights, the murmur of soft nurse voices down the ward. It was euphoria better suited for the great outdoors, for wide open spaces, for glorious sunrises, for rebirths. I wanted to scream with joy, laugh ceaselessly, beam at the world. I was alive! Life suddenly seemed outrageously fragile, and unfathomably precious. What a miracle it was; every breath of it a gift. I'd been given a second chance that I absolutely couldn't waste.

I spent a sleepless night re-evaluating priorities, my perspectives changing. What did I want from life? Was it really what I had: a sheltered suburban existence, with days that were safe and comfortable, routines that felt deadening, and work that lacked purpose; where I'd finish with a pension after forty-plus years of hard graft but would be too worn out to do anything with it? Was it really the pursuit of money, possessions, stability, security? Was life all about achieving status, being what others thought I should be? Did I really have to fit in with the system, follow the path that almost everyone I knew appeared to follow without question: travel from school to college to full-time labour to marriage to kids to mortgaged servitude to annual vacations to retirement? Was that really *living*?

Suddenly, it all seemed wrong. It was desolate. Empty. No, worse: it was ridiculous, and just because it worked for others didn't mean it had to work for me. I lived for mountains, for the simplicity of being in them, for the freedom they gave me to be myself, for other reasons I hadn't yet figured out. Mountains were the only places I felt fully alive. Why limit my time in them to annual vacations and snatched weekends? Vacations were too short. Life itself was too short! Couldn't there be another way?

What I yearned for flew in the face of everything I had been conditioned to from birth, went against all the advice I had ever been given, ran contrary to how everyone else appeared to live. No one had encouraged me to take risks. No one had suggested that following my dreams was an option. Quite the reverse. I was shy, a stammerer, and lacked self-belief. I was a product of a society that had taught me to do my bit, work hard, save for the future, fit in. And so my escape took weeks, months, half a year. It was a battle. There were doubts, fears. I made up my mind, then un-made it. The chains that bound me had been well set; the brainwashing went deep. But after the Hohtürli Pass there was no going back. I couldn't forget the second chance I'd been given, couldn't forget what had been revealed: that life was a gift not to be wasted, and finally, *finally*, I made my choice. No more the beaten path. I quit work, bought a replacement ice axe, pulled on my backpack, and set forth, leaving behind my suburban existence. It was the best decision I'd ever made. Afterwards, I wondered why it had taken so long. It was so clearly the right choice.

Decision made, I spent the summer of 1994 back in the Alps, walking 2,200 miles across the range from one end to the other, living the life I knew I was meant to live. After a winter of work back in London that now held real purpose—to fund the next adventure—I set out on a three-month walk through the Pyrenees the following summer. Once alone in the mountains I couldn't imagine a better life, couldn't picture one that taught more or gave so much back. I was glad I'd fallen from the pass. But it tormented me that the journeys had to end so soon.

Or did they?

Once home from the Pyrenees I began considering the possibility of something bigger. I wanted a journey I could lose myself in completely, something so long in distance and broad in scope it could become more than just a walk. I didn't want a journey that ended with the summer.

What I wanted was a new way of life.

PART I

GETTING THERE

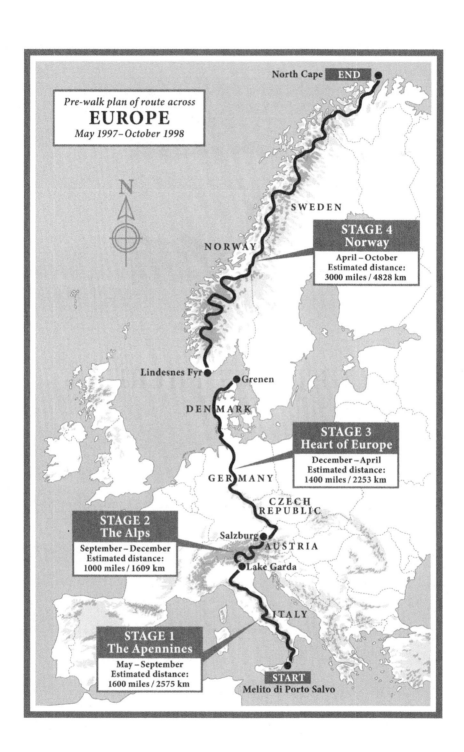

North Cape END

Pre-walk plan of route across
EUROPE
May 1997–October 1998

N

SWEDEN

STAGE 4
Norway
April – October
Estimated distance:
3000 miles / 4828 km

NORWAY

Lindesnes Fyr ● ● Grenen

DENMARK

STAGE 3
Heart of Europe
December – April
Estimated distance:
1400 miles / 2253 km

GERMANY

CZECH
REPUBLIC

STAGE 2
The Alps
September – December
Estimated distance:
1000 miles / 1609 km

Salzburg ●
AUSTRIA

● Lake Garda

ITALY

STAGE 1
The Apennines
May – September
Estimated distance:
1600 miles / 2575 km

START
Melito di Porto Salvo

LEVING
Chapter 1

AT THREE IN the morning on the day it began I felt sick to the depths of my being. Finally, after months of waiting, the Big Day had arrived: the day of departure to Calabria, to the Apennines, to the start of a walk that would stretch across an entire continent, and my knotted stomach was letting me know it. Nerves, excitement, a hint of terror; I couldn't sort one emotion from the other. I hadn't slept, hadn't come close, and the alarm wasn't needed. But I let the damn thing ring itself silly until it stopped, and then I lay for five minutes more—a final act of defiance against the future I'd willingly chosen.

When next would I sleep in my own bed? I was about to turn my back on home, on everything that was safe and familiar, and head alone into the wild. I'd be gone a year and a half, if all went well. It was exactly what I'd dreamed of but, suddenly, I didn't want to go. This wasn't how I was supposed to feel.

After dragging myself up, I pulled on the clothes I'd be wearing every single day for the foreseeable future. They were hard-wearing, quick-drying, sweat-wicking clothes: functional items, not fashionable. I stood before the mirror dressed for the wild, but relishing the softness of carpet between my toes, and felt like an imposter. Couldn't I just pretend to everyone it had all been a joke?

Breakfast brought home how much I was leaving behind. Today I had choices but tomorrow—and for the 550 or so days after—the choices would be notably reduced. Here, in my parents' kitchen, there were options. It was a thoroughly typical suburban kitchen filled with a typical range of foods, utensils and appliances, but on this morning of departure it all suddenly seemed both disdainfully excessive and painfully appealing. I felt an urge to throw open every cupboard and pull out every utensil, to plunder the pantry and empty the fridge. I'd bake fresh bread in the oven, cook bacon on the grill, set the coffeemaker percolating, the microwave radiating, the toaster toasting, the kettle boiling. I'd stand in the middle with arms outstretched, flipping pancakes with one hand, frying eggs with the other, balancing plates and bowls upon one foot, and rustle up the kind of breakfast I'd no doubt be fantasising about in a week or two.

Or perhaps I'd just have a slice of toast? In the end, toast was all I fancied, but once prepared I couldn't eat it. My stomach had gone on strike.

From now on my kitchen would be starkly different. It would consist of a small camp stove, one pot, one mug, one spoon. Food would be limited to what I could carry; water would come from streams. Thoughtfully, I wandered over to the sink, turned on the tap, and let hot water splash over my hands. I wouldn't be able to do that for a while.

I wouldn't see any familiar faces for a while, either. My parents, Valerie and Ken, lay sleeping upstairs, and although we'd made our farewells the evening before I was tempted to wake them for another goodbye. But it would be a mistake. The first goodbye had been difficult enough, although we'd been very English about it.

'Good night, sleep well, sweet dreams,' was all we'd said. None of us had wanted to make a scene.

In truth, a more emotional goodbye wasn't necessary. My parents had demonstrated their love often, especially with their support while I'd prepared for the walk, and with the help they'd offered for the months ahead. Not that my father thought the journey was the best choice I could be making.

'Look, I get why you went on that first long walk,' he'd said a week earlier. 'But I don't understand why that wasn't enough.'

I'd looked at him, wanting desperately to justify myself, but knowing from experience I'd fail. For one thing, I was certain he hadn't understood the first walk; if he had, he wouldn't be questioning this one. And for another, I always struggled to put my reasons into words. My motives made perfect sense to me, but whenever I aired them out loud they always sounded ill-considered and foolish, even to my ears.

'It's something I *need* to do,' I had finally offered, fully aware I was letting myself down with such a feeble response.

'Perhaps what you need,' my father had countered, 'is to move on. You can't do this forever.'

He had the best intentions—this I knew. Both my parents had gone above and beyond to give all their children the best possible start in life. It must have been exasperating to then see the opportunities spurned for an uncertain and risky future.

'All those other journeys,' he had continued. 'And now this one. Honestly, Andrew, I think you're mad. Where will it all end?'

It had been a rhetorical question. He and I had both known I hadn't an answer to give.

The answer was even more elusive now as I gazed around at the home I was leaving. The familiarity taunted me. This was the house I'd grown up in with my three brothers, and it was filled with nothing but good memories. It had always been a safe refuge. I was the second oldest, and the only one still here, which was fine. It worked for practical reasons: it was a hugely convenient base between trips. I paid my way when home, didn't have to maintain my own place when I was away, and I got on well with my parents —except when trying to explain my walks. The negatives were few, and the parental companionship and love were appreciated—and, perhaps embarrassingly, still needed. I didn't see my friends often, and when it came to romance I didn't know where to start; my stammer and a debilitating lack of social confidence held me back. Not that I dwelt on it. I had mountains, and nothing could compare with them. Under normal circumstances.

I took a final walk through the kitchen and living room, storing it all away, then hoisted on my backpack and stepped outside. Shutting the front door was such an everyday thing to do, but on this occasion the act held such momentous *finality*. The chill night air cleared my head, but the weight of my pack felt monstrous. I could sense my shoulders bruising even as I stood there. Swaying in the darkness, I felt mocked by all the silent suburban homes. They stretched away, row upon row, street after street. All those people, all those lives: perhaps they understood something I didn't. What was wrong with 'ordinary' anyway? Others lived lives of meaning here; why couldn't I?

A great lump rose in my throat, anxiety filled my gut, but I was saved from falling into panic when the taxi I'd booked the evening before arrived. The driver was a grumpy old sod, but a perfect distraction. Instead of wallowing in negative thoughts I made winning a laugh from him my mission.

As we drove towards London I tried out all the usual topics Londoners loved dissecting: the weather, the traffic, the government, the state of the economy, the awfulness of the health service, the enduring catastrophe also known as England's national football team. All I earned in response were grunts. But, when I outlined my walk, the driver finally grew animated.

'Hang on... you're doing *what*?' he exclaimed. 'Eighteen months of... exercise? Living outside round the clock no matter how hard it's pissin' down? And with *that* on your back?' He nodded at my rucksack, which filled the back seat like another adult customer. 'You must be off your trolley, mate. Sounds bleedin' miserable.' He paused a moment, considering it. 'Why the hell would you want to do that?'

I smiled. This wasn't my father. Frivolous answers were acceptable.

'Well, look at it this way,' I explained. 'For a year and a half I won't have to do a minute's work.'

He laughed at that. 'Yeah... that makes sense.' He went quiet as we pulled up outside Victoria station, the launching point for a long train journey to Rome. He seemed suddenly weary, as though resenting his day's work that stretched ahead. And then he spoke.

'So... can I come?' he asked.

THE CARPET BENEATH MY FEET
Chapter 2

I GREW UP not with the earth beneath my feet but with carpet, linoleum, tile, and pavement. For the first fifteen years of my life my feet didn't encounter a single surface that could truly be considered wild. Not that I cared. Why would I care about rock-strewn hillsides, mulchy forest floors, or spongy mountain tundra? You don't care about what you don't know. Or do you? Can you tell that something essential is missing, even if you don't know what it is? Do you instinctively recognise it when first you see it?

Home was a large house in the outer suburbs of London. It had three floors, six bedrooms, and an enclosed back garden with a soft lawn for play. Plenty of space for me and my three brothers. My father had worked hard to create a secure and comfortable existence, and my mother worked equally hard to maintain a clean house and keep her family well fed and dressed. Their achievements and gifts were extraordinary. As a child, I didn't know how fortunate I was.

Beyond our walls lay Pinner 'village'. It was a friendly place—a green and leafy garden community, well cared for, with a quaint high street of half-timbered buildings hundreds of years old, several parks, and even a dairy farm that helped locals pretend they were country folk. Residents were proud of Pinner's quiet ambience, and frequently talked up its village-like qualities, happily ignoring that it had ceased being a village in the 1920s when ever-expanding London had swallowed it whole.

As a child, I fully embraced the party line that Pinner was special, a true English village. It didn't bother me that London's background hum never ceased, or that an uncountable number of electric lights filled the night sky with a bleak neon glow, permanently hiding the Milky Way. No, I was unaware of such things. I took pride in Pinner's grassy verges, and in the tiny pockets of pseudo-countryside we saw during occasional family walks. As far as I was concerned, Pinner was idyllic.

For ten years, life passed without drama, and the vast majority of it took place indoors on carpet. My brothers and I weren't ever kicked out at dawn to explore. We were kept close, watched over, protected. And at no point did we question it. We were happy, knew we were loved, didn't doubt we belonged, and never felt unsafe. But for my persistent stammer, life was perfect.

The wild rarely entered my thoughts. Sure, I learnt at school that it existed. I understood that Everest, the Amazon, the Sahara, and the South Pole were all real places, but they were so distant they might as well have been made up. From what I could gather, they only existed so that we could 'conquer' them. What limited knowledge I had of wild nature was fed to me by others, and through books and the TV, where the wild was almost always an inhospitable environment people had to fight to overcome. My favourite childhood book—Tolkien's *The Hobbit*, read numerous times from the age of seven—enforced that theme. There were misty mountains to struggle across, Mirkwoods to get lost in, poisonous rivers to fall into —dangerous realms all. Of course, I knew the book was fiction, but TV news stories suggested that the real wild was the same. People were always having to be rescued from it. And then there were wildlife documentaries. They never showed people, and from that I assumed the obvious: people and the wild inhabited different worlds. Every single time the wild was mentioned it was done in a way that told me it was a hostile place to fear, an environment where the human species simply didn't belong. It had nothing to do with my life in Pinner.

Each summer my father booked a fortnight's holiday. He had a great knack for finding unusual places to stay: a cottage on an island in the River Thames, an old schoolhouse deep in the Devon countryside, a multi-storeyed harbourmaster's house leaning over a saltwater estuary. The holidays were the most exciting two weeks of each year, and once on them 'ordinary' life in Pinner was quickly forgotten. Life was simply better on holiday—a fact I picked up early. Why else would my hard-working parents spend half the year so eagerly anticipating them? Home was home, but travel was what life was really all about.

When I was ten the holiday took place in Devon in south-west England. And it changed everything. It was where I saw 'the wild' for the first time.

It happened as we motored uphill onto Dartmoor. Suddenly, there it was: a landscape so shockingly unlike the tidy gardens of Pinner I could scarcely believe it was real. Beyond the car window were sombre moors rising to granite tors, and dark, brooding hills stretching to the horizon. From the car I didn't have an opportunity to engage with this astonishing land—I merely saw it passing by—but I was profoundly impressed. I saw something beyond my experience that called to me and scared me in ways I didn't comprehend. I couldn't forget it.

In the years that followed, Dartmoor featured regularly in play, and the margins edging Pinner's manicured parks became tangled wildernesses. Around that time, one of my grandfathers began leading me and my brothers on short woodland walks. We only went four times a year, but these brief interludes into nature became cherished highlights. In my imagination, the walks were epic wilderness adventures. Of course, the woods weren't wild, not even close. There were no wolves lurking within the trees, no trackless reaches into which one could lose oneself for days on end. The woods were managed, they welcomed hundreds of visitors every day, and although you couldn't see suburbia from within the trees it was hard to escape its omnipresent background drone. But I pretended they were wild all the same.

It wasn't until I was thirteen that I plucked up courage to go by myself. The woods were located three miles from home, not far, but it was the farthest I'd dared venture alone, and the first time I'd been allowed. Despite all the previous visits, I had never truly experienced them—in company there had been too many distractions. But on that first solo visit I experienced significantly more, especially when I paused at the remotest spot to see how being there felt. And how it felt was unsettling. I stood still and quiet, and before long the trees seemed larger, the branches gnarlier, the shadows darker, the entire forest wilder. Strange shapes appeared in the undergrowth, and slowly the woods changed. They became aware. And that was when the fear hit. Suddenly, I felt eyes watching me, staring from the shadows and treetops, a thousand staring eyes—and all of them malevolent. It was more than I could take. I bolted. Heart pounding, I raced for home, powered by thirteen years of conditioning that had programmed me to separate myself from nature and fear it. I ran—like an intruder who had been discovered, like a visitor who didn't belong. I ran as I'd never run before, and it was years before I tried going back by myself.

A few months later I chanced upon a book by country vet James Herriot. Writing about his life in 1930s Yorkshire, Herriot introduced to me the radical idea that one could love wild places and find peace in them, not just fight them, conquer them, or flee them in fear. Herriot's deep affection for the Pennines had a profound impact, and by the time I had finished reading, re-reading, and then re-reading yet again all eight of his books I'd fallen hard for the rugged uplands he described. In comparison, Pinner had dulled and shrunk. From then on, it wasn't Tolkien's Middle-earth or Dartmoor that I fantasised about, but the Pennines. I longed to experience them for myself.

For two years, the closest I got was my daily pre-dawn newspaper round. It wasn't Pinner I cycled through but the wild, windswept Pennines, in my mind at least. My pleas for a family holiday in the hills finally paid off when my father booked a cabin near Snowdonia National Park in North Wales. As the vacation approached I could barely sleep from excitement, and my parents worried that the reality would disappoint. But they couldn't have been more wrong. When we motored into the Llanberis Pass, and I saw mountains rearing overhead in all their savage, rocky grandeur, I was swept away, captivated forever. In the Llanberis Pass my life's trajectory was set in stone.

Climbing 3,650-foot Snowdon merely confirmed it. It was the only time we ventured into the mountains on foot, and we did it via the easiest and busiest path, but I didn't notice the crowds, or the rack-and-pinion rail track that accompanied us to the summit. All I saw was the landscape, an untamed realm of plunging crags, cascading streams, and drifting clouds. Pinner it was not; gentle and familiar it was not. I didn't pause for a second to analyse what exactly it was, or question my reaction to it. I just gaped in adoration.

From then on, mountains became my obsession, although they remained far beyond my reach. The following year's holiday in the Scottish

On the way up Snowdon aged fifteen, July 1985.

Highlands was frustrating. I saw plenty of mountains, but looking at them from a moving car wasn't enough. My father, aware that he knew nothing of mountain craft, didn't want to drag his family into the heart of the wild and become just another accident statistic, and so our walks were few and short. Back home afterwards, I had to make do with cut-out calendar pictures of mountains taped to my bedroom wall, and dream about actually being among them. One day.

The long-awaited day finally arrived when I was eighteen and left home for college in Derby. The city sits just south of the Pennines, and that was why I chose it—not for academic reasons but so I could explore the Peak District National Park. A bus whisked me north on my first free day, and with a cheap canvas rucksack slung over my shoulders and stiff new hiking boots on my feet I strode towards the wild by myself for the very first time…

And ground to a halt on its edge.

It was laughable—how fiercely I'd longed to stand where I now stood, but how intimidated I suddenly felt. It didn't matter that I had a broad gravel track to follow, or that a town was close behind, or that the heather-clad moor only stretched ahead for three miles. What mattered was the fear I'd been conditioned to feel. What mattered was what I believed: that I didn't belong here, especially alone. *Never walk alone*—I'd heard the rule many times.

The trouble was, I *was* on my own. I would *always* be on my own. The stammer I'd suffered throughout childhood, and the resulting shyness, had made aloneness a defining part of who I was. Ordinarily, being alone didn't trouble me. In fact, I preferred it. In company, I cringed with embarrassment, but alone I was safe. But being alone here was the exact opposite of safe—at least according to everything I'd learnt from all the experienced adults who supposedly knew the mountains. *Never walk alone*. It was the cardinal rule. Who was I at eighteen to doubt it?

But I'd been dreaming of the Pennines for five long years. Steeling myself, I faced forward, but still wavered. Long minutes passed. It wasn't until three other hikers appeared on the track behind that I found the confidence to push on. And, of course, I didn't get lost or fall off any crags. Instead I walked in awe, lost in another way, and although the fear didn't entirely pass the exhilaration made it a stress I could bear.

For the next two years I spent every spare minute in the Peak District. Back in Derby among my college peers I was painfully uncomfortable, but alone on the gritstone moors I was free to relax and be myself. In the wild there was no one to mock my stammer the way it had been endlessly mocked at school, no one to belittle my choices the way adults had often belittled them, and no one to tell me what I could and couldn't do. Life on foot was simpler, exciting, and filled with endless natural wonder. Fear still occasionally struck, but the rewards usually overcame it.

When I returned to Pinner after college I saw that it wasn't quite the idyllic country village I'd once supposed. As weeks back home turned into months, and then years, dissatisfaction at my resumed suburban life evolved into anxiety. I had a job, a place to live, everything one was supposed to have—but I felt trapped. I was meant to be out in wild nature, not stuck in Pinner going nowhere. Every day I caught the same commuter train, walked the same streets, slept inside the same house. I escaped to the mountains one weekend each month, and for all my vacations. But the visits were too short. What else could I do? Jobs in the mountains were few, and I had no skills for any of them. My anxiety worsened when I began doubting myself. Perhaps I had it all wrong. After all, what was more likely to be correct: everything an entire society had told me about how to travel through life, or the ideas I'd dreamed up myself? Even worse was the shame I developed. I was arguably better off than most humans who had ever lived—how dare I complain about being stuck in Pinner with soft carpet underfoot? Was I that spoilt? And so I hid my anxiety as I hid my stammer. On the surface I smiled, pretending I was the happy-go-lucky mountain wanderer I longed to be, but on the inside I screamed and writhed in torment.

Years passed.

Thank goodness for the Hohtürli Pass.

ROME
Chapter 3

ROUGHLY 1,200 MILES from Pinner, I stood in Italy's capital city, sweating in hot, sticky air, a shock after London's finger-chilling dampness. A storm rumbled overhead, thunder echoing to and fro across the sky as though the gods were engaged in an apocalyptic tennis match. What would the augurs of ancient Rome have read into an omen like that, I wondered? Start a long campaign or not? March across Europe, or not?

In four hours I was due to leave for Calabria, but I had an essential task to complete first. Maps to track down. Despite many months of preparation I hadn't yet acquired detailed hiking maps of Calabria's mountains, although this wasn't entirely my fault. A specialist map store in London had generously promised to donate all the maps for the entire journey: a promise I'd celebrated. Back in 1997 there was no Google Earth, and GPS units were new, beyond my price range, and untrustworthy. Maps covering the entire continent would have cost a small fortune—the savings were immense. After making the offer, the National Map Centre had quickly provided a good selection for my route north of Tuscany, but none for the first 1,000 miles. Months passed. No further maps materialised. I'd checked in frequently, stressing the importance of maps for the rapidly approaching start, and each time was assured that *all* the maps were on the way. So I waited. What else could I do? The maps were free, a promise had been made, and my youth and English upbringing meant I wasn't capable of displaying anything but polite patience. I trusted that the maps would come. But they didn't.

And now I was just a train ride from the start with no maps to follow.

Still, the odds of finding what I needed in Italy's capital had to be high, and so, in a downpour, I splashed from bookshop to bookshop, parting the Roman crowds with my backpack. After three hours I finally tracked down a map of Calabria, although it didn't fill me with confidence. What I needed were accurate large-scale maps displaying the kind of topographical details that aid wilderness navigation, but what I found was a single small-scale sheet covering the entire region. It marked roads, towns and the coastline with some assurance, but seemed less certain about the interior. Blank spaces between roads were depicted with delicate crosshatching. No trails were marked. The rendering had been done with genuine artistic flair; I could only hope artistic imagination hadn't also been employed. But accurate or not, it would have to do.

At midday I entered the Stazione di Roma Termini and sat in a corner, watching the bustle. The sight of so many travellers in motion thrilled me, as it always does, and when my train was announced I leapt up with a burst of energy. Reggio di Calabria! The toe of the Italian boot! I looked around, but no one else appeared quite as enthusiastic about the destination as I.

Moving swiftly, I clambered aboard my train and claimed a spot in an empty compartment. It offered seating for six, or in this case five and a person-sized backpack. Soon, four other passengers joined me, each one examining my pack, and the ice axe strapped to it, with eyebrows raised.

'You are on the right train?' a businessman queried in Italian. He wore a loose, crumpled suit and a vibrantly colourful tie that no businessman in London would ever dare wear. His cologne filled the compartment with a sickly sweet aroma so strong it pushed me back against the seat and held me pinned by the shoulders. 'You are travelling *south*?' he asked.

'*Si*,' I confirmed.

'To Reggio?'

'*Si*.'

'But why the…?' And he pointed at the axe. Its sharp spikes had already wreaked havoc across Rome.

I threw up my hands, apologising for not yet having enough Italian to explain. The axe, the replacement to the one lost on the Hohtürli Pass, had accompanied me on all my walks since, even those not involving snow and ice. I'd named it Excalibur and it had become a trusted tool. Excalibur was long enough to use as a walking stick, sharp enough to dig into mud and use as a handhold on steep ground, fierce enough to wave at unfriendly dogs, and always useful on ice slopes to safeguard against another Hohtürli-style fall. But how could I explain all that?

Still, the businessman asked again, so I gave it my best shot, trying to hint at the scope of the journey: 'I... go... mountains... big walk... Calabria... to Norway.' To illustrate, I walked my fingers through the air.

'Mmmm... yes,' the businessman murmured, clearly not understanding. He paused for a moment, head to one side, considering my accent. 'You are from England, I think?'

One-word answers were definitely easier. '*Si*,' I replied, and the four Italians suddenly nodded, happy with Englishness as an explanation for the eccentricity. Who but an Englishman would need an ice axe in the Mediterranean?

The train juddered into motion and rattled from Rome. The four Italians all began talking at once, arms waving vigorously, not talking to one another so much as at one another. It was entertaining at first, but before long my head started to pound. The perfume-filled air soon seemed stifling, but when I gestured at the window, seeking permission to slide it down, my companions frowned. It wasn't healthy—too much of a draught could make one sick. For even suggesting it they looked at me as though I were several columns short of a full Colosseum.

I received a stronger version of the same look fifty miles later when my companions finally understood that not only was I planning on *walking* through Calabria, and planning on doing it *alone*, but also that I intended doing it in the *mountains*.

'But Calabria is dangerous. The mountains: extremely dangerous.'

'Why?' I asked, expecting the usual answers. People unfamiliar with mountains often seemed to fear them. 'Wild animals? Wild weather?'

'Oh, no,' came the reply. 'Wild men!' And my companions all laughed. But it didn't seem funny to me.

The businessman decided it wasn't a laughing matter either. He leaned forward, and his sudden seriousness sent a chill down my spine. 'In Calabria you will find many men with guns. Many *criminali*. The mafia is everywhere. They own Calabria. Your plan is not good.' He tapped his right forefinger against the side of his head. 'You must think about it… *very carefully.*' And so I did. For several hundred miles I found myself unable to think about anything else.

The train stopped frequently; my companions left, new companions arrived. Italy rolled by in a grey haze. The Mediterranean Sea was often in sight, but the view inland of Apennine foothills interested me more. I probed the hills for clues, imagining myself among them, but there wasn't much to see, just endless forests steaming with clouds. My eyes grew weary as I watched. Through heavy eyelids I noticed farms and villages growingly steadily poorer the further south we travelled. Whitewashed villas with flower baskets and terracotta roofs gave way to meaner buildings of crumbling plaster and grime. Naples was a teeming warren of narrow streets and ugly apartments stacked one atop the other, hung with dirty balconies, strung with endless webs of washing. After Naples the landscape became even harsher, even rougher, even spikier. For hours I sat and watched it slip by, obsessing about 'dangerous' Calabria. What had I been thinking? Perhaps I truly had made a monumental mistake.

THE IDEA
Chapter 4

I'D COME UP with the idea for the mistake less than two weeks after finishing my 1,000-mile traverse of the Pyrenees. The walk hadn't cured me of wanderlust, only increased it. The question was: where next? For a journey that was 'more than just a walk' it had to be somewhere special. The Rockies, Andes, and Himalayas all called, but I was also strongly drawn to thoroughly exploring my own continent first. Could Europe give me what I wanted? Was it big or wild enough? There were still two ranges I hadn't visited: the Apennines in Italy and the mountains of Norway. Could either of those work?

The Apennines stretch the length of the Italian Peninsula, forming a mountainous backbone 750 miles long and 9,500 feet high. Although lower than the Alps the range is significantly wilder. There are forests in the Apennines where wolves and bears still roam, and entire regions where hikers seldom tread. The Italy that most people know is a well-developed country tamed by thousands of years of civilisation and visited by millions of tourists each year, but the Apennines don't belong to *that* Italy; they belong to another place and time. Much of the range is sparsely populated, the communities isolated and horse-and-cart poor. In the wildest corners you can search a long time for evidence that other people have passed by before you, and completely fail to find it. The Apennines offer a ribbon of wild that most Europeans wouldn't even guess at, and the idea of wandering through it for months on end, and occasionally emerging into the better-known Italy as a bonus, was one I found immensely attractive.

But Norway was attractive too. Norway is Europe's least populated country and arguably the wildest. Stretching 1,000-plus miles from the Baltic Sea to beyond the Arctic Circle, Norway bears little resemblance to the industrialised, civilisation-ravaged Europe further south. Norway is a mountain kingdom beyond compare. From its ice caps and mountains to its fjords and forests it offers everything a wilderness connoisseur could desire, and I couldn't imagine a finer place to travel on foot.

But how was I to choose?

I was on my second day back at work, employed on a short-term free-lance contract, supposedly focused on the task I was being paid for, when a sudden thought occurred: 'Why not walk the Apennines *and* Norway in one go?'

'Because it's too far!' came a swift reply from a colleague seated at the nearest desk. Apparently, I'd spoken out loud.

Too far?

Well now, how could I resist that?

I considered it carefully, and the idea grew. Something about it felt right. I liked the idea of crossing the entire continent, progressing from one mountain range to the next, from one country to the next, from one climate zone to the next. Southern Italy is the land of the Mezzogiorno, the midday sun, a place of searing summer heat where the sun hangs directly overhead at midday and the dehydrating Sirocco wind can blast in from Africa. In contrast, northern Norway is the land of the *midnight* sun—a place so far north the midsummer sun never sets. The idea of linking the land of the midday sun with the land of the midnight sun was intriguingly poetic.

The more I contemplated the idea the more I found to like. I liked the idea of starting from the Mediterranean. It was where my Pyrenean traverse had finished so it would be like picking up where I'd left off. And I liked the idea of aiming for the North Cape at the top of Norway, the place beyond which one could Go No Further. Although reaching the end wouldn't be the point, having a famous destination would provide a satisfying sense of purpose. And I liked the idea of travelling north. The south offered sunnier skies and less challenging terrain (or so I thought), while the north offered harsher landscapes and colder winds: it oozed of the unknown. To head south would have felt too easy, but to head north smacked of adventure.

Most of all I liked how long it would take. At the pace I usually adopted —the kind of unhurried pace where one can notice details—it would take roughly a year and a half. And that was *exactly* what I was after. Definitely more than just a walk. And so I made up my mind: I'd tramp north across Europe, sleep outdoors for eighteen months, live a life of freedom in the Europe most people missed.

Ask anyone and they'll tell you: Europe is a known place. It is known, overdeveloped, and overcrowded—not a continent for adventure. But alongside that Europe is a lesser-known place, a parallel continent beyond the modern world's reach. The thing is, most people in Europe follow most of the same roads to most of the same places, but there are roads less travelled, and many places roads don't touch. The Europe that seems small by car or high-speed train becomes enormous on foot at three miles an hour. The Europe that feels crowded in towns and cities can feel empty in the roughest mountains. The Europe that seems tame and safe where the land has been tilled and built upon becomes wild indeed where nature runs free. Just try forcing your way through a trailless Apennine forest, or try crossing a remote Alpine pass in a blizzard, or try sleeping outside in the crackling depths of a central European winter, or try fording a storm-swollen river in the Norwegian Arctic, and you'll discover an entirely different Europe. An immense, uncrowded, and thrillingly wild place.

That was the Europe I planned to explore. The *other* Europe.

PREPARATIONS
Chapter 5

WITH THE IDEA fully formed I began preparations: gathering equipment, planning a route, figuring out how the hell to pay for eighteen months of freedom.

Equipment presented the first challenge. Although I already owned backpacking gear, most of it had been acquired seven years earlier at college. Since then, the gear had been heavily used, and much of it was now barely fit for a day hike, let alone a 7,000-mile journey. It needed replacing, but the cost was beyond me.

As winter rolled by I wrote a stack of begging letters to manufacturers, and to my delight several agreed to help. The British distributors of Italian footwear brand Scarpa donated several pairs of boots. Lowe Alpine donated waterproofs, clothing, and a backpack. Robert Saunders, manufacturers of superb lightweight tents, sent a brand-new Jetpacker, my trusted tent. And outdoor gear retailer Cotswold Outdoor offered a generous discount on everything else. By early spring I'd gathered a pile of equipment, and I divided it into gear needed for the start and gear needed further down the trail. The sight of it made the adventure feel thrillingly near.

Next came the route. With small-scale maps of each country spread before me I spent uncounted hours joining the dots, unlocking the secrets, imagining the adventures; I'd rarely had so much fun. Using maps and maps alone I worked out a plan. Back in the mid-nineties few other information sources were readily available, especially for the Apennines.

The internet was a fragment of the information powerhouse it is today. If planning it now I could pull up satellite images of the remotest valleys, read in depth about every region, village, valley, and hill, but back then options were limited. Which suited me fine. As I saw it, too much knowledge could ruin a perfectly good adventure. Sure, I needed to know *where* I was going —roughly anyway—but I didn't need to know too much about what I'd find when I got there. Finding out was the whole point.

Eventually, I sketched a route through the highest and wildest corners of the continent, avoiding civilisation as much as possible. It wasn't a route to stick to at all costs, but a rough guide from which deviations were to be allowed, if not actively encouraged. Using an old bootlace to measure distances I worked out a string of stepping-stone towns spaced roughly two weeks apart, put together thirty resupply packages filled with essential items not likely to be available en route, and addressed them to myself care of *poste restante*. My parents would mail them out. The system had worked perfectly in the Alps and Pyrenees, and I couldn't imagine it not working again.

The key to completing the walk would lie in timing: crossing the southern Apennines once the mountain snows had thawed but before summer grew too hot; crossing the Alps before winter's first storms blocked the passes; reaching southern Norway in spring once the deep snowpack had begun its annual retreat; finishing in the far north before the ferocious Arctic winter returned. It would be a race against the seasons, albeit a very slow race.

With the route chosen I moved on to the greatest challenge of all: money. The problem with money was that I didn't have any.

By trade I was a graphic designer, although it wasn't my true calling. Art had been my strongest subject at school and favourite activity at home, and when the time had come to pick a career the adults in my life had guided me towards graphic design. The idea hadn't excited; I'd sensed it was the wrong path to take, but I'd taken it anyway. As a teenager, I'd learnt to distrust my own instincts, had come to believe they weren't valid. Adults and teachers were forever smiling condescendingly at my observations, scoffing at my ideas, before saying they knew better and telling me what to do. Meekly letting others choose my path, I had studied graphic design at college, and once back in Pinner had found work for a small design business. But I'd hated it. My employer made me feel inferior and ignorant, the work seemed empty—it did nothing to make the world a better place—and I spent my work days feeling unfulfilled and trapped, dreaming of the hills.

At least before Hohtürli the job had provided a reliable (if modest) salary that had met my modest needs. But since Hohtürli my off-and-on freelance earnings between trips had been woeful. Staying on top of day-to-day expenses and paying my way at home was challenging enough, but saving for eighteen months of adventure was impossible. There was only one option: if I couldn't pay for the journey I had to find someone who could.

And so the search for a sponsor began, although with trepidation: would the commitments that come with having a corporate sponsor change the journey too much? Still, full of youthful optimism, believing I had much to offer, I mailed hundreds of finely honed propositions to hundreds of carefully selected businesses—and was turned down by all of them. A handful even let me know it. But I didn't give in. The walk *had* to take place; not just for my own sake but also for a promise I fully intended to keep.

The promise had been made to two charities based in central London that were helping the city's homeless. I had promised I'd use the walk to raise money for their work. My journey was essentially a selfish undertaking that served no practical purpose, but it presented an opportunity to do a little good—an opportunity that I was determined not to waste.

The idea of walking for the homeless occurred during my 2,200-mile Alpine summer. A moment of loneliness had prompted it. Before this, I had *never* suffered loneliness in the mountains. Sure, I'd been alone, but being alone in the hills was utterly different from being alone in the suburbs. In the hills it was a gift. The loneliness struck four months into the journey after eight days of torrential rain. Rather than spending yet another night in sodden clothes in a sodden tent, I took shelter in a remote cow byre, but the stench, filth, and isolation had a powerful effect. As darkness fell so did my spirits. Questions arose that had no answer. Why was I here, surrounded by muck, feeling cold and wet, tired and hungry? Why was I going without the comforts most people took for granted, living without a home, spending every minute alone? After Hohtürli I'd wanted to live life to the full, but was this really living? The more I thought about it, the more my journey seemed pointless, and the more unbearable the discomforts became. Suddenly, I saw myself for the fool I undoubtedly was—out of step not just with society but with common sense, walking a lonely path of failure and poverty when I could have been living in comfort. A desperate need for company, and for a home I hadn't seen in months, overwhelmed me, but both were out of reach. For two desolate hours loneliness crushed me. But then one of those profound eureka realisations hit, and it pulled me back from the brink. It was laughably obvious once I saw it: my situation was entirely self-inflicted. I could head home any moment I chose, but there were people in far worse situations who couldn't. The idea that others were stuck with this—stuck without a home, alone in big, crowded cities, surrounded by comforts but living in squalor—appalled me, and now I'd had a taste of what it might be like I vowed to do something one day to help. I'd make a difference in the world.

At first, I wasn't certain how, but when I visited The Passage and the Cardinal Hume Centre, and saw first-hand the difference these two charities were making, I knew I'd found my cause. Both charities treated the individuals they served with immense respect and a complete lack of judgement. It was the exact opposite of how society at large tended to treat 'the homeless'—as a faceless group of failed people who were probably getting everything they deserved. A Passage volunteer explained that many of their clients also ended up believing the same thing, that they were worthless and undeserving, an inferior species. In truth, the majority were victims of events beyond their control; they simply had no safety net to catch their fall. When I learnt that both charities didn't only meet the immediate needs of the individuals and families they served, but also helped them reclaim their place in society through job and housing assistance, and through a broad range of support systems, I was deeply impressed. It was then that I made my promise to help.

On my first visit to The Passage, the director—Sister Bridie Dowd—greeted me with a memorable line: 'So, you are the one who is going to do this wonderful thing for us?' I immediately felt like a fraud. For one thing, I hadn't yet decided which charity I was going to walk for; for another, it was she, her staff, and all the volunteers who were doing the wonderful thing—the real work. I was only planning a long holiday. I felt like a fraud again when my plans began generating publicity. The publicity always began with an explanation that I was walking to raise money for the homeless, as though it were concern for the homeless that had prompted the walk. This made me cringe. True, I *was* concerned, but altruism wasn't why I wanted to head into the wild. Not that it really mattered. If the misconception led to larger donations I could put up with it.

Using the walk to make a difference, however small, was the right thing to do. And unlike having a sponsor, there was little risk it would detract from the journey—only add to it. From the moment I made my promise, the journey developed extra meaning. There were other benefits too. Walking for the homeless would help with motivation once I was underway. When the going got tough, as it surely would at some point, I'd know I wasn't just walking for myself. And, even though it wasn't the reason for doing it, the publicity wouldn't hurt my search for a sponsor either.

Unfortunately, it didn't help. Months passed. Winter mellowed into spring, departure neared, but my search drew a blank. To fit in with the seasons the journey could only begin in spring, and when spring passed without a sponsor the adventure passed with it, leaving a gaping hole that Pinner couldn't fill. Distraught, I returned to freelance work, but continued with the search; I'd just have to begin the following spring instead, fulfil my promise a year later. A sponsor remained essential. Even another year of scrimping and saving wouldn't bring the funds needed. Two years might do it, but youthful impatience meant I wasn't capable of waiting such an unimaginable length of time.

And so the year passed with the dream, and my life, on hold. I escaped to the mountains for frequent short trips—my sanity demanded them—but otherwise it was a dull existence far removed from the adventurous life I longed to live. By autumn, however, the search showed promise. Perhaps my technique was improving, but the hook I dangled was nibbled more often, snagged a couple of half bites, and so I redoubled my efforts, pouring all my resources into the search. Everything else fell into place. My plan generated growing publicity: there were stories about the walk in local newspapers and magazines, I made two stumbling, stammering appearances on BBC radio, and a major national newspaper committed to printing a series of trail reports. With such prominent media coverage assured I felt certain I'd hook the big fish I needed. But once again time was running out. Winter flew by, spring approached a second time, and the May start drew ever closer. With six weeks to go I received a provisional 'yes' over the phone from a local business, and raced about afterwards like a delirious lottery winner, only to receive a curt follow-up letter three days later informing me that permission from head office had been withdrawn. There were two other gripping 'oh-so-nears' that had me on the edge of my seat, everything in place but the final commitment—which never came. Following leads and suggestions and 'I-have-a-friend-who-has-a-friend' tips I worked myself into a frenzy until the last-gasp moment when the final possibility somehow slipped from an 'Immensely keen, yes we'll do this' to an apologetic 'Sorry, but…'

And there it was again. I couldn't go.

But this time I couldn't postpone the journey. Postponement was *wrong*. I had a gut feeling that if I didn't start right now I never would. It was time to drop the excuses. Many dreamers spend a lifetime making excuses and then—after a lifetime has passed—realise it's too late to act out their dreams. No, it was time to be bolder. I had no responsibilities, no binding family ties, no partner to take into account. Apart from money, what was there to hold me back? I'd saved £2,000, enough for six months if I was careful, and I had to trust that once underway things would somehow work out of their own accord—that the mountain gods or the winds of fate or whatever it was that governed such matters would reward me for committing. It was a life-changing choice: go and risk running out of funds after six months, or don't go and risk the journey itself. In the end I chose 'go'. I chose to believe.

It was a huge leap of faith.

REGGIO DI CALABRIA
Chapter 6

SQUEALING METAL AND hissing brakes announced arrival in Reggio di Calabria. My watch showed 9 p.m.—the train was on time to the second. The two Italians with whom I'd shared the final 100 miles vacated the compartment first, wishing me *'Buona fortuna'* before leaving with a sympathetic shake of their heads. Once the exit was clear I heaved on my oversized pack and followed. This wasn't as easy as it sounds. The pack kept wedging itself into the narrow corridor, its straps catching maddeningly at every opportunity. I puffed, heaved, and cursed, then fell onto the platform when the train finally relinquished its grasp. It wasn't the most heroic arrival.

Night had fallen and a humid blackness pressed heavily upon Reggio. The walk's starting point lay thirty miles around the coast near the small village of Melito di Porto Salvo, but there were no connecting trains until morning. The map purchased in Rome led me to believe I could walk through Reggio swiftly and find somewhere quiet for camp beyond its edge. I didn't want to waste money on a hotel, and Reggio didn't look especially big. All I knew about the city was what I saw on my map.

In fact, Reggio di Calabria is a large, sprawling city of some 170,000 clamouring souls. It clings to the Straits of Messina across from Sicily and climbs from the coastline into a dense urban jungle. Reggio has experienced more than its share of troubles: in 1908 a catastrophic earthquake flattened the city, killing an estimated 25,000 people, over a quarter of the population at the time. Messina across the water suffered even more loss; 65,000 citizens died. Many residents fled for their lives, seeking safety at the water's edge, only to be engulfed by a thirty-foot tsunami, the first of several to follow the quake. It was Western Europe's deadliest natural disaster in modern times.

Recovery took decades, and it wasn't helped by devastating Allied air raids during World War Two. By the time I arrived Reggio was still an embattled city. Twenty-five years of organised crime, gang warfare, siphoned development money, and urban decay had left their mark. Aside from a few isolated pockets of prosperity, Reggio was a rough, poverty-stricken place. Illegally constructed concrete apartments were crumbling, public utilities were in a state of neglect, in poorer quarters open sewers still flowed, and an ancient water system meant city water was often unfit to drink. The economy was failing too: the port was losing trade, unemployment was spiralling upwards, and the only success story was the Calabrian mafia— the 'Ndrangheta clan—which wielded more power than official government bodies. Reportedly, the mafia extorted protection money from every single shop and business, controlled the city council, and dealt persuasively with anyone who crossed them. As the businessman on the train had explained, the mafia were in charge. And this was the city I planned to hike quickly across. How little I knew.

I sensed that things weren't going to run to plan shortly after leaving the station, and should have retreated right away, but didn't. British maps seldom lied about such details as a city's size; why should this map? Without any obvious major thoroughfare to follow I picked the best route I could, and it led into a labyrinth of dark lanes. Once away from the station Reggio appeared abandoned, as though some terrible apocalypse had occurred. Streets lights were dim, broken, or non-existent. Decaying buildings leaned over narrow, rutted streets. Black alleyways opened either side, graffiti and torn posters covered rough walls, and trash, bottles and jagged pieces of rusting metal lay in discarded piles. I walked briskly, trying to look as though I knew my destination, but who was I kidding? I stood out a mile. A shadowy group of men stared coldly as I passed; I could feel their eyes boring into my back. My pulse was soon racing: set into motion by angry shouts down an alley; by a sudden scream from behind an iron-barred window; by the blinding headlights of a car unexpectedly roaring into life;

by a snarling, snapping Cerberus that threw itself without warning against a chain-link fence. Impenetrable shadows filled with suggestions of movement left my nerves jangling. Sweat poured freely in the humidity and heat, and as I raced on into the darkness, determined to escape the city, I cursed the choices I'd made.

After half an hour I reached Reggio's edge—at least the edge on the map—but it was clear even in the blackness that Reggio stretched miles further, and grew rougher still. I lingered a moment, racked with indecision, surrounded by derelict warehouses and filthy tenements, and then succumbed to the panic that had been building for some time. Struggling for air, I dashed back the way I'd come, moving in as close to a run as my backpack allowed, menaced every step of the way by the violence that I knew lurked around every corner. My legs were shaking by the time I arrived back at the brightly lit station and checked in to a hotel opposite it. The room's nightly rate was equal to a twentieth of all I had saved, but to escape the nightmare of Reggio I would have gladly paid everything.

The room was cold, soulless, and spartanly furnished. It matched how I felt inside. I stripped off my sweat-soaked shirt and stood tensely, listening to sounds from the street. Many were unidentifiable. They weren't from my soft, safe, suburban world; instead they accentuated how far from home I was, and how alone. At one point gunshots rang out, and a wave of hopelessness followed them, sweeping away what little belief and optimism I had left. Despair reigned. Some adventurer I was. I couldn't cope with even a *single hour* of southern Italy; what chance did I have of walking to Norway? Angrily, I damned the idiot who'd come up with the idea for this ridiculous walk.

It was impossible.

I was saved, after a bleak age, by a cord hanging within my room's en-suite shower. It didn't appear to do anything, so I pulled it vigorously several times, using the mystery of it as a distraction. I gave up when I heard a rush of footsteps outside, followed by urgent thumping upon my door.

It was the hotel receptionist—I recognised his voice. 'Yes, yes! What is the emergency?' he cried, pounding harder.

'I'm sorry?' I answered. I quickly pulled on my shirt and let him in. 'Er... emergency?'

'You called?' he asked breathlessly. 'You are okay?'

'I called? I did? I don't think so. I'm okay.'

'But you rang.'

'Er… not me. Wasn't me.'

'Room twenty-three, someone pulled the emergency cord. Look…' And he showed me the emergency cord. There it was in the shower, still swinging.

'Oh,' I murmured as comprehension dawned. I felt my face colour, let fly a childish burst of laughter at his flustered face, realising too late that laughing was entirely the wrong thing to do. 'Oh, sorry,' I finally managed. 'I didn't know.'

Glaring, the receptionist looked me up and down; clearly a trouble-maker, this guest. 'Well, okay. This time. But remember: it is for *emergencies only.*' And with a final suspicious glance he left me to it.

I was still laughing when sleep claimed me.

MELITO DI PORTO SALVO
Chapter 7

IN BRIGHT MORNING sunshine Reggio wasn't the murderer-infested hellhole I'd imagined the night before, merely a city down at heel. All the same, I was happy to leave. The train to Melito di Porto Salvo carried me south-east around the sun-drenched Mediterranean coast and I loved every second of the ride. My nose was pressed to the window the entire way.

Melito sat at the southernmost point of the Italian Peninsula, sandwiched between rough hills and a wide sea. It was a compact little town existing for no obvious purpose I could see. There were no fishing boats, no signs of industry, no farms, just weary buildings squashed side by side and hundreds of half-built concrete structures that someone had clearly forgotten to finish. I instantly liked the obscurity of the place.

I dragged my backpack into a small café, bought juice and fresh bread, and after a stumbling start, began a conversation with a darkly tanned man. He told me he was a builder, but his posture suggested that café dweller was his full-time profession. His clothes and fingernails were spotless.

'So, is there much work here?' I asked, taking several comical minutes to do it in my faltering Italian.

'Ah, work!' he said fondly, in a voice that was coarse, slow, but wonderfully melodic. 'Yes, there is much work. I build houses. My friends, they also build houses.'

Several half-built concrete shells were visible through the café window.

'Why are so many unfinished?' I asked tentatively.

'Because we do not need them all.'

'But then why build them?'

'For the government. You see, the government pays extra money for each new house.' He swept both hands up towards the unfinished buildings in a gesture of immense pride. 'We only need to build so much for the money. So we have more houses, more money, and save building materials. It is very sensible.' I was glad it made sense to him.

His directions to the nearest campsite were equally nonsensical, but I found it anyway despite them. Located a mile along the coast, the cramped campsite was so close to the rail tracks it vibrated every time a train rushed by. Twenty-seven and a half slightly mouldy caravans and a utilitarian shower building left little room for tents, but mine—the Peapod Mark II —took up hardly any space, and soon a small patch of ant-travelled dirt was home.

The Peapod was a tiny tent, just three feet high and eight feet long. Called a Jetpacker by its manufacturer, Robert Saunders, the name I used had originated from a drunk Yorkshire camper seven years earlier. Stumbling across the English campsite after dark, he almost tripped over the tent.

'What the?' he exclaimed loudly to himself. 'By 'eck, that weren't there earlier. But is it a tent? Can't be! Too bloody small!'

He giggled for a moment, then continued, his words impressively slurred. 'Thou'd have to be a contorshioner... a conatorshion... a con... a...' and he ground to a halt, before inspiration struck: 'Thou'd have to be reet bendy to get inside that! Yeah, tha's no tent... it's nowt but a bloody peapod!'

Yes, I thought, lying within it, listening to the one-sided conversation outside: *the Peapod. What a perfect name.*

And now my second Peapod was pitched at the southernmost point of mainland Italy, in a campground entirely devoid of other campers. The only other occupant was a fiery-eyed hound of dubious lineage who paced to and fro outside a kennel on a well-worn patch of earth. He didn't appear to like campers; every time I moved he growled. I approved of the strong chain that bound him.

The summer season was still weeks off and I was the year's first visitor.

The emptiness created an atmosphere of expectancy, of things soon to begin; it felt perfectly appropriate.

It was time for final preparations. I returned to Melito and bought supplies from a cluttered food store staffed by two eager-to-please ladies. I was the only English customer they'd served in the twenty-eight years they'd worked at the store, and they fussed over me cheerfully while I rummaged along two disorganised aisles. Produce was limited, but I'd soon collected a mountain of provisions for the walk's first six days. When I came to pay, the price was shocking; at first I thought a mistake had been made.

'This is the correct price?' I gasped. 'For all this?'

'*Si, si.* This is correct. *Problemo?*'

'Oh nooooo!' I added quickly. The price was fine, just unexpectedly cheap. Six days' food here cost the same as one day's food back home. Such low prices filled me with optimism. Perhaps my pitiful reserves would last longer than I'd supposed.

I spent the afternoon back in camp dividing the loot into daily rations, wondering how on earth it would all fit into my pack. There was barely room for clothes and gear. The only solution I could see was to start eating there and then and worry about rationing later, so I stuffed myself silly, which wasn't a bad way to prepare for crossing a continent on foot.

Between bites I pulled out needle and thread and got to work on my backpack. I sewed on two extra straps to increase its carrying capacity, and repaired a shoulder strap already showing worrying signs of wear. The sewing was surprisingly therapeutic—until I stabbed a finger. Afterwards, while it bled into a sloppily applied bandage, I wandered down to the beach and sat staring out to sea, seeking some level of calm.

Gentle waves washed the beach, murmuring rhythmically. The sea and sky were grey, but a bright flotilla of clouds hung in the distance, obscuring Mount Etna, Europe's tallest active volcano. At my back, towering above the first Apennine hills, a huge anvil-headed cloud flashed and flickered with lightning, although I couldn't hear thunder. The unusual absence of sound gave the storm a serene, otherworldly beauty. But it didn't bring calm. In twenty-four hours I'd be up where it raged.

Sleep that night was hard to pin down. Melito was not quiet: scooters buzzed like angry hornets, church bells rang, dogs barked and bayed, crickets chirped, cats wailed, trains rattled by. But it was the rising excitement

The beach at Melito di Porto Salvo on the afternoon
before the walk began, April 30, 1997.

in the pit of my stomach that hindered sleep. I tried suppressing it, but the harder I tried the more it boiled, until soon it was like a fever, a crescendo of an emotion, as impossible to bottle as it would be to cork an erupting Etna.

I was about to begin a new life, become a completely different person. After waiting so long I was finally here, yet it seemed unreal. Too unlikely to be true. For a year and a half this had been a fantasy, a dream, but I wasn't dreaming anymore. For a long moment exhilaration overcame me: what freedom I now had! There were no longer any regrets, and all the doubts and fears seemed ludicrous. This was exactly where I wanted to be. More than that, it was where I was supposed to be.

A thought struck that this moment would only occur once, so why waste it trying to sleep? Out of my tent I climbed, and down to the beach I wandered, and before the sea I stood, one small figure alone on the edge of a continent.

A soft breeze brushed my face, and wave-washed pebbles chilled my bare feet. A bright moon two days off full shone upon the sea. Quite possibly, someone in Arctic Norway was staring at the moon that very moment, as was someone back in Pinner. The moon looked the same wherever one was, and I found comfort in that. It was a link to home; a link also to my destination. Unwisely perhaps, I found myself picturing the North Cape. It was impossibly distant, practically a lifetime away, but I couldn't imagine not reaching it. I could see the final day clearly, could imagine my lone figure tramping across snow to a dark headland above a churning sea. And yet I couldn't picture the Aspromonte a single day away. I didn't even know where I'd be sleeping tomorrow night! I sensed that the journey would be full of such enigmas.

I stood for an unmeasured age, and the magic of the night washed through me. I breathed it in, storing it away, curiously nostalgic for the moment even as it happened. Finally, yawns overcame me. I turned from the water and walked calmly back to camp.

PART II

THE APENNINES

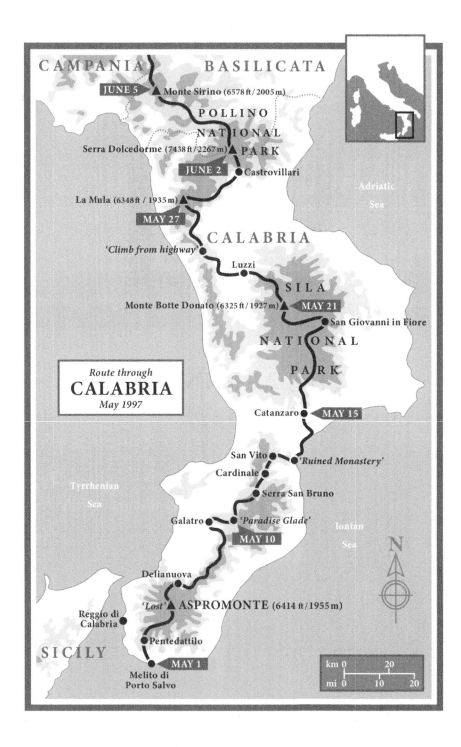

CAMPANIA   BASILICATA

JUNE 5 ▲ Monte Sirino (6578 ft / 2005 m)

POLLINO
NATIONAL
Serra Dolcedorme (7438 ft / 2267 m) ▲ PARK

JUNE 2 ● Castrovillari

La Mula (6348 ft / 1935 m) ▲

MAY 27

Adriatic
Sea

CALABRIA

'Climb from highway' ●
Luzzi ●

SILA

Monte Botte Donato (6325 ft / 1927 m) ▲ ◀ MAY 21
● San Giovanni in Fiore

NATIONAL

Route through
CALABRIA
May 1997

PARK

Catanzaro ● ◀ MAY 15

San Vito ●
Cardinale ●
● 'Ruined Monastery'

Tyrrhenian
Sea

● Serra San Bruno

Galatro ● ● 'Paradise Glade'

MAY 10

Ionian
Sea

Delianuova ●

'Lost' ▲ ASPROMONTE (6414 ft / 1955 m)

Reggio di
Calabria ●

● Pentedattilo

SICILY

MAY 1

Melito di
Porto Salvo

N

km 0   20
mi 0   10   20

FIVE SMALL PEBBLES
Chapter 1

MAY 1 DAWNED mild and bright, which was just as well. Had there been wind, rain, or even one small cloud I might have given in to temptation and hidden within my sleeping bag all day, a victim once again to emotions out of control. But conditions were perfect, offering nothing that could justify delay. There was no option but to get up and get going.

Dismantling camp took two hours, far longer than it should have—partly because I wanted to set a precedent for the entire journey by not rushing, but mostly because I couldn't fit all my food and gear into the pack. I spent ages trying, and in the end solved the problem by strapping much of the gear on the outside. The worst of it wasn't the sheer unbalancing weight—it was how it looked. It was just plain embarrassing.

Travelling light had never been my forte. I'd like to blame it on the heavier backpacking gear of the time, but that would be stretching the truth. The real reason was that I placed comfort in camp ahead of comfort on the trail. As I knew from previous walks, I'd spend twice as much time in camp as walking and there was no point making that time unnecessarily uncomfortable. Thus, my sleeping bag was warmer and heavier than needed, my sleeping mat thicker. And I packed more clothes than strictly necessary; there were clothes for walking, clothes for day's end. Food was approached in a similar way. I didn't want to get by on over-processed, chemically enhanced, dehydrated gruel for eighteen months. Fresh food was my fuel of choice. The journey didn't have to be an exercise in self-inflicted sacrifice. There was nothing noble in that. I wanted life to remain a pleasure.

For that reason, I also carried books and bulky camera gear: items not truly essential for progress, but indispensable items to me. Reading is one of the great joys of camp life, and photography wasn't merely for documenting the journey but a process to get me more involved, to help me see. Such items added to the load, but also added to the journey. I'd learnt I could carry half my body weight—seventy pounds—without excessive discomfort. Backpacking purists would likely scoff at such a load, judging it clear evidence that I didn't know what I was doing. But I did know, and I figured it was only too heavy if it distracted me from the journey or stopped me reaching the end. The only real difficulty lay in hoisting it onto my shoulders—which, until I grew practised at it, was touch and go. The first morning was no exception. Standing up took practically every ounce of strength I had, but finally I managed it, and stood upright, with Ten Ton on my back. The name came unprompted, but for some reason stuck. Wearing the backpack was like being massaged by a ten-ton forklift truck.

At nine-thirty I returned to the beach. As far as I could tell it was a morning like any other at Melito di Porto Salvo. As usual, gentle waves washed the pebbles; as usual, cloud-capped Mount Etna rose across the Straits of Messina; as usual, the old men of the village sat outside the tiny Bar Rosa, putting the world to rights. I was the only abnormality: a skinny, pasty-white foreigner wobbling under a monster-sized load. For me the morning was anything but ordinary. Outwardly, I was trying to project calm; inwardly I was tearing about like an over-stimulated hound. It's not every day one gets to start a 7,000-mile walk.

It was time to go.

Before turning north there was a ritual to complete. Bending down, I searched the pebbles at my feet for a token stone to carry to the North Cape. Once there I'd hurl it from the clifftop into the Barents Sea. This small piece of southern Italy would mark the journey's start and symbolically connect beginning to end, although why such a symbolic act was needed I couldn't say. But it seemed strangely meaningful, and therefore important. It was like the journey itself, perhaps even like life: it had no meaning, until meaning was consciously applied.

I took my time choosing, waiting for a pebble to suggest itself. At last

The start: sitting beside my monster backpack, Ten Ton, May 1, 1997.

one did. It was small, smooth, rounded, delightfully green, with a streak of quartz running through it, and I plucked it up before a wave could claw it away. But then another pebble caught my eye, pinkish-red this time, embedded with sparkling crystals; and then another, pale orange, flecked with grey. In the end I held five small pebbles and couldn't choose between them, so pocketed the lot. I wondered if the walk would be like that in its entirety. Would I always find more than I looked for, never less?

And so, finally, I took the first steps, but they were anticlimactic. There was no fanfare, no drum roll, no cheering crowds to see me off. I walked slowly, crunching across loose pebbles, and within 100 yards was already damp with sweat and breathing hard. Time for a break. I dropped Ten Ton, stripped to shorts, and plunged into the sea. Aside from a few items of floating trash the Mediterranean had looked inviting, but it gave an instant shock. Had I plunged into the icy Barents Sea by mistake? For a few seconds I toughed it out, hyperventilating, and failed to notice the only large wave for 100 miles, which came sweeping in and bowled me right over.

Spluttering, I resurfaced and scrambled onto dry land, hoping I hadn't swallowed anything toxic. A near drowning wasn't the most promising of starts.

I spent the next thirty minutes stretched out on the pebbles beneath the blazing sun, until it really was time to go. With a last look out to sea I turned inland and walked north.

'And we're off,' I murmured aloud. 'Mad Mountain Jack lives again!' Mad Mountain Jack—Mad Jack for short—was the trail name my three brothers had given me years earlier. Having a second name felt appropriate. Mad Jack and Andrew may have inhabited the same body, but they lived entirely different lives.

For the first mile I couldn't settle down, couldn't find any kind of rhythm. The simple act of placing one foot before the other seemed like the most extraordinary thing. 'Just look,' I spoke aloud again. 'I'm walking to Norway!' Laughing, I tried reminding myself that walking wasn't difficult or clever. Several billion people were probably doing it at that very moment. I had two legs, and they'd evolved for one purpose—forward propulsion. Remembering it helped. But at no point during the first day's march did the process feel ordinary.

My chosen route led uphill along narrow country lanes. Spring hadn't yet put leaves on the trees or green into the grass, and the landscape looked dried-up and dead. The only plant doing well was prickly pear cactus, an invasive import—and that such a desert-loving species was flourishing said a great deal about the aridity of the climate and poverty of the soil. A different kind of poverty was evident in unkempt buildings dotting the hillsides, and in litter and junk that lay everywhere. This wasn't the picturesque Italy of travel brochures, the *bellissimo* landscape beloved by artists. Life here looked hard. Material excess was notably absent, people clearly made do with what they had, and transport was less mechanised. I pulled level with a bent old lady clad head to toe in black. She was toiling up the road, pulling a huge load that dwarfed mine: a creaking handcart holding a mountain of hay. Respectfully, I tried engaging her in conversation, but my stammer thwarted my words, and the lady just looked through me with a perplexed expression as though she couldn't work out what type of creature I was, or where she'd seen one before. And I couldn't blame her. I was probably the first backpacker she'd ever seen. We parted without establishing any kind of connection, and it seemed a missed opportunity, the first failure of the walk. *You can do better*, I told myself. *You have to break through.* If I didn't it would be a lonely year and a half.

After a few miles I reached an ancient village, Pentedattilo, perched beneath thrusting towers of rock. Pentedattilo was first inhabited by Greeks in 640 BCE, and spent much of the next two millennia being conquered and sacked by invaders. Finally abandoned in 1783 after one of Calabria's many earthquakes, it was now a crumbling ruin, sinking back into the land. No matter how deeply established people had once been, the land had ultimately won out. Harsh winds, sterilising Mezzogiorno heat, infrequent rains, floods and landslides, poor soil, the trembling earth itself; some things could be coped with for a while, for 2,500 years even, but never overcome. There was a certain inevitability to Pentedattilo. It suited the landscape perfectly.

Pentedattilo, Calabria, May 1, 1997.

Calabria has endured a great deal, and it showed. Aside from the fierce climate and devastating natural disasters, the region has suffered war and neglect for thousands of years. Recorded history began with relative prosperity. The first settlers were the Itali tribe, the people that gave Italy its name. They were a peaceful people with long-term plans; they cultivated the land, growing grapes and other crops. After a few hundred years the Greeks joined them, establishing cities around the coast and the rule of law, turning the region into a well-run breadbasket. Arguably, this was Calabria's golden era, but it didn't last. Soon there were feuds, battles, invasions, conquests. Calabrians were pushed into the dirt. Tribes from the north conquered the Greeks, who were conquered by Romans, who eventually gave way to Arabs, who were followed by Normans. As centuries passed, Calabrians were never allowed the opportunity to govern themselves. Each time they tried pulling themselves up they were forcibly pushed back down. Throughout the Middle Ages distant rulers called the shots. Monarchs from Spain, Austria and Naples lorded it over the region, exploiting and taxing it heavily. These absentee landlords established a feudal system that did little to raise impoverished Calabrian peasants above their lowly status. Even the unification of Italy's separate states into one nation in the mid-nineteenth century, which should have benefited the entire peninsula, failed to benefit the Italian south. Power stayed in the north—as did all the wealth. The people from the rich, sophisticated, fertile, industrialised north came to look down their noses at their southern compatriots. Calabrians were considered backward, thick-headed, lazy, and they deserved everything they got, which was malaria, famines, earthquakes, epidemics, bandits, economic neglect, a mass exodus of its citizens, and ultimately the mafia. No wonder the hillsides looked abused, the buildings uncared-for, the entire landscape unfriendly.

Something of that unfriendliness was reflected in its people. The only realistic route on this first day lay by road. Traffic was infrequent, but when cars drove by several gave loud blasts on their horns. Youths filling one car shouted as they sped by, expressions taunting, making strange insulting gestures through open windows with their hands. Another car deliberately swerved at me, kicking up stones mere feet from where I'd jumped. Afterwards, I stood in disbelief, watching the car disappear, too shocked to react in anger. Had someone really just tried running me down? And it wasn't only people. Dogs ran out from every yard, snarling and barking, backing up only when I stooped for rocks. It was a relief to find a dusty trail leading towards higher ground and leave so-called civilisation behind.

By early afternoon dark clouds hung over the mountains and thunder rumbled ominously. Soon a steady rain began to fall. As I pushed into a secluded valley my legs were quickly soaked by rain-wettened grass, and I began thinking about camp. I'd only travelled thirteen miles, but the first day didn't have to be an epic—even though it felt as though it already had been.

Before camp could be made I needed water, but to my surprise there was none to be had. The distinctive shape of the valley suggested water had carved it, but there was no stream running through the valley, and the rain merely vanished into the dust. Such dry valleys seldom existed back in the British hills, or in other European ranges I'd explored. I'd grown so used to water being available that I'd taken it for granted it always would be. This was clearly a mistake: the first 'oops' moment, and probably not the last. Perhaps I wasn't as competent at this walking game as I liked to believe.

When an old stone lean-to appeared ahead I took shelter, and considered the problem. An inspired idea arose: why not collect rainwater? Pulling out the plastic groundsheet I carried, as well as a ten-litre water bag, I got to work, and soon had a channel of rainwater running into the water bag; within minutes I'd collected enough. The rain ceased shortly after, but that was okay, and I sat back smugly, belief in my competence restored. But the smugness only lasted until I picked up the water bag and discovered, to my horror, that it was now empty again. I'd sealed the top but had forgotten the valve at its base. *Sure*, I thought sarcastically. *I'm going to make it to Norway.*

Thankfully, fortune was on my side. A mile further I chanced upon a glorious sight: a spring gushing cold and clear into a stone trough, and a flat, grassy terrace right beside it. Everything in the world I needed. And how satisfying to know that my needs were so few.

After a day spent crossing unfriendly ground it was comforting to slip back into tried-and-tested camp routines, familiar from hundreds of mountain nights. First came pitching the tent, then unpacking gear and arranging it as I liked, then lighting the stove. After that it was sustenance: boiling water for tea, then more of the same for dinner. Dinner was pasta, roughly chopped vegetables, chunks of tinned ham, soup and potato powder, pieces of biscuit, and a dash of salt, all mixed together into a wonderful sticky glop. As usual, it wasn't an attractive sight, but my camping stews never were. 'Ugh, what the hell is that?' one of my brothers, Paul, had once asked in revulsion. 'Oh, only eat-it-if-you-dare stew,' I'd replied, digging in wolfishly. But it did the job. From here on I'd eat pretty much the same meal every night. Variation wasn't important; quantity came before quality; and so long as it was piping hot, stick-to-the-ribs-filling, and quick to prepare, it always hit the spot.

After dinner, the familiar routines continued. I rinsed the pot, licked the spoon clean, splashed water over my feet. I spent half an hour scribbling in my diary, another half hour teasing out the next day's route on the all-but-useless map, fifteen minutes practising Italian, and eventually came to the final—and best—part of my camp routines: doing absolutely nothing at all.

To do nothing, to rest in observant stillness for hours on end, was a large part of why I was walking. It's a luxury ordinary life rarely affords. As I saw it, the journey wasn't just about covering ground and getting somewhere—it was also about *being* somewhere. It was about opening all the senses, and connecting with each place. It was also about connecting with my own thoughts, and distilling life into something slower and simpler. It was about reaching beyond the surface for deeper truths, however vague they might be. Doing nothing gave me strength to go on afterwards and do something. It was always time well spent.

For the rest of the day I did nothing. The Peapod was too small for sitting upright, so I lay instead, staring out at the world. Rain began falling once again. I watched stems of grass bobbing and dancing as raindrops struck them, watched blurry-edged clouds spill over the ridge 500 feet above and pour downwards until swirling white fog hid the world. I listened to cuckoos calling, a familiar sound from countless camps back in Britain, and was transported in an instant to the Pennines, and to nights atop ocean bluffs in Cornwall, and to peaceful sojourns beside Scottish lochs. With fog filling the valley, rain drumming on the fly, and cuckoos calling, it suddenly seemed impossible that I was in Calabria. Surely I was back home at the start of an easier, shorter, friendlier walk?

For much of the day, the unfriendly miles had rekindled doubts and anxieties similar to those I'd suffered in Reggio. It was hard not to think about how far from home I was, hard to ignore the immensity of the challenge ahead. I was hopeful that the anxieties would fade, that they were no more than withdrawal symptoms from easier living. They'd darkened the first day's miles, but for now, with a soft blanket of familiarity draped across the landscape, the fears and homesickness slipped away.

THE ASPROMONTE
Chapter 2

CALABRIA IS A crinkled, folded, mountainous land. Less than ten per cent of it is flat. Most of its population lives along the coastal plains, leaving much of the interior uninhabited and undeveloped; perfect for mountain walking. Or so I expected.

The first high region on my route was the Aspromonte, the 'rough mountain'. Rising to 6,414 feet at Montalto, the Aspromonte is a labyrinthine wilderness of steep-sided valleys, twisting ridges, and remote summits. Forests of oak, beech, fir and pine cover the entire region, even cloaking the summits, and many of the valleys are so densely wooded that they are—to all intents and purposes—entirely cut off from the rest of the world. It's said that certain corners are so hard to penetrate and so seldom visited that those who have fallen foul of the law can safely seek refuge there for years on end. Tales insist that bandits still roam the wilds, as do large animals like wild boar and wolves. From the mid-seventies until the early nineties the 'Ndrangheta clan put the Aspromonte's inaccessibility to use, secreting away kidnap victims far from prying eyes. Supposedly, by the time of my visit, the practice had ceased. *Supposedly.* The 'Ndrangheta were definitely an organisation to respect. A vengeful inter-clan war between 1985 and 1991 left 600 people dead. To stumble across a mafia hideout deep in the Aspromonte would create a wilderness challenge unlike any I'd ever faced.

Not that I was worried. I knew nothing about the mafia's habits or the dense forests. My expectations were entirely based upon my less-than-detailed map, and on other Mediterranean ranges I'd previously walked. Elsewhere, mountains meant trails and open country where one could walk for miles and see a hundred more. Why should Calabria be any different? I assumed that, being so far south and so searing hot in summer, Calabria would offer barren slopes. It would be a harsh place, but accessible on foot. The only travel guide I'd found that even mentioned the Aspromonte confirmed it with two photos of open, treeless mountains. My assumptions were boosted further by the Aspromonte's status as an official national park, achieved eight years earlier. Every other national park I'd visited had been developed with pedestrian travel in mind. Some had even been overdeveloped, and I hoped the Aspromonte wasn't like that. But I needn't have worried; all my assumptions were wrong.

I reached the Aspromonte's edge at the end of the second day, thirty miles into the trip. Leaving the site of my first camp exactly as I'd found it, I wandered across fog-bound hills scattered with rocky outcrops and gorse-like shrubs, enjoying the rough terrain and the isolation. By this point my map made little sense—nothing on it remotely matched reality on the ground—so I resorted to compass work and educated guesses, and picked my way by feel, certain the Aspromonte's trails would ease progress once I reached them. After two miles I chanced upon a dirt road, and followed it north appreciatively, but it soon veered downhill back towards the sea, and I had to step away. Thus was the pattern set for the day: a few easy sections along dirt roads, followed by slower miles off trail. By the time I pitched camp I had only a vague idea where I was.

By the next camp I had no idea at all.

Progress on the third day was easy—at least to begin with. Unexpectedly, I stumbled upon a newly paved road so clean and bright it might have been finished the day before. Completely deserted, it twisted up-valley in the direction I wanted, and I followed it celebrating my good fortune. An easy mile passed. But then—without warning—it did what I was soon to discover many Apennine roads did: it stopped dead in the middle of nowhere. Ahead now was a solid wall of green. Surprised, I stepped towards it, and came face to face with an Apennine feature I'd soon get to know all too well. The infamous *sottobosco*.

The *sottobosco*—literally 'under wood'—covers great swathes of the Apennines. Dense, tangled and thorny, it takes many forms, but all severely limit progress (or stop it altogether). This first *sottobosco* was comprised of beech trees, but they were unlike any beech trees I'd previously seen. Common across central and southern Europe, beech woods are typically open and spacious, offering big trees, high canopies and soft carpets of leafy mulch. I'd experienced such woods during childhood walks with my grandfather, but this first Apennine beech wood was the opposite: not friendly and open but unwelcoming and closed. Progress was a battle from the first step, with the trees holding the upper hand. After just a few yards I was caught between interlocking limbs, snagged and hooked, and soon I was down on hands and knees simply to squeeze by, which struck me as crazy. I hadn't anticipated having to crawl across Italy. At that speed it would take eighteen months merely to cross Calabria. Wasn't Italy supposed to be civilised? *This* Italy was a jungle. I hadn't anticipated the difficulties beginning quite so soon.

It took two hours and several moments of near despair before I reached less tangled terrain. Dirty and scratched, I finally emerged into pine woods, relieved at the escape, only to realise I hadn't escaped at all. The pine woods weren't any easier. I'd climbed to 5,000 feet, and up here the forest floor was covered by snow. Speckled with fallen needles, the snow was leg-swallowingly soft where sunlight had reached it, and treacherously icy in the shade. Excalibur, laughed at on the train, was soon in use. With the axe in one hand and my compass in the other, I forged a route due north across the grain of the land, dropping into narrow ravines, fording rivers, climbing steep snow slopes, relying on Excalibur for purchase, forever descending and climbing, descending and climbing, never once knowing where I was. Tree limbs grabbed at Ten Ton; snowdrifts grabbed at my legs. Dense thickets demanded detours, and plunging ice slopes prompted retreats. It was impossible to follow a straight line or see any distance. The forest only thinned once, and all I saw ahead was more forest cloaking ridge after ridge, stretching away, snowy, wild, dark, and without a trail in sight. It wasn't what I'd planned.

Instead of relaxing into the land I worked myself into a frenzy. I'd hoped to climb to the Aspromonte's summit, but hadn't the foggiest idea now where it lay. *Perhaps I've already passed it*, I thought. The map, with its

'Lost' in the Aspromonte, May 3, 1997.

vaguely etched lines, was useless. Frustration grew. I was lost, and wanted the reassurance of being found. In the race to 'get there' I had forgotten every lesson supposedly learnt from all my years of mountain travel. I forgot that wild places don't care about expectations; they simply are what they are. I forgot that my role was to bend to the landscape, not expect it to bend to me. And I forgot that adventure was about uncertainty, about dealing with adversity with a positive outlook, making the best of what one has, changing what one can, accepting what one can't. Instead of focusing on where I was, I focused exclusively on where I wasn't, on how my expectations weren't being met, and the Aspromonte became a thoroughly testing place because of it.

Testing, and increasingly unsettling. The further I walked the wilder the forest became—less a European forest and more one from a continent that had never been explored. On one hand, it was exactly what I'd come for, but on the other it was too wild too soon. I wasn't ready, and it intimidated me. I started feeling that I didn't belong. As the feeling grew apprehension grew with it, and that only increased my frustration. Was I really still scared of the wild—even after all the mountains I'd climbed on previous trips? It bothered me. It was something I should have grown out of. Would I never manage it?

Pushing on, I thought about my flight of fear at thirteen, how a thousand malevolent eyes had chased me from tame suburban woods. And I remembered my indecision on the edge of the Peak District, how I'd wavered in doubt until other hikers appeared. The fear here reminded me of both occasions, although it was more insidious, more of a creeping dread that things weren't as they should be, and a rising compulsion to rush to make them right.

The problem was, unlike the wood I'd fled at thirteen, this forest genuinely was wild. And unlike in the Peak District, there was no chance other hikers would suddenly appear to give me confidence. There was no broad track to follow, no town close behind. The mountains stretched away on all sides for unknown distances. I was in deep with no easy way out. I was committed, with only myself to rely on, and this truth gnawed at my confidence.

I kept moving, following my compass north where the terrain allowed. My boots sunk into snow, branches grasped, twigs and pine needles caught in my hair. I began thinking about the old cardinal rule: *never walk alone.* I'd been breaking it for years—not just because I didn't have anyone to walk with but because I preferred walking alone. It had come to seem like a rule that imposed unnecessary limits, a rule that missed the point of why people head to the hills, a rule promoted by overcautious people who didn't understand the rewards that being alone brought. As I'd learnt at thirteen, places were experienced very differently alone. Back then, the experience had been terrifying, but in the years since walking alone had revealed treasures I'd never have found in company. Now, however, the *never walk alone* rule began haunting me. I couldn't push aside the idea that breaking it was wrong.

I was breaking another rule too: *always let someone know where you are going.* Goodness was I breaking that! No one knew where I was. I didn't even know where I was. And that only increased my anxiety further.

Before leaving home I'd marked my route on a map of Europe and had left it with my parents, for their benefit more than mine, and for logistical reasons rather than for safety. It included my resupply towns with rough arrival times, but it didn't show sufficient detail to help searchers find me if I didn't show up. Detail was impossible to give. Not only did I not have detailed maps, the route was certain to change daily depending on conditions. No one would know where I was at any given time. That would only change when I phoned home from each resupply town. Once every two weeks my parents would know I was safe.

Understandably, they worried, and for that I felt truly terrible, but I couldn't live an unfulfilled life because of it. My parents understood this, and to some extent they'd grown used to it during my previous journeys. To their credit, they never made it a big deal, although my father didn't keep entirely silent on the matter. 'Andrew, I think you're mad to take these risks,' he told me more than once.

Usually, being aware that no one knew where I was, that I was on my own, that there was zero chance of rescue, didn't trouble me. *I* knew where *I* was. *I* knew I was safe. *I* knew how much care I was taking. Hohtürli had taught me to watch every step, weigh every decision, and always consider the consequences. Thanks to the accident, I'd become an aggressively careful walker. As I saw it, I was far safer alone relying 100 per cent on myself than in a group relying on others. Groups brought a false sense of security, encouraged risks that would never be taken alone—as did knowing rescue was possible. Knowing there was no chance of help decreased the likelihood of needing it.

On previous walks I'd revelled in the self-reliance, but here it was different. The scale and roughness of the Aspromonte changed everything. Plus, it was a forest. I was a mountain walker, an above-tree-line walker, not a forest walker. Wide open spaces were home, not this dark, closed-in environment. I knew how mountains worked, but here I felt out of control, out of place, and out of reach of safety. Yes, it was definitely too wild too soon.

At least I had a plan: to head north. The Aspromonte had to end eventually. But until I reached that end I couldn't suppress my impatience, or my fear. I felt frantic and my speed increased. I knew I was behaving irrationally but couldn't slow myself, couldn't convince myself that I did belong here, or that I was safe. Was this one of the reasons I'd started the walk, to overcome my upbringing? Could I ever stand in a truly wild place and feel that I belonged? Would I ever move beyond this anxiety and fear?

At least I wasn't pining for home. The battle was so intense it left little room for homesickness. And, unsettling though it was, I'd never experienced a more absorbing set of miles. For ten gruelling hours I fought the *sottobosco* trying to find out where I was, hoping to stumble upon something that matched the map. When I made camp I still didn't know. The site I chose was a place of pine trees, snow and solitude—an entirely different universe to the seaside village I'd started from three days earlier. On any other occasion I would have revelled in the wild beauty, but I was too anxious to appreciate it for what it was.

Sleep wasn't restful—my dreams were disturbed. Dark shapes lurked within them, accidents occurred. In one dream I led a group of close friends up an ice-clad mountain in Norway. All at once they slipped and slid away, fingers reaching for mine, eyes wide with fear. One by one they plummeted over a precipice, vanishing without a sound. None had brought an ice axe, but I realised that was my fault—I hadn't told them to. I was supposed to be looking after them. I was the one who supposedly knew what he was doing. But did I?

Heavy water droplets thudding onto the tent woke me several times during the night. Outside, dense fog held the Aspromonte captive; appropriate conditions for a range also known as 'The Cloud Gatherer'. By dawn the fog had gone but, like my dreams, it lingered oppressively in memory for several hours.

The walk's fourth morning began as the previous day had finished. By noon I was beginning to doubt I'd ever reach the Aspromonte's far side, but to my relief the range began sloping downhill, the snowpack thinned, and by early afternoon I'd lost enough altitude that winter's old drifts had fallen behind.

Progress after that became significantly easier, and the anxiety started fading away. I entered a belt of beech woods as open as those from my childhood. The canopy was now high overhead, and it was softened by the first flush of spring. Gushing streams led to silver waterfalls, a thousand birds sang, and invigorating scents of new growth filled the air. In direct sunlight, temperatures were a few degrees above comfortable, but all it took to cool off was a pause at a stream. I could drink and cleanse my sweat-soaked body with one exuberant scoop, and the pleasure was all the greater for the battle and fear I'd just endured.

My goal in life had now become reaching the northern edge of the Aspromonte, specifically a minor road marked on my map, and at last—with a scream of joy—I reached it. Or so I believed. But this was Calabria, where roads on maps seldom match roads on the ground. Relaxing for the first time in two days I followed the unpaved road for a mile, but then tensed when it grew smaller, twisted in the wrong direction, and dwindled away entirely. Over the next two hours three further roads behaved the same way, promising escape but delivering me back into wilderness. A fundamental rule of Apennine travel was becoming clear: Apennine roads don't necessarily come from somewhere or go anywhere.

Late afternoon I finally burst free from the forest and landed upon the road I'd been seeking all along. From its edge I was granted my first long-distance view in two days: a sweeping panorama across foothills and hillside villages to the silver edge of the Tyrrhenian Sea. North-east lay my future: a long line of forested mountains rolling into the haze. It felt like cheating, being able to see so far.

But I still didn't know exactly where I was, although it looked as though I'd soon be able to find out. A hundred yards away I saw a shepherd. He was reclining beside the road, holding a large umbrella for shade, watching a few ragged sheep graze in a meadow. He looked up as I approached, stared at my backpack, and then—with appalling manners—burst into laughter. For a moment I was taken aback, but quickly accepted that laughter was probably deserved. By the shepherd's standards I'd seriously over-packed. All he carried was a leather flask, the umbrella, and a grubby woollen blanket; my load must have looked ridiculous.

I greeted the shepherd and held up my map. 'Please, could you tell me: where are we?' I asked in Italian.

The shepherd pulled the map towards him and stared long and hard, rubbing dirty fingers across the Aspromonte. He looked up, weathered face knotted with uncertainty, and shrugged, shaking his head. Where were we? Seems he didn't know either.

But I couldn't accept that. Surely he had to know?

Throwing my arms wide, gesturing to the mountain directly behind, I asked again, politely but with more emphasis. 'Where... are... we?'

There was a long silence. Even the sheep expected an answer now. Finally, the shepherd gave one.

'*Siamo qui*' ('We are right here'), he said simply.

I couldn't argue with that.

Calabrian shepherd, May 4, 1997.

YOU CAN'T ALWAYS HAVE WHAT YOU WANT
Chapter 3

THERE ARE THREE kinds of walking in the southern Apennines: the rough, the very rough, and the almost impossible.

Okay, so that's not strictly true, but it's not far off. There is a fourth kind of walking, if a northbound hiker wants to make solid northbound progress, and that's road walking. But this was something I wanted to do as little as possible. I hadn't come to hike roads; I'd come to hike mountains, to feel the earth beneath my feet. The mountains, however, weren't so easily hiked.

With the Aspromonte crossed I continued along the crest of the Calabrian Apennines, although 'crest' makes the range sound more dramatic than it really is. Instead of being a clearly defined ridge the Apennines became rounded, remained wooded, and began rolling like a confused sea. A few roads crossed the range, and a few others led along it roughly where I wanted, but they were unpleasant to walk upon, hot for my feet encased in heavy mountain boots, and severely limiting to the spirit.

Trouble was, roads were the only viable option. There weren't any trails. For a trail to exist someone would have had to plan it, pay for it, construct it, and then maintain it, but Calabrians clearly had more pressing matters to focus on. From what I could see, the locals weren't big on walking for pleasure. Given the nature of the land that was understandable. Impenetrable forests, searing summer heat, biting winter cold, frequent earthquakes,

Typical Calabrian scenery, May 9, 1997.

landslides, raging floods; historically, the land hadn't ever been welcoming. The land's many destructive forces had done more to keep Calabrians down than any wilful human influence. Although Italy is famous for its ancient civilisations, the peninsula is geologically young and highly active. Reggio's 1908 earthquake was just one of many to shake Calabria's foundations—hundreds of thousands more Calabrians have died in other quakes, mudslides, and floods, as well as in the epidemics and famines that followed. If Calabrians didn't rush into the wild for pleasure, and if they viewed the land with distrust, who could blame them?

At first, lacking trails, I tried pushing directly through the woods, but the woods were rather good at pushing back. Occasionally they granted passage—albeit begrudgingly—but more often they defended themselves with brambles, intertwined branches, and undergrowth so dense I couldn't see ten feet. Still focused on what I wanted the walk to be, I found myself growing increasingly annoyed with what it actually was. I grew annoyed with the reliably unreliable map. Why bother printing the damn thing if it wasn't to assist navigation? I grew annoyed with roads that led nowhere, with game trails that ended, with forests that tempted me forward but then shut me out. As I battled through teasing woods, snagged on spiny branches, drenched in sweat, swatting flies, I cursed. When roads curved the wrong way or dead-ended, I cursed. When I couldn't find water for camp and had to walk further than expected, I cursed. When savage-looking dogs charged at me with savage teeth and savage snarls, I cursed. And when the camps were small patches of earth crawling with ants in dense forests with no view, I cursed. This wasn't what I'd come for. My expectations had been altogether different.

The first week was supposed to have been a gentle breaking-in period, a time to gradually establish the walk's simple routines, to develop a connection with the land, but a gentle breaking-in wasn't granted. The roads were too wearying, the forests too rough, the sun too fierce, navigation too difficult. One thing I wanted above all else—more even than to reach the end—was to feel proud of the journey, to know I was giving the best of myself to it. To know I was walking in *good style*. Good style was sticking to a high-level mountain route and staying in the wild, and having fun while doing it, not walking on roads feeling anxious and frustrated. As the days passed I laboured on, head down, my attention so dominated by the task of making progress that I forgot almost entirely why I was there in the first place.

It wasn't until the seventh evening that I experienced a first glimmer of all the journey could be. For a week I'd been living among the woods and mountains. The music of songbirds, the sweet scents of spring growth, the shimmering patterns of sunlight dancing on leaves: it was all constantly with me. I hadn't noticed it, but it had sunk deep.

My seventh camp was made in a downpour, in the depths of a steaming gorge, with feet sore and shoulders bruised, and my shirt clinging to my back, and hunger gnawing at my stomach, and thirst scratching at my throat. But for once the discomforts seemed less noticeable, and I found myself thinking not of the start or future, but only of the present: the wild, dripping woods wrapped around; the pungent aromas and exotic sounds; the living, pressing, organic greenness of it all. And it was then, unexpectedly, that I noticed I was smiling.

It was a start.

PARADISE GLADE
Chapter 4

FOLLOWING THE TIME-HONOURED tradition of stuffy Victorian explorers, and for the childish pleasure of it, I gave every wild camp a name.

The first was 'Cuckoo Ridge', named after the birds responsible for the camp's reassuringly familiar soundtrack. The second was 'Snow Patch Camp', named for the first—but by no means last—snow patch of the journey. The third was 'Where The F*** Am I Camp', a name indicating my state of mind while lost in the Aspromonte. Other names had so far been 'Lumpy Terrace', 'The-Camp-Of-The-Seeping-Ooze', 'Brown Water', 'Windy Gorge', and 'The Little Red Bug Camp'. And then came the finest camp of the journey so far: 'Paradise Glade'.

'Paradise Glade' was reached at the end of a typical southern Apennine day. But the day hadn't begun typically; far from it.

It began, one might say, with a bang.

I was camped that morning many miles from anywhere, deep in the woods, peacefully alone. Birds were probably singing. Dawn's first rays were probably spilling through the trees. Not that I was aware of it. At 6 a.m. I was unconscious, lost within the kind of sleep so deep it is almost like death itself. But not for much longer.

One second I was unconscious, the next shockingly awake, adrenaline racing through my veins. The reason: a loud, blood-curdling scream —'YAAAAAAAARGH!'—followed by several gunshots, from somewhere *horribly* close: CRACK... CRACK... CRACKCRACKCRACK... and then nothing, just absolute silence.

I must have jerked instantly awake into a sitting position because that's how I found myself, without memory of sitting up. Hidden within the tent I couldn't see outside, but I could listen, and wonder. And so I listened, and wondered, unmoving, barely even breathing, ears straining, finding no sound to latch onto. Even the birds had shut up. The silence *throbbed*.

Several minutes passed with the gunshots echoing on through my mind. Questions raced. Was it hunters? Should I call out in case they hadn't seen the tent, green as the surrounding forest? I didn't want to catch a stray bullet. Shouting made sense, but I kept quiet. Why that first scream? Hunters don't normally scream before shooting. *I say, let's scream and give the deer a fair chance.* It didn't seem likely.

Not hunters, then. But who else could it be? Someone out for target practice? But why would anyone venture so deep into the woods at 6 a.m. just to shoot targets? And that scream? It was deeply unsettling. There had been no meaningful words, just pure emotion, piercingly primal. So I kept quiet. There was something about being entirely alone in a forest in wildest Calabria at dawn near persons unknown who had guns and had just used them that made me want to hide.

It was a bloody effective alarm clock, though.

I waited ten minutes, by which time the woodland birds had resumed their glorious dawn chorus, and then—with the stealth of a terrified mouse —packed away camp and stole through the trees, every sense alert. I placed every footfall with the greatest of care, desperate to remain silent; no broken twigs underfoot for me! After less than a minute I came upon a dusty lane I hadn't been aware of and saw, fifty yards down it, three brand-spanking-new sport-utility vehicles parked in a row. The vehicles were jarringly out of place. There'd been nothing like them since beginning the walk. Every other vehicle had been old, dented, and rusting, or at least covered in dust, but these were gleaming, with spotless black paint, tinted windows, and polished chrome. Peering cautiously from the trees I looked beyond them but saw no people, no movement. After a moment's indecision I darted across the road and merged like a shadow into the sheltering woods. And then travelled damn fast.

It took a while before my heart rate slowed to an acceptable level.

And I didn't stop for breakfast until I'd put three miles between myself and the site. I could live with not knowing.

To go on living, that was the thing.

The early start hadn't been planned, and the rest of the day didn't exactly go to plan either—although, to be honest, there hadn't really been a plan in the first place. There seldom was. Most days began with a possible destination in mind, a rough location on the rough map, but how I got there involved considerable spontaneity, and if—as often happened—a different destination suggested itself en route, so much the better. My walk wasn't about following an official trail devised by someone else, a designated route one felt compelled to stick to. No, my walk was a 'make-it-up-as-I-go' affair—an exercise in embracing chance. Not having a daily plan was one of the journey's founding principles. But still, some days didn't go quite as smoothly as others, and what the comment 'it didn't go to plan' really means is: 'if I'd had a plan, it sure as hell wouldn't have been this!'

As usual, the problems began with the map, creative work of fiction that it was. Three hours after the day's abrupt start the map guided me to a small settlement, although it wasn't located exactly where the map suggested. Nor did the road from it behave as indicated. It weaved south-east instead of north-west, downhill instead of up. Needing extra input, I sought help from three men just outside town. The men were short and stocky, wore rough work clothes, and they were inexplicably digging a massive hole where three roads met.

The hole intrigued me, but directions were more important. 'How do I get to Monte Crocco?' I asked in Italian.

My question prompted an animated discussion. There was much extravagant gesturing, scratching of heads, and raising of voices, until finally a direction was 'agreed upon'. One man pointed left, another right, and the third back the way I'd come. '*Grazie,*' I murmured. There seemed little point asking about the hole.

Walking on, I picked the most promising road. At first it looked good, until it swerved from the mountains gradually, as though trying to hide its intention. Foolishly, I stuck with it because it kind of matched the map —just the way the so-called map kind of matched a real map too—and because the heat left me reluctant to retrace my steps, and because the surrounding forests were too tangled for cross-country travel. But after several miles it became obvious it wasn't taking me where I wanted. And by then it was too late.

By late afternoon I was down at sea level and not, as planned, atop a 4,000-foot peak. Down here conditions were uncomfortably hotter and strikingly Mediterranean. There were palm trees and cacti, and green lizards with blue bobbing heads, and an evil-looking black snake that stopped me in my tracks and then slithered into the roadside jungle. But I was here, and decided to make the best of it. A town lay ahead, and I might as well stock up on fresh food.

At first glance, the town was typically Calabrian: old, rough-edged, and deeply attractive, with twisting side streets that called out to be explored, and ancient buildings that suggested stories I wanted to learn. But then I noticed a difference to other towns I'd visited, the way it appeared to be a town of two halves. There were signs of wealth and affluence: a jewellery store full of sparkling merchandise; pedestrians in stylish attire; several large villas immaculately maintained. I also saw signs of poverty: an elderly, emaciated couple slouched on a doorstep beneath a crumbling home; groups of working-age men in ragged clothes and flat *coppola* caps sitting despondently with nothing to do; trash piled in back alleys, rotten and reeking. How, I wondered, had the better-off half become so much better off?

As in every other Calabrian community, life was being lived on the streets. There were crowds of women on foot, dressed the way all Calabrian women above a certain age appeared to be dressed, entirely in black. There were high-spirited kids playing football—several barefoot, all in worn hand-me-down clothing. There were old men sitting on street-corner chairs, wearing ancient suits, gossiping, watching the world go by. And there were youths buzzing around on mopeds, shouting, posturing. It looked as though they were having fun, but the smiles seemed forced. I sensed immense boredom just beneath the surface.

Walking through town, I felt thoroughly out of place. My backpack and heavy leather boots drew frequent looks. But I wasn't as out of place as the three men walking down the street towards me. Broad and muscular, clothed in expensive suits that must have been exceedingly uncomfortable on so hot a day, the men looked plucked straight from a *Godfather* movie set. Each wore stern 'don't-mess-with-us-we-are-in-charge' expressions,

Galatro, Calabria, on a hot and humid day, May 9, 1997.

but for some idiotic reason I decided to try engaging them in conversation. As they drew level I spoke up. '*Buongiorno!*' I exclaimed cheerfully, grinning, but promptly wished I'd kept quiet. Only one of the men turned. The other two stared straight ahead. The one who turned—Scar Face—didn't reply with words; he did it with a stare, a cold, crushing, malevolent stare, a stare that put me down with the ants. Words weren't necessary, and the message was clear: 'Don't… ever… speak… to… us… again.'

Right, I thought. Lesson learnt. Don't try to engage the mafia in conversation.

In contrast, the town's storekeepers were talkative and friendly. They had questions-questions-questions: where was I from, what was I doing, why was I doing it? Foreigners, they explained, were rare; foreigners on foot, unheard of. I wasn't doing my walk to impress anyone, but I'm human—when someone was impressed I couldn't help but enjoy it. And yet I was careful to keep it in check, to avoid bragging, to state my objectives matter-of-factly, to throw in waivers, disclaimers and 'all-being-wells'. It seemed wise not to tempt fate. Since the first step I'd come to sense powerful forces in the background; forces of fate or karma or cause and effect that would balance boastful words with appropriate natural consequences. Obviously, such forces were beyond the realms of logic, but The Walk seemed full of them. Already I'd learnt that if I took an easy option a challenging obstacle would appear in my path, but if I put in real effort, stuck to my goal to walk in good style, and showed a little faith, I'd attain a reward. I sensed that any outright boasting would catch up with me, and so I tried to play The Walk down, but the storekeepers' admiration—and even more their disbelief—was fun to hear. For a short while I enjoyed being the centre of attention.

It was less enjoyable outside when a group of men surrounded me. Maybe that was instant karma for even mentioning The Walk inside. Because hunger had been in control, I'd purchased far more food than needed, and as I sat sorting through it the group slowly formed. Three men like them had shouted insults when first I'd entered town, but these locals seemed friendly enough, merely curious. On the other hand, their questions felt loaded. 'Are you travelling alone?' one asked, smiling. 'Where are you going next?' another asked, also smiling. 'Camping? Where are you camping?' a third said. 'What do you do for money?' a fourth enquired. 'Do you carry it all?'

Perhaps these were reasonable and genuine questions, but still…

Trying to hide my concern, I explained. 'No, I'm not alone. There are seven of us. The others are waiting outside town. It was my turn to get food. Just look at it all!' (And here I was glad I'd bought so much; who'd think it was all for one person?) 'Isn't it terrible, the price of food these days? I just spent everything I had.' Happily, my explanation appeared to do the trick.

The walk from town was uneventful, just long, steep and tiring. No one followed. Had I really thought anyone would? Who'd rob a scruffy, trail-scented vagabond anyway?

As I gained altitude, progress slowed, the extra supplies weighing heavily. Once again I couldn't fit everything into Ten Ton and much of the food remained in plastic shopping bags, carried in both hands. Over the next two hours my arms stretched out. I considered stopping early, but the only spots for camp were rough, brambly, and visible from the road. I was sure I'd find a perfect pitch if I walked on, if I displayed a little faith.

By early evening I was back above 3,000 feet and the moment the jungles fell away I escaped the road and began searching. I wasn't seeking perfection—all I needed was a water source and a flattish patch eight feet by three. At first, water was scarce and the search dragged on, but eventually I found a spot, and what a spot it was: a clear reward for faith and persistence.

It was an open glade in a beech wood, down in a shallow valley, surrounded by sheltering trees. The trees were all fully in leaf and leaned together, forming a lush canopy overhead and a glowing cavern of emerald light beneath. The floor was mattressed with leaves and moss, spotlit by sunbeams, and decorated with delicate crocuses. Curving seductively across it was a narrow stream, a sparkling ribbon of silver light. Birds sang, their notes echoing through the trees, and I was instantly bewitched. The glade felt like a sanctuary, like a sacred place—the most hauntingly beautiful location of the journey so far. I didn't need to walk any further. Paradise it truly was. Naming it was easy.

'Paradise Glade' proved almost impossible to leave. I slept late the next morning and once awake decided to stay put the entire day. I had a mountain of food to conquer, anyway—better to eat it than carry it. Stretching out, I spent hours in near silence and cool green shade, feasting on fresh bread and fruit, reading, relaxing, looking, listening, and above all feeling, letting the balm of the place sink deep. I did manage a few overdue chores—washing socks, practising Italian, writing my first trail report to hopefully prompt donations for the charities—but spent far more time on my back, staring upwards through the canopy to a deep blue sky. It was for such inactivity that I'd come. I wasn't on The Walk for the walking, I was on it for the non-walking.

Tearing myself away the following morning was even harder, but I succeeded, eventually. 'Paradise Glade' was the journey's first exceptional place, but I was certain of one thing: other exceptional places lay ahead.

I wouldn't find them if I didn't look.

YOU CAN'T GO *THAT* WAY
Chapter 5

AFTER 150 MILES I'd finally found some rhythm. Legs now ticked along, arms swung, and my entire body worked harmoniously towards one goal: progress at three miles an hour, with my mind roaming free. Walking was once again the most natural thing.

Alas, the surfaces underfoot weren't. For two days I'd been in lower country, in valleys more populated, stuck on pavement, and my feet weren't happy about it. The blisters had been small, and I dealt with them promptly, but even small blisters can remove joy from a stride.

On the plus side, populated valleys meant directions were easily gained. A labourer in an olive grove, a storekeeper in a village, an old man drinking from a roadside fountain, an inquisitive motorist keen to talk; directions came from varied sources. Not that all were accurate. Even locals became lost in these hills. A grocer told me about a trip he'd once taken to the Sila Mountains, a range I'd reach in a few days. 'Ah, I went for seven days,' he reminisced fondly, before adding the punch line: 'And I was lost every one of them. That's just the way it goes in Calabria.'

I knew I shouldn't feel bad about being lost so frequently when a Calabrian pulled over in his car and asked *me* the way.

Not all encounters were friendly. On a remote road near the village of San Vito a man driving by sent shivers down my spine. A spitting image of Charles Bronson, he slowed his car to a crawl and examined me head to toe with cold, wolf-like eyes. It didn't feel like passing curiosity. It felt calculating, as though I was prey. As the car pulled away I told myself not to worry, but when the car reappeared two minutes later and crawled by in the opposite direction I decided that concern was justified. By the third appearance I was ready. I'd stopped and detached Excalibur from my pack, and when the vehicle rolled by once more the axe was clasped firmly in my hand. I swung it aggressively with each step, letting it spark off the road, and it worked. I didn't see the car again.

Of course, the man might simply have been curious. Later, I cringed at the idea of him returning home to his wife and kids and telling them about the strange, sunburnt man he'd seen. 'He was carrying this absurdly big pack, and swinging an axe like a madman. And he wore the most unwelcoming of expressions.'

On the far side of San Vito I asked directions from a short, fancily dressed man. He wore tight jeans and a purple satin shirt, and sported a gold chain around his neck and a manicured moustache that he caressed lovingly. He asked the usual questions, I asked mine, and all seemed normal. But then, without warning, he reached forward and aggressively reached for my privates. Instinctively I pushed him back and saw anger flash across his face. He stepped forward to try again but I unleashed a stream of obscenities so colourful they shocked even me, and they stopped him cold. I turned and walked away, not looking back.

Three miles beyond San Vito I was finally able to leave pavement behind. A soft-surfaced forest track weaved ahead into the trees, and my tender feet laughed at the gentleness of it. For once the route actually matched the map. The prospect of easier miles set me singing, but alas it wasn't to be. Sometimes the direction a long-distance walker *wants* to go and the direction he is *allowed* to go don't coincide.

After a few minutes a police car appeared ahead, driving down the track towards me. It was the Carabinieri—the military police—out on patrol. I waved to be sure I'd been seen then stepped aside, giving the vehicle room to pass. But it didn't. It pulled level, then stopped.

A window hummed open and two dark faces peered out. Both were middle-aged, moustachioed, officious. The closer policeman began asking questions, but they were too rushed—I couldn't understand a word. I tried explaining the journey, but they didn't understand me either. Or perhaps the concept itself was too impossible to grasp. Heading to Norway? On foot? I might have been explaining a hike to the moon. Abruptly, one of them demanded my passport, and both policemen took turns inspecting it, leafing through it carefully, examining it from different angles as though it might reveal more if held upside down. While this went on I waited peacefully, trying to look as though being grilled by policemen was an ordinary, everyday event.

Eventually they returned the passport. But the Carabinieri weren't done. There was something I needed to understand, something vitally important.

'*Questi boschi,*' the nearest policeman said, urgently pointing ahead. '*Molto pericoloso.*'

'*Si,*' agreed the second. '*Criminali, molti criminali.*' He tapped his holster, pointed again at the woods. The meaning was becoming clear, but to be sure I pulled out my English–Italian dictionary, and for five minutes we passed it back and forth. Soon, I had the translation, and my orders.

'These woods, they are very dangerous. There are many criminals up there. Men with guns. We insist you go another way.'

Giving up on the soft track was upsetting, but what choice did I have? I went another way.

The next day, on the edge of another remote set of hills, a similar event occurred. Only this time it wasn't uniformed policemen that turned me back.

It happened where a road dead-ended, right where a rare trail began. Parked in front of it were two pickup trucks, and resting against them were two muscular men, dressed casually in clean jeans and polo shirts, looking thoroughly incongruous in so wild a place. They looked up as I approached, then stepped forward. I stopped. I had to; the way was now barred. But this time there was no stern warning. Instead I got smiles, warmth, and—amazingly—conversation in English, the first of The Walk. The men asked the same 'what, where, why?' questions everyone asked, and seemed genuinely interested in the journey, but when I pointed to the trail they crossed their arms and shook their heads.

'Noooo,' the tallest murmured in a deep, firm voice. 'No-no-no.' He smiled again, but shook his head once more. 'It is… ah… better you go another way.' His expression was earnest, sincere, and almost pleading, as though he were willing me to understand. 'Believe me,' he said with real emphasis. 'You should go another way.'

And so I went another way.

What choice did I have?

Deep in the Calabrian woods, May 12, 1997.

QUEST FOR A MAP
Chapter 6

DEEP IN THE frenetic hilltop city of Catanzaro I laid hands upon a treasure I'd forgotten existed: a good map. The long detour to find it, taken on a whim, had paid off.

So far, The Walk had included many detours, most unplanned. Going off-route by accident wasn't all bad—it certainly increased the adventure —but *not* going off-route remained an attractive idea. All I needed was an accurate map. Rumour had it that accurate maps existed; supposedly the Italian military had commissioned them. Nowadays, with the internet doing the legwork, tracking them down would be a piece of cake, but in 1997 it was a different game.

When I came within walking distance of Catanzaro, Calabria's capital, a thought occurred: if good maps existed anywhere then surely they would exist there. Making a spur-of-the-moment decision, I abandoned the Apennines and detoured downhill.

The new route led into densely forested foothills and steep-sided valleys. Closer to civilisation, piles of roadside trash marred the stirringly wild scenery. Several valleys had become unofficial communal dumps, with old television sets, mattresses, refrigerators, and other large items of household junk tipped into woods and streams. When I asked about it in Catanzaro I was told that Calabrians have two choices: pay an exorbitant fee to have junk hauled away, or dump it when no one is looking.

Evening light within the ruins, May 14, 1997.

Clearly, many Calabrians were electing not to pay.

Back beside the Mediterranean Sea, I spent an easy afternoon walking barefoot along the water's edge, boots tied to Ten Ton. In tourist mode I sat beneath palm trees, ate ice cream, and spent leisurely evening hours exploring a ruined monastery that I stumbled upon by chance. The ruins looked medieval and Christian, but could just as easily have been ancient Greek, Roman, or even Arabian for all I knew. Old ruins weren't really my thing—I preferred living villages full of vibrancy and life—but these were appealing for practical reasons. The overcrowded coastline offered no affordable accommodation, but the ruins were unfrequented and peaceful. And, even though there was probably a rule against it, they made for an atmospheric camp.

I entered Catanzaro the following morning. I'd grown used to woodland glades filled with birdsong, and small villages where time stood still; to my senses Catanzaro was a hot, steamy, pulsating metropolis of seething humanity. Here, 95,000 residents were going about their business right on top of one another. Breeze-block apartment buildings towered, alleys and roads twisted uphill and down, traffic roared, scooters raced, people rushed, voices shouted, arms waved, dirt clung, laundry fluttered, music howled, dogs barked. The chaos was awe-inspiring, but to the locals it probably seemed normal. Just another regular day.

I treated myself to a surprisingly affordable hotel room, deposited Ten Ton, then charged forth into the mayhem. As well as a map I needed food, but at first both quests seemed doomed. I found plenty of bars: bar after bar after bar. And then more bars. And then more still. Did Catanzaro's citizens live off alcohol alone? Inexplicably, no one seemed to know where a food store might be. After two hours I was flagging in the heat and humidity, and ready to retreat to my hotel if I could figure out which way to go, but then, by chance, I landed in a hidden piazza where not one but two small food stores sat side by side. The window displays were dingy, half empty, and displayed produce covered in dust, but I didn't care. I'd found food; mission half accomplished!

But this was southern Italy, and past noon. Siesta time. Both shops were closed.

'They won't open until morning,' a man across the square explained. He was standing outside an undertaker, an establishment that was, in contrast to the stores, fully open for business. It seemed appropriate—I felt ready for its services. The man introduced himself, bowing grandly. 'Nario, chief director of funerals, at your service!' Nario wasn't dressed as funeral directors usually are. He wore faded jeans and an extravagantly colourful Hawaiian shirt, out of which a forest of chest hair spilled. He laughed when I told him he didn't look the part.

'Pffft!' he said, dismissively. 'Death is just my business. *Living* is what I do best.'

Nario invited me into his office and poured me a glass of water. He'd lived in Ohio for ten years and was keen to practise his neglected English. With great enthusiasm he launched into a long story about his American life, describing the restaurant he'd worked in, and his American friends who'd become like brothers.

'Life in America was good,' he concluded. 'For a while. But in the end I missed the passion of Calabria. Americans are too much like Italians from the north. It is all work-work-work, and too much focus on things. And there is no excitement, no fire. Here we know how to live. We know when to take it easy and also when to—how can I say it—express ourselves! We know how to show emotion. Why hide your feelings? Life is too short! Of course, I saw Americans get emotional, but never about anything important. It was always for things like sports or celebrities or politics. Politics—pah! What a thing to get excited about! All that empty talk, all those broken promises! What a waste of energy! But what about life? What about family?

'Here we know what's important: our families, our traditions, our way of life. We have passion for day-to-day stuff: good wine, a sunset, beauty. We make time for each other. No one here is ever alone! Our families stick together. Brothers, sisters, cousins, grandparents, great grandparents, neighbours, friends, friends of friends; our families are huge. The Calabresi are poor by American standards, but money isn't everything. That's why I came back.'

Nario paused for a rare intake of breath, then continued. 'Not that it's perfect. My people can be so backward and superstitious. Some still live in the dark ages. I don't mean the church, although that's bad enough, with its saints for this and saints for that and endless rituals that make no sense. I mean the ideas people still believe about witchcraft and black magic and spirits. If you only knew how many ways there are to ward off *malocchio*, the evil eye! Some days I think science didn't make it this far south.'

Nario was on a roll, but all of a sudden I found it hard to focus. I'd just noticed something taped to his wall, the item I'd been dreaming of for weeks, the very thing I'd detoured to Catanzaro specifically to find, the treasure I'd just spent two sweaty hours seeking: a hiking map covering The Walk's next stage. I was so shocked to see it I couldn't take my eyes off it. It displayed contour lines, forests, lakes, springs, trails, campsites—the kind of topographical details that make getting lost next to impossible. It was all I could do to stop myself from running to it, tearing it from the wall, and sprinting away into the teeming city with an exultant whoop.

Eventually, I managed to interrupt Nario's flow. I pointed to the map, asked where he'd got it, explained my search, and the one-time Ohio resident shrugged and casually said that if I wanted the map it was mine, no big deal. I almost jumped forward and hugged him, almost kissed both cheeks, but British reserve intervened at the last second. I hoped my smile revealed just how much the gift meant.

It was a happy hiker who sat in his dingy hotel room an hour later, cooking on his camp stove, excitedly examining the next week of his life. The Apennines were revealed, and there were so many possibilities. The map transformed it into a different range.

After dinner I took my first shower since April and discovered that my 'suntan' wasn't quite as dark as I'd supposed. Sleep was difficult—the hotel bed wasn't soft like the forest floor, and the city sounds weren't lulling like woodland birds. But I didn't care. Neither did I care the following morning when the map revealed several minor inaccuracies—a trail printed in the wrong place, and a track that didn't exist at all. With larger topographical details marked, such as mountains that actually existed, the problems were easily fixed. That night, while lying in camp in a valley chosen in advance and navigated to with relative ease, I celebrated how The Walk had changed. A map was such a small thing, but what a difference it made.

Catanzaro, seen from my hotel window, May 15, 1997.

THE SILA MOUNTAINS
Chapter 7

AFTER 200 CHALLENGING miles the Sila Mountains were a welcome change. For a few days Calabria was almost easy.

La Sila is a friendly range. Almost as high as the Aspromonte, but more accessible, the Sila is a rolling upland of peaks, forests and serpentine lakes. The rocks forming it are different to those underlying the rest of the Apennines. Elsewhere, limestone dominates; in the Sila it is granite and sandstone. This leads to fertile soils, and surface waters that don't drain away, and a level of greenness entirely inappropriate for the sun-scorched Mezzogiorno. The lush, lake-studded Sila looks like a landscape stolen from the north, from Austria perhaps—a landscape kidnapped by bandits and secreted away where it shouldn't exist. It is Calabria at its gentlest.

As it turns out, the Sila *was* stolen from elsewhere; the rocks forming it came from France, far across the Mediterranean Sea. Plucked away by the same powerful tectonic forces that created the Alps, the granites that would eventually underlie much of Italy left France some thirty million years ago. Travelling south-east beneath the ancient Tethys Sea, they eventually collided with the Adria subplate, and over time rose above the waves. The Adria subplate is capped by limestone—a sedimentary rock formed by dead sea creatures settling on the seafloor—and after the collision it was limestone that primarily ended up on top. But in Calabria, a quirk of fate favoured the granite, which set the Sila apart. Of course, the story isn't done—the collision continues, as earthquakes across Italy attest. The plates keep moving, and Italy keeps moving with them, swinging across the Adriatic Sea like a leg preparing to kick a ball. And the Apennines keep rising, an inch every three years in Tuscany's Alpi Apuane—a significant amount in geological terms. I liked that the land I was travelling across was travelling too. Wait long enough and the Apennines would be an entirely different range in an entirely different location, although for now it sat exactly where I wanted: right beneath my feet.

Energised by my new map, I climbed swiftly into the Sila. Soon, sweltering Catanzaro lay far behind, replaced by cooler air and soothing greenness. The first Sila camp—'The Song Of Running Water Camp'—was made in a lush valley beside a bewitchingly musical brook. The following dawn sparkled, with moisture steaming from meadows and pine trees dripping with dew; and the following day, with its succession of lakes, woods and meadows, was a day of unfolding pleasures. Most pleasurable of all was the mighty thunderstorm that retreated before me. The storm was a monster, black as night and spitting lightning, but as I walked towards the clouds they steadily moved away, leaving behind a land watered and renewed. It was as though the mountain and weather gods were rewarding me for two weeks of solid perseverance.

Entry into the Sila took me beyond The Walk's first major milestone: two weeks underway. Two weeks was the length of a typical summer vacation, the annual escape from work, after which I'd usually return to an infinitely duller existence. But here, two weeks was merely the start—inconsequential compared to time stretching ahead. Awareness of all that freedom left me giddy with excitement.

After two weeks my suburban existence was slipping away, fading as though it were a life someone else had lived. What was the relevance of overcrowded commuter trains here in the Calabrian woods? What was the relevance of the depressing nightly news here, where the unfolding of spring was the headline story? This uncomplicated journey of day-after-day motion, of forever being outdoors, was becoming my life. Unlike a typical vacation, it didn't feel like a break from the real world—it was becoming the real world.

Routines were now less forced, tasks simpler, problems more straight-forward. Decisions faced each day were more basic. They revolved around food, water, progress, sleep. I rose with the sun and lay down at nightfall; sometimes sooner. I now knew where the moon hung in the sky, its phase, and where it would set. I was becoming more aware of the daily changes in the plants around me; of their subtle, intimate shifts. The landscape was no longer a pretty backdrop but a reality to stand within and explore with every sense. All the clutter of normal Western living, all the restrictions of everyday life, all the rushed moments and breaths were burning away like morning fog. Two weeks on foot and I was becoming more aware, more present.

Calabria's densely forested mountains hadn't been open and rocky the way I'd expected, but I was starting to let go of what I'd wanted them to be. I was growing attached to the beech woods with their sun-dappled glades, and to the rural landscapes and their silver-leafed olive groves and ancient hillside villages. And I'd come to treasure my brief exchanges with farmers, shepherds and shopkeepers. Few of them spoke English, and my Italian remained a low-vocabulary work-in-progress, but we still managed to communicate and begin to connect. The fact that I wasn't stammering helped. Italian is a beautiful melodic language, designed more to be sung than spoken, and I never stammered when singing. It was an immense relief to be able to approach people feeling less fearful that my stammer would get in the way. Even when I didn't know the right words I found a way through. Italians understand hand gestures better than most people, and they understood my smile. The smiles we shared helped us reach a simple human understanding, reminding us that—above anything else—we'd all rather laugh than frown.

After two weeks much had changed, which got me wondering: what changes would eighteen months bring? Would I keep growing closer to the land? Would I overcome my fear of the wildest forests? Who would I be in 7,000 miles?

Most of the changes were good, and yet not all was right. At night my dreams remained troubled. Nightmares continued to haunt them, with dark shadows, nameless fears, and terrifying Hohtürli-style falls. I couldn't understand it—they didn't reflect how I felt by day. Was it fear of the unknown, doubt in my abilities, concern about my funds? I wasn't sure, but hoped they'd soon pass.

After two weeks my fitness had noticeably improved. I hadn't exactly

Dewy morning in the Sila Mountains, May 18, 1997.

been unfit at the start, but there's only one way to get fully fit for a long walk: go for a long walk. The journey so far proved it. Ten hours of effort didn't tire me as it had, although the improvement had come at a cost. Aside from daily scratches inflicted upon my limbs by the *sottobosco*, and a three-inch scar I'd carelessly burnt into my arm on the stove, I'd also developed considerable pain in my left leg—a pain that ran from hip to heel with each stride. I couldn't pinpoint whether it was coming from muscle, bone, or nerve, but it seemed to be worsening each day. I suspected that road walking was the cause—too many jarring steps upon an unnatural surface the human animal hadn't evolved to walk—and I hoped the Sila's soft trails would clear it up. If they didn't, well, I tried not to think about it.

Less serious, and definitely more entertaining, was the transformation that my morning stools had undergone. They'd become great heaping country-pancakes your average 2,000-pound cow would feel righteously proud of. The cause was unknown, and there was no discomfort, but their arrival always added an element of extreme urgency to my morning routine. I aimed to leave each wild location exactly as it had been found, but my creations were making this a challenge. Normal six-inch-deep toilet holes were no longer large enough, and, preparation being everything, it was becoming essential to excavate them the night before. As time passed I grew better at repairing the surface, and began to approach the project with an artistic eye—even some artistic pride. My gut was creating a unique work of organic art, and at 7,000 miles end to end it was arguably Europe's longest.

One other change: after two weeks it was becoming harder to take myself seriously. My morning toilet, a work of organic art? It may not have seemed funny to others, but to me it was hysterical.

On May 19th I reached the mountain town of San Giovanni in Fiore, and another milestone: the first resupply parcel. It contained a number of useful items: three new novels, five rolls of Fuji Velvia slide film, dried vegetables, powdered milk, miscellaneous items of food, and a large-scale map of the mountains beyond the Sila. Of all the items the map was easily the most essential.

The parcel was addressed to me care of general delivery—*Fermo Posta* in Italian—and had been posted by my parents on May 1. The system had worked flawlessly during my previous big walks, but the moment I entered San Giovanni's post office I sensed that 'flawless' was a thing of the past. The interior was shockingly busy, bursting at the seams with a jostling, jabbering mob; everyone pushing, waving and shouting at once. Beyond the mob were four windows and four postal clerks, but I could see no obvious way of making an approach. In England there would have been orderly queues. Here it was shoulder-to-shoulder mayhem.

Intimidated, I dumped Ten Ton in a corner and joined the crowd. At first I stood back politely, waiting my turn, but after several old ladies had elbowed me aside I saw that English manners wouldn't cut it. Fighting every instinct, I began easing myself into any opening that appeared. Progress was slow—it was very much like swimming upstream—but although I frequently lost ground because of politeness I couldn't entirely shake, and although I probably said 'sorry' more often than a Calabrian typically would, I eventually landed before one of the windows. It had taken twenty minutes, but I'd made it: success!

Except it wasn't success.

A stern-faced female clerk tutted impatiently once I'd explained my need. 'No,' she scolded. 'For *Fermo Posta* you must go to that window, over there.' She pointed to a window identical to all the others, but on the far side of the crowd, and then stared at me impatiently as though I should have known.

'But,' I said, smiling sweetly, 'couldn't you just look for my parcel? Please?' The answer was a glare. Clearly, I was an idiot, and a time-waster too. Brusquely, she waved me away.

I launched myself back into the madness, and reached the correct window in a mere fifteen minutes this time, proud of my improved tactical manoeuvring. But the result was the same. At the window designated for collecting mail I was told there was no mail to collect. The clerk—short, balding, with a grey moustache and an executioner's eyes—wasn't remotely interested in helping. *Hand out mail?* his expression read. *Don't be stupid. Now go away. Leave me alone.*

Not that he actually said that. What he said was: 'There is no mail for you.'

'But how do you know?' I asked, fighting back manic laughter. 'I haven't even given you my name yet!'

Optimistically, I wrote my name on a slip of paper. With a deep grunt of annoyance he stood up, disappeared from view, and then reappeared five seconds later. 'No mail,' he said forcefully, before staring through me as though I'd ceased to exist. I protested, but might as well have tried talking to a wall. We were done. Aware of it, an old lady shoved me aside.

Outside, on the way from town, I visited several small shops, hoping the purchase of fresh produce would give my damaged morale a boost. But the only food available was over-processed, pre-packaged rubbish, not the locally grown fruits and vegetables I would have expected from rural Italy.

Seeking solace, I tried phoning home, but found only a continuously engaged line.

Salvation finally came when I passed a pub—an Irish pub of all things —and two pints of perfect stout, and the sympathetic conversations within, eased my disappointment. My alcohol tolerance had never been high, and The Walk must have diminished it further; my route back into the forests afterwards was more weaving than usual. My parcel had vanished, and I had no fresh food, but I felt like laughing.

'I'm drunk,' I slurred aloud at a passing tree, 'and I've got no apples!' And for some reason this inane observation, and the insanity of the post office, and the silliness of trying to walk to Norway, set me giggling uncontrollably, and it took several miles before I got myself back under control.

Two days later, at the start of The Walk's third week, I failed to reach my intended destination for the day. Such failures were becoming common, but this failure was more spectacular than usual. I'd planned on covering twenty miles; instead I managed fewer than three.

The normal reasons for such failures were numerous. Challenging terrain, soaring afternoon temperatures, flagging energy, cartographical inconsistencies, misleading directions, bad choices; they all played their part. But this time it was simpler, and due to a major character flaw: I was genetically incapable of passing by a perfect spot for camp and not making use of it.

The plan that morning was to climb 6,325-foot Monte Botte Donato, the Sila's highest summit, and afterwards push north. To begin with, it went well. The off-trail climb was swift and straightforward, and the beech woods were unusually accommodating, sparing me the epic struggle I'd come to know well. The only tense moment occurred when I stumbled upon three wild boar, the first of the trip. They were huge, all bristling hair and muscular shoulders, and the largest, a male with fierce tusks, probably weighed as much as me, Ten Ton, and a second Ten Ton combined. Wild boar are potentially dangerous—especially sows with piglets—and these first three were intimidating indeed. But so must I have been. One whiff of my scent and away they raced, crashing through undergrowth like runaway bulldozers.

When I reached Botte Donato's summit ridge I was delighted to find snow still lying on the forest floor. The trees were now in full leaf, and the juxtaposition of summer foliage and winter's old drifts was an unusual but strangely beautiful sight. Less beautiful was a small ski area beyond the ridge. The map had given no hint it existed, and the clutter of ski tows, rusty cables, broken fences, and trampled earth seriously detracted from the forest's pristine feel. I felt personally affronted by it, as though the ski run slicing through the forest was a scar upon my own body. The token stone I threw, which clanged harmlessly off a metal tower without leaving a mark, did little to help.

The ugliness was left behind on the mountain's far side, and it was there I found the perfect spot, a sheltered bowl at 6,000 feet. It had an unusually strong sense of place, as though it weren't just another random corner of the forest but the forest's very centre. Snow was piled around its edges, but the woodland floor in the middle was clear. One look was enough. I sensed an invitation I couldn't ignore.

After dropping Ten Ton I lingered awhile in stillness. Mulchy woodland scents filled the air, sunbeams chased through the canopy, countless birds sang, and there was no sign anyone had ever been there before. I'd barely begun my day, but how could I walk on?

I wasn't on The Walk to complete it as swiftly as possible, to set any records, test the limits of human endurance, or do something never before done. The journey wasn't about bragging rights afterwards; it was about experience at the time. It wasn't about rushing; it was about finding a natural rhythm, and stopping when it seemed natural to stop. And it wasn't about collecting places; it was about finding them, and then savouring them. My goal was to seek out the continent's special places, the places of natural wonder that few know exist, and this woodland bowl was clearly one such a place. Not for all the riches of civilisation would I have walked on.

For the rest of the day I wallowed in one spot, losing myself to its sights, sounds and scents. I sat, explored, touched, rummaged. I examined the details: insect life on the woodland floor; translucent designs on each backlit leaf; the soft velvety texture of moss-covered beech bark; the trampoline feel of fallen leaves beneath bare feet; patterns of light made by a dancing canopy; the aroma of damp earth and rotting vegetation. The more I looked the more I found. The more I opened myself the more I experienced. Soon, I was filled with an incredible sense of belonging, as though I were home, but home in a way I'd never been back in Pinner.

This gentle place wasn't the Aspromonte, that was for sure.

Sitting quietly, I considered the journey, examining my slow, meandering approach. Before starting, several people had expressed surprise at how long I had said it would take. 'I could do it in half the time,' someone had even disparagingly observed.

Possibly I could have too, but successive twenty-five mile days weren't the point. It would have been a poorer journey, a rushed journey: very much a wasted opportunity.

At home in the Sila Mountains, at the 'Four Seasons' camp, May 21, 1997.

HARD DAYS, HOT NIGHTS
Chapter 8

ON MAY 25 I walked off the map, but had to laugh: how many travellers get a chance to say that? I smiled at an imagined headline. 'Mad Mountain Jack: Boldly Leaving the Known World!' Except of course it wasn't like that. More accurate was: '*Mapless* Mountain Jack, the Cartographically Challenged Explorer'.

I was reluctant to leave the Sila. Life there had been good, and the soft ground had partially healed my left leg. But with the range crossed and Nario's detailed map stretching no further, and with the replacement map swallowed by Calabria's postal 'service', the journey was once again about to become more adventurous.

Which, I reminded myself, was one of the reasons I was doing it.

There was nothing for it but to return to roads, loathed though roads were. Assisted by the poor excuse for a map I'd bought in Rome, and relying on not-always-accurate directions from locals, I trekked north. There were many wrong turns. But at least I was engaging Calabrians in conversation. At least I was learning more about them with each encounter.

Two mornings beyond the Sila, on the edge of a village not appearing on my map, I sought directions from three people standing outside the first home. Bedraggled after a sweat-drenched night, and mildly frustrated after a succession of wrong turns, I was happy to stop. Not only did I need directions, but a pack of mean-looking dogs were on the loose fifty yards ahead, snapping at passing cars, and I hoped a long-enough pause would give the hounds time to vanish. Ah, *optimism not based on reality*: an essential character trait for any long-distance walker.

The conversation began much as others had. 'Excuse me,' I said. 'Could you tell me how to get to Tarsia?' I always asked about the next town now, never further. Further caused too much confusion. And I'd learnt to never mention Norway. Fun as the reaction might be, the mountain gods were always listening.

'Tarsia?' one of the Italians replied. 'Why would you want to go there?' It was a typical response.

'Well, I'm on a long walk. Mostly I walk in the woods, but…'

'In the *woods*? These woods! On your *own*?' It was another normal response, accompanied by normal expressions of horror. 'That is very dangerous. There are many bandits. You should not be doing such a thing!' To many Italians the woods appeared to be an alien environment, a place to fear and avoid. Not that I was worried about bandits, just worried about taking yet another wrong turn.

Shrugging away their concerns I asked for directions again, but the three Italians couldn't help; they were visiting from further south. Instead, they called for their landlady—'the lady of the house' as they described her—and her response was definitely not normal. Plump, serious-faced, and commanding, the lady was a true Italian matriarch, used to getting her way. After listening carefully and peering at the map she frowned, shook her head, stepped into the road, waved down a passing car, argued passionately with its driver, turned back to me, and commanded that I get in—the driver would take me wherever I needed to go. The poor driver sank low in his seat. It looked as though he hadn't been given a choice. I felt for him.

It was quite an offer: a quick car ride, a few easy miles? But I didn't consider it for a second. My journey had one rule above all others: that I walk every step of the way. Once it was done I wanted to look back and see an unbroken line of footsteps stretching across the continent. Sure, I'd allow myself ferry rides where walking wasn't possible, such as across the Baltic from Denmark to Norway, and breaks from the trail when necessary, so long as I began again exactly where I'd finished. The continuous line of steps was paramount. Nothing else would do. Cheating would be easy;

who'd ever know? Who'd even care? But *I'd* know. *I'd* care. If I broke the line of steps The Walk would lose all meaning; it would no longer be a walk. Travel by car, bus or train and I was just another tourist. Skip even one mile and I might as well skip them all. A single mile missed might seem like a small thing, but the effect on me would be profound. And if I was doing The Walk for any reason it was for its effect on me.

Of course, explaining this wasn't so easy. The lady of the house didn't understand. In fact, she grew quite cross. After creating the opportunity for my ride she didn't want it wasted. She insisted, loudly. But after the motorist saw his chance and sped off, and after my umpteenth explanation, she finally came round.

Reluctantly, she gave directions, but then, as I turned to go, she caught me off-guard. 'So, have you had breakfast yet?' she asked sternly, as though I were a naughty schoolchild not taking care of myself the way I should. I told her I had but was ordered to wait, and what could I do but obey? After ten minutes she returned and thrust a bulging paper bag into my hands. 'For you,' she urged, glaring fiercely to quell any protest. But then her face softened, and the transformation was remarkable. All of a sudden she became like anyone's loving mother. 'For you,' she murmured. 'Because you are so *alone*.' She stressed 'alone' as though it were the most terrible thing in the world.

I ate my second breakfast a mile further on, stretched out in the shade of an olive grove, for once unmolested by dogs. Like a child at Christmas I emptied the bag, laughing as the spoils tumbled to the ground. There were two cans of fruit juice, a huge chunk of cheese, a packet of sliced salami, an assortment of biscuits, a triangle of fruit cake, a tin of tuna, a bottle of orange soda, four thick slices of home-baked bread wrapped in foil, and a bottle of beer.

I started with the beer.

Calabrians, I decided, may not understand the journey, may even disapprove, but when it came down to it they weren't so bad.

In punishing heat I strode through a rural valley. An orchard sat to one side, an olive grove to the other, and woodland smothered the surrounding mountains. In the far distance, climbing a steep hillside, was a medieval village, from which church bells rang. It was the kind of bucolic Italian landscape one might fantasise about, a place for easy living, but for Mad Jack plodding through on foot it wasn't easy at all.

It wasn't what I had expected, but as I now knew, little in the southern Apennines would ever match my expectations. Before starting, I had thought that rural country would offer easy walking, high mountains harder walking, but the reverse was true. The valleys made everything harder.

Down in the valleys route options were limited. Pedestrian-friendly tracks were scarce, and where they existed most were private and closed. Fences and barriers blocked routes. Open spaces for straightforward travel didn't exist. Lying between farms were numerous uncultivated thickets, places so wild with brambles they were genuinely impenetrable. Every time I tackled the *sottobosco* I experienced the full thrill of jungle exploration, and rarely made it far. I lost pounds in sweat, and all I gained were extra perforations in clothes and skin.

Camping in the valleys wasn't any easier. Finding a spot for my tent took ingenuity and, as most land was private, I had to use great stealth. Water was scarce. Streams were few and most were polluted by livestock. Potable sources existed, mostly in the form of roadside fountains, but camping near them wasn't practical—they were surrounded by farms and houses, not woods where I could hide. And the camps themselves were uncomfortable. Ants, mosquitoes, and other biting insects made it impossible to sit outside and relax. Mosquitoes forced me into the zipped tent, which became a claustrophobic, airless sauna every single night. Sleep rarely offered much rest. I tossed and turned, melting in the heat, and was often more wasted at dawn than I'd been the evening before.

Then there were the dogs: farm dogs, sheepdogs, village dogs, and plain old crazy wild dogs. They were everywhere, keeping me awake at night with their ceaseless baying, hassling me by day, suggesting with snarls, bristling fur and low-hung tails that I move on, however much I needed rest. I grew tense every time I approached a farm building, anticipating the next attack. No one else was out walking for fun. It was easy to see why.

But the worst part was the roads—the flaming-hot open-to-the-midday -sun roads. They left my legs sore, my soles tender, my heels raw, my spirit drained. When they led where I wanted they were taxing enough, but

Rural Calabria, May 12, 1997.

when they led me astray and added extra miles I finished the day ready to keel over, too far gone to think, too exhausted to find any pleasure in The Walk. There were many hours when I simply didn't care. About anything.

I couldn't wait to return to the mountains.

The next high range—the Pollino National Park—lay 100 miles ahead. In the Pollino, I was told, grassy heights rose clear above forests, the air was cooler, water was plentiful, and a tent could be pitched wherever one wished. Such descriptions turned the Pollino into the promised land, and I rushed towards it in haste, travelling further and faster each day than was wise, wearing myself down. Anything to escape the lowlands. For a week life was rough.

Of course, it didn't have to be. Many valley towns offered small hotels. A cleansing shower, a soft bed, an air-conditioned room; these would have eased the discomforts significantly. But I couldn't afford such luxuries, which was appropriate, I told myself, for someone walking for the homeless. I didn't want to fail because I'd frittered away my limited funds on hotels, because I was too soft to cope with a few discomforts. But how different The Walk would have been with a reasonable budget. It would have turned southern Italy into an entirely different place.

It wasn't just the budget, but the method of locomotion too. A visitor touring Calabria by bus, car, or bicycle might find it a gentle, welcoming place. But I was travelling on foot, and on foot I saw Calabria up close, warts and all. I saw the beauty, and felt the pull of the region's multi-layered past, but I also saw the roadside trash, and the corners of poverty, and I bore scars from its unwelcoming thorns. I experienced the good and the bad, glimpsed more of the story. It was one of the attractions of foot travel —even if it unarguably made life hard.

A deliberate choice made it harder still: I refused to ask for help. Asked directly, farmers might have granted permission for camp, might have provided water, even food. And village residents might have opened their homes. But I didn't ask. If help were to come I wanted it voluntarily offered; it would mean so much more. And beyond even that, I didn't ask because I wanted to stand on my own two feet and prove to myself I had what it took. I didn't want to take the easy option. I wanted to feel worthy, to earn whatever rewards lay ahead. I had no doubt that great riches lay down the trail, but finding them wasn't guaranteed. Only the purest approach would do it. And for that approach I suffered.

Late one scorching afternoon I followed a minor road into the depths of a steep-sided gorge. Once again the map had misled. Where it showed nothing but forest filling the gorge a major four-lane highway now roared. Heavy with traffic, the highway wasn't crossable, and so I followed its shoulder, seeking a way out. Briefly I considered turning back, but couldn't face losing my hard-won miles. Retreat would have been the smart choice, but I was too weary and sun-fried to recognise it.

After a long mile the highway entered a tunnel. Only fifty yards long, it was unnerving to negotiate. I dashed through, pressed hard against the walls, cars and trucks speeding by mere feet away, horns blaring in anger. A second tunnel appeared soon after. This one was longer—its end was out of sight. Too fearful to head into it, too weary to turn back, I chose the only other option: a climb from the gorge. Directly beside the tunnel's entrance a vegetated slope led upwards, and that was the route I took.

It was, without doubt, the worst decision I made in the Apennines.

Clutching at loose rocks, plucking at roots, kicking boots into earth, I scrambled upwards. Soon I was twenty feet above the road on a slope disturbingly steeper than it had looked from below. The slope traversed directly above the tunnel's entrance, and what the motorists below must have thought of the man with a huge pack inching along overhead I can't imagine. Not that I was worrying about them—focus had narrowed. Three ideas dominated my mind: the empty space beneath my feet; the dire consequences of a fall; and the absolute certainty that I had to hold on. It felt like Hohtürli all over again, but with traffic beneath. When I tried reversing I discovered that I couldn't. The only escape lay upwards. Carefully, moving only one limb at a time, hoping shrubs and grass wouldn't tear free, that loose earth wouldn't give way, I gained height. Time behaved as it had back at Hohtürli—slowing, horribly. With the roar of traffic filling my ears a great surge of anger overcame me. This was supposed to be a *wilderness* walk. What the hell was I doing risking my life above a road? A slip would finish the journey, and what an embarrassing way to fail it would be.

But, through great care and immense patience, I escaped. The steepness relented, and I scrambled to safer ground, but not ground that was easier. The hillside above the tunnel was so knotted with razor-sharp brambles that it took an hour to cover 100 yards. Progress was desperate. But oddly, in the midst of the struggle, with blood flowing from numerous cuts, and sweat washing the blood away, I found myself coming alive. I began laughing and screaming—the situation was so utterly ridiculous I couldn't help myself. Laughter eased the pain, and screaming raised my energy and increased my determination. I developed a grim pleasure in the battle, pride in my refusal to give in, and satisfaction in each yard gained. Progress became so absorbing I thought of nothing else. It was like a journey within a journey, a life within a life. The situation wasn't remotely what I wanted The Walk to be, and yet for an hour it was everything The Walk could be. I'd rarely lived more in the moment.

And it would certainly make future miles up in the mountains all the sweeter.

The balancing moment came two days later, on La Mula, a mountain on the Pollino National Park's western edge. There, I burst above tree line for the first time on The Walk and danced with joy beneath a big sky.

It didn't matter that it was just one mountain, or that I faced another epic battle descending from it through more *sottobosco*, and then more sole-destroying miles on roads. All that mattered was that for twenty-four hours I could live in absolute freedom. I'm not sure I had ever appreciated a high mountain more.

By the time I reached Calabria's last town, Castrovillari, I was a physical wreck. Being scratched and torn, dirty and fragrant, sunburnt and exhausted was the least of it. My left leg had worsened again. Great spasms kept erupting from behind my knee, running up my thigh, shooting down my calf; and my left ankle had swollen exactly as it had after being fractured on the Hohtürli Pass. Somehow, I completed a gruelling twenty-eight-mile day to reach Castrovillari before stores and services closed for the weekend —most if it done with a painful, hobbling limp. When I stepped into town I thought *to hell with the budget* and splashed out on a hotel. I still believed the mountain gods would ultimately reward me, but on this occasion I reckoned I'd earned the right to reward myself.

Open mountains at last, La Mula, May 27, 1997.

PARCO NAZIONALE DEL POLLINO
Chapter 9

FRANCO GIROVAGO WASN'T happy. I could tell from the stoop of his shoulders when first I saw him; from the light that came to his eyes when we began discussing the Pollino National Park. He tried arguing otherwise, but I wasn't buying his story that he could live without mountains. Some people can't.

I met Franco early on my first morning in Castrovillari, shortly after discovering that Calabria's dysfunctional postal system had swallowed my second resupply parcel whole—book, maps, film and all. In search of replacement film I followed directions to a small photography store hidden down a side alley near Castrovillari's bustling central piazza, and in it met its owner, Franco: not just the first Italian who understood the journey, but the first who wished he were doing it himself.

After learning about my walk Franco wanted to talk, and I was happy to let him. To give my failing left leg time to recover I'd decided to extend my Castrovillari stay to two nights, and couldn't think of a better place to spend some of it than with a man who knew the next range like the back of his hand. Franco had spent his teens and early twenties exploring the Pollino, wandering by himself for weeks on end.

'It was all I wanted to do,' he explained. 'I had no interest in being anywhere else. My friends thought I was *lunatico*, but—hah!—I didn't care. They could keep their football and silly girlfriends and the *passeggiata* every night—I had something better, *libertà di spazio aperto*, the freedom of open space.'

Franco had lived his entire life in Castrovillari, but from as far back as he could remember had felt drawn to the mountains looming over town.

'At school I'd stare at them through the windows, imagining myself up there. No one else ever seemed to notice them—I couldn't understand it. But now I do. People here are only interested in human things, not natural. I'll never forget the first time I went by myself. It was like suddenly I could fly! I came to love winter best. Down here everything was hot and dusty but up in the snow it was another world. Castrovillari isn't large like Napoli, but it can be so crazy-busy. But in the mountains all is peace. Pollino is like the pause between breaths...' and Franco stopped, searching for the right metaphor. 'It is like that moment of silence at the end of an opera before the audience begins to cheer.'

But now it was a world denied. Ten years earlier Franco had fallen in love, married, fathered three children, and his sole focus now was supporting his family. Money was tight. There was little room for mountains. He worked six days a week—the seventh was dedicated to church and family. He loved his family passionately, said he'd make the same choices again, but still pined for what he'd given up.

'I haven't visited the Pollino in three years,' he said with a sigh. 'Just imagine it. Sometimes, when I think about it too much, it is like all the music has been stolen from the world.'

Naively, I asked about working in the mountains. Wasn't there some way to return more often?

'Ah...' he replied, smiling ruefully. 'Become a shepherd, perhaps? A forest worker?' I didn't have an answer, and shrugged. 'In Calabria we are people of tradition,' he went on. 'Change is not always so easy. A shepherd makes shepherds. A forester makes another forester. But my father was a shopkeeper. And my family has to eat.'

My heart went out to the man. I remembered how trapped I'd felt before Hohtürli had changed my life, and also when I'd postponed The Walk for a year, but how much worse must it be for Franco: living within sight of the thing he desired, but kept from it by his own honourable choices. How many years would pass before he could again wander freely? Denial of freedom and suppression of dreams can cause more suffering than mere physical wounds. That Franco's suffering was self-inflicted only made it worse.

Franco and I spoke for some time. Eventually I bought four rolls of slide film—at a discounted price, Franco refusing any profit. As I left he suggested I return the next day, and when I did he handed over the only English-language paperback he owned, as well as hiking maps of the Pollino and the hills directly beyond. The maps were black-and-white photocopies, but more than adequate. Franco had highlighted his favourite routes, and spent an hour pointing out secret corners I might otherwise have missed. He couldn't return to the Pollino himself, but wanted to make certain I experienced the best of it.

'It will make me happier than you can know,' he said as we parted. 'Just imagining you up there. I will be walking with you. Enjoy it for me.'

I climbed into the Pollino a different person, a backpacker renewed.

Aside from the post office, Castrovillari had treated me well. Its citizens had been friendly and helpful, chores had been accomplished with ease, the town laundry had washed my clothes for me, the supermarket had been well stocked with quality food, and upon hearing my story the hotel manager had sliced my room rate in half, then in half again. Instead of struggling to get things done I'd been free to rest and recover. By the morning of departure my injuries had practically vanished. I was deeply impressed by how quickly the human body could bounce back.

The thrill to be underway again was so great that I burst into song the moment the town fell behind. After looking around to make certain I was alone I let it rip, only to stop when three wild dogs exploded from a roadside shrub directly beside me and dashed away in terror, tails between their legs. Heart beating, mouth open, I looked around suspiciously; were there dogs beneath every shrub? And then I started laughing. Clearly, my singing was worse than I thought.

The ascent into the Pollino went well, despite taking two wrong turns. But Franco's maps put me right, and soon I was zigzagging up a narrow trail into forests of black pine, leaving the sun-blasted plains behind. In eight miles I gained 5,000 feet of altitude, swapping a Mediterranean climate for one that was essentially alpine. It was like being transported 1,000 miles north.

From the first pass—the evocatively named Passo della Lupi, the Pass of the Wolves—I stared into the heart of the range, at a mountain landscape unlike any I'd so far seen. Before me now was a broad upland meadow strewn with wildflowers and scattered with stones. Surrounding the meadow were dark beech woods, and soaring above the woods were rugged mountains of rock and snow. The largest mountain in view was 7,375-foot Monte Pollino, sporting a great cirque that had clearly been carved by an ancient glacier. It was the first mountain of the journey that deserved to be labelled one. At the sight of it I couldn't stop grinning.

The Parco Nazionale del Pollino is Italy's largest national park. Covering 743 square miles, it forms an immense natural barrier that in centuries past effectively cut Calabria off from the rest of Italy. Built from limestone, carved by water and glacial ice, the Pollino is a range of untracked forests, deep gorges, and sun-bleached peaks. During the last ice age the ice sheet that covered Italy extended this far south, but no further, and the Pollino still boasts Calabria's coldest environment. Snow can bury it half the year. Even summer's midday heat fails some years to entirely banish winter's deepest drifts.

The Pollino is famed for being the last holdout in Italy of a rare tree— the majestic, thick-trunked Bosnian Pine. It is also a stronghold for other threatened wilderness species, including golden eagles and wolves. Several of Castrovillari's citizens had warned me about Pollino's wolves, but Franco, the only person I'd met who had actually visited the range, had told me not to worry. 'To even see one,' he said, 'you'd have to be incredibly fortunate. You won't have any problems, probably.'

Unsurprisingly, it was the 'probably' that stuck in mind.

The idea of travelling alone where wolves roamed was unnerving, but thrilling too. With wolves present the wilderness possessed extra depth, an *edge* missing elsewhere. The Walk was a search for Europe at its wildest, and where could be wilder than a place where sharp-toothed predators lived? And the truth is that wolves are aggressive predators. Killing and eating other animals is what they do best—their survival depends on it. And yet, throughout untold centuries of conflict with another aggressive predator, there's little doubt which species came out on top. You have to look back two centuries to find Europe's last documented wolf attack on a human, but human attacks on wolves in that time? You couldn't even count.

The fear some people still have of wolves is understandable, even if it is based more on superstition and folklore than fact. Then again, the fact is that wolves did once prey upon humans—the historical evidence is undisputed. Back in prehistory, when human survival depended upon overcoming nature, wolves were a genuine threat. But that was then. In modern times, lone travellers have little to fear. Wolves are not unintelligent—their preference is to avoid people. Given their experiences with hunters, poachers and shepherds over the years it's not hard to see why.

At one time wolves padded across the entire continent—barely a habitat existed that didn't echo to their howls. But as the human population swelled wolves were pushed back, until they clung on only in isolated pockets, barely surviving, and more often dying out altogether. By 1970 Italy's wolf population was so reduced it had reached endangered status—only 200 were estimated to remain along the entire Apennine chain. But changing attitudes and the passing of protective laws have since allowed a modest recovery, and revised estimates in the mid-nineties suggested the population had rebounded to 400, and was still climbing. Wolves remained rare, but their recovery prompted real hope. After all, never before in recorded history had their numbers increased, or their territory expanded. A recovering wolf population was a monumental thing.[1]

Members of the grey wolf family, Apennine wolves are smaller than European wolves further north, and typically form smaller packs, often consisting of just an alpha pair and the most recent brood of pups. By necessity they have evolved into elusive, adaptable creatures, able to make limited territories work, capable of dealing with disturbances that would drive other wolves away. Their diet consists primarily of boar, deer, chamois and rabbits, as well as occasional plants and berries rich in fibre. They also take sheep—and who can blame them?—but not long-distance walkers. As Franco had said, I probably wouldn't see one. And yet, the nervousness remained, not just because of my upbringing but also because tens of thousands of years of shared human experience have pushed some fears so deep that rational thinking can never entirely overcome them.

1. At the time of writing, December 2020, estimates suggest Italy's wolf population has risen to between 1,200 and 2,000 wolves.

That a large carnivore roamed the Pollino wasn't something I could forget. But also, it wasn't something I wanted to forget. It prompted a different level of disquiet to the dread I'd felt in the Aspromonte. It wasn't bad, but good. It was why I was here.

From the Pass of the Wolves I trekked a mile further, loping over a rolling meadow. Halfway across, down in a hollow, I came upon eight wild boar, for a second thinking they were wolves. They scattered in an instant, heading for the woods, hooves pounding like thunder. Camp was made at 6,000 feet in the heart of the wilderness, right upon the Calabria–Basilicata border. It offered everything I desired: a wild, unpeopled land spread around, a view towards snow-draped cliffs, and a small stream gushing from a nearby snowdrift. For a month water had often been a challenge, but not here; for a month relaxing outside had been impossible, but not here! There were no flies, no mosquitoes, and the air was refreshingly cold. Instead of sweat I developed goosebumps and had to pull on my fleece. 'Base Camp Pollino' was as perfect as any wild camp could ever be; a suitable reward for 480 miles of effort.

Breezy afternoon at 'Base Camp Pollino', June 1, 1997.

I spent the evening outside. Wrapped in my sleeping bag I listened to cuckoos calling, to large creatures rummaging through the forests below. Were they deer, boar, wolves? I couldn't tell. Clean air blew against my face, and the surrounding mountains slowly grew familiar. The mountain closest to camp was southern Italy's tallest, 7,438-foot Serra Dolcedorme. *Dolcedorme* means 'sweet sleep', and after all the sultry nights at lower elevations I certainly did.

Dawn, June 1, brought whirls of frost to the inside of the tent, layers of ice within my water bottle, and bright, crisp sunlight. It wasn't a day for striking camp and moving on—it was a day for packless wandering. Following many of Franco's suggested routes, and making up several of my own, I stravaiged without real purpose across meadows, through woods, up lonely ridges. My eyes stayed wide open, all senses alert, but I saw no wolves, only a single set of fresh canine prints angling across a sun-softened patch of snow. Had a wolf left them? It didn't honestly matter. The near-pristine quality of the wilderness was the only thing that did. Just being in it was enough.

June's second day was the fourth anniversary of my Hohtürli fall, and to mark it I set out from 'Base Camp Pollino' long before sunrise, heading for Dolcedorme's summit. In pre-dawn gloom I made my way appreciatively uphill, thinking back to four years earlier. Then, I'd begun downhill, nervous of what lay ahead; here I was heading uphill, excited to find out. Around me now was a landscape as hushed as Switzerland at altitude had been, but a landscape significantly richer. It slowly came into focus as daylight increased: beech woods falling away, rough mountain grasses underfoot, the silhouette of Dolcedorme directly ahead. As I travelled I sensed the land holding its breath, awaiting rebirth, throbbing with promise and expectancy, and a rush of childlike joy overcame me. There was nothing to fear here, only gifts to embrace.

Soon, a soft glow lit the mountains. Patches of frozen snow passed underfoot, glowing from the light. Then came sharp-edged limestone, the handrail of a rising ridge, cold to my fingers. With mounting excitement I scrambled towards the summit, the world below dropping away and dawn growing ever nearer. This was better than bouncing down an ice slope in Switzerland! If only Franco could see it.

I summited at 5 a.m. and perched in stillness, higher than anyone else in southern Italy. For twenty minutes I watched and waited, and then it came: a flash on the horizon, followed by brightness and warmth. I stared outwards across a huge swathe of Italy to three seas—the Ionian, Adriatic, and Tyrrhenian—and gave my imagination permission to roam. There's no traveller like the imagination, and no better place to grant it freedom than a high summit at dawn.

Since Hohtürli I'd considered June 2 my adopted birthday; it marked my second chance at life, and here, on Dolcedorme, I knew I wasn't wasting it. The summit was the perfect birthday gift. To the wilderness spread around, to the mountains and forests and sky, to all the wolves I'd never see, and even to fear itself, I offered my heartfelt thanks.

As with 'Paradise Glade' and the Sila, leaving was a wrench. Discovering such places was why I was on The Walk, but leaving was clearly going to be one of its torments. Moving on, always moving on; it was what made The Walk a walk. But how foolish it seemed when I'd found what I was looking for. I wondered if I'd ever find a way to ease the conflict of it. Could I learn to fully enjoy each place, but not cling; to celebrate each moment, and then let it go?

With the Pollino behind I descended into sun-dappled beech woods identical to those traversed during The Walk's first week, only this time they felt welcoming. On the northern edge of the national park I passed an official sign: 'NO CAMPING IN THE PARK'. Oops. But who'd have thought it: a wilderness where overnight stays were banned? The idea of it rankled. Mountains were places of freedom, but rules create limits, and freedom with limits isn't freedom at all. In any case, there was nothing I could do about it; I'd already broken the rules.

My approach to wild places was the same whether official rules existed or not: it was an approach of absolute respect. The plants growing in the wild, the animals calling it home, the living earth underfoot, were all elements not to be disturbed. I didn't want to leave even a single footprint if I could help it, nor any sign of my visit. I lit no fires, never deliberately approached wildlife, never moved rocks or plants to make a camp possible. My goal was to leave a place exactly as it had been found, or better, and to this end I packed out trash left by others, broke apart old fire circles, returned rocks to holes they'd been pulled from, did whatever I could to keep the wild… wild. If my visit left any part of the natural community diminished, that was wrong, but it had nothing to do with the rules.

Of course, my very presence was a disturbance, I could see that. But as a creature of the planet didn't I have as much right to be present in the wild as any other creature? As long as my presence did no damage and caused no stress. The chief difference between my right and that of, say, an Apennine wolf, was that my right came with a responsibility to go another way if harm was likely. My right didn't override the wolf's; the wolf had nowhere else to go.

Looking back objectively, I couldn't believe my quiet two-night occupancy and careful passage had caused harm. It would have been different if I were one of a hundred, or a thousand, and if we'd all camped wild, but clearly I wasn't. If there had been crowds, if the land was being devalued, if its inhabitants were being stressed, there would have been clues, and I would have behaved differently. But this wasn't a crowded place.

I was visiting these uncrowded places to escape rules and regulations, to live a less restricted life. Clearly, civilisation wouldn't function if everyone broke the rules, but breaking them in the wild seemed a part of being a wilderness traveller. This wasn't a human-dominated place and human laws didn't necessarily apply. There were higher natural rules to obey, and if every visitor followed them official rules wouldn't even be needed.

As I saw it, the camping ban was alienating. Follow it, and true knowledge of the wild could never be gained. To know a mountain only by day is to only half-know a mountain. By night it is an entirely different place, offering entirely different experiences, touching the senses in entirely different ways. Had I known about and obeyed the no-camping regulation my experience of the Pollino would have been immeasurably poorer. The rule would have had me behaving as a visitor. But mountains weren't just places to visit. Mountains were where I belonged.

Sleeping and walking where both were banned was an unavoidable part of The Walk. This was Europe, a continent carved up by private land ownership, and progress was going to be impossible without some trespassing. But I'd always do it softly, with all the care I could muster, and no one would ever be able to tell I'd passed through. The ability to trespass discreetly and camp gently had served me well so far, and I wasn't about to give it up now.

This wasn't my country, but these were my mountains. They were mine, they were no one's, and they were everyone's. And I'd go on treating them with the respect they deserved.

Morning light high on Serra Dolcedorme, June 2, 1997.

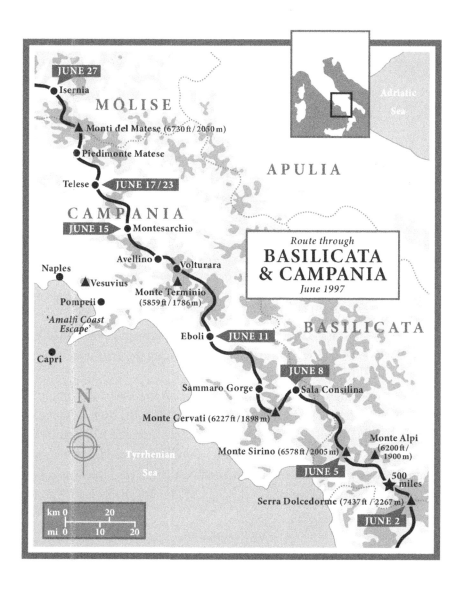

JUNE 27
Isernia
MOLISE
▲ Monti del Matese (6730 ft / 2050 m)
Piedimonte Matese
Telese
JUNE 17 / 23
APULIA
CAMPANIA
JUNE 15
Montesarchio
Avellino
Volturara
Naples
▲Vesuvius
Monte Terminio
(5859 ft / 1786 m)
Pompeii
'Amalfi Coast
Escape'
BASILICATA
Capri
Eboli
JUNE 11
JUNE 8
N
Sammaro Gorge
Sala Consilina
Monte Cervati (6227 ft / 1898 m)
Monte Alpi
(6200 ft /
1900 m)
Tyrrhenian
Sea
Monte Sirino (6578 ft / 2005 m) ▲
JUNE 5
500
miles
Serra Dolcedorme (7437 ft / 2267 m) ▲
km 0   20
mi 0   10   20
JUNE 2

Route through
BASILICATA
& CAMPANIA
June 1997

Adriatic
Sea

103

BASILICATA
Chapter 10

BASILICATA: A WHOLE new region, in essence a whole new walk. I entered it travelling at three miles an hour, not fast in the scheme of things, but fast enough to deliver change. As The Walk was demonstrating, three miles an hour can change everything.

The first Basilicatan encounter was memorably different from any in Calabria. There, I'd feared the dogs, but in Basilicata the dogs feared me. At least, the first three did.

I ran into them mid-morning, down a narrow cart track hemmed between tall earthen banks. I was heading downhill, the dogs heading up. They were all outdoor dogs; large and ragged, with matted hair that clearly hadn't experienced soap and water in a very long time. Travelling with them was a large flock of sheep and goats, the latter with massive curved horns like those of an ibex, and at the sight of so many menacing horns and three menacing dogs I stopped dead. But so did the animals. With Ten Ton on my back I probably looked menacing too.

For half a minute little happened. It was a Basilicatan standoff: man versus dog. The sheep and goats milled in confusion, baaing and bleating, neck bells clanging, kicking up dust. The three dogs stood dangerously still, ready for action. After a month of unpleasant canine encounters I felt nervous. Apennine sheepdogs have a fierce reputation. Bred and trained to protect sheep from wolves, they often act aggressively when people approach. The three before me all wore traditional *roccale* collars—thick iron collars studded with lethal spikes designed to offer protection from a wolf's bite—and each dog fixed me with a cold and intense stare. They looked strong, capable, and extremely mean.

Keeping still, trying not to reveal any fear, I considered my options. All were based upon not triggering an attack. Further seconds passed. Tension grew. Distressingly, a nervous itch developed on my nose, and soon I couldn't ignore it. Carefully, knowing it wasn't wise, but unable to stop myself, I moved my right hand ever so slowly upwards to scratch.

And that was all it took.

Suddenly, the dogs sprang to life, muscle, bone and tooth energised. With shocking speed they launched themselves—backwards. At first my mind couldn't compute. Yelping with fear, the dogs turned tail and fled into the flock, and when I realised the truth it was such a relief, and so unexpectedly comical, that I burst into laughter. This set the sheep and goats off too. Panicked, they climbed over one another in a scramble to escape, and the pandemonium made San Giovanni's post office crowds seem peaceful and orderly.

Feeling awful, I turned to retreat, but at that moment a shepherd appeared, riding forward on horseback. When he saw the cause of the ruckus he stared first to the heavens, then disparagingly towards his dogs, now cowering far to the rear.

'*Inutile cani*' ('Useless dogs'), he muttered.

I stood quietly and apologetically to one side while the shepherd drove his flock past. But the dogs refused to budge. They hung back, slunk in circles, making as if to rush by one moment, then losing nerve. The shepherd hurled insults at them, pleaded, begged, cajoled, but nothing worked. Finally I mountaineered up the steep bank and hid from view. At that the dogs dashed by. The shepherd gave me a resigned look, nodded his thanks, then rode after them. Basilicata was off to a cracking start!

An hour later, I reached the first village, Rotonda—a significantly *un*Calabrian place. It was cleaner and better maintained than any village I'd seen in Calabria, with recently plastered walls, immaculately tiled rooftops, and showy flower baskets hanging from balconies. The care lavished on appearances spoke of prosperity and pride. In Calabria I'd felt too clean for the grimy villages; here I felt too dirty.

The general store was notably different too. Although as small as most Calabrian stores I'd visited, it was far better stocked, not just with fresh food but with an item not available further south—a detailed, recently published topo map of the next set of hills. Clearly, the Pollino *had* been a barrier. I'd entered a whole new land.

Thrilled by the changes, I pushed on, and other differences soon emerged. One was a woodland track. In Calabria it would have dead-ended, but here it led onwards for the rest of the day. Celebrating, I followed it through peaceful chestnut woods, over grassy hills, and across meadows splashed with poppies. Overhead, skylarks sang; beside the track stone water-fountains appeared every mile or so, a treat Calabria had only bestowed near villages. Even camping was different. I found a pitch without difficulty—a comfortable spot in a hidden meadow with a view back to the snow-splashed Pollino—and as I settled in I marvelled at the change three miles an hour could bring.

Basilicata, as I discovered over the next few days, was different from Calabria in many ways. In the Pollino, the Apennines had coalesced into one massive range, but in Basilicata the range sprawled outwards, separating into mini ranges that stood far apart. Instead of endless rolling hills Basilicata offered greater variety: limestone gorges, grassy uplands, craggy ridges, steep-sided mountains, deep valleys. There were more orchards and olive groves, more hilltop villages, more tended land, but also more land *un*tended: longer stretches of forested wilderness. I wouldn't have thought it possible, but Basilicata offered even more trees than Calabria. The region was once known as Lucania—a name possibly derived from *lucus*, the Latin word for 'wood' or 'grove'. It would make perfect sense. No region in Italy is more covered by trees.

Of course, Basilicata was still part of the Mezzogiorno, and in the Mezzogiorno some things are set in stone. By noon on the second day it was painfully clear that Basilicata's midday sun was easily equal to Calabria's. It was also clear that its hills were as steep, its *sottobosco* just as tangled, and its hounds every bit as ferocious after all. And on the second night I discovered that campsites could be just as hard to find, and equally uncomfortable; and that its mosquitoes were as bloodthirsty, if not worse. The shape of the land may have changed, but certain characteristics of the Mezzogiorno never would.

Like the maps.

Full of optimism, I began following my new topo map north, but quickly discovered that it contained just as much cartographical fabrication as any Calabrian sheet. Indeed, so impressively inaccurate was it that I soon began thinking I might have been better off with no map at all.

The first major error occurred two evenings into Basilicata, on a mountain named Monte Sirino. The map marked a lake halfway to the summit, and beside it a *rifugio*, and the idea of both was so deeply appealing I let anticipation rule my emotions—only to suffer when I discovered the truth. Alas, there was no lake, no refuge, just a steeply pitched slope, barely usable for camp. Cursing, I settled into 'The Refuge That Never Was Camp', and was mobbed by flies for my trouble.

The second major error appeared the following morning: an entire town that didn't exist. Clearly marked two valleys north of Monte Sirino, San Pietro Nei Boschi wasn't the sizable town shown but an empty plain. I'd detoured to the town to resupply, but gained nothing but extra miles for my trouble. In Mezzogiorno heat, extra miles weren't a bonus.

That evening, after ten hours of toil, I trudged towards a fifteen-mile-wide plateau that contained nothing but green on the map. Promising solitude and shade, it looked like the perfect place for camp. Reaching it took the last of my energy, but when I completed the climb I discovered not a forest or a plateau but a broad valley; not solitude but roads and farms. Sure, it was attractive and full of rustic charm—an unforgettable vision of Europe from a bygone era, with a pony and trap on the road below, and a farmer ploughing a field with horses—but it wasn't what I'd sweated uphill for. It wasn't what the map had promised. Deflated, I slumped back to a spiny thicket passed a mile earlier, cursing the cartographers with each weary step. I could forgive them for mislocating trails, even for adding lakes and refuges that didn't exist, but not for missing every single detail of a wide valley. They were no doubt getting paid for their work, but were clearly just making things up! Whoever they were, I hoped my dark thoughts reached them.

But perhaps I should have been more forgiving. It wasn't only cartographers that got it wrong, but long-time residents too.

My fourth day in Basilicata was brain-bakingly hot. Early in the afternoon I reached Bugiardo, a small village tucked beneath Monte Falso, a limestone mountain. Wilting from the heat, I paused for a break in the central piazza, slumping with a sigh into blessed shade. Across the cobblestones a church tower reached towards the harsh white sun, its crumbling stone walls looking a thousand years old. Despite the temperature the piazza was bustling: women in black heading home from Mass; suited men gossiping in small groups; ragged children chasing one another in circles. I watched mindlessly, trying not to think about walking on. My destination lay miles further, beyond Monte Falso, but I wasn't certain how best to get there. The map was typically vague. I wondered if a local might be able to help.

Eventually, an old man strolling by paused to talk. Dressed in rough outdoor clothes, deeply tanned, heavily lined, he looked wise and knowledgeable, and proudly told me he'd lived in the village for seventy-eight years. 'These mountains?' he said, sweeping an arm around. 'I know them all.' It was exactly what I wanted to hear: if any man could provide accurate directions, here he was.

And so I asked: 'Which road should I take for Santo Antonio?'

'Ah,' the man replied confidently. 'You want that one.' He pointed to the piazza's east corner, and beyond it to a road snaking uphill.

'You are sure?' I checked, and the man nodded with absolute certainty. Relieved, I set off.

The road was narrow and twisted as though unable to decide where it wanted to go. After half a mile it passed an outlying house, outside of which an even older man sat—a toothless citizen who might have seen an entire century pass. Playing it safe I asked for directions again, and the man confirmed that all was good. '*Si, si, si,*' he said while nodding vigorously. 'Santo Antonio, heh-heh-heh!' It was like an evil wizard's laugh, and how I later cursed it.

On I went.

Hours passed. The temperature soared above ninety. My usual three miles an hour dwindled to two, dropped closer to one. Soon, my eyes stung from streaming sweat, my soles ached from searing pavement, and my legs hung heavy from gravity's strengthening pull. Feet shuffled along, and my focus altered. A vision drifted into view. I saw a mountain lake, cool and crystal clear, and I saw myself plunging into it, floating gently on my back, imagined the delicious chill enveloping my body. But then I stumbled and returned to harsh reality: sun-baked mountains, blinding light, shimmering heat. For a moment I fantasised about stopping, perhaps for days, to wait for cooler conditions, but I didn't. Stopping wouldn't help. Summer was only going to grow hotter.

Time dragged; feet dragged with it. At the completion of each mile I paused, pulled off my boots, aired my soles, drank conservatively from my water bottle, and wrung out my saturated shirt. But I congratulated myself. At least I was heading the right way. The last thing I needed on a day like this was to go wrong or gain unnecessary height.

After four miles and 1,000 feet of ascent I came upon two men. They were on the road's shoulder near a parked car, standing in the shade of an umbrella pine. Eyebrows raised in surprise at my appearance on foot, they beckoned me over, and I didn't hesitate. '*Fa caldo*—it's hot!' I gasped, sweat dripping from my nose. Both men agreed, nodding seriously. For a minute, nothing more was said. The shade was glorious.

Eventually, one of them spoke. '*Dove vai?*' ('Where are you going?')

'Santo Antonio,' I answered wearily.

'Not on this road you're not!' one of the men exclaimed. 'You want that valley, over there.' He pointed far to the east.

No, I thought. *Noooo…*

'You're sure?' I asked, praying it was a joke. It had to be. It was too hot to have gone wrong.

'Sorry, we are certain. This road will take you nowhere. Up to Monte Fermare only, and then nowhere. The woods are too closed. There is no way through.'

A wave of dismay washed over me, and it must have shown for the men offered to help. 'If you like we will show you the correct way. We could even drive you to Santo Antonio if you like?'

I would have liked it very much. *But*.

'Thank you,' I replied. 'Thank you very much. But unfortunately…' And I began my impossible explanation, outlining The Walk's number-one rule. Of course, they didn't understand. Why would anyone walk when they could travel by car? Both men looked at me with concern, perhaps wondering if I'd spent too long out in the sun. A long moment of silence followed, and then the men reached a decision. They began moving back to their car. Clearly, they had a lunatic on their hands. Closing the car doors

Hot work in Basilicata, June 7, 1997.

they wished me good fortune, but then motored swiftly away. Through the rear window I saw them engaged in animated discussion, shaking their heads as they left.

The return to Bugiardo was painful, but downhill at least. Soon I was back in the piazza, slumped in shade where I'd slumped before. The wise seventy-eight-year-old was nowhere to be seen—perhaps just as well for his sake. But I pushed him from mind. I hadn't walked 580 miles just to let bad directions ruin The Walk's continuity. I was going to leave behind an unbroken line of footsteps across Europe, no matter what it took.

And so, four hours after leaving Bugiardo for the first time, I left it again, this time in the right direction. Or so I hoped.

For six days I crossed Basilicata, walking across the grain of the land. The variety kept things interesting, but progress remained a challenge. Temperatures continued to grow hotter. I couldn't fathom how my body kept going day after day. I drank gallons but couldn't drink enough. My T-shirt developed a permanent salt stain; my pee was permanently yellow. As before, my left leg began failing. I jarred it on a rock and felt an intense stabbing pain. Distressingly, my left ankle swelled once again.

Different surfaces passed beneath my hot feet: gravel, trail, grass, earth, rock, pavement. No two miles were the same. I progressed from a chestnut wood to an olive grove to a pine forest to an open ridge to a tangled thicket. Stony ground led to a dusty path and then knee-deep thistles. I was grabbed at by brambles, negotiated a barbed-wire fence, followed a woodland path that dead-ended, became ensnared in a thorny thicket, landed back on a road. My arms and legs soon bore a latticework of scratches; a record of the journey, a scabby testament to challenges overcome. But I didn't mind them. I wore the tattoos with pride.

Daily, flies grew worse: black flies by day, midges and mosquitoes by night. There were ants too, and they got everywhere. The fifth Basilicatan camp was so overrun with ants they were still climbing out of Ten Ton a week later. Each night the forest floors came alive with thousands of insects and bugs: hairy millipedes inches long, giant armour-plated beetles, creeping lice, a multitude of spiders and ants, insects shaped like leaves or sticks, glistening slugs and worms, leaping fleas, long-legged grasshoppers, and countless other unclassifiable multi-limbed monsters. A veritable army of miniature aliens from another world. Fascinated, I inspected many up close, getting down low to examine them eye to eye. The variety was truly astonishing—nature's creativity a wonder to see. But the presence of so much life defeated my wish to sleep out under the stars, tentless. The insects, and an occasional passing snake, made it impossible. The mosquitoes alone would have sucked me dry.

The whining of mosquitoes became the sound of the Apennines. The Italian for mosquito is *zanzara*—plural *zanzare*. It's a vigorous-sounding name that suits them perfectly. Ferocious and unrelenting, *zanzare* have impacted Italy's history, and caused more deaths and misery than any other creature. Until recently, they carried malaria, and because of it some parts of Italy were once practically uninhabitable. At the start of the 20th century 20,000 Italians were dying from the disease every year. Ancient Romans believed the disease was caused by foul air hanging over swamps; hence the Italian name, *mal aria*, which literally means 'bad air'. It wasn't until the late 1800s that mosquitoes were identified as the carriers, and not until the late 1940s that serious eradication attempts began. It took many years, but by the 1960s malaria was beaten, until the warming climate of the late 20th century brought a return—albeit on a much smaller scale. Although it was extremely unlikely I'd contract malaria from Apennine mosquitoes I saw no reason to willingly donate blood. Before sleep each night I'd remove all *zanzare* from the tent. I'd sweep my searchlight about as though hunting enemy bombers and smear them against the walls once they were found. Mosquitoes that had already feasted left red streaks; the unfed left dusty black smudges. By lights out it often looked as though some terrible bloody massacre had just taken place.

Because of the *zanzare* I went many nights without leaving the tent after dark, but on the sixth Basilicatan night, at a camp I'd named 'Insect Central', I caught a glimpse through the tent wall of a moving pinprick of light outside, and opened the zip to investigate. And was glad I did. Travelling through the blackness were a thousand yellow-green lights flickering on and off, drifting gently like a neon snowfall. It was mesmerising, otherworldly, and beyond beautiful. I guessed at once they were fireflies, even though I'd never seen them before. Either that or I'd woken up in a dream.

Fireflies are small flying beetles capable of producing a luminous glow in their abdomens. Created by a chemical reaction known as bioluminescence, the blinking on–off light is a male firefly's call to mate. It must surely work—I wasn't a female firefly, but I couldn't look away. Spellbound, I watched for a long while, entirely forgetting the mosquitoes. It was as though an entire galaxy of tiny stars were floating through the forest; as though a scene from a fairy tale had sprung to life. I'd put myself through many discomforts since Melito, but suddenly they all seemed worthwhile. *To see this*, I thought, *I'd do it all again*. If the goal of travel is to experience places utterly unlike home then the fireflies helped me achieve that goal. If another goal is to find moments of sheer wonder, the fireflies helped with that too.

Fireflies emerged again the following night, entrancing me once again. Perhaps locals who grew up seeing them every year would feel blasé about such a phenomenon, but I doubted I ever could. I felt fortunate beyond words. You have to take the rough with the smooth, I reasoned, the cursed with the magical. *Zanzare* and fireflies—the yin and yang that summed up two complementary sides of The Walk.

My final camp in Basilicata was in an apple orchard among trees hung with nets. I moved in at dusk and would be gone at first light, leaving no sign of my stay. No one would ever know.

Trying to ignore the mosquitoes I stayed outside after dark, losing myself in another firefly display. In delight, I stepped gently through the orchard, spinning slowly, arms wide, firefly-stars at my fingertips. Eventually, floating on gratitude, I retreated to the tent and, as usual in the sultry Mezzogiorno heat, slept on top of my sleeping bag, not in it. At two in the morning I was woken by a sudden burst of birdsong so loud it had to be coming from directly overhead. For a second I cursed, but only for a second. The song was like the fireflies: beautiful, unlike any I'd ever heard. It was more complex, more varied, more compelling—the work of a virtuoso, an absolute master of its craft. It contained warbles and trills, chirps and whistles. Tone and tempo continuously altered. Short staccato bursts became liquid outpourings that flowed like cascading streams. Notes soared and spun into space. Simple repeated melodies evolved into rich, multi-layered themes.

I lay in silence, as entranced as I'd been by the fireflies, never happier to have been plucked from sleep. For nearly an hour the bird offered its serenade. It had to be a nightingale. What else could produce such a work? The bird wove its spell, and I celebrated every note. How fortunate I was to be where I was, I decided. How fortunate that I couldn't afford hotels and wasn't shut away inside.

UPS AND DOWNS IN CAMPANIA
Chapter 11

THE FIRST SIX miles in Campania were fast; the fastest of The Walk so far. Perhaps it was the plunging 3,000-foot descent, or the promise of fresh food, or the idea of taking a day off, or the hope that the next resupply parcel might possibly have arrived, but I practically ran down the steep-sided mountain from Basilicata into Campania and landed in the town of Sala Consilina with a resounding thump, dust billowing from my clothes.

Sala Consilina didn't look large from above. From the area it occupied I guessed at a maximum of 500 inhabitants, not the 13,000 I found. As I was coming to see, the citizens of the Mezzogiorno appear to like living on top of one another. Wide spaces might exist all around, but why use them when everyone can squeeze onto one small hill? In medieval times compact hilltop towns were easier to defend; in modern times building up is clearly favoured over building out. Sala Consilina contained numerous soaring apartment buildings and tower blocks. They rose shoulder to shoulder, and their inhabitants displayed the frantic energy of ants whose nest had just been disturbed. Or so it seemed to me, fresh from the woods. London, with its teeming millions, had nothing on Sala Consilina for bustle.

Battling culture shock, I navigated to the post office. Unexpectedly, the interior was calm, the officials efficient and quick. When a clerk handed over a parcel and several letters as though he did such a thing every day I almost fell over in shock. The parcel's brown paper wrapping was shredded, the address label hanging on by the slenderest of threads, but there it was, containing everything it should. It felt like Christmas in June.

Outside, I found a phone box and called home to share the news. Base Camp—as I now called my parents—were delighted to hear that their behind-the-scenes support was finally paying off. And Base Camp were doing a great deal behind the scenes: not just mailing out the resupply parcels but also keeping the charities updated on progress, chasing sponsors who hadn't fulfilled promises, and managing many of the details of the public fundraising side of the journey. They told me that The Passage and Cardinal Hume Centre had received early donations—over £1,500 so far. This was fantastic news, and it would provide extra motivation if I needed it. Motivation wasn't usually in short supply, but when I followed bad directions, was misled by the map, and got lost in the *sottobosco* I didn't always manage zen-like calm. But knowing that funds for the homeless were coming in? It would be something positive to focus on.

After Base Camp had shared all their news I had my turn, describing recent highlights—the fireflies, the nightingale. But I didn't touch on everything. Since the first call home I'd avoided describing the worst hardships, and never touched on the risks, gunshots in the woods, or encounters with the mafia. It seemed important to consider my parents' feelings. Heading alone into wild mountains was bad enough, but giving Base Camp extra details to worry about would have been unforgivable.

From Sala Consilina I weaved north-west. Monte Cervati, Monte Alburno, Eboli, wild Monti Picentini; mere names on the map became real places to touch and smell. I treasured how The Walk was transforming a one-dimensional line on the map into a multi-dimensional reality. The further I travelled the more I understood. How the range fitted together, how it worked, what it was; the Big Picture was developing. Although I was only scratching the surface and could never know individual corners as intimately as the locals did, I was learning what lay beyond each corner, beyond each mountain, beyond a hundred mountains after that. My final perspective of the range would likely be very different from that of anyone else alive.

The Apennines I saw didn't seem to match the Apennines apparently seen by other writers. Where others had found deforestation I found lush forests. In his 1915 book, *Old Calabria*, Norman Douglas uses words like 'dark and barren' to describe mountains that to me had been bright and verdant. He even included an ominous warning towards the end of his narrative: 'This is not a land to traverse alone.' In Carlo Levi's famous memoir, *Christ Stopped at Eboli*, the landscapes of the south were dark and mysterious, frequently inhabited by creatures not known to the Christian world. His descriptions were vague, but they were also powerfully and poetically evocative. He painted the landscape as shadowy, monotonous and desolate; as a realm lacking trees; as a forlorn wasteland comparable to a sea of chalk. There was a bottomless sadness to it, and a weariness, as cold winds spiraled up from ravines and mountains hung like islands above black veils of mist. According to Levi, it was a world apart. It was shrouded to most people, accessible only to the peasants who lived there, and closed off to everyone else unless they possessed a magic key.

Levi was writing about the southern Apennines of the late 1930s. He had been exiled to the region by Mussolini for anti-Fascist activities, and discovered a level of poverty below anything encountered in Italy's prosperous north. This backwardness, the unusual geology of the specific location he was confined to, and the restrictions of exile itself, may well have coloured his impressions; often, what we see is based on what we expect to see. Levi's descriptions were understandable, but I wondered how much they had influenced other writers. 'Barren, desolate, oppressive, desert-like'—had the authors of these words, all more recent, actually visited the range?

The Big Picture I was forming was based on complete immersion in the range. I wasn't just seeing it from the side of a road, but also from beyond even the trails, from deep in the woods. Even though I'd come expecting an open, sun-scorched land, I'd moved beyond those expectations. My level of immersion had revealed the truth, and it definitely wasn't barren.

If the Apennines had taken shape, so too had The Walk itself. It had developed character of its own, stood separate from previous journeys, and now felt utterly separate from life in London. It was defined by its details, by the insects, thorns and sweat, by the constant desire for water and shade, by the fierceness of the sun, by the ever-changing textures of the earth beneath my feet. It was defined by scents; the smell of crushed fruit in orchards, the sweetness of pine resin in forests, the pungency of dense vegetation in the *sottobosco*. There was a rhythm to The Walk now. It had momentum. What it stood for was becoming clearer. It stood for freedom to move at my own pace, and freedom to think my own thoughts. It was about connection with the land and with myself. And it was about the discovery that I could stand a lot, that I could stand myself, that I could get by without many of the things I'd once considered essential, that my body and resolve were tougher than I'd supposed. It was about discovering that even hardship and discomfort had worth.

The difficult moments had been stored away. Unexpectedly, I found myself recalling the worst of them with fondness. That I'd overcome them filled me with pride. It struck me as ironic that the journey's least pleasant moments had become the most pleasurable in hindsight, even while daily discomforts continued to hurt. But at least I'd learnt a few coping tricks. When my feet screamed I tried turning it into achievement—positive evidence of how far I'd come. When mosquitoes chased me into my stifling tent I sought gratitude that I had a tent to hide within. When thirst hit I told myself it would only make water taste sweeter the next time I found it. When I ended up lost I told myself it would make being found all the better. Not that I managed a positive outlook in every situation, and not that it always worked, but I had come to accept that discomforts and difficulties were essential traits of the journey. Without them the Apennines wouldn't be the range it was, and The Walk wouldn't be the journey it was. Easy travel would have been, well, easier, but also far less interesting. Or so I tried telling myself.

I was coming to suspect that I was on The Walk to learn some fundamental lessons. This wasn't why I'd begun, but I could see it was perhaps something I'd needed. I felt stronger for the lessons and tricks so far learnt: more confident, more resilient. I wondered about the lessons that lay ahead. Would I learn to find positivity in *all* situations? Would The Walk's lessons prove useful beyond the trail, back in ordinary life?

One thing I'd learnt for sure was that I had been right all along—that this simple wandering life was the life for me, even with the difficulties. In the mountains of Campania, after six weeks on foot, I felt like a seasoned veteran, ready for everything and anything that lay ahead.

Typical Campanian scenery, June 13, 1997.

It was morning, the forty-fourth of The Walk, and on the surface similar to the mornings before it. And yet it wasn't similar the way mornings back in Pinner had been. Here, I woke in the same tent, but in a new forest. Here, I was on the same journey, but faced an entirely new set of miles. Here, the similarities only accentuated the differences.

As usual, sunlight pulled me from sleep. Or perhaps it was the baying of distant dogs, or the chiming of church bells from a nearby village, or simply because I'd had enough sleep. But whatever the cause, I woke into instant alertness, ready to face another gruelling day. Sure, my body held some residue from the previous day—from all the previous days—but less than I would have once expected. The human body's ability to repair itself overnight astonished me.

Woodland birds sang. Sunlight danced upon tent walls. The air was cool and fresh, spring-like, optimistic. What a joy it was to wake naturally instead of by alarm, feeling alive instead of jaded, and excited by the day ahead instead of bored at its prospect. How remarkable it was to not know what lay ahead. The new day could bring anything.

I lit the stove without getting up. Breakfast in bed: one of the journey's many perks. It was Monday. At least, I thought it was. *No, it's Tuesday. Or maybe Wednesday?* The more I considered it the more I realised I didn't know, and the realisation filled me with satisfaction. Who cared, anyway? Who needed labels? Here on The Walk a day was just a day, a blank slate that would be whatever it would be, filled with things to discover and experiences to be had. Back home a day was too often defined—and limited —by its name, but on The Walk there were no such limits.

After tea and cereal I dismantled camp. Unlike on the first morning, it took less than thirty minutes, and that was without rushing. I spent half the time lost in the view: a rural valley and beyond it wooded mountains. Each morning I woke to a new view, each night lay down somewhere fresh. The restless gene, the human desire to see if the grass truly is greener beyond the next hill, was being well fed.

From camp I strode forth, and could have burst from the freedom of it. I felt capable of anything, of Herculean feats, of conquering the world. It was how I felt most mornings. I loved pulling on Ten Ton and striding into unknown country. It had become an everyday occurrence, but it remained extraordinary. *I'm really here!* I thought. *I'm really doing this!* It still seemed like a dream.

The first couple of hours were effortless, but soon the hard physical reality of Mezzogiorno walking brought me back to earth. Joy and optimism remained, but they were tempered by heat and effort. As I now knew, emotions could change significantly mile by mile. A day on foot was often a roller-coaster ride. High one moment, low the next—a mountain walk was a thing of frequent ups and downs.

From camp I lost height and reached a road. It twisted down-valley, through a small village, up the far side. As was usual now, people stared at me in the village. Locals stopped what they were doing; heads turned; eyes followed. In a land that saw few tourists the stares were understandable, but they made me uneasy, especially those that revealed distaste at my trampish appearance.

I would have preferred being the observer, not the observed, but it was seldom allowed—especially not in the second village. Its piazza was hopping with mid-morning life, a fascinating drama to watch, but watch I couldn't. Despite retreating to a quiet corner I was followed by five scruffy urchins. All I yearned for was a few minutes' rest, but when the children positioned themselves around me, standing only an arm's length back, the opportunity vanished. Smiling and joking, I tried breaking the ice, but gained no response. Ten large round eyes stared back, unblinking. Ignoring them didn't work, either; how could I relax when I felt like an exhibit in a zoo? After a few minutes I couldn't take it any longer. Reluctantly, I heaved on Ten Ton and trudged wearily on. The stares followed me.

Back in Calabria the staring had been minimal, but since entering Basilicata the stares had barely stopped. They'd become wearing, although not as wearing as an endlessly repeated question: '*Dove vai?*'

At first, '*Dove vai?*' ('Where are you going?') had seemed perfectly reasonable, and I'd answered as best I could. Trouble was, my replies were seldom listened to, let alone comprehended. No matter if I said 'The next town', or 'Just for a walk', confusion or disinterest usually followed. I understood the confusion—as I'd seen since Melito, few Apennine residents deliberately walked any distance for any reason. But the disinterest was more perplexing. People wanted to stop me, wanted to ask '*Dove vai?*', but that was all they cared about: the asking, not the listening. Still, at each '*Dove vai?*' I tried my hardest to explain, but the attempts were draining. In truth, they took energy I often didn't have. And, worse, having to stop —again and again and again—broke my stride. '*Dove vai?*' I'd be asked on the way into town, and in a store when all I wanted was a cold drink, and outside when I was desperate to slump into shade, and when I stood up to go, and as I was building momentum on a climb from town, and when I was weary to the bone and simply wanted to keep moving and have the day done. I'd be asked time after time, day after day. It didn't stop.

If the question had led to deeper conversations I would have welcomed it. I longed to connect with the people as deeply as I was connecting with the land. Local insight would have added layers to the journey, and '*Dove vai?*' gave me a way in. But I wasn't breaking through—most likely my fault, not theirs. I didn't have the right skills, language or social. I couldn't figure out the trick. This failure frustrated me. I had no doubt there was a great lesson to learn from it, and felt sure there must be a positive way of looking at the problem, but unlike with other difficulties I'd overcome I couldn't see the positive or the lesson. Perhaps this wasn't surprising. After all, 'communication' and 'people' had never been my strengths. Even if I didn't stammer when speaking Italian, I still had a stammerer's hesitancy, and an introvert's reticence. Conversation would never be easy for me. *'Dove vai?'* kept coming, and it was wearing me out.

The questions and the staring made relaxing in villages impossible, and relaxing away from villages was becoming impossible too. Dogs, flies, and mosquitoes always moved me on soon after I'd stopped. The only real moment of peace came at dawn, before the sun grew too hot and insects too numerous, and perhaps that was why mornings felt so peaceful and so exhilarating. But the peace was always fleeting. After weeks of intense effort the need for a full twenty-four hours of quality rest—a simple day off—had become overpowering, but it was a need that now seemed impossible to meet.

From the second village I returned to the woods, leaving the stares and questions behind. A gravel track led uphill, then a path. I approached navigation in a more instinctive way now; intuition often served better than untrustworthy lines on a map. As I later discovered, many Apennine maps were based on surveys carried out during World War Two. Vegetation can change significantly in half a century. Easily navigable paths from the forties could be decades overgrown fifty years later. When I discovered that Apennine maps weren't representations of the present but snapshots of the past their untrustworthiness made a great deal more sense.

Fortunately, the Campanian woods were easier to negotiate than woods further south. There were more tracks and trails—clear evidence that others visited the woods, although I never saw them. So far, since the very first step, I hadn't seen a single other person on foot in the mountains, only on roads, near farms, and in villages. It had truly made the woods feel remote. The 'other' Europe that I'd come to find was far more 'other' than I'd expected.

The trails now available helped in many ways, but also presented a novel problem: there were almost too many of them, and most choices still led to dead-ends. Which is where intuition and instincts developed over the miles came in. A path's shape, the amount of leaf litter upon it, evidence of recent passage, the density of surrounding undergrowth, the possible purpose a path had for existing; all these details hinted at how a path would likely behave. Sometimes, however, even these clues weren't enough, and I resorted to a failsafe navigational method: a flipped coin. Heads I go right, tails left. Choosing the future on the toss of a coin seemed illogical, but it matched the traveller I'd become. It was deeply satisfying, sportingly unscientific, thrillingly random. I'd learnt to trust chance, and the funny thing was chance never let me down.

On this day I spent five hours traversing the woods, often making instinctive guesses, twice resorting to the trusty coin. For once progress went well. I reached the ridge I'd been aiming for without incident, then began the day's final descent. Just as I was starting to believe I'd manage a first—an entire day without a wrong turn—I took one. It happened late afternoon, with a storm threatening and humidity dripping from leaves. Tiredness led to a poor choice: I didn't toss the coin, and the result was a path that died. Still, I'd been in this situation before. All I needed now was faith. Wilting from the heat, dirty from the miles, scratched as usual, unpleasantly footsore, I eased through the *sottobosco*, laughing ruefully at the morning's unbounded optimism. Conquer the world? The world was conquering me. The day had become like most others: a test of endurance, a sweat-fest in the trees. If I were to remember anything of the southern Apennines in later life it would be this, the tangled forests and myself entwined within them, drowning in green. This was the Italy few outsiders knew. This was the Italy most insiders avoided.

Pushing on, I began longing for things I didn't have, too weary to remember lessons supposedly learnt. I longed for day's end when I could collapse in camp. And I longed to be clean. Weeks had passed since my last shower, and I could feel the grime upon my skin. I always gave my feet a thorough splash each night, but seldom had water spare for anything else. The uncomfortable stickiness of summer was getting to me. No wonder I attracted so many flies.

It wasn't until evening that I escaped the trees and found water for camp. I came upon a road, and a short distance along it found a parking area and a fountain—cold water dribbling from an ornate metal pipe into a stone bowl. Nearby, an unusually good trail led back into the woods, and 100 yards down it I chose a hidden spot for camp. The trail bore Italian Alpine Club waymarkings—it was the first waymarked trail of the entire walk—and a sign along it declared the area a nature reserve. Camping was probably banned, but it seemed unlikely that my quiet camp so close to a parking area would cause harm. Three cars were parked, but there was no one about. With luck I'd spend the night undetected.

I felt like a fugitive as I pitched the Peapod—a familiar feeling. Most of my Basilicatan and Campanian camps had been illegal, stolen on private ground. Other options had been limited. Hotels remained too costly, and organised campsites didn't exist, although the maps had broken my heart several times by promising them. In an ideal world I would have camped deep in the wild each night, but the lack of surface water across Campania's limestone mountains made this difficult. Often, there had been no option but to settle close to civilisation, relying on water carried from town. Trespassing respectfully, I'd pitched my little green shelter in orchards, olive groves, and woods, often within earshot of settlements, always being careful with tent pegs and metal cookware lest they rattle, mindful of my headlamp's light after dark. Voices had passed close by from time to time, and dogs had barked in my direction, but I hadn't yet been discovered. Having to hide away each night added extra stress to the journey. I couldn't relax in villages because of the attention, in the mountains because of flies, or in camp in case I was found and moved on. I was starting to feel like an outcast—a vagabond living beyond society's edge. It seemed appropriate. Perhaps this was how London's homeless sometimes felt.

I stole back to the fountain, checked that there was no one around, and began filling my water carrier, trying to ignore the guilt that suggested I was doing something wrong. As the water bag swelled, I found myself recalling the words spoken by a Passage volunteer during one of my visits to the charity. 'The longer someone spends living outside without a home, the more normal that way of living becomes to them,' he had said. 'It varies person to person, of course, but becoming institutionalised to homelessness doesn't take long. Often, people end up fully believing that living rough is all they deserve. When a person is judged by their appearance, by how dirty they look, or when they are treated as though they don't even exist, it's hardly surprising that someone comes to feel like a lesser being, different from everyone else.'

I could believe it. Although I was living away from home by choice, I felt different too—and not always in a healthy way. Occasionally, I'd found myself believing that the hardships I experienced were deserved. I'd even considered the possibility that I wasn't worthy of the home I'd left behind. On the surface I knew it was ludicrous—as ludicrous as it was to compare my journey with homelessness. But I couldn't entirely dismiss the idea that I deserved what I had. What if it were true? And what if I was becoming institutionalised to my grimy, rootless, solitary way of life? Every day I experienced hunger, thirst and tiredness. Every night I hid myself away from other people, and curled up in my sauna tent, sweating, unwashed and alone. Living in any situation for a long period changes a person. Wasn't it inevitable that living apart from society would change me?

I'd wanted my walk—I'd chosen it. I'd thought it might change me. But it hadn't crossed my mind that the changes might be bad.

I had almost filled my water bag when a man suddenly emerged from the trees. Wearing olive-green fatigues, he resembled a forest ranger, and for a moment I thought the game was up. But I couldn't have been more wrong. Acting furtively, the man's posture suggested he was hiding something under his jacket. After glancing my way a couple of times, he must have realised I wasn't a ranger either because he visibly relaxed, grinned, and strode over. He opened his jacket and proudly revealed three rabbits 'acquired' in the woods, and was about to share the tale of their capture when a car motored into sight. In a flash he turned away, tucked his bounty from view, and stole back to his car. Instinctively, I hid my water carrier too.

But I needn't have worried. The new arrivals were a young couple from Rome, touring the area—not park rangers seeking rule-breakers. They walked over to talk, and when they learnt I was English they broke into instant smiles. I was keen to retreat into the trees but found it impossible to make a quick escape. The couple had a lot to say, and seemed genuinely interested in The Walk. But then the conversation turned farcical.

'So, where are you staying tonight?' they asked.

'Down the valley a mile or so,' I lied, not wishing to give away my exact location. 'I'm camped in the forest.'

'Camped in the forest? You have a caravan?'

'No, a tent.'

'A tent? But what kind of camping is that?'

'Well... it's just camping.'

'What about a car?'

'I don't have a car. I'm walking.'

'No car? But where is it parked?'

'It's not parked anywhere. I don't have one.'

'But *where* are you staying, then?'

'In the forest.'

'But what are you *doing?*'

'I'm walking. Up the Apennines. Like I explained...'

'Up the Apennines?'

'Yes.'

'And you are going by car?'

Thankfully, the questions ceased when an elderly man appeared and tapped me on the shoulder. He wanted me to move my car! And then another young couple emerged from the bushes, brushing grass and leaves from disarranged clothes, doing up buttons. It seemed like a good time to escape. I pointed the elderly man towards the poacher, bid a hasty goodbye to the Couple With Many Questions, and retreated back down the trail to the sanctuary of the woods.

Later, I considered returning to the fountain to wash, but wasn't brave enough to risk it. I spent another sultry night sweating in the tent, hunted by *zanzare*.

Another mosquito-haunted night in the jungle. 'Camp of the Creeping Weed', June 14, 1997.

Two days and forty miles later I descended from wild woods into the Valle Caudina: a valley so wide and flat it almost qualified as a plain. The mountains several miles distant on the other side were barely visible in the heat haze. Three miles of road walking took me to Montesarchio, the first of the valley's two towns, and once there I climbed a rocky outcrop in its centre to a small castle and looked out across the valley. Spread like a map below, Montesarchio radiated outwards in all directions, its roads like spokes on a bicycle wheel. Though only a small town, like many such towns it was doing a fair impression of a medium-sized city. Its hum filled the air.

Towns like Montesarchio had become appealingly familiar. Like other towns it offered the usual blend of ancient and modern, of narrow alleys and open piazzas, of teeming streets and empty corners. Like other towns it looked thoroughly *lived in*. Centuries of hard living had left cracks in masonry, stains on walls, chips in stones, grime in cracks. Balcony railings were bent, walls leaned at odd angles, weeds grew. The narrow streets and jammed-together apartments gave it a built-up appearance, and with the dirt and noise it could have been ugly, but it wasn't—it was hugely attractive. The town seemed organic, as though it had grown from the landscape, from the very bones of the mountains. And it had a level of style that towns back in Britain seldom achieved. Every building sported some kind of classical architectural flourish, and all the buildings somehow matched. Red tiles covered most rooftops; wall colours complemented one another. Montesarchio was a work of art.

After descending from the castle I paused in a large piazza, trying to ignore the usual rude stares. A church steeple towered overhead, and at my back large stone lions rested on pedestals, water gushing from their mouths into a pool of shimmering blue. It was all I could do to stop myself plunging in.

Minutes passed. No one came close, but I wasn't surprised. I was now as dirty as any long-distance hiker has ever been. God alone knows what I smelled like. It was probably my imagination, but even the flies had started keeping away. Time to do something about it.

I hadn't managed a day off in nearly three weeks and 250 miles. I'd planned on several, but circumstance hadn't allowed them. A week

Montesarchio, June 15, 1997.

previously I'd begun staring hungrily at hotels, imagining their cool rooms and clean sheets, fantasising about their cleansing showers. Montesarchio looked large enough to offer several hotels. It was time, quite literally, to splash out.

Following directions from a helpful teenager I marched enthusiastically to the first hotel, picturing the comforts ahead, but discovered on arrival that the place was closed, and looked as though it had been for years. A gap-toothed vendor at a nearby fruit stall gave me directions to the next hotel, assuring me it was open. It lay a mile across town, but that was nothing to a man who'd just walked 700. I was on a mission now—nothing could stop me, not even two typically aggressive Apennine dogs. On a street with several dead rats in the gutter the dogs attacked, snapping at my bare legs. In defence I kicked out with practised efficiency, and after a long half-minute of strategic action an old lady appeared from a house and called the dogs home. She glared at me as though it were entirely my fault.

Half a mile further I reached the second hotel, also closed, and shortly after it a third. It was called the Hotel Jolly, and it was—thankfully—open. Gasping from the heat, sweating from my battle with the dogs, I stepped inside.

The sun-blasted day faded in an instant. Inside, all was cool and dim, clean and polished, comfortable and refined. I instantly felt out of place. I hadn't been indoors somewhere like this in a very long time. I'd peeked into old churches, wandered the aisles of village supermarkets, but that was the extent of time inside. I hadn't seen such plush chairs, ornate light fittings, or fancily decorated walls since April. At first glance it all seemed gaudy and ostentatious, if not downright silly. But I couldn't wait to enjoy it.

A sharp-suited man with oil-slicked hair and an immaculate moustache stood behind the front desk. He eyed me carefully as I approached. 'Yes?' he drawled in Italian once I stood before him. 'Is there a problem?'

His greeting struck me as odd, but I forged ahead, thinking only of the shower I'd soon enjoy. 'I need a room, please—perhaps for two nights. What is the nightly rate?'

The receptionist inspected me deliberately, making no attempt to hide his examination, and concluded it with an expression of immense disdain. I instantly felt like a lesser being. 'For you,' he finally sneered, 'I make a special price. Only four hundred thousand lira. Per night.'

I made a quick mental exchange, and was shocked at the price: £160. The shower and clean sheets receded from grasp. But then I saw what the man was doing: judging me for how dirty I was, disregarding me because of it. Anger flashed through me, overcoming the thought that being turned away was deserved. I opened my mouth to protest, but stopped, sensing that it was pointless. An argument would achieve nothing but waste energy I didn't have. I was tempted to stay anyway, just to prove a point, but it would have been a hollow, expensive victory.

And to be honest, I understood. Would I let someone like me anywhere near clean sheets I owned? Would I voluntarily sit next to someone like me in a restaurant?

'Well,' I responded meekly. 'Are there any less expensive hotels in town?'

The receptionist snorted and stuck his nose in the air. 'No. In Montesarchio we only have four-star hotels.'

So much for the Hotel *Jolly*.

Across town I found two more hotels. One was closed; one was full. Desperate now, unable to let the night of comfort pass, I pushed on to the Valle Caudina's second village, and approached its only hotel. It was a sensational place, gleaming in the sun, surrounded by immaculate gardens and lawns, with palm trees offering shade, and exotic flowers spilling from tidy flowerbeds. A swimming pool sparkled seductively. Sunbathers lounged on reclining chairs; swimmers splashed and laughed. It was a vision. I'd never seen anything so fine.

A sign out front announced that there were vacancies, and I strode confidently to the receptionist, determined to reclaim my place in society and earn an honest rate. But it wasn't to be. My position as an outcast was set. I wasn't worthy, and I definitely wasn't wanted.

'No vacancy,' the receptionist curtly explained. I could see her examining my appearance, comparing it with her own. She was polished to a shine. Not a hair on her head was out of place, and her jacket looked as though it cost more than everything I owned.

'But, but, but...' I stammered. 'The sign outside...'

'Is incorrect. We have a large wedding tomorrow.'

And the manager, when called upon, confirmed it. He and the receptionist exchanged a telling look.

I finished the day camped on a scrubby hillside above town, wiping off ants, broiling beneath the evening sun. The 'Tiny Ant Terrace' was another illegal camp. Not only was I an outcast—I was also a criminal.

While filling my water carrier from a fountain in the centre of the village a policeman had approached me. He wanted to know what I was doing. 'Vagrancy is against the law,' he told me firmly, accusation in his eyes.

'But I'm a hiker,' I explained. 'From England. I'm on holiday.'

'Your passport,' he demanded, and, intimidated, I handed it over.

While the policeman inspected it, I stood in temporary captivity, seething at the injustice of it. Not having a home was criminal? I was here by choice, but what if I weren't? What if I were living out of a backpack because I'd lost a job and couldn't keep up payments on a home? What if I'd run away from abuse, from a dangerous situation? What if had nowhere to turn? Waiting submissively before the policeman, I felt a growing urge to stand up for myself. I wanted to argue. But once again I sensed that it would be futile. And risky. The policeman might find a reason to arrest me. Perhaps he'd do it anyway, for camping illegally in the woods. It was better to stay submissive, however much I hated it. However small it made me feel. I didn't want to do anything that might threaten The Walk.

The policeman finally accepted that I was who I said. But he remained suspicious. 'Where will you go next?' he demanded.

'Montesarchio,' I lied. 'I'll find a hotel there.'

'Good. Do not go over the mountain. It is closed.' He considered things for a moment, staring at my bulging water carrier. 'What is that for?'

'Oh,' I answered quickly. 'To cool off. I'll dump it on my head outside the village.' And I mimed the procedure. To my surprise he bought it, and wandered away.

The water, of course, was for dinner and breakfast, and to drink, and to sprinkle over road-weary feet. As night rolled in I hid within the tent, hunted as always by bloodthirsty mosquitoes. Sweat dripped, and the uneven ground pushed rocks against my side. Dogs barked, crickets chorused, and sleep wouldn't come. I was too weary, too dirty, too upset, and felt too rejected. My head throbbed. I began cursing southern Italy. I swore and swore, venting my fury into my diary, four-lettering across an entire page. The heat, the flies, the dogs, the rude hoteliers, the policeman, the stares and endless questions, the road walking, the useless maps, the tangled forests, the entire bloody range: I hated it all.

Even Base Camp rejected me the next day. I called home, desperately needing to talk, but on this rare occasion was let down. 'I really can't talk,' my father said quickly. 'I'm waiting for a very important call.' And he hung up, leaving me on my own, feeling unimportant and abandoned.

For another day and a half I wallowed in anger, frustration, and exhaustion, feeling like an absolute failure. So much for all the lessons learnt, for all my coping tricks, for all my positivity. And so much for considering myself a seasoned veteran, ready for everything and anything. The

Mezzogiorno was beating me. I'd had enough. Homeless people don't have the option of an easy escape when their situation becomes too hard to bear, but I did. When I reached the town of Telese, and saw that it had a train station, I did what every serious self-respecting stout-hearted never-give-up adventurer would do: I caught a train out of there. Mad Mountain Jack in full retreat.

The train carried me to the coast, and what a dazzling sight it was. I camped in a real campsite, showered away the filth, became a member of society again—clean, unjudged and invisible. I joined tourists in Napoli and Pompeii, swam in the clear waters of the Mediterranean off the Amalfi Coast, explored emerald Capri, and—above all—relaxed.

My journey was nothing more than a glorified vacation, but I needed a vacation from it.

I took five blissful days.

MEASURE OF THE SOUTH
Chapter 12

I PICKED UP the trail *exactly* where I'd left it. Back in Telese I took great care to place boots to the inch where they'd been placed before. Yes, I'd left the trail, but the line of steps would remain unbroken.

Five youths loitered outside the station. Tall, oozing machismo, sleeves rolled high to reveal bulging biceps, they leaned against a stone wall. 'Hey, where are you going?' they shouted in Italian with teasing but unthreatening smiles. I dropped Ten Ton, wandered over, and explained. Perhaps they'd provide the kind of send-off that had been lacking back on Melito's lonely beach.

One of the youths pointed to the backpack. He asked if he could try it on.

The pack, loaded with water for the night and five days' food, was back to its heaviest. It weighed at least sixty pounds; lifting it wasn't easy. I led the youths to it, then stood back to enjoy the show.

The first youth swaggered forward, bent down, heaved and... nothing happened. He looked up in surprise. Trying again, he widened his stance, tightened his grip, strained, grunted, managed to raise Ten Ton two feet off the ground, and then staggered about in circles trying to manhandle the awkward load onto his back. The other youths laughed. After a valiant attempt, he lowered the pack and admitted defeat. One by one the others stepped forward, each certain he could succeed where his friends had failed—and one by one they discovered the pack was heavier than it looked. It was the same each time: cocky confidence, an expression of surprise, neck muscles popping, rueful acceptance of defeat. '*Mamma mia!*' they exclaimed in turn, shaking heads in disbelief.

'So, show us!' they demanded, after all had failed. They knew they were stronger than I was. It was obvious from the comparative size of our arms, from my skinniness compared to their bulk. It was clear I was going to fail too.

Enjoying the moment, I stepped up. Lifting the pack had nothing to do with strength. It was all technique, and I'd had two months to perfect it. Momentum was key; using a leg for extra lift helped; a particular twist at the right moment was essential. Trying to look casual, I leaned over and swung the pack onto my shoulders in one smooth motion.

'*Porca miseria!*' one of the youths exclaimed.

'*Madonna!*' cursed another.

'*Cavolo!*' swore a third.

They looked at me with new respect. 'You are carrying *that* through the mountains?' There was no teasing now.

One of the youths struck an exaggerated body builder pose. 'You are made of steel,' he said.

It was a fine way to return to the trail.

From the station I wandered through Telese, footsteps echoing along deserted streets. It was siesta time, and the town was silent, as though time itself had stopped. Blinds were drawn, shutters were clamped shut, shops were closed, traffic was non-existent. I couldn't help but compare the stunning quietness to the busyness of the places I'd just visited. Was it really possible that both extremes belonged to the same Italy?

Leaving Telese, I returned to familiar Apennine landscapes: olive groves, beech woods, limestone mountains, everything softened by hazy afternoon light. Progress felt easy. Ten Ton's considerable weight seemed strangely inconsequential. The break had been a physical necessity—I'd been driving too hard—and the rest had allowed complete recovery. But it was more than that. The retreat into the better-known Italy had confirmed, just when I was starting to doubt it, that the quieter Italy was where I belonged.

My boots paced out the scalding Mezzogiorno afternoon, taking me through woods to a town, San Savaltore Telesino, then onwards around a large mountain to another town. I arrived at 4 p.m., with siesta time over and locals emerging. To my surprise they were friendlier than other Apennine folk had been just six days before. Every single person returned my smile of greeting, there were no rude stares, and no one stopped me to ask '*Dove vai?*' Something had changed. Was it because I was cleaner? Was it because I was more relaxed now that I'd taken a break? Was it all *me*? I wondered if the people had been friendly and welcoming all along, but The Walk's unrelenting challenges had stopped me from seeing it. Was it possible I'd missed opportunities because I'd been too worn down to look? Had I felt like an outcast simply because I'd been tired?

The landscape felt friendlier too, the mountains more accessible. They looked bigger, with dark forests, steaming clouds, and ribs of bare rock, and the path into them was softer underfoot and easier to follow than any path before it. I even found the heat—as high as it had been anywhere south—entirely bearable. I saw deer among the trees, spied two wild boar, and camped in sweet solitude, thoroughly at home with the mosquitoes and fireflies. The *zanzare* weren't exactly relaxing, but they weren't the curse they'd previously been.

The five days away had put the Apennines into perspective. Compared to the mayhem of Naples the landscape was beguilingly unrushed; compared to the brash commercialism of Pompeii the villages were peaceful and dignified; compared to the superficial honeypots of Sorrento and Capri everything felt authentic. This land of mountains, villages and farms wasn't a destination, a package designed for visitors, a place altered by marketing for consumption—it was a lived-in landscape that simply was what it was.

Lying in camp that night I re-examined the time away, trying to pin down why *here* felt better than *there*. The better-known Italy hadn't disappointed. It had delivered exactly what I'd sought: an escape, relaxation, a few famous sights, and even great beauty. That Amalfi Coast sunset, witnessed from a marble-pillared terrace, with the sea below a rippling sheet of gold, would be hard to beat. But something had been missing. Perhaps it had all come too easily, presented on a platter. Given, not earned.

Perhaps finding out for myself was what made the difference.

For me, finding out was a key ingredient of travel. The urge to find out, to push beyond horizons, to travel into the unknown, is part of what makes us human. It is an urge that led our species out of Africa, into Europe, across Asia, over the Bering Sea, down the spine of the Americas. It is an urge that led us to the remotest, highest, hottest and coldest reaches of the planet. It's an urge that even carried us to the moon, and may one day propel us light years beyond it. It's an urge that makes us ask the deepest questions. To deny it is to deny ourselves. To limit it is to limit all we can be.

Back on the Amalfi Coast my fellow tourists and I had received exactly what we'd paid for. Most visitors seemed perfectly happy with it, and there was nothing wrong with that. But a few appeared to sense that travel could offer more. Outside Pompeii I'd watched an English-speaking herd disembark stiffly from a coach and follow their prim tour guide into the ruins, her bright yellow umbrella a rallying flag. Tagging along behind, I had eavesdropped, hearing a litany of complaints about heat and dust, aching legs and pounding heads. 'I wish the guide would slow down,' a middle-aged man had complained. 'How are we supposed to actually see anything if we never stop?'

It was a teenager scuffing along in the rear who offered the most revealing remark. 'I'm bored,' he whined. 'I wish something interesting would just bloody happen.' His father gave him a harsh glare, but I knew exactly what he meant. Clearly, the teenager wanted more.

Me too—I wanted more, and that was why I travelled on foot, inching slowly across the surface one laborious step at a time. What I wanted was active participation, not passive observation. What I wanted was uncertainty, discomfort, challenge; the very qualities I'd run from. I'd just needed a reminder.

<hr/>

The southern Apennines and the Mezzogiorno were all but crossed; ahead now were bigger mountains. The first range—Monti del Matese—was already in view, a bald crest rearing above forested foothills, marking the south's end. Beyond it was the fabled Abruzzo National Park, and beyond that the mighty Gran Sasso d'Italia—the Great Rock of Italy—pinnacle of

135

the entire range, an edifice of rock unlike anything further south. Anticipation made sleep each night increasingly difficult to find.

After two months in the south, and after time away to consider it, I reckoned I finally had the measure of it. Unexpectedly, I even began to miss it. The Mezzogiorno hadn't allowed easy passage, and had I known in advance what lay ahead I might have made other plans. But now I looked back with gratitude, half-wishing I could do it all again, especially with the knowledge I now had. For the final few miles I savoured every step. Familiarity was an odd thing. The Mezzogiorno was now familiar, and I was loath to let it go.

I even reckoned I'd solved the dog problem. The final Mezzogiorno pack appeared ten miles before the Monti del Matese, and the encounter began as many others had. In searing noon heat I paused in woodland shade for rest, but moments after pulling off my boots and socks to air tender feet an angry barking erupted below and grew rapidly nearer. *Here we go again*, I thought, and sure enough a typical pack of Apennine hounds soon appeared.

There were five of them, mixed breeds all, and they came to a halt ten feet away. Barking, baring teeth, dripping saliva, they began pacing to and fro. *What are you doing here?* I could see them thinking. 'GO AWAY STRANGER!' they barked. But I didn't. For once I stayed put.

For two months such creatures had been the bane of my existence, but this time, instead of heeding their threats, I ignored them. I leaned back, stretched out my legs, and gazed peacefully at the woods as though the dogs didn't exist. I avoided their eyes, tried to still my galloping heart, and waited.

And it worked. Non-reaction deflated their aggression. It took a couple of minutes, but eventually the barking lessened, grew half-hearted, ceased altogether. One by one the dogs flopped to the earth and sat quietly, watching me intently at first, but soon losing interest and looking about elsewhere. Birds began singing again. A companionable silence settled between us. The dogs lay peacefully, panting in the heat. One snapped at a fly; another dropped its head onto its paws and stared sleepy-eyed into space. Through the corner of my eye I watched them settle, and allowed myself a moment's self-satisfaction. I really had come far. I felt that I'd just conquered the entire Mezzogiorno.

After a while it seemed safe to address them, and I murmured softly to each in turn. Ears pricked up, tails twitched and began thumping, and after I tossed a few crumbs to each dog I had friends for life. When I stood to go the dogs sprang up too—not to bark or snarl but to accompany me through the woods. Clearly delighted to be led on a walk they kept pace for several minutes, darting after squirrels, sniffing beneath bushes, bounding ahead then looking back to make certain I was still in sight. This was more like it. Mad Mountain Jack finally had company on the trail.

But it couldn't last. After ten minutes I began growing concerned: how would they find their way home? Although dirty and flea-bitten they weren't wild dogs—four of the five wore collars. At last, reluctantly, I stopped and pointed back the way we'd come. 'Go!' I said, '*Va' Vai!*' I made a shooing motion, but the dogs wouldn't shoo. They tilted their heads, waited patiently. *Why have we stopped?* I could see them puzzling. *Let's just get going.* 'Look,' I said with a sigh. 'I'm going further than you realise. Our relationship is doomed.' But the dogs didn't care. All they wanted was to walk and explore, and I understood that entirely.

After another ten minutes I decided that enough really was enough. The companionship was wonderful, but for their sakes I couldn't let it go any further. As before, I tried shooing them away, but my commands and gestures failed. So I resorted to yelling, and charged at them a couple of times, hating myself for it. 'Go home,' I barked. 'GO AWAY!' It was ironic how the tables had turned.

The dogs finally got the message, but didn't understand it. I could see confusion in their eyes, even hurt. *Why?* they seemed to be saying. *What did WE do?*

A last rush sent them scattering, but still they wouldn't leave, although I thought they had. Twenty minutes later I discovered them still tagging along behind, furtively keeping pace back in the trees. I was now genuinely concerned. Befriending them had been a mistake—I should have let them chase me off right at the start. I'd messed with the natural order of things, and look at the result. The last resort was to throw small stones—nothing that would hurt, just scare—and that finally did it. Predictably, once they were gone I missed them; the woods seemed empty. Ridiculously, I even hoped they wouldn't bear me any ill will. I considered their long journey home, hoping they'd find their way. I vowed to never look at, talk to, or feed an Apennine dog again.

Clearly, I didn't have the measure of southern dogs—or the south—after all. The Mezzogiorno was too complex. Mastery of it could never be more than an illusion.

The Mezzogiorno. Fascinating, challenging, beautiful... and impossible to master.
Malvito, Calabria, May 25, 1997.

MAPLESS IN MATESE
Chapter 13

IT SEEMED FITTING that the south's final resupply parcel should fail to arrive. If I hadn't needed its contents I would almost have approved.

The clerk in Piedimonte Matese's post office was a short, jovial man, as round as he was tall. Smiling welcomingly, leaning forwards, rubbing his hands together, he wanted nothing more than to please, but a positive attitude couldn't conjure my parcel into existence. After a lengthy search he returned empty-handed, visibly upset. '*Mi dispiace tanto,*' he murmured. 'I am so sorry.'

When I phoned home, Base Camp confirmed that the parcel had been posted four weeks earlier. It should have arrived. 'Try again,' my parents urged, and with nothing to lose I followed their advice. The clerk jumped to it without hesitation, thrilled to have a second chance to please, and this time had moderate success. He returned bearing a look of immense surprise and a solitary envelope. He presented it with reverence. 'Well, how about that?' he said with a laugh, eyebrows raised.

And so I sent him off again, and this time he returned with a second letter, and after that a third. The surprise he wore each time was priceless. *Hey, this is a funny game, isn't it?* his expression read, as though finding mail in a post office were the most extraordinary thing.

I finished up with five letters from England—all gratefully received— but no parcel. For the mail he'd unearthed the clerk beamed with pride, and for his sake I hid my disappointment. Who was I to deflate anyone's happiness or self-worth? That wasn't why I was walking at all.

For the next hour I wandered Piedimonte Matese's cobbled streets, seeking maps and film. The film was swiftly acquired, but a *carte dei sentieri* remained elusive. An unsympathetic official in the tourist office finally crushed my hopes. 'There is no such publication here,' he declared with finality, waving away the idea as ridiculous. 'Hiking maps are available in Isernia,' he added, as though that solved my problem. It didn't. If I made it over the Matese to Isernia I'd no longer need a map of the Matese.

Frustration surged—would the map curse never end? But I let it pass. When I considered the problem I realised that I wasn't entirely bereft of navigational aids. I carried a map of the entire country—sparse in detail, maybe, but still a map—I had a functioning compass, possessed my trusty coin, and still had all the skills and instincts I'd developed during all my mountain walks. Two years earlier, on a week-long walk in the Scottish Highlands, I'd intentionally travelled without using my map. The aim had been to see if a mapless approach could work, and it had, especially up high where open country meant I could see ahead. The mountains of the Matese were open too, not forested like much of the south. Perhaps it was time to try mapless exploring once again. It was either that or take the safe option, the easy option, and go around the mountains. But easy and safe didn't appeal. It definitely wasn't good style. It wouldn't earn the rewards I was here for.

In trepidation, I picked a road that looked as though it led the right way, and followed it from town. Via a succession of tight hairpin bends it climbed towards the mountains. My optimism grew. Soon, it was impossible to imagine the frustrations from a week earlier. Had I really fallen so low? Striding forward, I began singing at full volume, unable to believe I was here, even though I didn't know exactly where *here* was.

Miles passed with no wrong turns. I reached a hilltop village wrapped about a small, round-towered castle, and should have paused to explore it, but I was on a roll. Onwards I paced, flowing through a landscape even more idyllic than usual. I passed tidy fields, well-tended orchards, and neat olive groves—a rural paradise—and stared up at the rugged Monti del Matese, a paradise of another kind. It was the contrast between tamed and untamed that made the landscape so idyllic. Each environment increased the beauty and worth of the other, the way sunlight increases the value and beauty of shade.

The lack of map increased the beauty too. Not knowing, but finding out, enhanced each new sight—especially as I encountered no dead-ends.

In golden sunlight I reached a second village: San Gregorio Matese, a sign declared—a compact community draped across steep, wooded slopes. On the road from it a car pulled over and two grinning men in their early twenties climbed out. 'We found you!' they exclaimed. 'We've driven everywhere!'

At first their faces drew a blank, but then I placed them: from outside the supermarket back in Piedimonte Matese. We'd spent an entertaining twenty minutes together while I'd sorted food and repacked Ten Ton. Fascinated by my backpacking gear, the men kept picking items up and examining them. The compass, stove, headlamp, first-aid kit, other such tools; all were carefully scrutinised. 'What's this for?' they'd asked repeatedly, curious as children. Now, hours later, they'd driven up the mountain to offer a ride.

'So, where would you like to go?' they asked cheerfully. 'We want to help.'

For once it was hard to decline. I wanted to accept the offered ride, for their sakes. I thought back to Calabria, where I'd avoided asking for help, wanting it to come voluntarily, knowing that it would mean more. Well, here voluntary help was, and it meant a great deal. It was a boost, even if I had to turn it down.

'I am *so* sorry,' I explained. 'I have to walk. Long story. But you *have* helped. You really have.'

Unsurprisingly, the men didn't understand, but we parted as friends.

'You are a crazy Englishman!' one of them shouted, big grin on his face. They drove off, arms waving madly out of open windows. 'Give our regards to the Queen!'

Energised by their kindness, grinning, I trekked on, still gaining altitude, still avoiding dead-ends. The bludgeoning humidity and heat of the lower valley had faded, although evidence of it lived on in my clinging shirt. It instantly chilled me when I paused for a break, goosebumps appearing for the first time since the Pollino. My thermometer read seventy Fahrenheit, twenty-one Celsius, but so hot had conditions been for so many weeks that seventy now felt cold.

At last, rounding a corner, the entire Matese range appeared: huge, dark, and bare of trees, capped by ominous clouds. At the sight I stopped dead and experienced two thoughts: *Oh yes!* instantly followed by *Oh no!* The mountains were a sight for sore eyes—for weeks I had been dreaming of them. But they were also intimidatingly massive, and the idea of traversing their tops without a map kindled a familiar spark of fear.

A few minutes later I chanced upon a managed campsite, the first in the Apennines since the Sila. It was a welcome sight as well as a complete surprise. Showers, a restaurant, easily available water, a soft lawn for my tent—the luxuries were a thousand times finer for not being expected. The fee for staying was surprisingly high, higher than the hotel room back in Castrovillari, and the restaurant was well beyond my means. But I chose to stay anyway, declining restaurant food in favour of my standard eat-it-if-you-dare stew.

Across the lawn, a Scout troop was also camped. They were a busy, industrious bunch, forever coming and going, collecting firewood, playing games, singing and storytelling, and, for a long while, cooking. Shortly after nightfall one of the adult leaders invited me over. 'Come join us for dinner,' he said. 'We have plenty.' *Sure,* I thought; *why not?* I could squeeze in a little more. And so I feasted in company, enjoying the kind of friendliness and hospitality that hotel receptionists back in the Valle Caudina had forgotten how to give. I'm not sure what entertained the Scouts more: my mispronounced Italian, the stories I shared of wildest Calabria, or the numerous second helpings I devoured.

'*Signore,*' a small boy finally said, his eyes wide with awe. 'I thought my mamma ate a lot. She's big. But I have never seen her eat as much as you!'

I woke the next morning to a rare thing that summer: dense fog swirling around the tent. Loving the atmosphere, but intimidated by the prospect of setting out into it mapless, I took my time over breakfast, and the tactic worked: by the time I'd dismantled camp the fog had burnt away.

With the Matese rising overhead it was clear which way I had to go, although a tightly woven beech wood stood in the way. According to the

Scout leader, a trail led through the trees and up the mountain, but I didn't find it until after I'd battled through the wood. Sweating and scratched, I finally spotted a splash of red-and-white paint on a rock, and followed the barely discernible path it marked for a few minutes until it faded away. Not that it now mattered. I'd reached open country, and trails weren't really needed. Up here I could wander unrestricted, and the freedom couldn't be measured. This wasn't the Mezzogiorno anymore.

The slope angled towards a distant summit—an obvious goal, although it looked as if approaching clouds would beat me to it. I was tempted to race them, but instead took it easy, savouring each step. I'd waited a long time for this, and there was much to savour: ever-broadening views to the horizon, and wildflowers and lichen-decorated rocks closer at hand. Soon, a familiar old elation began bubbling up, increasing with each step. It was an emotion I often felt on high mountains: a feeling of release, of chains falling away, of cutting loose from the world. After so many weeks enclosed in trees I revelled in the space.

Fog smothered the summit by the time I reached it, and within moments of arrival a chill wind forced me into long trousers, a fleece, and a warm hat. There was no view, but the fog brought pleasure, not disappointment. After so much blinding sunlight it felt like a gift. It was comforting like a blanket; it made the summit feel more remote. Back home in the regularly wet British hills I'd often dreamt of Mezzogiorno-like sunshine, but now that I'd endured so much of it I decided that fog and damp weren't so bad after all.

I sat still a long while, losing track of time. Without a map I didn't know the summit's name or its altitude, which made it feel even higher. But not lonelier. I shared the summit with thousands of ladybirds. Bright red and in constant motion, they swarmed within cracks in the limestone, looking thoroughly out of place in so harsh an environment. *So this is where all the world's ladybirds came from*, I thought. *Who'd have guessed?*

Eventually, it was time to go. My compass pointed me off the summit on a northerly bearing, down rocks treacherously slick, until I'd lost 500 feet of altitude and burst free once again into a world of sweeping views. Velvet-green mountains now rolled ahead across a land that looked well watered, although I couldn't spot any streams. Limestone regions often lack surface water; the rock dissolves easily and water quickly sinks away.

There are rivers in limestone country, but they often run far beneath the surface. I'd walked across limestone hill country before, back in England's Peak District and the Yorkshire Dales, and the Matese bore a striking resemblance to both national parks. It had the same bright and airy ambience, and yet it was vastly bigger. It prompted a disorienting moment of déjà vu. I felt at home here, but also thrillingly far away.

The Matese could have been traversed in one long day, but that would have been a waste. Far better to spend a quiet night in the heart of the range. Although surface water was scarce I travelled in faith, trusting that I'd find some, and when I reached a high valley after an adventurous journey across the grain of the land I was rewarded by a trickling stream. It was barely fifty yards long, and cattle had soiled it, but its source within a fern-draped grotto was out of bovine reach, and I judged the spring water perfectly safe to drink.

I set up camp to the chime of distant cowbells. Clouds still smothered the summits, and other clouds raced eastwards in a brisk wind. Grass swayed; flowers danced; patches of sunlight surfed across rolling slopes. Skylarks sang, filling the air with cascading brightness, and a solitary cuckoo called. At the valley's upper end I noticed a broad snowdrift resting beneath a crag, and the air felt almost winter cold. I pulled on thermals. When darkness fell I climbed *into* my sleeping bag for the first time in a month. Was this really the Apennines? With no mosquitoes to hound me, and the air chill enough that my breath showed, sleep that night was deeper and more restorative than it had been since the Pollino.

Dawn came early—5 a.m.—and I woke raring to go, charged with an energy not normally present at such an early hour. Mountains awaited, but I couldn't! I rushed breakfast and was packed up and moving before first light spilled onto the highest slopes. Some days seem destined to stand apart, and I could tell from the first breath that June 26 was going to be one of those days.

In air sharp and clear I followed a grassy stairway upwards to the high spine of the Monti del Matese, and soon stood in sparkling light, the Central Apennines revealed. From the huge bulk of yesterday's summit, to

Camp chores. Waxing boots in the heart of the
Monti del Matese at 'Skylark Alley', June 25, 1997.

a hundred-mile-distant horizon, to valleys far below filled with morning fog, to the sawtoothed skyline of the Abruzzo region to the north, I didn't know where to settle my gaze. And so I didn't. I let it roam: along ridges, across forests, into valleys, over summits. In the crisp air colours seemed unusually intense, details supernaturally sharp. Villages 5,000 feet lower and tens of miles distant seemed touchable. And yet I felt utterly removed from them, as though my ridge belonged to a separate world.

Not owning a map was no problem up here where I could see forever. I didn't even need my compass—the sun made it clear which way was north. I pushed on, keeping to the highest ground, and no single stretch since Melito had been easier. Singing and laughing, I danced along my ridge in the sky. Steep ground fell away either side, plunging to wild cirques. In places, old snow still hung in cornices over great drops, and I stopped several times to scoop up snowballs and hurl them into the void. No doubt the morning was already broiling hot down in the lower valleys. Farmers' shirts were probably clinging to backs, commuters were likely sweating in buses, brows were being wiped, shade was being sought, flies swatted away.

But up here I had snowballs to throw, champagne air to breathe, the entire world to myself. I had space to throw my arms wide—space to spin, space to scream if I so desired. I was free to be myself, to act like a raging intoxicated maniac if that suited me. There was no one to judge me or set limits. *This* was freedom. I walked on, in good company with myself, a mountain underfoot, skylarks overhead, high on life, and if some people still thought me foolish for choosing this unconventional path through life then I couldn't have cared less.

It truly was a day apart, shining because of all that had gone before. The unpaved earth felt softer for all the hard surfaces I'd crossed. The mountain air tasted fresher for all the sultry Mezzogiorno air I'd breathed. Everything up here felt earned; everything seemed like a reward. It was as if the mountain gods had taken stock of all my actions since Melito and had decided to grant all my wishes at once. Of course, there were no mountain gods—it was a childish idea—but I still couldn't dispel the notion that powerful forces were at work. I'd been sensing them since Calabria. For 800 miles they'd been rewarding effort, punishing weakness, keeping me on track, helping me stay true to my goal, to walk in good style. Silly or not, the idea of them was part of The Walk's growing mythology, and this was just another example of their work. Here I was, high on a mountain even though I didn't have a map, and look what I'd earned!

My feet soon delivered me to the highest point: Monte Miletto, as I later found out. Radio masts and a weathered crucifix marred the summit, but these ugly intrusions couldn't dent my contentment. I feasted on the isolation for almost two hours, and moved on only when it seemed right, stepping away with a sigh of satisfaction. A quarter of a mile below the summit I came across a few splashes of paint, and followed the route they marked down difficult, ankle-breaking terrain. A valley of shattered rock gave way to forests rippling with green light. Next came farmland where horses grazed, followed by a field of sheep, watched over by two huge Maremmano sheepdogs as well as a friendly old shepherd who, thankfully, had the dogs under control. The shepherd wanted to know where I'd come from and where I was going. Where was I going? I couldn't rightly answer—not without a map—and I didn't honestly care! This way, perhaps? Or that way? I shrugged, laughed. What did it matter?

I sauntered through the afternoon across a glorious Italian dreamscape, a Renaissance masterpiece of rolling hills and emerald woods, golden fields and wildflower meadows, old stone farms and small settlements. Roadside fountains refreshed me. I chose my route by flipping the coin. The Monti del Matese fell away but the limestone giants of the Abruzzo rose ahead. Just a few days more and I'd be up on even higher mountains, alone above the world.

And I'd have the earth beneath my feet just the way I liked it.

A morning apart. Looking south-west from the Monti del Matese, June 26, 1997.

MARCHE

AUGUST 3 ▲ Monte Pennino (5154 ft / 1571 m)

UMBRIA

SIBILLINI
NATIONAL
PARK

▲ Monti Vettore (8123 ft / 2476 m)

Castelluccio/Piano Grande ●

JULY 28

Adriatic
Sea

'Crazy shepherd' ●

▲ Monti della Laga (8062 ft / 2458 m)

GRAN
SASSO
NATIONAL
PARK

Corno Grande (9551 ft / 2912 m) ▲ JULY 21

L'Aquila ● JULY 18

ABRUZZO

N

★ 1,000 miles

Monte Velino (8159 ft / 2488 m)

Monte Amaro
(9170 ft / 2795 m) ▲

Celano ● JULY 11 / 15

LAZIO

Scanno ● JULY 5

● ROME Simbruini Mountains
(7072 ft / 2156 m) ▲

Monti
Serrone ▲

ABRUZZO
NATIONAL
PARK

Route through the
CENTRAL
APENNINES
July 1997

Monti della Meta
(7378 ft / 2248 m) ▲

Isernia ●

JUNE 27

km 0   20
mi 0   10   20

Monti del Matese
(6730 ft / 2050 m) ▲

CAMPANIA

148

LAND OF ORSO
Chapter 14

I'D REACHED THE Abruzzo, the undisputed mountain heartland of the Apennines. What little I knew of the region was exciting. I knew it was home to the tallest, steepest, and sharpest mountains in the Apennines; mountains that had been chiselled and sculpted by glaciers of old. I knew that it was a region of hilltop villages, small farms, extensive forests, and treeless alpine heights. I knew that it was a remote region—a region that until recently was one of Italy's least accessible, second only to Calabria in isolation. I knew it was richer in wildlife than any other area in the Apennines, and that it offered quality wilderness, with a larger percentage of its surface area protected by national parks and reserves than any other in Europe. I knew it was immense, covering over 4,000 square miles, and complex, made from many separate mountain groups.

And I knew with absolute certainty that it required a detailed map.

I began searching for one in Isernia, a large town south of the Abruzzo National Park, and I was helped by a girl I met on the town's edge. She caught me off-guard, approaching from behind while I was trying to squash a small bag of rubbish I'd carried down from the hills into a large overflowing bin outside a restaurant.

'Excuse me,' she said in a concerned, gentle voice. 'Are you okay? Do you need help? Are you... hungry?'

'I'm sorry?' I answered. 'Hungry?'

For a moment I didn't understand, but then saw the scene through her eyes. Oh my! She thought I was raiding the trash for provisions.

'I'm always hungry!' I said, laughing. 'But I'm not that desperate! I'm on a long walk. What I really need is a map.'

The girl spoke reasonable English, and offered to help with the search. Short, with soft brown hair, she guided me into town, walking closer than necessary, often brushing right against me. I'd never experienced such close attention—it made me uncomfortably self-conscious. She smelled clean and soapy, but I was all too aware of my ripe mountain aroma. The girl, a graphic design student, was surprised when I revealed that I was a designer by profession. 'You don't really look like one,' she observed candidly, tilting her head to one side. I wondered if what she really meant was that I didn't *smell* like one.

After a year in Isernia she knew the town well, and led me to stores I might not have found. She did most of the talking, explaining my need for a hiking map, but alas, the search drew a blank—a real surprise given that Isernia was just ten miles from one of Italy's premier hiking regions. The girl was surprised too. And disappointed.

'I am *so* sorry,' she said. 'Really, this town is too small to be of any use to anyone. I wish I was in Rome or Milan.'

Success came the following day at an official campsite, the second stumbled upon by chance inside a week. The map was fixed to a wall outside the site's office, sealed within a Perspex case. It was faded from sunlight, and a few sections were barely legible, but it still covered the next week of The Walk in enticing detail.

Inside the office a dark-haired man stood behind a desk. 'The map outside,' I asked in excitement. 'Do you have any more for sale?' The answer, unfortunately, was no. Hiking maps had been 'on order' since the previous summer, but this was Italy—they'd arrive when they arrived. The man, Luigi, listened to my story, and after a long pause told me he'd see what he could do. And early the next morning he did it. Wearing a wry smile, he strode to my tent and handed over the map. 'For you!' he exclaimed. 'No charge.' I turned and looked towards the office; the frame was no longer on the wall. It lay on the ground, broken in half. My show of gratitude was casually waved away.

I put the map to good use within an hour. Following it, I climbed into wild woods, accompanied by a cloud of black flies. To my delight the map passed the first test most Apennine maps failed: the path I had chosen existed not just on paper but also on the ground. It was overgrown and several fallen trees lay across it, but it matched the map perfectly, and that made all the difference in the world. Thrilled, I entered the Abruzzo National Park.

The Parco Nazionale d'Abruzzo was the second national park to be established in Italy. It was created in 1922, born during a period in the history of Italian nature conservation when real progress was being achieved. At that time, progressive liberal thinking had Italy at the forefront of environmental conservation in Europe, until Mussolini came along and demanded a more utilitarian approach.

Still, the park survived being treated as a resource, and so did many of its natural inhabitants. By European standards the list of residents is long and unusually distinguished. All the usual Apennine species are present: wolves, golden eagles, wild boar, deer, and European wildcats. And then there are species not so easily found elsewhere in the range, such as lynx and porcupine, as well as sure-footed chamois.

Chamois, a goat–antelope mix, are most at home on the highest slopes. Like wolves, they were once native across the entire Apennine chain until humanity hounded them to the brink of extinction. Efforts to save them began in the early twentieth century. Their future looked promising when the park was established, but with Fascism's rise, and a world war raging, their numbers plummeted to critical levels. By the late 1940s it was estimated that only thirty chamois survived, living against the odds in one small corner of the park. Apennine chamois are a subspecies, genetically unique to the range; once gone there would have been no bringing them back. You could in theory recreate the Colosseum from scratch if it were destroyed, but no amount of painstaking work could recreate an extinct species. Recognising this, true Italian heroes took up the fight, and they dragged Apennine chamois back from the brink, growing the population into the hundreds, helping them spread beyond park borders. As with Apennine wolves it was a modest success story, a reason for optimism. If wolves and chamois could be saved, why not the world itself?

I thought fleetingly about chamois as I walked, wondering if any would cross my path. But I thought about another animal significantly more.

It was an animal that was even rarer, an animal I wanted to see but was nervous of seeing. It was an animal that could weigh 500 pounds; that possessed long claws, sharp teeth, and never turned down meat when it was available; that could break me in two with a single swipe if it so desired; an animal that truly put the 'wild' into wilderness. It was the Marsican brown bear.

Large, powerful, intelligent, *Ursus arctos marsicanus* is a magnificent beast. Like Apennine chamois, the Marsican bear (*orso*, in Italian) has lived in isolation long enough to evolve into a genetically unique subspecies. A member of the brown bear family, it gets its name from its home, Marsicana, as the Abruzzo was formerly known. The Marsican bear shares a similar story to wolves and chamois: it once roamed the entire range, until humans began wiping it out. Ancient Romans slaughtered them by the thousands in gladiatorial arenas, as did shepherds defending their flocks, and peasants out of ignorance and fear, and royalty in the name of 'sport'. They remained numerous 200 years ago. Hunters in the early eighteenth century were reportedly able to kill bears, wolves, chamois and foxes without intermission from morning to night. Even in the early twentieth century bears were still hunted, and authorities paid a bounty for every individual killed. By the time I reached the Abruzzo an estimated 100 individuals were left. In theory, enough genetic diversity remained for the subspecies to survive, providing the population held steady. The Abruzzo National Park was supposedly achieving this. According to park authorities the population was even showing signs of bouncing back.

Despite their size, Marsican brown bears are impressively gentle. Shy, intelligent and sensitive, they go to great lengths to avoid people. Like most apex predators their reproductive rate is low. A mother usually gives birth to twins, and spends three years raising them. But it is a tough childhood. Typically, only one cub will reach maturity, *if* it is lucky. Population growth is hard to achieve.

Adult bears are solitary wanderers, preferring their own company (something I could understand). Their territories extend over vast areas —several hundred square miles in some cases. Plants make up ninety per cent of their diet, but meat is never turned down, and occasionally is actively sought, as Abruzzo shepherds still attest. The traditional pastoral way of life in the Abruzzo has long helped Marsican bears survive. Over the years they've come to rely on occasional sheep, and even more on fruit from orchards. Without vast quantities of fruit, the fat reserves they require for hibernation would be near impossible to attain. It wasn't always so—at one time the wilderness provided—but the modern wild isn't what it was. Dependency on our food has become a staple of their life.

Marsican bears are as un-aggressive as bears can be, but they'll still defend themselves if surprised, cornered, or provoked. Mothers with cubs can be especially defensive. Although exceedingly rare, maulings have occurred. Where bears roam, individual human beings are clearly not top of the pecking order—a detail very much in my mind as I walked. I knew the odds of seeing a bear were low; the odds of a violent encounter barely calculable. Bears were few, the forests vast. But it wasn't impossible. I might encounter one.

The way we react to wilderness has little to do with logic or scientific fact; instincts and emotions have far more impact. A wilderness inhabited by bears prompts an entirely different response to a wilderness without them. Without bears a forest is just a forest, a mountain just a mountain. But with them a forest and mountain are so much more. And that makes us more too. Ancient, half-forgotten instincts return to life. Our own fragility becomes more apparent. Our true place in nature becomes clearer. Sleep becomes lighter; senses sharpen; alertness grows. We become more attuned to the environment around us. The difference is so huge it is beyond calculation. To walk where bears walk is to become more *human*.

I entered the 'Land of Orso' on the last day of June. Broadleaf forests swept upwards, and they were more than just forests. At first I proceeded with caution, peering around corners, studying the undergrowth with great concentration. Of course, I saw no bears, nor any sign of them, although possibly I wouldn't have recognised evidence of a bear even if I stood in it. But what I did notice were details I might previously have missed: textures and patterns, sunlight and shade, moss and lichen, birds and squirrels. From looking so hard the forest was truly revealed.

Many of the beech trees were gigantic, sporting trunks ten feet thick. A few, with wrinkled bark and spreading crowns, looked ancient. Certain beeches in the park have been dated to 1,000 years—it seemed possible I was in the presence of trees that old. In reverence, I brushed my hands against several trunks, and once, when I came upon a tree that seemed unusually sentient, I halted my steps and discarded Ten Ton. Respectfully,

I wrapped my arms around the beech, closed my eyes, and let the tree's calmness overtake me. I sensed immense strength, pulsing energy; experienced a deep, timeless reassurance that went beyond words. Tree-huggers are mocked by some, but the laughter says more about those that mock, nothing about those that hug. *Let the mocking come*, I thought, accepting the old tree's many gifts. Those with narrow minds were the ones missing out.

After two hours the trail reached tree line and my wise arboreal companions fell behind. Open country now lay ahead. Mad Mountain Jack country. It began with a glacier-carved valley, its floor littered with boulders and old moraine ridges, the savagery softened by acres of rippling grass. At the valley's head were fans of broken rock, ribbons of snow, and soaring cliffs. It was the start of the Monti della Meta range: a ten-mile-long ridge snaking north above the trees. Within an hour I was striding its roller-coaster crest, and it was like the Matese all over again, only higher, grander, wilder. The possibility that bears were rummaging through the forests below added distance to the isolation and a level of mystery that had been missing further south. Because of *orso* the entire landscape felt like a place only recently created, like the original primal wilderness. Even if it wasn't beyond humankind's influence, it felt it. And the feeling is what matters most of all.

In a rising wind I picked my way carefully over jumbled rocks, my boots insecure on steep ground and loose stones. Across the valley on a distant summit I noticed three tiny dots—the first other people I'd seen in the mountains since I'd begun The Walk. I hoped they were feeling the same joy that was surging through me.

At 7,356 feet I topped out on La Meta, The Walk's highest point so far. The summit sprouted a strange iron construction, an out-of-place work of industrial modern art that frost, wind and lightning were slowly wiping from existence. Several miles north was my next destination—Monte Petroso, a few feet higher—and in every other direction was a sea of peaks. I felt like the king of the world.

The day had started clear but clouds now blew in on a rising wind. Thin mists began forming a few hundred feet below La Meta's summit, thickening, then curling upwards in my direction. Tentatively, they brushed my lonely perch, retreated, but finally grasped the summit in a tight fist

Chamois on the Monte della Meta ridge, June 30, 1997.

of fog. Daylight dimmed as though evening had arrived early. The wind strengthened. It surged around the summit rocks with a mournful sigh and the fog rushed past at speed, horizontal to the ground, creating the odd sensation that the summit was moving, not the clouds, as though I were standing on the bow of a ship. *Well, that's it for the day*, I thought, views obliterated. But I was thankful for all I'd already seen.

The wind and damp soon had me shivering, and I moved on, downwards through the murk until I burst unexpectedly back into clear air. Strangely, the ridge ahead remained cloud free. It twisted north into sunlight. It turned out to be a perfect ridge for walking: narrow, but not too narrow; rocky, but not too rocky; undulating, but not too undulating. Hands in pockets I sauntered casually onwards, distance passing easily, the panorama constantly unfolding. I felt detached from the world, elevated, and wanted to run and sing, but held myself back from both, sensing that the land deserved a gentler approach. Anything other than quiet reverence would be a crime.

Halfway along the ridge I noticed movement ahead on the skyline. I pulled out my camera and focused on a deer-sized animal. Its coat was beautiful, reddish brown; stylish dark stripes ran from eyes to snow-white muzzle; two sharp black horns curled over its head. A chamois, wandering the ridge in peace. Unaware it was being watched, it posed perfectly for half a minute before moving higher up the ridge to stand silhouetted against the sky. Five more chamois appeared and drifted towards the first, then all disappeared from sight, hooves making no sound whatsoever. Full of gratitude, I paused to give them time and space to move away.

The ridge led on, unmarred by trail, footprint, or even a single scuff-mark, creating the illusion I was the first person to ever walk it. I wondered at that; didn't people visit these mountains? Wasn't this a national park? In Britain such a ridge would have been busy, indented with a deeply worn path. The solitude here was extraordinary. Undoubtedly others walked here—I couldn't be the first—but I felt as though I were, and in appreciation stepped lightly. Perhaps the next visitor would feel as much like an explorer as I did.

Easy progress ceased a mile before Monte Petroso. Suddenly, the ridge narrowed and two deep notches required a hands-on approach. The map had given little hint that difficulties lay ahead—the sheet wasn't perfect after all. Hesitantly, I pushed on. Since Hohtürli I had struggled with exposure. Whenever slopes grew too steep the memory of falling came rushing back. In an attempt to overcome them I'd taken up rock climbing, but with a rope attached exposure never felt the same. It was worse when back-packing; worse still with a pack as large as Ten Ton. Clutching the ridge tightly, feeling top heavy, I scrambled up sixty-degree steps, worked over small pinnacles, eased myself downwards above unnerving drops. My legs quivered, unsettled by the space beneath, and my breath came in shallow gasps. A lone chamois hissed at me from a ledge, perhaps afraid that I was a hunter. But it had nothing to fear. 'Don't worry *Signore* Chamois,' I panted. 'I've other things on my mind.'

The ridge narrowed further, becoming a sharp-toothed spine of rock. Directly ahead a tower blocked the way, and I approached it warily, fearful I'd have to retreat. But the limestone was solid, offering plentiful holds for hands and feet, and soon I was astride it, fear suddenly—inexplicably —gone. In amazement I scrambled on, grinning with delight. For the first time in my life I felt completely at home in a situation where a single misstep would see me plummeting to my death. I didn't comprehend it,

Along the pinnacled ridge, June 30, 1997.

but celebrated it all the same. At the highest, spikiest, and most precarious perch I finally gave in to temptation and screamed at the top of my voice. The elation couldn't be suppressed.

The final stretch to Monte Petroso was easier. On the 7,378-foot summit I gazed back along the difficulties, enjoying a feeling of achievement. Under ever-darkening clouds the ridge looked oddly familiar, and the longer I stared the more I felt I'd been here before. Had I followed an identical ridge elsewhere, I wondered, scrambled over similar pinnacles on another walk? I was certain I hadn't. The déjà vu strengthened, and then I got it. The ridge was no longer just 'a ridge', no longer mere scenery to look at; it was a ridge I'd touched and had grown on; a ridge I now knew. It had become a part of who I now was.

I slept in the valley that night, not above tree line as planned. As in the Pollino, wild camping in the Abruzzo National Park was outlawed, but my map showed an unstaffed refuge below Monte Petroso and I figured I could sleep there. I changed my mind when I saw it. Instead of a welcoming shelter I found a depressing hovel, a crumbling shell of a building surrounded by trash and filled with rodent droppings—an ugly human intrusion in a pristine place. Disappointed, I continued down through the woods, eventually landing at a campsite near the medieval village of Civitella Alfedena. The site had only been open two nights and I was the season's first paying customer. Well, almost the first paying customer. The owner let me stay for free.

I returned to the mountains the following day, and the day after, establishing a new rhythm for The Walk: airy limestone ridges by day, valley campgrounds by night; earth, grass, and rock underfoot, roads a forgotten torment. For the first time the journey felt like a true mountain walk, although the camping ban made it less than it might have been. For five nights I adhered to the regulations, until I couldn't take them any longer, and finally slept in freedom at 6,000 feet. A rule-breaker I may have been, but I was gentle with the land, and left no trace of my passing.

I travelled gently by day as well, and was rewarded for it, spying a porcupine in the woods, more chamois on the ridges, and several birds of prey. On one summit I chanced upon a golden eagle perched fifteen feet ahead on the edge of an abyss. For thirty seconds I stood and watched, barely daring to breathe. The eagle was facing away, its attention elsewhere. It twisted its head side to side in abrupt jerks, surveying the valley, allowing me quick glimpses of cold, hard eyes and a fierce, curved beak. A gusting wind ruffled its dark brown feathers, revealing gold beneath. Fearsome talons curved over the rock at its feet. As the minutes passed I sensed the certainty the eagle had in its own power, as though it knew it was master of its environment. I even felt a dash of disquiet—a reaction to the eagle's predatory nature. The moment ended when I began backing away, hoping to retreat from sight and return with my camera, but the eagle sensed movement and launched itself with a single beat of massive wings. I dashed to the edge and looked down. There was the eagle, soaring away on wings spread wide, already far below. In moments it became a distant speck.

Miles passed. I saw deer in the woods, spotted two foxes, and had a memorable encounter with a family of wild boar. Somehow I didn't notice the boar until I was practically on top of them. Surprisingly, they didn't notice me. They appeared on the path forty feet ahead—a large sow and three striped piglets moving in my direction, snouts down, snuffling through leaf litter, grunting deeply at each edible find. The moment I saw them I skidded to a halt, remembering the many warnings I'd received about how ferociously adult boar defend their young. From the huge size of the sow's shoulders it wasn't difficult to imagine the damage she could inflict.

Aiming for absolute silence I began backing away, eyes fixed on the sow. Time slowed the way it always does when attention becomes truly focused. Just when I thought I was going to make it everything went wrong. The path behind had a slight curve to it, a curve I didn't spot until it was too late. Without noticing, I veered off the path, backed towards a fallen tree, caught my heel on it, lost balance, flailed madly, and fell backwards into the undergrowth with a crash. But my luck was in. The boar were so surprised they practically jumped out of their hairy skins. For a second they stared in my direction, their tiny eyes as wide as boar eyes ever go, then they turned and fled as though all the hunters in Italy were on their heels. They crashed through the undergrowth, the sound lasting an impressive length of time.

Of *orso* I saw no sign, though I never once forgot them. But that changed late one night, outside the park borders, in a beech wood, far from the nearest road.

It was late, I was asleep, and then, suddenly, I wasn't. I heard a sound —sounds—approaching, moving downhill towards camp. Sticks snapped, leaves crunched, the undergrowth rustled. Large rocks were overturned, possibly inspected, then dropped. And there was a growl, deep and throaty. It wasn't aggressive or hungry—it was ponderous, a thinking growl. But still, in the blackness of night, it was ominous, as unsettling as approaching thunder. It came with every breath the animal took. I heard a hiss of air inhaled, a rumbling huff of air expelled. It filled my head, emptied it of rational thought. And it drew ever nearer.

I lay in absolute silence, holding my breath. My heart raced: ka-boom, ka-boom, ka-boom, to my ears as loud as a pounded drum. Would my heart give me away? So far as I could tell the creature wasn't aware of me, a state of affairs I hoped would long continue. *But what was it,* I wondered, *this growling, huffing beast?* Did I even want to know? For a moment I considered making noise to scare it away, but didn't, couldn't. Instinct wouldn't let me. The creature neared.

Suddenly, its shadow appeared upon my tent's wall, a dark shape cast by the waning moon. Seen from my lowly position on the ground, the shadow made the animal appear enormous. It loomed over me—broad and lumbering—but I couldn't make out anything distinctive in the shape to confirm the creature's identity. The growl continued, rumbling darkly, and the animal walked right by the tent, passing perhaps an arm's length away. Incredibly, and wonderfully, it didn't stop, just kept on going, heading slowly but purposefully downhill. I listened, breath still held, as it descended towards the valley. Slowly the sounds faded. A few more rocks looked under, a few more crashes in the undergrowth, and then nothing. Silence.

For five, ten or fifteen minutes I lay motionless, straining to hear. Finally, when I was certain it had gone, I let out a long exhalation of air. And then slept. What else was there to do? Waiting and worrying seemed pointless. And packing up camp and leaving seemed even worse; I didn't want to bump into anything out in the night. So I slept. But at 4 a.m. the situation repeated itself. Something large approached, along with the same distinctive growl, but this time heading uphill not down, away from the valley and back to wilder haunts. Once again it passed near the tent, although not as near as before; once again it showed no interest in my camp; and once again it faded away into the forest. Afterwards I lay awake for hours, heart pounding, wondering.

The following morning I inspected the ground around camp, and found little evidence that a nocturnal visitor had passed. I could see where a few large rocks might have been moved, but no footprints. The forest floor was covered in leaves, not mud, and the leaves revealed nothing.

Down in the valley half a day later I described the sounds to a knowl-edgeable-looking shopkeeper, but he quickly dismissed the possibility of it being a bear. 'Cinghiale,' he said with certainty. 'Wild boar. Bears are very rare, but boar are everywhere.'

But I wasn't so sure. I'd heard boar several times. They grunted and snuffled, never growled and huffed. And then there were the rocks. Does a boar pick up rocks?

I'll never know.

What I did know was that I had experienced something most visitors to Italy never imagined. International tourists filling Rome's piazzas and museums just two hours away probably had no idea that in woods nearby wild things growled in the night. Perhaps most Italians didn't know either, or care. But they should. Forget the Sistine Chapel, forget the Colosseum —the wild things in the Land of Orso are the country's greatest treasures. They are irreplaceable.

Wild country: ridges and woods in the 'Land of Orso', July 7, 1997.

SCANNO
Chapter 15

OUT OF FOOD, legs weary, clothes dirty, body unwashed, chores undone, I turned for the valley. After a week of constant motion it was time for a day off.

I reached the village of Scanno early evening. The final miles were eased by fantasies of all the food I'd purchase and devour, but reality fell flat. It was a local holiday, some saint's feast day, but not mine—Scanno's stores were all closed. The local campsite office-cum-store was closed too. 'Campers, please pay in the morning,' a handwritten sign suggested. Peering through the window I gazed hopelessly at a shelf laden with pasta, sauces, veggies, fruit, chocolate. So much food. So near, but it might as well have been in Norway.

All I had left for dinner was a horribly bruised apple, but fellow campers saved the day. A group of lean Germans halfway through a three-week cycling tour invited me over for pizza and beer. The feast was hugely appreciated, as was the evening of laughter that followed. I explained to my new friends that I'd been mistaken for a German practically everywhere I'd walked in Italy so far.

'So,' one of them replied, smiling mischievously. 'You must have taken that as quite the compliment, yes?' We all laughed.

I returned to Scanno early the next morning, heading first to the only bank, needing cash to purchase food. Disappointingly, its ATM was out of order, and under no circumstances could the clerks change my traveller's checks. Not today, anyhow—it would have to be tomorrow, for reasons the clerks couldn't explain. But to my relief the village supermarket confirmed they could take payment by card, a rare thing back then in small Apennine villages. Hungrily, I wandered the aisles, filling my basket to the brim, and then presented my VISA. 'Well, we do take cards,' the owner explained apologetically. 'But not *that* card.'

Fortunately, Apennine shopkeepers recognise hunger when they see it. 'How about you take the food and pay tomorrow,' the owner suggested casually, as though letting complete strangers walk away without paying for produce was the most common thing in the world. For the trust alone, the food tasted sensational. I paid the next day.

With food gathered, and some of it consumed, I considered the many rest-day chores that needed addressing, but put them all off. More important matters demanded my attention. Like Scanno itself. What I had seen of it while shopping had me yearning to see a whole lot more.

Since Melito, I had passed through a succession of hilltop villages, but hadn't fully explored any of them. It was time to make amends. Scanno was as perfect a hilltop village as any I had seen: compact, ancient, attractive. Scanno's arches, alleys and stairways formed a veritable maze. The village's history dates back to Roman times, but it wore its age well; its heavily weathered buildings revealed character, not Mezzogiorno neglect. Stepping into Scanno was like stepping back in time.

For much of the day I wandered Scanno's cobblestone passages, climbed stairways, ducked under arches, and cut down alleys. From the lowest level to the highest, from piazza to piazza, from stone building to stone building I roamed, visiting the nooks, crannies, alcoves, and secret corners. Unpredictable turns meant that I frequently passed over the same ground twice—often several times and from different directions, as if I were on Escher's eternal staircase. If any local residents noticed me they must have wondered what the hell I was up to. Perhaps they thought I was lost, really lost, and had a good laugh at my expense. If ever '*Dove vai?*' were justified it was here, but Scanno's citizens were too used to nosy tourists like myself to ask, and far too polite to stare. Not that I would have noticed. Scanno had me under a spell and I was oblivious to all else.

To a traveller who loved to explore, Scanno was addictive; it offered

Compact, ancient, attractive: Scanno's alleys and stairways
formed a veritable maze, July 5, 1997.

endless scope for exploration. And to a traveller who was also a photographer it was even more addictive. The village was a work of art, a medieval
masterpiece that did what all great works of art do: it transported, fired
the imagination, set creativity loose. And to a traveller on foot Scanno
was a kind of vindication, proof that going by foot was a normal, natural
thing. Unlike most towns, Scanno wasn't hospitable to cars, and the best
of it could only be reached on foot. It was approachable and intimate, a

people-first village. In short, my kind of place.

After so much walking I finished my day off wearier than I'd begun it, and to compensate I took the next day off as well. It was another of The Walk's perks: complete freedom *not* to walk whenever I wished.

I dedicated the second day to chores. The first was writing—reports were due to several newspapers, magazines, and websites. The most urgent was a full feature owed to *Spotlight Verlag*, a magazine published in Germany to help English-language students improve their English. *Spotlight* had recently become a part-sponsor, offering much-needed financial support in return for a series of trail reports. But writing the reports was an intimidating task. Students would be learning English from my words. What if I made grammatical errors? What if I got the basics of English wrong? I had visions of students failing exams because of me, pictured entire careers going down the tube. Fighting back a childish urge to invent words and phrases anyway, I got to work. I felt the pressure to get it right.

Once the writing was completed, I moved on to other chores: repairing torn gear with needle and thread, waxing boots to keep them supple, sorting food into daily ration packs, visiting the post office to mail film and handwritten reports home, making a series of phone calls. The chores seemed endless.

The phone calls brought good news, mostly. The first was to one of Britain's national newspapers, *The Sunday Express* (arguably a more substantial newspaper in 1997 than it is now). They had agreed to print my trail reports, but there'd been no written contract, nor any talk of payment, and I had no illusions about what they'd do if my words weren't up to scratch.

'Yes, we got your first report,' the travel editor replied. 'And I'm glad you haven't been eaten by wolves. We're running it on Sunday.' For a moment I held my hand over the mouthpiece, looked away, and let fly a jubilant scream. My words, to be read—potentially—by millions; I could scarcely believe it. What a boost for the charities the publicity would be.

The second call, to Base Camp, brought more good news. A story I'd written months earlier before The Walk for a mountaineering magazine had been published; payment was already in the bank. I'd also received a modest deposit for photograph sales from Rex Interstock, a London-based photo library who were developing all my slides for free during the journey and who held many of my images from previous trips on file.

I now had sufficient funds to make it across the Alps, perhaps even halfway up Germany—if I continued living frugally. The decision to start when I hadn't the means to finish, the great leap of faith, was being rewarded instalment by instalment.

Good news also came when I rang the charities—£3,000 in donations had now been received. These donations entirely benefited the homeless, and I found it humbling that people should feel prompted to give away their hard-earned cash because of something I was doing. It made time spent writing reports far less of a chore.

The final call, to the photo library, delivered the only bad news: only two of the four parcels of exposed film I'd sent back had arrived. Missing were all the photographs from the Sila to Monti del Matese. They were lost, probably forever, just like my missing resupply parcels, and I cursed the Italian postal system as vigorously as I had previously cursed Italian cartographers.

The final chore was washing weeks of dust and sweat from my clothes. I shared the *lavanderia* with several people: a tight group of old ladies, all dressed in black, chattering at warp speed; and a small, grey-bearded man, Pietro, a photographer from Milan on assignment in Scanno for a travel magazine. Pietro and I spent two wash cycles discussing photography, travel, mountains, wildlife, and eventually bears. When I told him about my nocturnal visitor he agreed that it could have been a bear: 'It certainly sounds like one.' He looked at me quietly for a moment as though unsure whether to continue, but then made up his mind.

'It seems you care about these mountains,' he observed, a trace of sadness in his voice. 'So I'll be honest. The Abruzzo bear: he is nearly finished. The national park says there are a hundred left, but I have spent time with the scientists who study bears and they say there are only forty, at the most optimistic count.' He paused a moment, letting the number sink in. 'You look upset,' he continued. 'Perhaps you would prefer I pretend everything is okay, the way they do in the national park?'

I gave no answer. I was wondering if forty meant the gene pool was too small for the species to survive.

'The authorities exaggerate the numbers to bring in tourists. But the bear, he is having a rough time. His home is being destroyed. Every year there is more development, there are new resorts; every year he has less space. Life here is changing fast. Farming is dying out. There is no money to be made from it and young people aren't interested. Fewer farms and orchards mean less food for the bear. And the wild boar population is growing—they too are crowding him out. Plus, illegal hunting still takes place. Bears are poisoned, sometimes by accident, sometimes on purpose. And bears die at night on roads. Others drown after falling in water tanks. According to the experts Abruzzo's bears will last two more generations, but then they will be gone. If it was a bear you were fortunate. Soon, no one will ever see or hear our great bear again.'

And the Abruzzo National Park will be just an ordinary national park, I thought, no different from any other. I hoped Pietro was wrong. The Abruzzo without bears would be a lesser place; incomplete, forever broken.[2]

From Scanno I walked north-west, immersed in my wandering life. The Parco Nazionale d'Abruzzo fell behind, but I still had mountains aplenty to cross. July was now in full swing; the sun burnt down with increasing ferocity, drying out the land before my eyes. Storm clouds built every day. Dark and menacing, rumbling with thunder, they threatened great violence. Fearful of lightning I scurried to lower ground, but the storms were imposters, failing to deliver the goods. I longed for rain, but none fell. Water remained scarce, especially above tree line. Without snow, dug from old drifts and melted on my stove, camping high would have been impossible. Back in England torrents were falling. 'It's like February,' Base Camp revealed. 'All the flowers are rotting.' I couldn't imagine it.

Day by day, flies grew worse. Black flies plagued me during daylight hours, getting in my face, into my ears, up my nose; *zanzare* filled the nights. In mid-July a new fly appeared: a dark-grey monster with bulging eyes and razor-sharp mandibles. A sudden stabbing pain on my upper

2. At the time of writing, December 2020, Marsican brown bears are still somehow clinging on. Estimates put the population at 50 to 60 individuals spread across the entire Central Apennines, with perhaps only 13 females at breeding age. Although conservationists are hard at work, the challenges remain numerous, and the bear's existence hangs on the brink. Hope remains, but significant changes in culture—in how land is managed and developed, and in how wildlife is regarded—are needed. A growth in ecotourism may offer a viable-long term solution, but expanded ski resorts, which further reduce and fracture wildlife habitat, are still being proposed. A visit to the Abruzzo to support organisations that offer guided nature and wildlife-viewing tours may make a real difference.

arm marked the first encounter. With a yell I turned and found myself eyeball to eyeball with a nightmarish alien, its great bug eyes glowing green like something from a horror movie. In revulsion I brushed it away, and watched blood trickle from the hole it left behind. From then on, whenever my guard was down, they struck. I began suffering several bites a day. I never heard them coming; they landed with a gentleness mosquitoes must envy. And they were persistent buggers: hard to squash, never giving up. Not knowing their true identity I came to call them Terror Flies, and I grew to fear the evil, blood-sucking beasts.

Monte Lorio, Monte Serrone, the Serra Longa; the Abruzzo and its mountains passed beneath my feet. I had originally planned a route into the Maiella National Park and up Monte Amaro, the second-highest mountain in the Apennines, but from a distance Amaro looked like a desolate lump, and I detoured over the more shapely Simbruini mountains instead. In place of Amaro's karst deserts I crossed a rich and varied landscape of woods and meadows, deep valleys and crinkly ridges, and celebrated not having a route set in stone.

There were highlights: sunset from Monte Lorio, with beams of golden light spilling across forests and ridges; five shared miles with the first fellow backpackers of the journey, two Romans out for a weekend; and realising one evening that after ten weeks on foot I had finally reached the same latitude as Rome. But, in truth, every single step upon the wild earth was a highlight. It was curious how each step was such a small thing, so repetitive, so ordinary, but each day I felt my appreciation for all of them growing.

On July 11 I reached the town of Celano and collected the fifth resupply parcel without difficulty, just as I would for the rest of the journey. And then I hopped on a train to Rome. It wasn't to escape hardships this time—such an escape wasn't necessary—I was simply too close to Rome to pass it by. What if I never came this way again? Rome didn't disappoint; it was a magical, exhilarating, and inexpressibly romantic city. But it wasn't all play. With considerable legwork I tracked down all the hiking maps needed for the rest of the Apennines that my map sponsor back in London hadn't found, divided them into parcels, and sent them on ahead. No more thrashing through the *sottobosco* for me. I bought several items of gear that couldn't be found in Apennine stores: two new cooking pots to replace the scratched, pitted pots I'd been using; new shorts that weren't dangerously threadbare at the back; a new headlamp that didn't flicker unpredictably; extra tent pegs to replace those I'd lost. And I found a barber willing to tame my shaggy locks. The beard I'd tried to cultivate—a sparse and dismal failure—also had to go. I may have been living like a wild man of the woods, but that gave me no excuse to look like one.

And then, scrubbed, rested, and done once again with crowds, I hopped back on a train and returned to my real life.

Evening light upon the Abruzzo, seen from Monte Lorio, July 7, 1997.

THE GREAT ROCK OF ITALY
Chapter 16

ON JULY 17, two days north of Celano, I completed The Walk's thousandth mile. The weather gods found a dramatic way to mark it.

It was another day of imposter storms. Three times storm clouds built, and three times I retreated—once from the summit of 8,159-foot Monte Velino, once from a treeless plain, once from an exposed ridge—and three times the imposter storms dissolved without a whimper. But at midnight the real deal finally erupted. A mighty KER-RACK ripped the night clean in two, waking me in an instant. Lightning flashed, thunder rolled, torrents pummelled my flimsy home. Soon, the world was in turmoil. Trees tossed and churned as though the storm were trying to suck them into the heavens.

This was no imposter storm! Fireworks to celebrate 1,000 miles, and they were deeply appreciated. The storm's uncontrollable wildness was everything I was walking for. These were conditions to put me in my place, conditions deserving of awe, but not conditions to fear—not here in the forest where lightning wouldn't likely strike. The storm roared, and I lost myself within its drama, let the crescendo of sound and motion sweep me away. When the scent of dampness drifted into the tent I breathed deep. I'd been waiting for dampness a long time.

For six hours the storm spit fury at the land. At times the ground actually shook. Sleep was impossible; the night was too loud, and reading wasn't an option either—entire pages passed without a word sinking in. As time passed I simply lay still, feeling small as a speck of dust, but also hugely grateful: grateful for the moisture; grateful such a storm hadn't struck during one of my exposed camps above tree line; grateful for *not* having four solid walls and a roof cutting me off from the elements; grateful for the experience itself. When the storm finally relented shortly before dawn I felt a stab of disappointment. Part of me hadn't wanted it to end.

I slept late and didn't get away until nearly noon. Dark clouds prowled the sky, a blustery wind whipped across the valley, and a few spots of rain fell. The tops of surrounding mountains were lost in fog, and I shivered, partly from the uncharacteristic cold, partly from the hostile atmosphere. Wild mountains deserve wild weather. The Apennines were better for the scowling skies and for the wind and wet. They felt bigger and harsher, and they reminded me of home. On the northern side of the Velino range I walked in nostalgia, imagining myself back in British hills.

Conditions remained stormy for several days, down through the earthquake-prone Aterno Valley and the city of L'Aquila, right up to the edge of the Gran Sasso d'Italia, the Great Rock of Italy. And then, as if by some command of the mountain gods, the cloud curtains were drawn aside. It couldn't have been stage-managed better. The Great Rock of Italy suddenly appeared, rearing overhead. It was pure theatre.

The Gran Sasso d'Italia is appropriately named; it truly is a great rock. At 9,554 feet it stands head and shoulders over its neighbours. Its closest rival, Monte Amaro, is an undistinguished lump in comparison. On Gran Sasso, rock walls soar 3,000 feet. There are buttresses, cliffs, gullies, needles, ridges, slabs, pillars, towers. There is rock: everywhere rock, acres of it, filling the sky; exposed, solid, and unyielding. The Great Rock of Italy dominates the landscape with such vertical abruptness that it looks out of place. There is nothing else like it in the Apennines.

It had to be climbed.

I walked towards it, warily at first, unable to forget the violent storms of preceding days, but the excitement of rising rockscapes and ever-clearing skies soon banished my nerves. From steaming pine-scented forests I climbed onto open hillsides bright with wildflowers. At first, I walked alone, but at 7,000 feet I came upon crowds. The southern edge of the Gran Sasso e Monti della Laga National Park is easily reached by road and cable car.

The Great Rock of Italy, suddenly revealed, July 20, 1997.

At Campo Imperatore there are buildings and car parks, ski runs and fences, cables and machinery, signs and regulations, masses of people and thoughtlessly trampled margins. For a few minutes I watched the mayhem; was this really the Apennines? *My* wild, unpeopled Apennines? It wasn't the crowds so much as the infrastructure that shocked me. Such crowds were only possible because developers had built a road and cableway. Build, and they will come; the majority to look for a few minutes, take a photo, use the facilities, spend money on a gift or meal, then drive away, knowing little of what the mountains can offer. For this, a wild mountainside had been ruined.

For a few minutes I watched the crowds, smiling at the irony of sight-seeing the sightseers. Then I turned my attention to the clutter of buildings: an angular cable car terminal, an observatory with two prominent silver domes, and an austere red-bricked hotel that looked like a prison. At one time, that was exactly how the hotel had been used. In the summer of 1943, following the Allied invasion of Italy, Mussolini was deposed by his own people and imprisoned here in great secrecy. But the Nazis learnt of his location and set a rescue mission in motion, and on September 12 a small force of commandos flew to the Gran Sasso in gliders and landed close to the hotel. Two hundred well-armed Carabinieri awaited them, but the warning to stand down or be shot for treason allowed the Germans to take command without a single bullet being fired.

The drama of Mussolini's imprisonment and rescue had perhaps increased the crowds. The hotel was little changed from 1943, but the surrounding landscape had altered considerably, with the industrial junk of the ski industry befouling it most. If Mussolini could have seen the modern view he may not have recognised it.

Thoroughly disoriented by the crowds, I continued uphill. Happily, solitude was easily found on the far side of a grassy ridge, in the wide basin of the Campo Pericoli. As in other Apennine national parks, camping was probably banned, but having just seen Campo Imperatore I felt rebellious, if not angry. I wasn't doing any harm. How did my gentle bivouac compare with park-sanctioned refuges, roads, buildings, ski tows, and pylons? If camping was banned, shouldn't these intrusions be banned too? I would soon be gone, leaving no trace; could the operators of refuges and cable cars say the same thing? Remove all the buildings, clean up the scars, unpave the pavement, teach every visitor how to tread softly, make it harder to get into the mountains, not easier, and *then* ban camping. Except by then, such a ban wouldn't be necessary.

Breathing out, I settled down for a lazy afternoon. From the way the map showed it I had expected Campo Pericoli to be a harsh arena of glacier-scoured rock, but what I found was a gentle, grass-softened paradise made vibrant by daisies, primroses and delicate saxifrages. Leafing through my English/Italian dictionary I translated the name: *campo* was field, *pericoli* danger. On that benign July afternoon the description couldn't have been more inaccurate. 'Campo Not So Pericoli' was one of the friendliest wild camps I'd made.

Stretching out bare feet, I relaxed, and soon discovered that I didn't have the location entirely to myself. First, six chamois wandered by. They stopped when they saw me, heads up, alert. I sat still as rock, and within half a minute the tension left their bodies. They turned away and began grazing, untroubled by my presence, keeping me company for several hours. Next, alpine choughs flapped in, seeking scraps. When none were forthcoming they left with coughs of disappointment. Soon, smaller birds began flittering about, filling the air with light-hearted conversation. They had me smiling before I realised it.

Hours passed, and I filled them with a favourite occupation: cloud and mountain watching. In view was Corno Grande, the Gran Sasso's highest summit, and also a striking rock pyramid: Monte d'Intermesoli. Careful not to crush any flowers I leaned back and watched the ebb and flow of light upon the peaks, the growth and dissipation of clouds beside them. Monte d'Intermesoli was a cloud maker, growing them on its huge east face. Clouds formed, spilled across the valley, broke apart, reformed all over again, and the drama kept me entertained all afternoon. Later, sunset was equally captivating. An unusual cloud formed above Intermesoli's summit and shone with neon-green light. A *green* cloud: whoever heard of such a thing?

Sleep that night came without effort. The hush of high mountains was a comforting blanket, the peace of the wild a mattress for the soul.

Monte d'Intermesoli, making clouds, July 20, 1997.

The next day began early—the silence of the Campo Pericoli was shattered by my 3 a.m. alarm. The early start wasn't strictly necessary, but I wanted the summit of the Apennines all to myself. Nothing else would do.

Barely able to contain my anticipation, I lit the stove to boil water for breakfast. This was a day I'd been dreaming about since beginning The Walk—summit day—and summit fever had me in its grip. I was a child on Christmas morning again, scarcely believing the big day had arrived. Was adult life supposed to feel so full of optimism and promise?

While water boiled I lay quietly, savouring the moment, aware that too many of life's best moments are rushed. I wanted to soak in the details: the way steam swirled in candlelight; the way my sleeping bag's rustles accentuated the hush outside; the way excitement churned like a fever. I wanted to grab it all and store it away so that I'd have this moment available for all time. As my hands clasped my mug of tea I savoured even that, relishing the warmth in my hands, the taste of hot tea. The mug I held was the same mug I'd been using for eight adventurous years. It linked me to every camp I had ever made, to every mountain I had climbed. I felt connected to them all.

I set out shortly before 4 a.m., leaving the Peapod and most of my possessions behind. A heavy dew lay upon the earth and the air felt crisp and still. I pulled on gloves for the first time since leaving England, and wore a headlamp, but didn't turn it on—it would have limited my world to a small circle of light. I'd timed summit day perfectly. The moon was full and climbing into the sky behind me, bathing the land with silver light. The clarity was phenomenal—bright as daylight, only more fantastic, more dreamlike. The fierce silhouette of Corno Grande's summit ridge rose ahead. There was magic afoot, an atmosphere almost too perfect for this world. This was a land few people knew, a time of day seldom visited. This pre-dawn Gran Sasso felt nothing like post-dawn Gran Sasso. It didn't belong to the same range, the same world, or even the same universe.

Campo Pericoli's slopes swept upwards like a grass-covered glacier, a reminder that an actual glacier still nestled within a deep bowl on Corno Grande's far side. As glaciers went, the Ghiacciaio del Calderone barely registered in significance, and it was shrinking fast each year, but as the southernmost ice sheet in Western Europe—and the only glacier in the Apennines—it remained a notable feature. The existence of a glacier made the Gran Sasso itself greater, just as the Abruzzo was greater for possessing bears.

I gained altitude at a measured pace, stepping with reverence. The sounds of boots crunching on stone and Excalibur ringing against rock were sharp and hard-edged. A shooting star streaked across the night sky directly ahead, showing the way; a good omen if ever there was one. Soon, I reached the rough path that led towards the only reasonable breach in Corno Grande's southern defences, a scree slope between walls of rock. I had studied the slope from camp and its Hohtürli-like steepness had concerned me, but like most worries I needn't have entertained them. Although the path was loose and steep it was also broad and easy to follow. There would be no bouncing down mountains today.

The first glimmering of dawn now lit the horizon. To the north, 8,711-foot Corno Piccolo came into view, its rock needles looking alpine against a paling sky. I paused to take photos, to sample the throbbing silence, to store away yet more of the morning. Then, leaving the main trail, I turned east towards the Cresta Occidentale, Corno Grande's airy half-mile-long west ridge—a sporting route to the summit. Soon, Corno Piccolo and every other mountain lay below. Empty space fell away either side, the drop half a mile deep on my right. As with the scree slope the ridge had filled me with apprehension, but once upon it I experienced none of the old Hohtürli fear, only a thrill from the exposure, a deep satisfaction from how I was dealing with it, and ever-increasing exhilaration for being where I was. Progress was uncomplicated, the limestone solid, hands only occasionally required. Enjoying myself immensely, I picked my way towards the summit, half-hurrying to reach it before sunrise but wishing the moment could last forever.

A bright yellow streak now lit the horizon and I could feel the immediacy of dawn in the air, the promise of new beginnings and unbounded possibility. Far below, the smoky-blue Apennines stretched away to distant horizons, and at my fingertips the limestone appeared to glow from within. The rock had been formed beneath the sea—tiny sea creatures had given up their calcium to make it. The idea of it forming beneath waves, of it once being alive, was difficult to grasp. It didn't belong to the sea now! From the way it hung in the sky it didn't even belong to the earth. I was scrambling across the heavens.

Soon—too soon perhaps—I reached the top. It was 5.45 a.m., and four minutes later the sun crested the horizon. Suddenly, the rock at my feet was on fire, luminous as the sun itself, and for a moment I wasn't standing on a mountain—I was perched on a pinnacle of pure light. As the light strengthened, Corno Grande projected a long shadow west across lesser mountains, a deep blue triangle that soon stretched for forty, fifty, sixty miles. For a few minutes, only Corno Grande caught the light, so high was it above its neighbours, but then the new day touched other peaks one by one, painting their summits gold. It was like watching fires being lit one after another, a message of victory being relayed across the land. *Look: night has been banished, evil overcome, death conquered! Spread the word, celebrate!* Soon, daylight was spilling down slopes near and far, moving so swiftly I could grasp the spinning of the planet from it. Below, a mile and a half lower, the valleys remained deep in shade, night still holding sway. The darkness down there only increased the feeling of incredible, untouchable elevation up here.

On the summit of Corno Grande, July 21, 1997.

I stood alone atop the highest rock in the Apennines, grinning like a fool. I think I laughed; I may have yelled, but I can't be certain. I wasn't paying attention. I was lost, entirely consumed by the moment. Where I ended and the world began I couldn't have said. There was no separation.

I spent an hour and a half on top, and it passed in the blink of an eye. From up there the world looked entirely different. It *was* entirely different. And I could see so much more of it.

Change your perspective and you change everything.

Later, when I returned to Planet Earth and clambered back to camp, I did so with an extra spring in my step. It would be a stretch to say that the summit completely changed me, but it had a lingering effect. How could it not? We are the sum of our experiences, and I could feel the truth of it. This was the thing about the entire journey: every second of it, every step, every mile, every moment comfortable and uncomfortable, every single experience good and bad was all adding up, becoming part of who I was. Step by step, my knowledge of the world was expanding, my appreciation for it increasing, my place in it altering. I'd grown up as one thing back in the suburbs, but was becoming something else.

It was a thrilling thing to feel.

SHEPHERDS AND STORMS
Chapter 17

FOR TWO DAYS more, sunlight spilled upon the Gran Sasso. I made the most of it, weaving this way and that in anything but a straight line. Straight lines are for urban planners and mathematicians, not long-distance walkers. By the direct route, Calabria to North Cape is only 2,500 miles, not 7,000. The direct route would obviously be faster, and possibly even saner, but it would miss too much. Deep within the Gran Sasso I came up with an equation that perfectly explained my meandering approach: *the shortest distance between any two points is equivalent to a wasted opportunity.* I laughed aloud when I thought it. Yes, give me curves, loops and detours. Give me the path of most resistance. Give me the longest route between any two points.

And so I followed the longest route. It led into the Val Maone, where I stopped to climb on massive limestone boulders, playing like a child while summer's warmth shone on my bare back. It led to the Valle Venacquaro, where I hid Ten Ton and explored sweeping slopes without a care in the world. And it led to the Val Solange where I discovered a cascading stream, the first high-country watercourse since the Pollino—a gift to taste, splash in, and savour for an entire afternoon. Why rush on? Why worry about what lay ahead? The year of effort still to come, the winter to be faced, the certain discomforts to be endured: these things weren't a concern. I'd worked hard for the treasures I'd found, for the emotions that had been

Descending into the Val Solange, July 23, 1997.

unleashed, and I milked them for all they were worth.

For two sunny days I sang while I walked, and walked while I sang. I couldn't keep my contentment locked away.

'Someone is happy!' a voice called late one morning when I thought I had the mountain to myself. Stopping mid-note I looked around, and finally spotted four people a short distance below. They were perched on a steep slope, harvesting a wild, cabbage-like vegetable, or had been until my song interrupted their work.

'Don't stop!' one of them teased. 'It is *bellissimo!*'

I laughed, but couldn't bring myself to resume until out of earshot.

The singing reflected my mood, as did my dreams. The dark nightmares from the first weeks were now long gone—replaced by dreams so light-hearted I actively looked forward to them. Some dreams were so entertaining and so filled with comedy that laughter shattered them and spilled over into wakefulness, lasting for minutes more, ringing out into the night. You know life is going well when laughter interrupts sleep.

Feeling alive and cheerful, fit and strong, I paced up steep mountains that seemed less steep, carrying a Ten Ton that now seemed misnamed.

Two days after summiting Corno Grande I suddenly realised that my left leg was free of pain. Looking back, I couldn't recall when last it had hurt. The Abruzzo region had distracted me, and perhaps even healed me, proving what I already knew: that the human animal isn't designed to walk on paved surfaces, but on the soft and forgiving earth.

Wild valleys, high passes, and two more summits; the Gran Sasso gave it all. There were even companions; mountain shepherds, plying their unhurried upland trade. I'd been running into shepherds since Calabria, and had come to consider them a breed apart. They all shared a distinctive appearance—ragged sun-bleached clothes and leathery tans—and they all possessed a similar untroubled air, living as though neither time nor the world's problems were of concern. Their possessions appeared few, their lives looked visibly hard, but their wisdom seemed immense. It was as if they knew something the rest of us did not.

I met the first two Gran Sasso shepherds on an open hillside. They were standing side by side, one tall and thin, one short and stocky, and they were sheltering from the sun beneath a faded yellow umbrella, although it didn't appear to be working; they were burnt as dark brown as any white-skinned person has ever been burnt. Their sheep grazed far below, wandering slowly away, but the shepherds appeared unconcerned. From their relaxed postures they might have been on permanent vacation. I soon understood why. Compared to the war they'd escaped, their mountain existence was a life of absolute peace.

'I am Goran,' the taller of the two shepherds said, his moustache rising at the edges as he smiled. 'And I am Obrad,' the shorter shepherd added, his face warm and open, his smile broad. They offered their hands.

'We are from Yugoslavia,' Goran explained with the cadence of someone who has the entire day spare. 'You know about the war?'

I nodded. The Yugoslav Wars hadn't escaped my attention, even though most news stories did. The conflict had featured genocide and all manner of atrocities, and from my understanding Yugoslavia no longer existed.

'We were in the centre of it,' Goran observed mildly. 'But it had nothing to do with us. Our home, our village, our families... they do not exist anymore.' He spoke without sadness, and shrugged as though the loss were of no consequence. It might have been a misplaced button he was describing, not a world torn apart. 'We have lived here three years now.'

He looked around at the landscape, grinning with pride.

Obrad nodded. 'We will never go back. This is our home.'

'Just look,' Goran said slowly, spreading his arms wide, and he didn't need to add anything else. Green slopes swept towards soaring mountains, wildflowers grew as though sunshine itself had taken root in the soil, and the troubles of the world seemed a million miles away. I understood. A few months here would cure anyone of all the world's ills.

'Take our photo,' Obrad suggested, noticing the camera slung over my shoulder; so I did, but it failed to capture their calmness and contentment. When I looked at the photo once The Walk was done the tanned faces were deep in shadow, the expressions barely visible.

The next day another photo did a better job. I noticed a solitary shepherd across the valley, lying on a hillside beneath yet another yellow umbrella. When I closed to within a quarter of a mile I pulled out my camera, and with the zoom at maximum photographed him from afar, feeling guilty at the invasion of privacy, but not letting it stop me. The image captured a man at ease in a wild place, living as untroubled an existence as anyone ever could. Photo taken, I walked on, not wishing to disturb his peace. It was only later that something odd struck me: there had been no sheep! Had they wandered off? Had the shepherd been too relaxed? I laughed at the possibility of it.

Changes came on July 23 when I left the Gran Sasso. Within an hour dark clouds swept across the sky, and a humid, pressing atmosphere built. On the climb into the next range, the massive Monti della Laga, the tension in the air became a palpable thing, oozing menace. The Monti della Laga is as wild and unfrequented as any corner of the Apennines, and is another location where bears reportedly roam. The possibility of *orso*, the reality of hassling flies, and the threatening atmosphere transformed the climb into a journey to the edge of the unknown. Despite all the months spent in the range's remotest corners without anything bad happening I suddenly felt a surge of fear, just as I had back in the Aspromonte, just as I had in the woods as a thirteen-year-old standing alone in nature for the first time. *You don't belong*, a voice in my head insisted; *BEWARE!* Of what, the warning didn't specify. I was disappointed in myself, and also confused—why did some places still have such power over me? What did I have to do to make the wildest places feel like home?

I didn't make my first Monti della Laga camp where planned, beside a spring clearly marked on the map. The spring existed, but 100 yards before it I came across the rear half of a cow, torn and bloody. At the spring I found the front half of the carcass, and from the look of it the kill was recent. Had wolves been feasting? Would they return after dark? Or had something larger dragged half the heavy carcass across the hillside? The nearby forest provided no clues, just impenetrable shadows. Playing it safe, I filled my water bag and camped miles further on. I slept lightly, thunder rolling in the blackness.

My unease grew stronger the following day. Instead of climbing far above tree line as planned I chose a lower route, scurrying through the trees like a timid mouse. To save face I tried using weariness as an excuse, but the argument wasn't convincing. In truth, the fear had won. The oppressive atmosphere, the dark and unknown mountains, the memory of the butchered cow, the voice insisting I didn't belong; they all combined to produce a feeling of dread, and I couldn't overcome it. I longed to explore the crest of the range and continue in good style, and I loathed taking the coward's option, but I couldn't do anything about it. More powerful forces were in control.

By day's end the air felt primed to explode. I made camp fifty yards from an abandoned refuge: a dirty, doorless shell, but a reassuring back-up shelter this time, not a befoulment of the wild. Sleep was fitful, and at dawn the storm finally erupted. Shortly after sunrise the skies blackened as though night was barrelling back in, and thunder grew louder and nearer —an approaching tsunami of sound. I barely had time to dismantle camp and dash into the refuge before the show began. And what a show it was, an event of biblical proportions: a flashing, deluging, crashing maelstrom of light, sound and motion. For three hours the world might have been coming to an end.

Cowering inside the refuge, I shuddered at the onslaught. Fog outside flashed white every few seconds, each explosion leaving an afterimage, each peal of thunder so loud I half-expected the ceiling to cave in. I imagined myself up on the Monti della Laga's exposed crest as planned, and celebrated my cowardice. How fortunate I'd stayed low! But then again, was it fortune? The more I considered it, the more I realised that it wasn't. Instead, I saw that a lesson had been offered. A demonstration that fear has its uses. Was that what I needed to understand, that fear was something the human animal had evolved for good reason, an instinct I'd forgotten how to use, an instinct I needed to relearn?

Perhaps.

Why then did I still feel it was getting in the way, holding me back, limiting me? Why did I feel that by skulking in the valley I was letting myself down?

The storm raged on. From within the refuge I imagined similar conditions striking Gran Sasso. Would I have attempted Corno Grande? Unlikely! Violent storms had preceded Gran Sasso, and had now followed it, but conditions had been perfect for my visit. Fortune had granted me the summit of the Apennines.

The storm eventually faded, although rain continued to fall. Sensing that another storm was possible I avoided exposed ground when I moved on, and kept to the valley. Sweating freely in waterproofs, I covered long miles until mid-afternoon brought a return of thunder. But the timing was perfect. At the first rumble I spied a stone hut a short distance ahead: shelter, exactly when needed. Fortune *was* on my side.

Straw and muck filled the single-roomed hovel, but it gave a grand view. From the entrance I watched sheets of rain tipping down. Thunder echoed; mist settled upon the hills; distant horizons blurred in the deluge, and then disappeared altogether. I settled in for the duration.

Long minutes passed and my eyes grew weary, but then movement caught my attention. Far down the valley I spotted a lone figure surrounded by a small flock of sheep. Slowly, the figure and flock drifted closer, until I heard neck bells chiming, heard a man's voice surging in song. Rain was still teeming, but the figure didn't appear to be hurrying towards shelter. He seemed happy where he was, splashing in puddles, throwing his arms wide, singing and hollering in excitement. To be honest, he didn't look entirely sane.

And then he spotted me.

'Aha!' I heard him exclaim with delight, as though he'd just discovered gravity, and over he splashed, chattering with excitement.

I stepped back to give him room to enter, but he stopped outside the doorway, despite rain pummelling his shoulders. From head to toe he was as bedraggled and unkempt as anyone I'd ever seen. He wore old wellington boots so worn that bare toes poked through. On his legs were rubber overtrousers, old and torn, held up by frayed braces; and on his scrawny body was a threadbare shirt, half undone, clinging wet. Completing the outfit was a dirty woollen sweater worn like a cloak, arms tied about his neck. Thick yellow hair lay plastered on his head, and his face was burnt red, his lips dry, split in the centre. He looked like someone who hadn't been indoors or taken a shower in *many* months. Perhaps that explained his delight at the rain.

But the feature that struck me most was his simple, powerful, radiating happiness. It oozed from every ounce of his being, surrounded his body, lit his eyes. Strikingly blue, with whites clearer than any I'd ever seen, his eyes revealed raging contentment. Just staring into them made me feel happy. He stood before me, smiling as wide a smile as anyone had ever smiled, as though life could not have been better. He ignored the rain, showed no embarrassment at his appearance, displayed no reserve at meeting a stranger—just smiled and laughed and burbled with innocent, baby-like glee.

And it was deeply contagious. I couldn't help but smile, and eventually laugh, right back.

Beaming with delight, the shepherd reached out, clasped my right hand tightly in both of his, and began pumping it up and down, showering me with water.

'*Mio amico, mio amico!*' ('My friend, my friend!') he exclaimed, over and over, grinning.

He shook my hand for what seemed like an age. Finally, he calmed down enough for introductions, although the broad smile never left his face.

'Demetri,' he said, stabbing a thumb against his chest.

'Andrew,' I replied, and at that he shook my hand again, clapped me on the back, and laughed even louder. I crossed my arms when it looked as though a hug was about to follow. Unconcerned, he turned and stared at the rain, chuckling every so often. For a while nothing more was said. We stood in companionable silence, sharing the moment as though we were brothers, or friends of long acquaintance who had no need of talk. No awkwardness marred the silence. It seemed like the most natural thing in the world.

Of course, I was the one to break it. Demetri clearly needed nothing more—his contentment was complete—but I managed to begin a conversation anyway, although it wasn't easy and didn't last long. Via Italian even more rudimentary than mine I learnt a few basic facts: he was Romanian; he had been a shepherd for three months; and he had a wife and children back home, to whom all his earnings went.

But that was all I got. The conversation ended when an especially loud clap of thunder exploded overhead. Demetri raised his arms and wailed with laughter and, naturally, I wailed along with him. Then, after sharing a final radiant smile, he squelched casually back to his sheep, singing gustily with each step. A hundred yards away he spun and waved a final farewell, and then vanished into the downpour, leaving me staring into the greyness in bemusement, wondering if I'd imagined the entire encounter. He must have been the craziest man I had ever met, but also, by some considerable margin, the happiest. Singing in a thunderstorm! Laughing at a deluge! I wondered if laughter interrupted his dreams too.

Obrad and Goran, Apennine shepherds, July 23, 1997.

LEGENDS OF THE SIBILLINI
Chapter 18

FOR THE NEXT three days thick clouds smothered the Apennines. Twice the sun tried pushing through, but it merely generated greenhouse heat, more thunder, and more rain. After the entertainment of losing a path one afternoon and battling through a rain-drenched *sottobosco* I then experienced all the joys of setting up camp in a downpour. Even though I had walked in waterproofs, my clothes were soaked from sweat, and once the tent was pitched it was fabulous to dive inside and peel them off. Pulling the still-wet clothes back on again the following morning was significantly less pleasurable. But I chalked it up as good practice for Norway.

In spite of this, I welcomed the rain. It was still a novelty after the Mezzogiorno, and perhaps something I would never again take for granted. It also kept the flies away. When rain wasn't falling, flies were becoming hellish. With great concentration I could just about maintain my sanity when they settled on my arms and legs, but when they crawled over my hair and face, and when I swallowed them, sanity deserted me. As time passed I realised they were chiefly attracted to sweat. Stop sweating and the swarms drifted away. But this didn't help. Tramping up mountains in humid midsummer heat with Ten Ton on my back meant sweat was an unavoidable part of my life.

The final major mountain range in Abruzzo—the Monti Sibillini—now rose ahead, but with fog smothering the land it looked as though I would not even see it, let alone reach the highest point. On the evening before arrival a hint of sunshine sent me scampering from camp to a minor summit, where I stood in thinning mist, willing the clouds to break. For a brief moment they did. Clear sky materialised overhead and sunlight shone upon my perch, casting my shadow onto a bank of fog. A Brocken spectre appeared around my shadow, a glorious halo of rainbow colour and light, but within seconds it vanished. I sat awaiting its return, camera ready, until dense fog rolled in and approaching thunder prompted a hasty retreat.

Dawn brought more fog, but it seemed thinner and brighter, and without any sense of foreboding I climbed through it onto open slopes. Before long the reward came. The fog thinned, sunlight filtered through, and finally the clouds broke apart as they had on the edge of the Gran Sasso, revealing a day so clear and bright it was barely conceivable rough weather had ever existed, or ever would again.

A line of grassy hills curved north from my feet, and to the east the Sibillini towered, smooth-sloped and monumental in stature. But it was the valley below—the Piano Grande, the Great Plain—that most caught my attention. In a realm of mountains it was like a great hole in the landscape, fifteen square miles of dead-flat, utterly featureless grassland; without doubt the most unexpected and unusual landscape I'd seen. It was the space that captured my imagination, the immense *openness*. I gave heartfelt thanks that the fog had cleared.

Gathering ever-increasing numbers of flies, I strode the rolling crest skirting Piano Grande's western edge. It was Sunday, and other hikers were about—even more of a novelty than rain. Embarrassingly, the flies only seemed interested in me, but I found a sneaky way to escape my tormentors. Near the crest's northern end, above the hilltop village of Castelluccio, I came upon another shepherd and flock. The shepherd was as easy-going as every other shepherd before him. He let me photograph him and his amicable sheepdog, and then I dashed swiftly on before the flies realised I was on the move, leaving them with man, dog, and flock. I felt a little mean, but tried not to worry. It would take more than a few extra flies to dent an Apennine shepherd's saint-like calm.

Down in Castelluccio, crowds of Sunday tourists filled the cobbled streets. For a while I sat and watched them. They quickly shattered my notion that all Italians knew how to dress. Garish colours, jarring patterns,

Shepherd and flock above the Piano Grande, July 27, 1997.

figure-hugging clothes on bodies not ideal for flaunting; a fashion horror show paraded by. But the irony that judgement was being passed by Mad Mountain Jack didn't escape my notice. I wasn't exactly a picture of sartorial elegance. My clothes were now so sweat-stained and trail-worn they barely retained any shape or colour. But at least they helped me blend in.

I found a discreet spot for camp a mile from town, near Piano Grande but hidden in a beech wood. Several groups and families were also camping wild. The campers sat beside their tents, some sunbathing, some cooking, all apparently untroubled by flies. I envied them. After leaving Castelluccio I'd somehow acquired another fly cloud, and I cringed when I saw the campers watch me and my cloud pass by. I could only imagine their thoughts. *Just look at that poor man. He must be filthy!*

I set out early the following morning in a vain attempt to escape before the flies woke up, but it didn't work. They must have guessed my plans because they were waiting, and they'd brought reinforcements: a gang of the evil Terror Flies I hated most of all. Unable to stop and rest I covered six miles and climbed 2,000 feet in one ferocious push, crossing into the heart of the Sibillini at a high pass, the Forca Viola. Salvation from torment came at the pass. A fierce wind blasted through it, so strong it almost blew me over. The flies didn't stand a chance. Finally free of them, I entered the Sibillini in a more relaxed frame of mind.

The Monti Sibillini, like much of the Apennines, is rich in myth and legend. It's hardly surprising that mountains that have seen civilisations rise and fall over thousands of years should boast many ancient stories, but perhaps it is unusual that so many of the Sibillini's are of a dark and magical nature. The range is named after a wise prophetess—one of the three sibyls of classical mythology, or so some historians claim. According to legend she fled the underworld and took refuge in a remote cave, the Grotta delle Fate, or Cave of Furies. Knights, philosophers and truth-seekers undertook perilous journeys from far and wide to gain an audience with her, seeking her wisdom. Supposedly, favoured visitors willing to stay a year were granted immortality and a life of ease and pleasure, although at a price—thereafter they could never leave. Another legend tells how the body of Pontius Pilate was dragged from Rome by oxen and cast into the cold waters of Lago di Pilato, a small glacial tarn resting in the heart of the range. The lake became an accursed place. Throughout medieval times witches, wizards, necromancers and devil worshippers were said to have gathered beside it. Rumour has it that rocks inscribed with occult symbols can still be found on the shoreline, and folklore insists that modern-day necromancy, devil worship and witchcraft still take place. Local place names are suggestive. Rising sheer above the lake for 1,000 feet is the Pizzo del Diavolo, the Devil's Point, while a short distance away is the chasm of the Gola dell'Infernaccio, the Gorge of Hell. Even the map of the Sibillini hints at the region's dark reputation, bearing a disquieting number: 666. Was the number mere coincidence, a cartographer's joke, or something more sinister?

In bright sunlight the legends seemed ludicrous, of course, as such legends do; no more than tales for children. But I understood where they came from. It wasn't many generations ago that mountains were regarded with dread. Ignorance and superstition populated them with ogres, demons, and all manner of supernatural beings. Mountains far less forbidding than the Sibillini had been feared. Even beneath an azure sky, with slopes green and verdant, the hulking Sibillini possessed an imposing aura, and it wasn't difficult to imagine superstitious peasants being intimidated. Only days before, after all, the Monti della Laga had intimidated me. I was a well-educated twentieth-century hiker armed with science and a decent map, but I'd been touched by a menace I couldn't name and had cowered from it.

The legends I learnt throughout the Apennines were all mildly diverting, but present-day reality interested me most. The stories from history were all well and good, but, quite simply, they were done. Few nations have as rich a history as Italy. Countless lives had been lived, epic deeds done, loves found and lost, battles fought, blood spilled, and civilisations come and gone, all upon the very soil I trod—even the remotest stretches where human history lay thinnest. The land had been touched by it all, and still bore the scars. Evidence lay everywhere if one only looked. The Sibillini's open slopes were an obvious example: once densely forested, they were now bare. Centuries of felling by woodcutters, charcoal burners and shepherds had completely altered their appearance. But history and legends only take one so far in understanding a place. The problem I had with our human story was the way it was almost always told out of context, focusing exclusively on us. What about us *and* the environment? Just as we've reshaped it, so it has utterly shaped us. And what about natural history, geological history, the collision of continents, the pushing up of ranges, the evolution of species, the carving done by glaciers? Don't these stories reveal more? Compared to geological time our history is just a snap of the fingers, barely relevant. But even knowledge of natural history fails to match knowledge gained from actually walking across a mountain— from sleeping upon it, touching it, and sitting still with questing senses and open emotions. Actively experiencing it. Mountains, forests, plains—all wild places—have a unique spirit, and there is only one way to truly know it. As I saw things, my journey wasn't about delving into the human past; it was about exploring and fully experiencing the present.

The legends and myths that appealed most were those of my own journey. The Walk was perfect for personal legend-making—its scale and setting provided an epic backdrop that suburban life could never match. Back home, adventures took place vicariously, through books, movies and on the life-force-sapping TV, but out here the adventure was real, and it was taking place in my very own Middle-earth sprung to life. Here the difficulties and discomforts weren't imagined, and the risks had real consequences, and one way of dealing with them was to weave them into my own legend and imbue them with purpose and meaning. The myth that the mountain gods were granting rewards for good style wasn't just light-hearted fun; it was also a useful motivator. The idea that storm clouds were being pulled aside for my benefit as a gift for good behaviour was clearly utter nonsense, but it made the elements feel less fierce and less indifferent. I supposed this was how most superstitions started: from wanting to believe that the uncontrollable could be controlled, that random events had meaning, and that personal behaviour made a difference. Perhaps my own legend-making was nothing more than delusional self-aggrandisement, but from the way the rewards occurred it often felt more than mere chance. Of course, I knew it was only a fantasy, but it was far more relevant to me than old myths about cave-dwelling prophetesses, devil-worshipping wizards, or any of the countless other fantasies humans have invented and believed since history began.

When I reached Lago di Pilato I paused, hoping to sense something haunted in the atmosphere, but all I found was the natural grandeur of a wild mountain cirque on a warm summer's day. The cliffs and talus slopes of Pizzo del Diavolo reached down to the lake's edge, and sunlight set the water sparkling. The number of mountain lakes I'd visited since Calabria could be counted on one finger. The temptation to plunge in was hard to resist. I'd swum in similar lakes many times during previous walks, but my body was dirty, the lake small, and I had read that a rare crustacean inhabited it, so rare it lived nowhere else in the world. Tiny and orange, the shrimp-like *Chirocephalus marchchesonii* was visible when I peered into the water. A swim might pollute the water, and it seemed poor manners to engage in an activity that might harm or even wipe out an entire species. So I did nothing more than look.

I camped above the lake at 7,200 feet—the 'I Ain't Afraid of No Necromancers Camp'—and shortly before sunset climbed Monte Vettore, at 8,123 feet the fourth-highest Apennine peak. With no pack as ballast, just a camera over my shoulder and an apple in my pocket, the ascent was as effortless as an ascent could ever be. Vettore's summit was a benign place, washed with warm light, caressed by a breeze so gentle it barely moved the

Benign evening on the summit of Monte Vettori,
looking east towards the Adriatic Sea, July 28, 1997.

air, and hung with a faint rainbow directly overhead. To the south, thirty miles distant, Corno Grande thrust its sharp summit skywards, and forty miles east the Adriatic coastline made a wide, sweeping curve. Hundreds of square miles of lower hill country were spread below, villages glinting seductively in evening sunlight; and as I studied it all, matching villages and mountains with names on the map, I realised that I was no longer in Abruzzo but on the border of Umbria and Marche. A real feeling of progress overcame me. Footsteps were such small things, but they added up. The surrounding mountains still looked huge, but the entire Apennine chain felt curiously reduced. Walking its length suddenly seemed the easiest thing in the world.

The dark, legend-filled Sibillini granted me a peaceful night and a serene second morning. I returned to Vettore for sunrise, this time carrying Ten Ton, and then followed a long ridge over a succession of fine summits. Wild mountains had rarely passed underfoot with such ease, but by early afternoon the heat and miles had become taxing, the flies had returned, and worsening weather drove me down. Clouds that began as insignificant white puffs grew within a short hour into black cumulonimbus, and by late afternoon they were spitting forked lightning. It was sobering to see lightning strike the ridge I'd just crossed. A potent reminder of nature's power.

The rain when it came was like water from a hose, but it no longer mattered. I'd climbed the mountains I'd wanted. Once again, fortune had granted me perfect conditions exactly when I needed them. A storm twenty-four hours earlier would have denied me Vettore's summit, would have turned a peaceful high-altitude camp into an uncomfortable, possibly dangerous affair. The mountain and weather gods were on my side—it couldn't now be denied. For persevering in the Mezzogiorno I'd earned their favour, and they were now showing it. This *was* the stuff of legends.

A two-hour trudge in heavy rain dampened my fantasies a little. By early evening I was ready for camp, but I found nowhere for it. The ground was either too steep, too rocky, or too awash. Shortly before nightfall I chanced upon another stone hut, larger than others I'd seen. It looked habitable, but when I tried the wooden door it was bolted, and the shutters wouldn't budge. The hut was built onto a steep hillside, and underneath it on the downhill side I saw a small basement with a doorless opening. A quick inspection revealed a passable home for the night. It wasn't the cleanest accommodation, but it was preferable to pitching the Peapod in ever-deepening puddles outside.

With rain hammering down I moved in. Old straw and muck covered the floor, and small pellets scattered in corners suggested there would be rodent company later. A stack of bricks and several planks lay piled against a wall. I used these to build myself a table and bed high enough off the floor to keep mice away, then unrolled my sleeping bag, and pulled out the stove. I had food, water, and shelter; what more could Mad Mountain Jack want? Home sweet home.

Night fell, darkness hid the rain outside, but I could still hear its percussion. Lying on my makeshift bed, cocooned in the sleeping bag, I read by candlelight. I'd grown to prefer candlelight to the headlamp's beam. The headlamp was cold and impersonal, the same as every other electric light, but the candle's flame was warm and organic. Almost alive. It danced, flickered, and comforted, almost like a companion—although perhaps you've spent too long on your own when a candle becomes a companion.

But I wasn't on my own for long. Out of nowhere a presence materialised in the room. I sensed it overhead in the shadows. It began moving in circles, and I caught sight of a dark shape, wings, a vague impression of flapping, of a creature in erratic flight, of something panicked that had entered by mistake and couldn't find the exit. To see better I sat up, accidentally knocked over the candle, and was plunged into blackness. The thing darted past my head and I yelped.

Scrabbling for my headtorch I flicked it on, and cast its searchlight beam around the room, seeking the creature. And at last I saw what it was.

Heavens—a bat!

I knew it was a bat because all of a sudden it flew straight at me, reared before my face with long-fingered wings stretched wide, grinned a disturbingly demented grin, hung still for an eternal second, and then darted away. On it raced around the room in stuttering circles, setting the air in motion. It shattered the sense of peace and well-being I had developed. Apennine bats can carry rabies, and I knew I'd never get to sleep with it in the room. It was a rodent, after all, and I couldn't push from mind the image of its ugly, leering, pug-nosed face.

I descended from the bed and tried guiding the bat towards the exit with the book I'd been reading. But the bat wanted none of it. It didn't want to be out in the rain any more than I did. Growing desperate, I began chasing the bat, swinging the book like a fly swatter. And so the Great Bat Chase began. Stumbling over the bed, leaping over Ten Ton, hurdling the room's assorted junk, round and round I chased the bat in crazy circles. And crazy it was: if someone months earlier had told me I'd find myself alone in a remote hut chasing a bat with a rolled-up book I wouldn't have believed them. How long the Great Bat Chase lasted I can't say, but it finally ended when I made a desperate lunge, missed spectacularly, and crashed into an unyielding stone wall. I stood, hands on knees, gasping for breath, while the bat flew on.

Trying a new tack, I took up position near the doorway and swung at the bat every time it passed. It outclassed me utterly. Strike one, strike two... strike twenty... strike fifty. I even tried holding the book motionless, hoping the bat would crash into it; not a chance. Eventually I lowered my arms, weary, defeated. Now unchallenged, the bat increased momentum, making ever faster circuits, and then it commenced dive-bombing runs, swooping low and pulling away at the last moment, each time making me duck. I swear I heard it laugh. By the time the damn thing finally grew bored and darted out the doorway I was a nervous wreck.

With the bat gone I stood still, staring into the night, praying it wouldn't come back. A minute passed and I began to relax.

But then: bloody hell, I nearly jumped from my skin! A human face appeared suddenly, right in the doorway. A face!

It was framed with thick black hair, wore a bushy moustache and a furious expression. Eyes glared. I couldn't see a body. My heart nearly stopped.

'NO!' the face shouted, shaking from side to side. 'No-no-no-no-no!'

The face moved closer and a body appeared beneath it. I noticed rough clothes and bare forearms knotted with muscle. The man looked hard as nails.

He spoke again, a demanding question, but I couldn't understand the words.

'I don't understand,' I stammered in Italian. 'Do you speak English?'

He shook his head. Still glaring, he spoke again, harshly, and although I couldn't grasp a single word the meaning was obvious: 'Who are you? What the hell are you doing in my hut?'

With a beckoning finger he ordered me out. I couldn't believe it—an Apennine shepherd, behaving this way. Where was the calm? Where was the friendliness? Was he really throwing me out?

Frowning, he gestured that I follow, and I felt I had no choice but to obey. Outside, rain still fell. Sheep milled in the dark. Holding a torch, the man led me up the slope to the hut's front door. My heart hammered in my chest, and I began trying to explain, but he held up a finger for silence. He produced a key, unlocked and pushed open the solid door, and stepped through, making sure I followed. We entered a narrow room—a kitchen, I saw. The man began talking, but with less urgency and anger, and shone his light about as though conducting a guided tour. The beam swept across a large sink, a countertop, a stove with two gas burners, on to a shelf stacked with plates, mugs and glass tumblers, and settled on a small metal pot. The man took it down, screwed off the lid, and pulled out a large box of matches. He then directed the light towards a door and guided me through.

The second room was larger, and I caught a glimpse of furniture, felt a soft rug beneath my boots. The man laughed—he sounded friendly now —and he passed over the torch. Showing where to point it, he struck a match—it broke—struck another, and held the flame to a lamp hanging from the ceiling. The lamp caught and a warm orange glow pushed back the shadows. The room had seen some hard living, but compared to the filthy, bat-haunted basement directly underneath it was palatial. There were tables, chairs, a large wood-burning stove in one corner, a radio and even a small television of all things, and bunk beds with real mattresses.

He pointed at one, and then to me, smiling broadly, nodding. Comprehension finally dawned. He wasn't throwing me out; he was giving me a bed for the night. If only all the world's homeless were treated so well! With simple sign language he told me to go and fetch my stuff. I was back with it in seconds.

The evening that followed was the most enjoyable of the entire summer. Tomas, the Slovakian shepherd, treated me like royalty. We had no common language—he only possessed ten words of Italian, and certainly no English—but words weren't needed. Sign language and actions spoke more clearly, and where they failed we resorted to pen, paper, hieroglyphics. Tomas pulled the rings off two cans of beer, then disappeared into the kitchen and began reheating a stew. Soon, a heavenly aroma filled the hut. A few minutes later he delivered two bowls filled with a rich, steaming gravy, afloat with tender chunks of meat, and it was incredible. Tomas clapped when he saw my delight. Through questions and answers drawn in pictures I learnt some of the ingredients: venison, wild mushrooms, tomatoes, cream from a goat, peppers, a great heaping pile of wild herbs and spices. Later, I regretted not learning them all. It was the culinary masterpiece of the journey.

After several more beers Tomas and I were laughing like old friends. The pictures we drew to communicate grew increasingly wobbly and ever harder to decipher, and before long we were in stitches. The rest of the world, the rain and dark night outside, The Walk itself—it all faded away. We sat in warmth and companionship within the soft glow of the oil lamp, the last two people on the planet, and hours passed like minutes. Yawns eventually overcame us both. Midnight was late for a shepherd, Tomas sketched, just as it was for me. When I lay on my bunk the mattress swallowed me, and sleep came in minutes, laughter spiralling downwards into glorious oblivion.

———————

Tomas was already up when I woke bleary-eyed and hung-over shortly after seven. He looked as though he'd been awake and active for hours, and seemed none the worse for all the beer he'd drunk. Sensing that he was keen to get outside and on with his day, I packed Ten Ton swiftly and stepped out into a crisp, dewy morning. Sunlight streamed across the meadow and hundreds of ragged, long-eared sheep were grazing, their chiming bells heart-wrenchingly exotic in the chill air.

Tomas spoke in Slovak as he shook my hand. Somehow, I understood his words perfectly. 'Well then, you take care...'

'Thank you, for everything,' I replied in English, and he obviously understood too.

I left reluctantly. Such encounters weren't everyday events, not even on this journey, but it was time to go. For the first time I felt a sense of urgency to push north. August had arrived, and at this altitude a hint of autumn hung in the air. My Apennine summer wouldn't last forever.

EMILIA-ROMAGNA

N

AUGUST 22/24

Vernio

Scarperia e
San Piero

AUGUST 17

San Bernedetto in Alpe

**FORESTE
CASENTINESI**

Monte Falco (5436 ft / 1657 m)

Florence

TUSCANY

Badia Prataglia

Badia Tedalda

MARCHE

AUGUST 11

Monte Dei Frati (4767 ft / 1453 m)

Route across
**UMBRIA,
MARCHE,
& TUSCANY**
August 1997

Pietralunga

AUGUST 6

Monte Serra Sante (4701 ft / 1433 m)

Monte Pennino (5154 ft / 1571 m)

AUGUST 3

km 0   20
mi 0   10   20

UMBRIA

Adriatic
Sea

LORD OF THE FLIES
Chapter 19

IN THE APPENNINO umbro-marchigiano—the Umbrian and Marche Apennines—The Walk entered a new phase. It became a quieter journey, lower key. The massive, glacier-sculpted peaks of the Central Apennines fell behind, and lower, forested mountains took their place. In July, the journey had been legendary in scale and deed; in August, it was back to being a plain old long-distance hike, a simple walk in the woods.

I walked mostly through beech woods, less often on open ground, but to my great surprise discovered I didn't mind. Before beginning The Walk forests had been second-tier environments to me, places to pass through en route to the only landscapes that really mattered: high mountains. But as the Sibillini fell behind I discovered that my perception of forests had changed. Now, after hundreds of miles alone in them, forests had become an essential part of the mountain environment, not a mere prelude to it. I'd grown so deeply attached to being among trees that I started yearning to remain in them when I left them behind. I'd come to love the way they gave shade and shelter. I loved how I disappeared when I stepped into them and became anonymous. And I loved how they wrapped themselves around me as though they were places to wear, not just places to visit.

As I slipped quietly through the Umbrian forests I thought back to the Aspromonte, remembering all the doubts and fears I'd suffered during that first encounter with wild Apennine woods. Back then, before becoming a 'forest walker', the sensation of being somewhere I hadn't belonged had been a constant, nagging, and deeply unsettling companion. But now, 'you don't belong' no longer applied—at least not here among the trees.

It was nature overcoming nurture, I suspected. Nature was what I was—a member of a species that had been entirely shaped by the natural environment. And nurture was what I'd become growing up with carpet underfoot, separated from nature by four walls and a roof. I thought back to my first lone encounter with woodland at thirteen, how I'd fled like an intruder; and then I looked around at the Umbrian woods, finding nothing but comfort and security. *This* was nurture too; nurture by direct experience, nurture by deep immersion, nurture by choice, and it was profoundly changing me. Sure, the Monti della Laga had revealed that I had some distance to go before I belonged everywhere in wild nature, but progress was definitely being made.

The more I considered it, the more I saw the size of that progress. Feeling that I belonged here was huge. After all, unlike the woods I'd fled from at thirteen, these forests genuinely were wild. Here, creatures like wolves weren't just imagined—I hadn't seen any, but they were known to be present. And here, I could lose myself for days at a time if I so desired. But, wild as these forests were, I also saw their reality, saw that they weren't filled with menace—only with trees. Eyes watched as I passed, that I didn't doubt, but they weren't malevolent like the eyes I'd imagined as a child. At worst they were indifferent; most likely the eyes belonged to forest creatures wary of me. From imagining that a forest was out to get me I'd grown to see it as a sanctuary, and it fascinated me how far it was possible to come. I'd crossed a barrier that I hadn't known existed, a barrier my own species had built, and now that I was aware of it and had lived on both sides I could see it for the artificial construct it was.

Of course, I'd only stepped partway across. It was one thing to feel relaxed in these sun-dappled beech woods, or to feel at home on the green mountains of the Abruzzo under benign summer skies, but quite another on bigger mountains in fiercer conditions. Would I still feel so relaxed in the Alps when the first blizzards hit, or in Central Europe's dark forests in the frigid depths of midwinter, or on Norway's wilderness fjells during lashing Arctic gales? That would be the test—and I had a hunch, from how

I'd cowered beneath the Monti della Laga, that it wasn't a test I was yet ready to take.

For now, I tramped northwards, as relaxed as one could be with flies in unceasing pursuit. For three weeks and 280 miles life became more straightforward than it had been at any stage since Calabria—which didn't mean it was easy, just easier. Some things would never change. Hunger, thirst, heat, and weariness remained constants; they just didn't seem as extreme.

Hunger was quickly dealt with here in the Appennino umbro-marchigiano. Villages were closer together, and instead of carrying a week's food I was able to replenish supplies every two or three days. In theory, this meant I didn't have to carry such a heavy load, but in reality I carried the same amount and simply ate more. I'd developed an appetite worthy of three people, and Ten Ton had space—it was difficult to resist utilising it.

Drinking water was more readily available too. Frequent fountains and springs meant I could fill my bottle several times a day, and there were even streams in the deepest valleys: a treat I could never again take for granted. The increased availability of water came at a good time. Although August's temperatures didn't match the soaring extremes of the Mezzogiorno, increasing humidity made conditions feel hotter. I drank gallons, but could never keep up with the sweat I lost, and my T-shirt was often so wet it looked as though I'd been swimming. Without the extra water sources I'd have dried out and shrivelled away, and without the liberal spoonfuls of salt I lobbed into my nightly stew, hyponatremia and heat exhaustion might have swiftly ended The Walk.

The abundance of water made a real difference to progress, as did a far more extensive network of tracks and trails than had existed further south. Some tracks were ancient, once traversed by muleteers, pilgrims and bandits; some were modern and reasonably well maintained. The increase in trails meant there was a corresponding increase in people. I saw mushroom pickers and woodcutters in the woods, and other visitors also walking for pleasure, although they carried daypacks—not eighteen-month packs—and few ventured far from road's end. The better-maintained trails shortened the miles, but I still found myself taking occasional unplanned detours into the *sottobosco*. This was still the Apennines, after all! And I still followed roads occasionally too, but not often, and usually only because a town, and fresh supplies, lay right ahead.

Monti dei Frati; typical forested mountains in the
Umbrian and Marche Apennines, August 11, 1997.

The promise of food always made pavement bearable.

Although more rounded and far lower than the Central Apennines, the mountains remained attractive. It was merely a different kind of beauty: softer, subtler, and more intimate. The land revealed itself not with a grand flourish but slowly and seductively. There were beech and oak woods filled with birdsong and shimmering light, and chestnut woods with prickly forest floors, and pine woods softly carpeted with needles and filled with the heavenly aroma of pine resin. I walked through meadows that hummed with insect life, crossed ridge-top grasslands that were open to the sky, and descended into limestone gorges that echoed to the sound of running water. Best of all were the deepest V-shaped valleys. They were filled with such a rich variety of different tree species that for once I wanted a companion, if only to see the pleasure I could feel mirrored on someone else's face.

My route weaved along Italy's high spine, a more noticeable feature now that the range was narrower. Here, tamer country always lay closer than it had further south, rarely more than half a day's walk away. I made one notable detour down into it, tramping into the kind of postcard-perfect landscape most people picture when Umbria and Tuscany are mentioned. The detour delivered me to Pietralunga: an immaculate village perched atop a small hill. It was scrubbed clean with nary a stone out of place, bedecked with scarlet flags and fluttering banners, but when I wandered its narrow streets it didn't feel authentic—it reminded me of the Amalfi Coast, existing more for visitors than residents. I found myself pining for the more genuine charms of Calabria and Basilicata's rougher villages.

At least the frequency of villages introduced more people into the mix, and I benefited from their generosity several times. I enjoyed an invitation to dinner, a few laughter-filled nights in campsites sharing food and wine with Italians my age, and one warm night in an old stone church courtesy of a Dutch couple who'd rented it for their vacation. I wasn't stared at in the villages the way I had been further south, and was only occasionally stopped for the old standby, 'Dove vai?' At last I was able to rest undisturbed in village centres and watch daily life unfold. I'd grown fond of what I'd seen of the Apennine way of life; the easy, laid-back, *Italianness* of it. Even here in rough mountain villages life was lived with style and a certain theatrical flair. I found myself falling for Apennine civilisation and society as much as I'd already fallen for the wild.

For the first time since the journey had begun my route coincided with not one but three official long-distance trails: the SI (Sentiero Italia), the E1 trans-European trail, and the GEA (Grande Escursione Appenninica). The knowledge that I was now following a beaten path altered my perception of the land a little, unwilding it to a degree, but nothing on the ground really changed. The trail wasn't exactly a major thoroughfare, overrun with teeming crowds. Even though it was now August—the month most Italians reserved for their vacations—I met no other long-distance hikers. Day-trippers ventured a couple of miles from roads, but I still had the remote corners entirely to myself. The E1 and SI appeared prominently on my maps, but waymarkings on the ground were often scarce—especially where I needed them—and were comically inconsistent. Not that this troubled me; I'd dealt with far worse in the Mezzogiorno. And at least here there were trails—most of the time.

The E1 trans-European trail was part of a growing network of long-distance trails criss-crossing the continent. On paper it led from the

Tyrrhenian Sea near Naples to northern Norway, but what had been imagined by its founders, the European Ramblers Association, was still thousands of miles from actually existing. The Sentiero Italia—the Grand Italian Trail—was in a similar state. First proposed in 1983 by a group of Italian hikers, and developed with the assistance of the Italian Alpine Club, the trail theoretically traversed Sardinia, Sicily, the complete length of the Apennines, and then the Italian Alps. When I began my journey in Calabria I hadn't a clue such a trail existed, and until the first SI sign appeared in Tuscany I'd seen zero evidence of it on the ground, despite walking many miles along what I later learnt was supposedly its route. I first heard about the trail back in L'Aquila, beneath the Gran Sasso d'Italia.

'So, you are following the Sentiero Italia?' a store owner asked, after quizzing me about my walk.

'Er, the what?'

'The Sentiero Italia, the Great Walking Path of Italy. It is a famous route.'

'No, I'm just making up my own route. I didn't know there was a Sentiero Italia.'

'But how could you miss it?' The man laughed, holding his hands up at my apparent blindness. 'It is fully established. Even in Calabria.'

'Well, have you seen it?' I asked politely but firmly. After three months on foot I had finally developed sufficient confidence to stand up for myself. 'Have you walked in Calabria?'

'Me? No! I would never walk there—it is much too dangerous. And the Calabrians: so backward! But there is a good path. I know this for a fact.'

I had a similar conversation in a village two weeks later, and again several times once I'd reached the Alps, where people who had never visited the Apennines swore that the SI had been blazed in its entirety. The truth, however, was clearly different.

Even though the official trails were often elusive, progress was generally uncomplicated. But occasionally—on days when temperatures soared, and the trail petered out, and the *sottobosco* ensnared me—it was as though I'd returned to the south. Ever-increasing harassment by Apennine flies added to the unpleasantness of those moments, as did dogs once again, a hassle I thought I'd left far behind. On August 7, while guiding a cloud of flies along the E1 as it followed the crest of a steep-sided ridge, I came upon three impressively massive Maremmano sheepdogs. White and shaggy as polar bears, the dogs were guarding a flock grazing on the ridge, and the trail led straight towards them. I approached cautiously, practising all my well-honed dog-coping tricks, but three strategically placed bodies, three sets of bared teeth, and three deeply menacing growls—sounding like volcanoes preparing to erupt—made it clear that I wasn't going to be granted permission to pass. A long detour through the surrounding *sottobosco* followed, and it was every bit as traumatic as usual, although marginally better than being savaged by polar bears. But it took time. A hundred-yard stretch of the E1 that should have taken thirty seconds ended up taking a sweat-soaked, arm-punctured, fly-bedevilled hour.

A second forest detour was forced upon me later that afternoon when the E1 reached a pocket of overgrown farmland—and vanished. It stopped at a field being worked by an old farmer. The man belonged to an earlier time. He was dressed in heavy clothes as rough as sackcloth, and was toiling backwards and forwards, pulling a rusty iron plough by hand. I called out a greeting, asked about the E1, but he knew nothing of it, nor the Sentiero Italia, the Grande Escursione Appenninica, nor any other trail, and waved me and my flies away.

So it was back to the woods, and another wearying hour in Apennine jungles. But eventually I burst free at a muddy track. A coin toss took me right, and a few short minutes of squelching progress delivered me to a paved road where an E1 trail marker stood glowing in the sun. I was back on track.

Just down the road three men stood beside a parked car, smoking and laughing, enjoying the view down a forested valley, its depths lost in late-summer haze. One of the men glanced up when I emerged from the trees. He wandered over. Sure enough, it was time for another '*Dove vai?*'

I smiled. Now that the question was asked less frequently I enjoyed answering it. 'Badia Tedalda,' I explained. 'The village. Down the valley.'

'No,' the man replied with a frown and a shake of his head. He opened his mouth to speak, and I expected to hear that there was no village, or that this was not the valley to it, but his words were far more memorable. 'It is *too far*,' he stated earnestly, looking worried on my behalf. 'It is ten kilometres away!'

Struggling to keep a straight face, I described how far I'd already walked, but, as usual, the concept of hiking any distance wasn't grasped.

'It is not possible,' he declared.

'Well...'

'There is a bus that comes through here. You must take the bus.'

'But you see...'

'Definitely better.'

'But I'm only travelling by foot.'

'Well,' he finally murmured dismissively. 'You can walk... if you want.' And he gave me a disparaging look that said anyone walking from here to the village deserved everything he got.

But the last laugh was on me. In a way it was too far. The black flies haunting the valley were so numerous, and the squadrons of Terror Flies so persistent, that the short walk down the valley felt like 100 miles of purgatory. It almost unhinged me.

The flies and sultry heat continued the next day, but the day after that a thunderstorm banished both, for a few hours at least. Pounding rain stripped leaves from trees and turned the trail into a cascading river of mud. Dripping mists followed, filling the woods with sombre light, and the following dawn brought a chill so cold it raised goosebumps on my arms and set excitement coursing through my veins at the prospect of the autumn soon to come.

But the cold snap didn't last. A scorching sun soon returned, along with even more merciless airborne companions. I was their lord, and they seldom let me forget it.

My dedicated followers belonged to five main species. First, there were blood-sucking *zanzare*, filling the nights. There were occasional ticks, collected during off-trail detours through long grass and woods. Then there were tiny midges, each one packing a sharp little bite—uncomfortable individually and distressing in their hundreds. And then there were black flies, *moscerini*, always in multitudes too numerous to count. They didn't often bite, but their lack of respect for personal space was maddening. They hovered before my face, crawled through my hair, landed on my arms and shoulders, buzzed in my ears. They were at their worst on long climbs when I moved too slowly to outpace them. With no shelter, no opportunity to rest or escape, many uphill stretches became torturous grinds. Insect deterrent was useless; it poured off with my sweat. Sweat was their nectar. It drove them wild. The more I sweated the more *moscerini* I attracted, and the more *moscerini* I attracted the faster I was forced to walk, and the faster I walked the more I'd sweat. At least on descents I could outrun them—and run sometimes I did, laughing at the madness of long bounding strides. But with Ten Ton on my back I couldn't run forever, and the flies always caught up eventually. Windy days were treasured for how they kept flies away, and rain was a blessing, even though I knew dampness would ultimately boost their numbers. All told the *moscerini* had real impact, often keeping me from appreciating the land, sending me far away into daydreams about cooler, flyless places.

And then, of course, there were the Terror Flies—the large bug-eyed monsters I'd first encountered in the Abruzzo. I hadn't yet found anyone who could tell me the name of the species, although I'd asked many times. Not that a name would have helped. They'd still land just as softly, still bite just as painfully, still evade my defences and attack again… and again… and again. As names went, Terror Flies did the job just fine.

As August progressed their numbers increased. They were particularly aggressive when thunderstorms approached, and I went out of my way to avoid farmland where cattle grazed. Even detours into the *sottobosco* were better than facing the swarms of Terror Flies near cows and horses. Not that the Terror Flies could be completely avoided. They were everywhere. They attacked in the open and chased me into the woods. And they attacked in the woods and chased me back into the open. Their persistence and agility would have been impressive if they hadn't caused such anguish. Trying to swat them away was a waste of time. My waving arms merely signalled to all the other Terror Flies who hadn't yet joined in. The thing was, their bites really hurt; there was always blood, and an itchy red lump that lingered for days.

Later, once The Walk was done, I figured out that they were horseflies, *tafano* in Italian, and a particularly aggressive breed. Research turned up revealing snippets of information, including terrifying close-up pictures of knife-like mandibles used to rip apart flesh. There were rumours about swarms drinking enough blood from cattle to leave their prey fatally weakened, and details about various diseases some could transmit: a

parasitic worm, and even anthrax! Of course, they have their place in nature, as all life forms do. Supposedly, in some parts of the world, they are
important flower pollinators, but this knowledge wouldn't have stopped
me from eradicating every single one of them if I'd had the means.

August 10 brought a typical Terror Fly attack. For a while life that
day had been good. A two-hour climb in cooling shade led to an open
ridge, and blowing across the ridge was a strong wind that kept all the flies
away. For once I travelled without sweating, leisurely enjoying long views
east to the silver hem of the Adriatic Sea. Inevitably, it didn't last. By early
afternoon the wind dropped, and Terror Flies returned with a vengeance.
They attacked in a cloud, landing on my arms, legs, hair, ears, mouth, neck,
and eyes—dive bombing without pause—and I had to wipe each off in
an instant before it bit. The rest of the day passed in a living hell. Hell, I
decided, is being too hot and perpetually drenched in sweat, with biting
Terror Flies all around, and no earthly way of escaping the torment.

It wasn't until late August that I finally found a local able to supply
a good regional name for the flies. The man was an old forester, and undoubtedly knew the correct scientific and common name of every species
in his region.

'What do I call these flies?' he answered, looking at me with a grim,
harassed air, as several of them homed in. 'They are... *BASTARDI!*' he
cried, which, really, said it all.

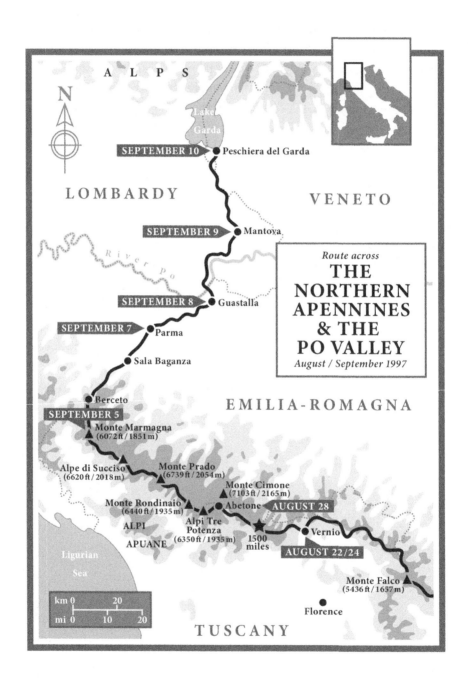

Route across
THE NORTHERN APENNINES & THE PO VALLEY
August / September 1997

A L P S

N

LOMBARDY

VENETO

Lake Garda

SEPTEMBER 10 — Peschiera del Garda

SEPTEMBER 9 — Mantova

River Po

SEPTEMBER 8 — Guastalla

SEPTEMBER 7 — Parma

Sala Baganza

Berceto

SEPTEMBER 5

Monte Marmagna
(6072 ft / 1851 m)

EMILIA-ROMAGNA

Alpe di Succiso
(6620 ft / 2018 m)

Monte Prado
(6739 ft / 2054 m)

Monte Cimone
(7103 ft / 2165 m)

Monte Rondinaio
(6440 ft / 1935 m)

Abetone

AUGUST 28

ALPI

Alpi Tre Potenza
(6350 ft / 1935 m)

1500 miles

Vernio

APUANE

AUGUST 22/24

Ligurian Sea

Monte Falco
(5436 ft / 1657 m)

km 0   20
mi 0   10   20

Florence

TUSCANY

INTO THE CLOUD FORESTS
Chapter 20

MY BOOTS, AFTER 1,500 miles, were beginning to show the strain. The leather had cracked open in several places, leaving gaping holes that small stones and thorns leapt into at every opportunity. They wouldn't last much longer.

I, on the other hand, felt in fine form. Physically, I doubt I'd ever been stronger, but the sense of well-being went far beyond muscles and lungs in top condition. Spirits were high. I found myself laughing at little things, even things that went wrong. Laughter frequently pulled me from sleep. I sang for hours while walking, unable to contain the contentment. On the edge of San Benedetto in Alpi a girl leaning over a balcony heard my song and playfully joined in. We waved happily. It was wonderful to share the exuberance.

With August nearing its end, change was afoot. The weather see-sawed daily from broiling hot to cool and damp, and the torment of flies finally lessened—a monumental change. Autumn's closeness was palpable in browning vegetation and wilting flowers, in dry scrub oak leaves that crumbled to dust when I grasped them, in growing morning dews, in the way the sun hung lower in the sky and gave light that was softer and more golden. Regular rains dampening the forests, thick fogs enveloping the highest slopes, and finger-nipping dawns made it clear that summer was fading fast.

When I reached the town of Vernio on August 22 I jumped on a train to spend a few days in Florence, but for all the city's artistic brilliance the stifling low-altitude heat, round-the-clock noise, and inescapable crowds were too much to take, and I didn't stay as long as planned. Afterwards, settling back into my simple existence, I decided that the forest cathedrals of the Apennines were easily equal to Florence's famous Duomo, and a hell of a lot more elevating to the soul.

A tight knot of excitement built in the pit of my belly as August's final week progressed. It fermented with similar intensity to the excitement I had felt before the journey's start, only this time there were no accompanying nerves. In less than two weeks I'd be done with the Apennines. It wasn't that I wanted to be finished with the range. Quite the opposite—leaving would be hard, as saying farewell to the familiar and loved always is—it was more an excitement based on the closeness of completing the task I'd set myself. The traverse of the range had been a long and difficult undertaking. On many occasions it would have been easy to give up. Not that giving up had ever been truly considered, but the difficulties—the gruelling physical challenge, the discomforts endured, the endless mental battles and spiralling emotions—indeed every single thing encountered and experienced since the first step, from the highest summit to the most persistent fly, had all come together to create a task that held immense meaning. Completing that task was a prospect too thrilling to contain.

And then there was excitement at what lay beyond the Apennines: the Alps, Europe's premier range. Startling glacial scenery, clean alpine air, a chance to revisit a few favourite corners visited before; if that weren't enough to excite a mountain vagabond then what would? Sure, winter was also drawing nearer, with discomforts greater than any I'd yet faced, but I'd learnt that discomforts only increased the rewards. The Alps and winter would likely test me in ways I hadn't yet guessed, but that was all part of the process. I now knew I'd become more than I currently was because of them.

It wasn't just the long-term future that thrilled, but the short-term future too. Not far ahead, the northern Apennines rose above the forests into a near-continuous ridge that coasted on for days on end. Along this crest, this high Crinale, were several peaks over 6,500 feet high— mountains comparable in stature to those of the Abruzzo. With luck and benign conditions I'd be able to traverse them all. Below the Crinale numerous lakes filled steep-sided cirques, each one a potential location for a memorable wilderness camp. The Crinale boasted a newly opened national park, the Parco Nazionale dell'Appennino Tosco-Emiliano; it offered the longest above-tree-line ridge in the entire Apennine chain. A fitting grand finale to the summer. My stomach knotted with anticipation as I considered it.

Before reaching the 'Grand Finale on the High Crinale' I faced one more week crossing lower mountains, stumbling on and off the easy-to-lose Grande Escursione Appenninica. The GEA weaved through cloud-smothered forests, dropped to small villages, climbed to remote passes. A succession of mountain refuges lay along the route, some only a few hours apart. These refuges were the only places where I saw other people. I met no one on the trail itself. All the other hikers appeared to make refuges their destinations, either for lunch or the night, making the shelters busy, noisy places. When rain fell hard I was tempted to sleep in them, but I doubted the crowded dormitories would be restful. Instead, I camped alone, deep in the woods that I'd grown to love. Human company after so long alone might have been beneficial, but I preferred listening to birds chatter than human beings. My evenings were peaceful. At a camp I named 'The Cathedral of Spiders' I spent long hours watching spiders enveloping my tent in elaborate designs, claiming it as part of the forest. It seemed appropriate; I felt I was part of the forest too.

Not all the refuges were inhabited and in good nick—some were rough shells, decaying back into the wild. I passed one that three cows had occupied. As I approached it a bovine face appeared at a window. The eyes that watched me pass had a snobbish, lord-of-the-manor air to them, a look that said: *what the devil are you doing on my land?* Another abandoned refuge was home to more squirrels than could be counted. I peeked in, wondering if it would make a passable home for the night, but the sight of so many squirrels racing around the walls put me off in an instant.

August 27 was a typical day of forests, fog, and refuges. I woke early, to birdsong as usual, feeling refreshed despite interrupted sleep from a string of thunderstorms that had swept through overnight. I paced uphill in fine drizzle, partially sheltered by beech woods, but was soon sweat-soaked beneath waterproofs. And yet the dampness was no hardship. The morning

'Cow refuge' along the GEA, August 26, 1997.

air was as sweet as new life, the decaying leaves underfoot a gentle path, the soft rain welcome and cleansing. Perhaps by Norway the pleasure of rain and dampness would have worn off, but it hadn't worn off yet.

My climb took me through layers of shifting mists until finally I was wrapped in fog so dense I could only see halfway up each tree. According to my map a refuge lay ahead—the Rifugio Monte Cavallo—and I considered ending the day's walk there if it were quiet. But it wasn't—it was bulging at the seams. Still, I paused inside for a few minutes, perched in front of a crackling fire, steam rising from my clothes. I was joined by two blond Californians in their early twenties, both working at the refuge for the summer. They'd just spent a week off in the Dolomites: my favourite corner of the Alps, a corner I'd reach in five weeks, all being well.

'They were soooo steep and jagged,' the Californians exclaimed, still awed. 'And these forests feel so remote. We had no idea Italy was like this.'

We chatted for a while about shattered expectations, until they had to get back to work. But before leaving they asked if I wanted a shower. An Italian who had greeted me at the door, as well as an older couple at a nearby table, had also asked the same question. I decided it was probably a good thing that I wasn't sleeping in crowded dormitory rooms.

Back in the fog I picked up a westbound trail, heading towards another refuge, Rifugio Porto Franco. Although the signposted trail number didn't match the number on my map all seemed well. Trees came and went on the fog-bound ridge. Sounds were muted. Shrouded in the murk, I felt 100 miles from civilisation, even though one refuge lay half a mile behind and another three miles ahead. The fog gave the woods a pillowy softness, and it was hard not to smile. I was walking in clouds, and it felt as though they were half supporting me. This definitely wasn't the Mezzogiorno.

But the easy travel didn't last: it never does in the Apennines. Perhaps it was carelessness on my part, perhaps I could blame it on an inaccurate map, or perhaps it was the gods of fate punishing me for showing too much pride in my journey back at the Rifugio Monte Cavallo, but whatever the reason, the following three hours were an absolute debacle.

It began when the trail I was following turned unexpectedly towards the valley. It worsened when I struck away from it directly into the forest to find myself drowning in the rain-soaked *sottobosco*, slipping and sliding on steep slopes of streaming mud. And it worsened further when I reached another trail that bore no relationship to anything on the map. For three hours I persevered, becoming as muddy, ragged and exhausted as I'd ever been. The morning's easy miles might have belonged to another life.

Relief came when a signpost loomed out of the fog. But the delight quickly passed. 'Rifugio Monte Cavallo', the sign declared, '0.25 km ahead'. How could that be? I was almost back at the refuge I'd left three hours earlier! But my compass—repeatedly checked since leaving the refuge—confirmed it: somehow I was now heading entirely the wrong way. East, not west. And so I laughed, long and loud and hard. What else was there to do? These Apennine forests clearly wanted to keep me in my place.

Happily, my second attempt to reach the Rifugio Porto Franco was more successful, and I finally arrived four hours later than originally planned. It didn't sit where my map showed it, and it wasn't 'open and unstaffed' as the Californians at Cavallo had assured me it would be, but staffed, busy and prohibitively expensive. But at least I knew where I was. More or less.

With sunlight now burning into the fog, and temperatures climbing, I set out to cover the day's final miles. A third refuge lay three hours on, according to the Porto Franco's warden; I set off towards it. The route led upwards to open ground, the first outlying stretch of the mighty Crinale. Marking the border of Tuscany and Emilia Romagna, the Crinale twisted westwards, far above tree line. Hesitantly at first, I climbed into bubbling clouds, smelling ozone in the air, feeling a rising sense of trepidation. Electrical storms weren't part of the day's official forecast, but my own tingling instincts suggested otherwise. Unable to ignore them, I set a punishing pace through the fog. I sensed great drops plunging away either side, but all I could see was rough grass and grey rock at my feet. Repeatedly checking my compass, I raced on, and was relieved to drop from the crest and reach the refuge two hours ahead of schedule. Arriving so quickly wasn't a surprise. When was route information ever accurate in this range?

This refuge was boarded up, which suited me fine. Happy to have the mountain to myself, I pitched the Peapod within sight of a small lake, swapped my stinking clothes for the dry set I kept for camp, and slowly the day's misadventures receded. After cooking and devouring my typical throw-everything-in stew I lay peacefully in the tent entrance, and stared dreamily out at rugged slopes climbing into the clouds. Rain began in earnest, and a cold wind tugged at the guylines. I chuckled with appreciation. This was weather I knew well from home. But I hoped it would clear before I reached the main Crinale.

I woke the next morning wondering if I'd dreamt the starry skies I'd marvelled at during the night. Dawn was grim and soggy. Fog still enveloped the land. A brisk wind pushed through long grass, and pine trees lower down the slope moaned and tossed. By the time I'd struck camp, my fingers were stiff from the cold, and I wore gloves for the first mile until my digits came back to life.

Leaning sideways into a strengthening gale I regained the Crinale and struggled along it for a mile, but when I reached a jumbled mess of machinery and bulldozed tracks that looked like the remnants of some awful trench war I decided that enough was enough. Fog-bound, wind-blasted, and covered in the junk of an out-of-season ski resort, the ridge wasn't a pleasant place. I'd planned to follow it a mile further to Monte Cimone, at 7,103 feet the highest peak in the northern Apennines, but all I'd see in the fog when I got there would be the radio towers and concrete buildings that cap its summit. And there'd be no joy in that. Instead, making a spur-of-the-moment decision, I plunged down a ski run, passing beneath pylons strung with long cables that whistled mournfully in the wind. The earth was littered with discarded wooden posts, splintered planks, and rusty scraps of metal; it was criss-crossed by broken snow fences, and vandalised by hard-edged ski runs—all of it a depressing sight. Hundreds of feet lower I stepped from the ruined landscape into a soulless resort. My footsteps echoed about empty apartment buildings. A solitary car drove by, a few harsh German voices cut through the fog, and a lone figure loomed from the gloom and was swiftly swallowed. Nowhere in the Apennines had been more desolate than here.

Feeling cold and dispirited, I tramped on, down a narrow forest lane transformed by fog into a dark tunnel. The lane led past a lake of unguessable size, with grey wavelets receding from a reedy bank into foggy nothingness. A lone angler sat hunkered down on the shoreline, immobile as stone. A few minutes later I came upon a shepherd, waiting with a muzzled sheepdog beside a field. Sheep drifted about on the edge of vision, bedraggled and sodden, and the shepherd turned my way.

'*Fa brutto*' ('It's ugly'), he murmured despondently, which was just about right. Even Apennine shepherds could only take so much gloom.

The lane led downwards, and finally emerged beneath the fog. After so much confinement the view brought on mild agoraphobia. A massive V-shaped valley stretched ahead, forested on its flanks, dotted with farms and small villages, dark and elemental beneath mountain-capping clouds. Stirred by the sight, I strode down the valley feeling more cheerful, the miles now passing swiftly, until I took a well-earned break in one of the valley's many hillside villages. It was a quiet place, but not completely inactive. From a vantage point on stone steps beneath an old church I took time out to watch village life. The three-act play that unfolded was more colourful than anything I would have seen back home on TV.

The first act was an old lady in black who waddled across the piazza, head bent low, mumbling religious incantations as though keeping some great evil at bay. The second act was three workmen who pulled up in a truck and set about unloading metal scaffolding. But the scaffolding wouldn't unload—it was wedged in place. Theatrical curses, arguments, and animated gesturing followed, and after ten minutes' effort the workmen suddenly and unexpectedly threw in the towel and walked off, frustrated voices fading. I believe I heard the question '*vino?*', but I may have been mistaken.

The final act appeared after a five-minute intermission. It began with the clip-clop of hooves on cobblestones, and then, from around a corner, the most powerful-looking horse I have ever seen appeared. A deep chestnut colour, rippling with muscle, the horse towered over me as it passed. But even more impressive was its rider. Perched far above the ground, riding bareback, was a boy so small the scale of horse and human seemed impossibly mismatched. The boy couldn't have been older than six, but his expression was unusually mature, like that of an adult who had seen everything of life there was to see. The boy effortlessly brought the horse to a halt beneath a building to my left, and with a summoning tone hailed a second-storey window. In a moment an old man appeared. Grey haired, heavily lined, with a hooked nose and prominent chin, the old man called back; impatiently it seemed to me, throwing his arms to the air to wave the boy away. But the boy was unmoved, and spoke again, with urgency and command. It was as though normal roles had been reversed: the boy was the adult, the old man a reluctant child. After a brief exchange the old man gave in. Whatever he was needed for he'd come. Expressionlessly, the boy turned the giant horse with a flick of his small wrists and rode from the piazza. Moments later, the old man appeared through a door, clutching a leather bag and pulling on a heavy coat, and followed in the boy's wake. I watched him depart, wondering. I felt an entire novel could have been written around the scene I'd just witnessed.

All these different lives, I thought, *all these stories*. The more I saw on The Walk the richer the world became.

From the village I set forth for the day's destination: the large ski resort of Abetone. I took small roads and tracks, travelled past fields and through forests. I walked in hot sunshine, interrupted by sudden downpours of rain. Progress was steady, but I took another break from it to stalk a lizard. The lizard was basking in sunlight upon a steaming woodpile, and after noticing many such lizards I decided the time had come for a closer look. These lizards were usually skittish, darting away at the slightest movement, so I approached with stealth. Barely moving, but inching ever closer, I managed to position my face just twelve inches away. At such close quarters I was astounded by its beauty. From a distance the lizard had appeared dull, but up close its scales were streaked with oranges, greens, and blues, the patterns arranged in complex fractals. Like a miniature dinosaur the lizard stared back inscrutably, flicking its tongue, until it grew bored and skedaddled. Smiling, I stood up. How wonderful it was to have time enough spare to examine the world's details.

Abetone, when reached, was another unattractive ski resort, at least to my eyes. Its modern buildings and multi-storey hotels didn't compare favourably with the smaller Apennine villages I'd grown to love. But it had all the amenities I needed: a well-stocked supermarket, a laundry, a bank, and a post office that provided my latest resupply parcel. I camped with well-practised discretion in the forest above town, and spent the next day working through my usual chores: cleaning and mending gear, writing trail reports, preparing food for the next week of my life. The Crinale was now directly overhead, and once upon it I didn't plan to detour from it. I wanted to finish the Apennines in style. Seven days' food should be enough, and with that in mind I went on a shopping spree, only realising I'd bought too much once I was back in camp. Buying too much was now a familiar problem, but a hard one to solve. I'd come to crave food, and often obsessed about it while walking. Resisting everything on offer in food stores was beyond my powers of self-control.

Fog remained fixed to the mountains: a permanent cloak, impenetrable and sombre. Rain still fell in sudden showers, and even midday seemed as gloomy as dusk. The camp's name—'Mirkwood'—perfectly summed up conditions. How, I wondered, would my final Apennine week go if the murk continued? I'd been told that the Alps could be seen from the Crinale, and I longed to find out if that were true. But conditions weren't promising. They'd been unsettled for a month now, growing worse as August progressed, not better. September was two days off—why should things improve? All I hoped for was one brief snatch of clarity, but it seemed unlikely. And yet, the mountain gods had granted perfection in the past, exactly when it was needed: on the Matese, on the Gran Sasso, and in the heart of the Sibillini. I'd put in an immense amount of work since then, shown great faith, persevered and stuck to the wildest path.

Would there be a reward?

GRAND FINALE ON THE HIGH CRINALE
Chapter 21

CONSCIOUSNESS ON THE morning of August 30 arrived suddenly. One moment I was lost, the next fully aware, all senses razor-sharp, details tumbling in thick and fast. The scents struck me first, piney and intoxicatingly clean; and then the temperature, unusually cold; and then the brightness, a half-forgotten thing, sunlight shimmering on tent walls. In an instant I was up, reaching through a cloud of my own breath for the tent zip, and pulled aside condensation-soaked flaps to peer outside.

What a morning I found! Sunlight streamed through the forest canopy, catching on a million droplets of water that hung like pearls on every pine needle, on every frond of bracken. Steam rose from the forest floor, spectral wisps that drifted upwards in silvery spirals. The morning looked and tasted like the first morning ever, untouched and untarnished. I celebrated while, overhead, forest songbirds celebrated with me.

I climbed from Abetone in a state of feverish excitement. For once I didn't notice the ski runs and chairlifts; all I saw were sparkling forests, and above them the Crinale, clearly defined against a deep blue sky. With minimal effort I gained 1,500 feet despite a load on my back greater than any carried all summer. In no time the forests fell away, and in their place were open slopes sweeping upwards in a great wave, decorated with gushing streams, shining pools, clumps of bilberry, and freshly washed grass. Soon, I stood upon the high crest of the Crinale, and strode along it in un-

The Alps, my future – in view from the Apennines, August 30, 1997.

bounded freedom, feeling like a lord of the Apennines, like a king of a realm that bore no connection whatsoever to the ordinary world other people trod.

Momentum carried me to 6,350-foot Alpi Tre Potenza, the first of the week's many summits. The panorama was everything I'd hoped for— and more. I stared north eagerly, and there they were, far in the distance, hanging in the sky like clouds above the great basin of the River Po, shimmering white and magically pristine: the Alps, my future. At the sight my emotions brimmed over and, once again, I screamed my elation into the mountain air. Ordinary life just never did this kind of thing.

I spent some time feasting on the views. In the opposite direction, the silver shoreline of the Ligurian Sea curled against dark land, and southwest the Alpi Apuane range—a small offshoot of the Apennines—rose into the sky. I'd barely noticed the Alpi Apuane on my map, but I noticed it now. Its mountains were steeper-sided than the mountain I sat upon, and they gleamed strangely in the sunlight, as though lit from within. As I later learnt, this was more than a trick of the light. The Alpi Apuane is famous for its high-quality marble, which has been quarried since ancient

Romans first discovered its treasures. The Pantheon in Rome began its existence there, as did Michelangelo's David. London's Marble Arch, Washington D.C.'s Peace Monument, plus numerous other monuments, palaces, cathedrals, temples, and mosques around the world feature Alpi Apuane marble. The price, of course, is mountains gutted, but I could see little of the damage from my perch, and knew nothing of the quarries. From where I sat the range was merely a dazzling backdrop, an extra bonus adding to the brilliance of the day.

And brilliant it was. In sharp light and welcome warmth I picked my way along the airy Crinale, enjoying every rise and fall, every step. Deep valleys fell away south into blue-green forests; dramatic cirques plunged north, some holding lakes that looked like mirrored doorways to another world. But it was the Alps I stared at most. In my imagination, I was already among the glacial peaks. I even heard the familiar high-pitched whistle of alpine marmots, or at least imagined I did. Marmots are ground-dwelling squirrels similar in size to beavers. They live in alpine environments around the world, and at one time had thrived in the northern Apennines, but the twin onslaught of hunters and ever-warming temperatures had wiped them from the range. Marmots can be comical to watch; they have a great capacity for play. They'd entertained me often during my Alpine and Pyrenean journeys, and the Apennines had been poorer without them. I missed them—so much, it seemed, that I was now imagining their calls. But hang on; that *was* a marmot! A sharp-pitched whistle rang out, a warning to other marmots that danger was near: hawks, eagles, or long-distance hikers. I looked around quickly, and spotted a rump of golden-brown fur disappearing into a boulder field. I was overjoyed. Marmots may well be ordinary rodents to some, but to me they'd become synonymous with the wild, and cherished because of it. A single marmot whistle can evoke everything I love about Europe's wildest mountains.

By mid-afternoon my energy was finally waning. When a small tarn, Lago Baccio, appeared below I descended to it, clambering across loose scree and acres of tussocky ground. A near-perfect lawn of short-cropped grass lay close beside the water, and no camp I'd made anywhere in the range was finer than the 'Marmot Mountain' camp. Tent pitched, dinner consumed, I rested with my back against a boulder, basking in late-afternoon sunshine, surveying the wild haunt. Monte Giovo's east face towered overhead, alpine swifts soared above its screes, and marmot calls echoed about the crags. Marmot fur was once prized for its insulating properties and softness, and marmot fat supposedly contains a natural cortisone and has been used for centuries as a remedy for rheumatism. For me their value didn't lie in what they could be used for but in their presence alone. In 1954, foresters on Monte Cimone must have felt the same. They reintroduced the species to Cimone's slopes, and the species thrived—and spread. As with Abruzzo chamois and Apennine wolves it was another rewilding success story, a claiming back of the land, a turning of the tide. For the next week marmots were constant companions. I listened to them, watched them, dined and breakfasted with them. For bringing back marmots, Monte Cimone's foresters have my eternal thanks.

An hour before sunset I returned to the Crinale and lingered atop 6,440-foot Monte Rondinaio, munching on an apple while the western sky glowed. Evening haze now hid the Alps, but alpenglow striking the Apennines was ample compensation. Legend has it that Rondinaio's summit is haunted by witches and ghosts at sunset, but no place I'd visited all summer was less haunted than this. Later, in near darkness, I carried the absolute peace of the Crinale back to my tent, and on into my dreams.

Evening light on Monte Giovo, seen from Monte Rondinaio, August 30, 1997.

The following week was arguably the finest of the summer. The Crinale wasn't quite the unbroken crest I'd expected, but the short breaks from it only added to the pleasure. The lakes I swam in below the ridge were rejuvenating, the beech woods were familiar and cooling, and the wild raspberries now ripening made a sweet supplement to my rations. Every location whether high or low was now a location to savour. I was nearly done with the Apennines, and I'd miss every part of it.

Monte Giovo, Monte Prado, Monte Alto, Alpe di Succiso, Monte Osaro, Monte Marmagna; I traversed the summits along the ridge one by one. Up down, up down; peak col, peak col; my aerial skyway led onwards. On my right the land plunged north towards the Po Valley and Italy's industrial heartland; on my left it was south into the rustic Tuscan hills, the land of *La Dolce Vita*. No other ridge I'd ever walked had felt more like a natural border than the Crinale. Progress was straightforward, but never fast. The Crinale was often rough underfoot, several exposed sections required a steady head for heights, and the narrowest stretch presented borderline climbing, but I welcomed these obstacles. They were play, not problem. Physically, the week should have been draining, and I did finish each night feeling spent, but progress was so absorbing that I barely noticed the effort. My body, trained on all that had gone before, responded with strength and vigour I didn't recognise. In my eyes I was still a 140-pound wimp, but the months had strengthened me. On the Crinale I was healthier, happier, and freer than I had ever been in my life.

I spent each night camped in glorious solitude, increasingly connect-ed to the land. The more time I spent upon it without interruption the more immersed I became. There *were* other people about—a smattering of tourists at passes where roads crossed the range, a shepherd astride a dirt bike watching his sheep, a few walkers on summits, a lone blueberry picker—but conversations stretched no farther than '*Buon giorno*' and they didn't disrupt the flow. A string of small refuges sat below the ridge, often near lakes I might otherwise have slept beside, but I avoided them. Refuges were permanent structures—intrusive to my eyes and the opposite of all I sought. By avoiding them I turned the Crinale into the wildest stretch of the summer, and it lifted me to another level of existence. And yet I knew

A spectacular perch along a narrow section of the Crinale, September 2, 1997.

it paled in comparison with the scale and remoteness I'd find in Norway. If I felt this liberated from ordinary life here, experienced this sense of belonging, what effect would Norway have? I couldn't imagine, but loved knowing that I'd one day find out.

From ridge in the sky to emerald lake to sun-dappled wood I roamed. Even a break in the weather on days five and six didn't dampen my spirits. Increasing heat and haze became rolling thunder, rain, mist, and then drizzle, but so what? I'd received clear passage where I'd wanted it, and if it rained non-stop for the next two months I would still have counted myself fortunate.

The week became the summer's highlight, but two moments still stood out. The first occurred on the second morning, on the 6,528-foot summit of Monte Giovo. The day before had given extraordinary views, but on Giovo I summited earlier into air that was colder and sharper, and the view stretched so far it was, quite frankly, absurd.

Using my compass and my small-scale map of Italy I identified all the prominent mountains in view. South-west, back down the Apennines, was Monte Catria, 120 miles distant. South-east, across the Ligurian Sea, rising sharply into the Mediterranean sky, were the mountains of Corsica, an impressive 150 miles away. And due north were the Alps, shining white above the industrial murk of the Po Valley. The soaring Adamello group was 140 miles away, the glaciated ice kingdom of Piz Bernina 20 miles further than that, and most distant of all, etched in white against the horizon, was the Rheinwaldhorn—the source of the River Rhine—an astounding 180 miles from where I stood.

It was quite a thing, seeing so far. A panorama 300 miles wide. It delayed progress for some time.

The second highlight came at the final summit, Monte Marmagna. Determined to make the most of my final Apennine mountain, I decided to sleep on top. Not only would this be the last Apennine summit but also the range's last wild camp—definitely a bittersweet occasion.

I'd already tried one summit bivvy. Four days earlier I'd stopped late in the afternoon on 6,739-foot Monte Prado, intending to spend the night, but the peak was home to thousands of ant-like flies, and within seconds they were everywhere: on my clothes, arms, legs; in my hair; swarming over my backpack. Fighting back revulsion I had brushed them away and moved hastily on.

Monte Marmagna, fortunately, was unsullied by such beasts. I picked a flat spot below jumbled summit rocks, unpacked Ten Ton, but did not pitch the Peapod. I'd been longing to sleep beneath the stars for months, but conditions—mosquitoes mostly—hadn't allowed it. But September was four days old now and the season for *zanzare* was passing. At 6,073 feet, Marmagna's highest point was too high, dry, and breezy for them; at last my opportunity had come. As I ate dinner my only companion was a plump marmot, peeking bashfully from behind a rock. He looked confused. Most two-legged visitors came during the hottest and brightest hours of day. What was this one doing, sitting motionless with the sun so low in the sky?

The weather had cleared again, another gift from the gods. Although a thick haze remained, conditions seemed benign. A great sense of ease washed through me as I stretched out, but as dusk approached tension suddenly grew. Clouds began forming, curling over my summit, and I sensed the air grow heavy and oppressive. Suddenly, I felt a strong desire to be elsewhere, and I didn't argue with it. This wasn't irrational fear. I knew enough now to trust my instincts—they'd become tuned in. Throwing my gear into the pack, I vacated the summit at considerable speed, and made a new home in a protected hollow 600 feet lower. In my diary I jokingly labelled it 'Coward's Camp', but vindication came at midnight when rain pummelled the Peapod and lightning flashed across the mountain.

That, of course, wasn't the highlight. The highlight came at dawn.

Silence woke me at four. Peering from the tent I looked up into a dazzling arc of stars, and knew I couldn't waste the next few hours asleep. Some moments only occur once, some moments are *key*, and the trick is recognising them for what they are. With controlled haste I struck camp and retraced my steps to Marmagna's summit, then set up a comfortable bivvy at the highest point. Sleep was still a possibility, but I didn't consider it. Sleep would have been a crime.

And so I sat on my last Apennine summit, wrapped in my sleeping bag, pushing aside the urge to take photos, to move from vantage point to vantage point, to be active, to 'do'. It's not easy to dedicate a special time to stillness, or to keep at it when confronted by the demands of everything we think there is to be done. Deliberate stillness had been an exceedingly rare thing back in London. Even on The Walk I'd spent less time in stillness than perhaps I should have. There were often distractions: chores to work on, books to read, reports to write, photographs to take, food to prepare, maps to examine, progress to make. But taking time out to just sit and become fully open is essential if a place isn't to pass by unseen and unfelt, and although I had done it every day to some degree, most often at day's end, on Marmagna I saw that I hadn't done it nearly enough. And so I sat still, and pushed from my mind all I'd been through, and banished all that was still to come, and slowly the pulsating magic of pre-dawn in the mountains spilled into my being and took control.

Time slowed, and everything around me changed as though a mask had been lifted. The rocks I sat among were soon more than mere rocks; they became curiously familiar and welcoming. Next, the brittle night-time silence softened, and from within it I heard a gentle breeze whispering across the summit, carrying stories from far below of water rushing, of creatures stirring, of birds calling. And the great space stretching before me changed. It pulled me into it until it no longer seemed like a great space but like a part of me, and me a part of it. And Marmagna was transformed from a static peak into a feature as impermanent as an ocean wave, existing

—like each of us—for just a fleeting snatch of time. As I lay there I sensed the great mass of rock beneath me, and the colossal forces still pushing it up, but also sensed the unstoppable elements that were tearing it back down. As the first streak of orange flashed across the horizon, and as the stars wheeled overhead, I clearly witnessed the spinning of the planet. In stillness I saw motion, and in that motion bathed in stillness.

Dawn came as slowly as only dawn can when it is watched for. But its arrival was inevitable, and soon the Crinale was washed in rich morning light. And that was when the time for stillness ended; the photographer within could no longer be suppressed, and he dashed about trying to capture the sight and emotions and sheer beauty of the morning. And what is photography anyway but just another way of connecting with the world?

Soon it was a new day—bright sun, blue sky, high mountains—and time to move on. But still I lingered. In the end I didn't leave until morning was nearly afternoon. When the time finally arrived the elation remained, but reluctance and longing dampened it. I belonged here now, but when would I return? Would I ever? To the west the Apennines continued towards their final foothills above the Mediterranean, offering perhaps another week's walking, but my path lay north. Dragging my heels, I scrambled from the summit, into the woods, and for a while felt overcome by loss.

The two-day walk out from the range led through a series of 'Apennine lasts'. Last beech wood; last unplanned excursion into the *sottobosco*; last camp; last village; last set of inaccurate directions from a local; last '*Dove vai?*'; last Maremmano sheepdog; last Terror Fly. As the altitude decreased temperatures rose from cool and autumnal to searing and summer-like. Too quickly the ground levelled off and the Apennines fell behind, and from down here on the edge of the hundred-mile-wide Po Valley the mighty mountain range that had been my home for the entire summer looked small and insignificant; barely even hill country, a land with little character, not worth bothering with at all.

But I was glad I'd bothered.

Fulfilment on the Crinale, September 1, 1997.

ACROSS THE FLATS
Chapter 22

THE VAL PADANA—the great valley of the River Po—was a flat place, a straight lines place. The horizon was flat, the roads straight, the landscape divided into hard-edged, squared-off fields. Humankind dominated down here: nature fitted in with us, not we with it. Water ran where we desired, along irrigation ditches to fields covered in plants that we had chosen. Trees didn't grow in forests but in isolation, where we wanted them: as barriers, in orchards, or as mere decoration. And aside from people in fume-spewing machines the only mammals moving were commodities—slaves destined to be milked, sheared, ridden upon, and slaughtered. The Val Padana confirmed what I already knew: that I preferred untrammelled places, landscapes filled with life and freedom. And it reminded me, once again, that I loathed walking on roads.

Oh yes, how I loathed roads. How I loathed their hard surface, and how limiting they were, how repetitious, how unnatural. Tougher long-distance walkers have spent entire journeys following roads. Continents have been crossed via them. But I would have failed. Pain and boredom would have defeated me. I needed contact with the earth; I needed to follow a natural line of my own choosing with forgiving surfaces beneath my feet: sand, rocks, soil, leaves, grass. But here I was, back on roads, my soles already tender after the first five miles, my left ankle and knee throbbing as they had in the far south. Heavy mountain boots, searing heat, and unyielding pavement were never meant to go together. I'd guessed the Val Padana crossing was going to hurt, but I hadn't guessed how much.

And it wasn't just the road but the heat too: goodness was it hot down here! The sun hung high overhead, white and burning. When I crumpled into shade to rest, the little keyring thermometer I carried read ninety-four Fahrenheit, thirty-three Celsius, although the actual temperature may have been higher. A large electronic thermometer fixed prominently to a wall on the edge of one town displayed thirty-eight Celsius, over a hundred Fahrenheit; hotter than the Mezzogiorno. Not that mere numbers meant anything. What counted was how it felt, and after the gentle breezes and finger-nipping dawns of the Crinale, the polluted, humid Val Padana felt like the inside of an oven.

But the Val Padana had to be crossed—the Alps lay beyond it. And so did Base Camp. My parents were due in Italy in five days. They'd booked two hotel rooms in Torbole, a village on Lago Garda's northern shore. There was a room for them, a room for me. The plan was to take a full week off to relax, feast, laugh. Seven days with a soft bed, restaurant food, a swimming pool, company, and parental love. After all I'd been through it was quite the incentive to progress. I didn't want to miss even an hour of it.

But the heat tried to slow me.

I walked in spurts, stopping often. Two hours at a time were all I could manage before shade and rest became essential. Mile by mile, hour by hour, my feet grew worse. Despite fierce attempts at preventative bandaging my heels and soles developed blisters, the first since Calabria. I punctured them with the needle I kept for such a task. I drained, disinfected, and dressed them, but the blisters returned—and worsened. Initially, for the first few hours each day, the discomfort was just about manageable, and I found some pleasure in the land. The landscape may have been straight edged and cultivated but it wasn't entirely without charm. It was still an *Italian* landscape, still somehow romantic; and there was some wildness left, surviving in the margins. Fierce-looking dragonflies droned above irrigation canals; butterflies floated like a magical confetti through rare undisturbed strips of land where wildflowers still found footing; unshackled birds filled the air with song; magnificent herons perched motionless on reedy banks watching for frogs and rodents, their stabbing sword-beaks ready for the killing plunge. But my interest in the wild margins faded as each morning

'Where did the mountains go?' Unpleasant road walking
in the Val Padana, September 10, 1997.

progressed, as discomfort morphed into genuine pain, and soon I noticed little, and thought only of when next I could stop. Breaks from walking brought great relief, but it was always only temporary. I'd pull off boots, unpeel socks, splash a little water from my bottle over my burning feet, and rest—but when I began again my raw feet protested all the more at the shock of it, and until numbness returned the first few hundred yards were not pleasant.

I crossed the Val Padana in four days, twenty-five miles at a time. The first night was spent in Parma, a vibrant, throbbing city that deserved more attention than I was able to give it. A campground sat in the heart of the city in the Cittadella: a pentagonal-shaped park contained within the walls of a sixteenth-century fortress. At dusk the park came alive with humanity, with the fabled *passeggiata*, the evening promenade—a nightly event common across Italy where locals take to the streets en masse to walk, talk, and be seen. Amorous young couples, playful families, arm-in-arm seniors, boisterous youths; the *passeggiata* was in full swing. Sports venues lined one edge of the park, and on a basketball court I saw an energetic game in motion. Muscular players twisted, passed, and shot with incredible skill, the movement of fit bodies in the floodlit night like a choreographed dance on a stage. It was a thing of beauty and artistry, improved further by the voyeuristic pleasure of seeing people other than myself working up a hard sweat.

I spent the second night in Guastella, a smaller town of old buildings and bicycle-filled streets. My destination had been the youth hostel, but it was closed, and I finished up in a sauna-hot room in a crumbling hotel that cost three times the amount I'd planned to spend. To save money I cooked dinner in the room on my camp stove, but the heat from it made the space barely habitable. I awoke from a fitful sleep the following morning with a splitting headache; I was in pain now at both ends of my body.

I crossed the mighty River Po early on the third morning, and stared down at its swirling waters with respect. The Po drains a huge catchment area, 27,000 square miles; tributaries pour into it from half the Alps. Although it's no Nile or Amazon it *is* a powerful force, and when it bursts its banks the cost to humans can be high. Just three years earlier, in 1994, a November deluge in the Maritime and Cottian Alps had delivered over half a year's rainfall in just four days, and once the super-saturated ground could soak up no more water the runoff had cascaded into the Po, filling it to the brim, and then bursting over its banks. Before the flood waters had subsided—which in some places took three months—10,000 people had lost their homes and 70 their lives. The storm hadn't just been a distant news story for me; I'd lived right through it. I'd been a week from the end of my six-month trek across the Alps, and had found myself directly beneath the cloudburst. Hammered by the maelstrom for four wild days I'd stayed put on high ground, watching as tiny mountain streams became raging torrents choked with mud, listening to giant rocks thundering downhill beneath the waters, discovering later the washed-away roads and bridges that bore testament to the storm's fury. It had been a stark and unforgettable reminder that nature could do what it wished.

On the third night I reached Mantova, and entered the city in a bad way, hobbling on pulverized feet, stained with salt, weary to the bone. My map showed two affordable options for the night: a campground and a youth hostel, but I was told that both had been closed for five years. Too far gone to care, I found another hotel that would have seemed cheap to most people but was distressingly expensive to me, and spent the first half-hour of my stay in the shower. I set the water to cold and willingly embraced the shock of it. For a while the endless miles, and all the sweat and pain, receded from mind.

By dusk I was back on the streets seeking dinner, not wanting a repeat of the night before. I walked gingerly, an old man in all but age, and chance led me to Mantova's *centro historica*: a warren of cobbled lanes, piazzas, medieval buildings, and Renaissance palaces. It was a fascinating, beautiful place, and if my body could have stood it I would have explored all night. Instead, I slumped in one spot—at a pizzeria tucked into one corner of an ornate square—and feasted hungrily at an outside table, although it's hard to say what I enjoyed more: the pizza, the thick and frothy Lambrusco wine, the surrounding architecture, or the *passeggiata*. Mantova's citizens were out in force once again: young, old, friends, families; all strolling by. An atmosphere of casual joy accompanied the pedestrians, as though the parade were a special one-off celebration, not a regular nightly routine. I envied the citizens their sense of ease; I envied them their pain-free steps; and I envied them the companionship they all shared. The waiter serving me was my only companion, and we only had one short conversation, although it was memorable. Upon learning I was English he commiserated with me over Princess Diana's recent tragic death, stepping back in surprise when he discovered I hadn't even known. She'd died nine days earlier.

'But you must be the last person in Europe to find out!' he exclaimed. 'Where have you been?'

I was too tired to explain.

The final day in the Val Padana was one I'll never forget. As the hours passed the pain in my heels and soles grew, soon surpassing any pain I'd previously felt. That it was entirely self-inflicted didn't help; that I could have eased it by taking more days to cross the Val Padana taunted me; that potential car and bus rides passed by every few minutes only increased the torture. Hard questions arose. What was I doing here, away from the mountains? Why this path of loneliness? Why was I punishing my body, enduring such physical anguish, behaving with such unreasonable masochism? I was on

*Leaving Mantova on the morning of September 10, 1997,
sensing the anguish that lay ahead.*

the journey to connect with the natural world—a mild goal—not test my endurance or cleanse my spirit through self-flagellation, nor purge myself of some past trauma or sin that could no longer be borne. Until falling down the Hohtürli Pass my life had been as trauma free as any life could ever be, and even Hohtürli was nothing compared with the trials many of the world's citizens face on a daily basis. Was there guilt in that, perhaps? Guilt for resenting my comfortable life in Pinner? Guilt that I'd dared compare The Walk's hardest moments with homelessness? Was I punishing myself now for having it so easy for so long? Was I trying to prove something I wasn't even aware of? Were there unguessed-at insecurities so deeply buried that the only way I could overcome them was to drive myself mercilessly along a hard Italian road beneath a ridiculously huge backpack and a burning Mediterranean sun? I doubted it, but still, here I undeniably was, and the miles *were* punishing, and there was *something* within that stopped me from easing up. I walked in immense pain, toiling at my absolute limit; but instead of behaving rationally and slowing down I fought back with rising madness, with a grim I-will-not-succumb stubbornness, with a determination to overcome. The fire in my feet, the fatigue, the raging thirst, the more reasonable inner voice that cried *enough!*—none of these would triumph.

The task became all-consuming and the questions faded, blurred by effort and pain, perhaps to be answered another day. Soon, my thoughts were simpler. They became mere reactions to stimuli, reduced but focused. I didn't look ahead beyond each of the many breaks I took, and I noticed little of the landscape. There was a concentrated *nowness* to the miles that ought to have given delight—delight that I was once again living in the moment—but I was numb even to that. At the start, on a busy main road leading from Mantova, I walked in fear for my life as huge lorries thundered by inches from my side. To escape, I attempted a cross-country shortcut, but obstacles hindered progress: leg-wearying fields of ploughed earth and cloying mud; hard-to-cross irrigation channels; barbed fences; legions of mosquitoes that revealed even the Po Valley could be truly wild. Defeated by the human-arranged landscape, I retreated to pavement and found smaller roads that carried less traffic, but they weren't any softer or cooler underfoot. Long, straight, and unshaded, the pavement led north. Each step pushed white-hot daggers into my soles and heels. The day's heat, debilitating as it was, now paled in comparison to the burning heat underfoot. The fiercest fire came from a huge blood-red blister that had formed beneath the ball of my right foot, and to avoid pressure on it I walked with my foot angled sideways, using the outside edge; in no time a blister formed there too. Without the breaks, now hourly, and lasting longer each time, I would have ground to a halt. But even during them the pain didn't significantly lessen.

Time and miles passed with agonising slowness. The day stretched into infinity. I took each step slowly and deliberately, one by one, hobbling from village to village, from fountain to fountain. Each step was a curse, an agony of unwanted sensation. Desperation reared. Failure began to seem attractive. I tried escaping into fantasy, imagining reunions with friends, things I'd say, stories I'd share. I imagined having unlimited funds, and no stammer, and even a girlfriend—something that truly was a fantasy. But pain always triumphed, bringing me back to earth. By early afternoon I'd sunk so low I was yelling aloud at myself, swearing my head off, bullying myself onwards to the next pit stop, the next heavenly moment when I could collapse into shade and air my butchered feet. I became a swearing, ranting, sweat-drenched, limping madman beside the road, oblivious to the world around me, lost within my own ridiculous self-created purgatory.

Frame by slow-moving frame, late afternoon became early evening, and the final miles were the worst. When the blood blister burst without warning I almost fainted from the gunshot intensity of it. But by that point I'd come too far to give in. Snail-paced, I came upon the rushing Mincio River, the outlet for Lake Garda, and at the sight of its cool waters I felt emotions rising that so nearly had me adding tears of relief to the river before me. Barely daring to believe that the pain might finally end I pushed on, and the surrounding world came back into focus. I noticed well-cared-for holiday villas, tall cypress trees in tidy rows, a hauntingly romantic sun sinking into an orange sky, and the masts of yachts. *Yachts?* I stopped, did the classic double take. The yachts were too large for a river, which meant… I was almost done! I screamed with relief, the loudest scream of the journey so far. It only took one more minute of effort, and there suddenly it was, wide at this southern edge, fjord-like in the hazy distance where it cut into the Alps, Lake Garda, my destination, the true end to the journey's first stage, and my salvation from torment.

The emotions that overcame me were unlike any I'd experienced before, more powerful even than those felt beneath the Hohtürli Pass. I'd pushed myself to the edge while crossing the Val Padana, and now I plunged over it, into joy, laughter, and tears. In the midst of the outburst I discovered answers to all the questions I'd earlier asked, but they were answers that words can't truly express because such words don't exist. The answers were things now *known*; realities now *understood*; truths now *felt*. For all I'd unreasonably endured—not just over the past four days, but elsewhere since the journey's first step—for all I'd put myself through, for all I'd worked so hard for, I now reaped the reward. And it had nothing to do with silly notions about mountain gods granting rewards, everything to do with real experience, everything to do with interest now received on massive deposits made. I'd pushed far beyond comfort, had created a task of immense meaning, and the reward for completing the task was a crescendo of achievement and fulfilment that surpassed measure.

I camped that night near Peschiera Lago Garda, sharing an official site with late-season vacationers. The site had its own restaurant, sparing me the immense effort of having to cook, and I hydrated and feasted like a starved wolf, for once uncaring of the expense. A boisterous gang of Italian youths sat with me, a TV before all of us, and on it an international football match played live, my own nation jousting with tiny Moldova. England won with ease, and my Italian companions couldn't understand why I didn't jump up to celebrate each of England's four goals. 'Where is this legendary English passion for football?' they teased.

I'll never forget their reaction when I pulled off my boots and showed them my feet, evidence of *my passion*.

The next morning I caught a bus to Torbole at Lake Garda's northern end, and the reunion with Base Camp was a fitting climax to the Apennine stage of The Walk. My parents were waiting outside the Hotel Dolce Riposo, sitting in café chairs and sipping tea, and the second I saw them they jumped up, instant smiles lighting their faces. My mother practically screamed.

'There he is! He made it! Andrew!'

Arms wide, I hurried towards them, my fiery soles temporarily forgotten. Ten Ton's bulk thwarted our first hug, but I quickly jettisoned the load—a symbolic act, like throwing off The Walk itself—and the hug that followed took me straight back to childhood, to having a home, to comfort and security, to the reassurance of knowing I was no longer alone. For four and a half months I'd met only strangers. I'd gone without friends and family, without the kind of deep connection that's only possible with people one has known for years, and I'd never fully noticed how hard the going without was—until now. My eyes moistened even while the three of us laughed.

'Mum, Dad! It's *so* good to see you. Seems like thousands of miles! You look… wonderful, amazing.'

We stepped back and held each other at arm's length, sizing one another up.

'You don't look so bad yourself,' my father said, smiling. I noticed that his eyes were moist too, and perhaps it was wishful thinking, but I thought

I detected a hint of pride.

'You made it!' My mother squealed again. 'All those miles. Well done you!'

'If you *are* my son,' my father joked. 'That's quite a tan you've got there.'

'But you look well,' my mother quickly added. 'Lean, though. We'll have to fatten you up.'

I jumped on that. 'Oooh—yes please! Let's get right to it.'

'An early lunch, then? We've so many questions… but they can wait.'

Swept away by the love I'd deliberately left behind 1,600 miles earlier, I swung Ten Ton onto my back as though it weighed nothing, and let Base Camp shepherd me into the hotel. For a fleeting moment, Mad Mountain Jack rebelled at letting others choose the path, but I brushed his protest aside. Meekly, I followed my parents into shade and comfort, and left Mad Mountain Jack behind, standing alone beneath the harsh Italian sun.

Arrival at Lake Garda, late on September 10, 1997.

PART III
THE ALPS

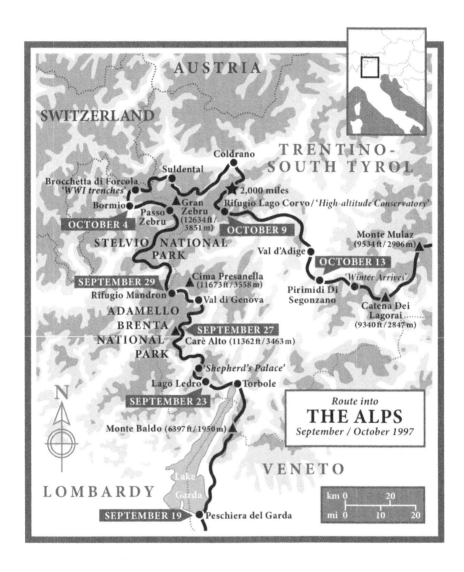

AUSTRIA

SWITZERLAND

TRENTINO-
SOUTH TYROL

Coldrano

Suldental

Brocchetta di Forcola
'WWI trenches'

★ 2,000 miles

Bormio

Gran
Zebru
(12634 ft /
3851 m)

Rifugio Lago Corvo/'High-altitude Conservatory'

Passo
Zebru

OCTOBER 4

OCTOBER 9

STELVIO NATIONAL
PARK

Val d'Adige

Monte Mulaz
(9534 ft/2906 m)

OCTOBER 13

'Winter Arrives'

SEPTEMBER 29

Cima Presanella
(11673 ft/3558 m)

Pirimidi Di
Segonzano

Rifugio Mandron

Val di Genova

Catena Dei
Lagorai
(9340 ft/2847 m)

ADAMELLO
BRENTA
NATIONAL
PARK

SEPTEMBER 27

Carè Alto (11362 ft/3463 m)

'Shepherd's Palace'

Lago Ledro

Torbole

N

SEPTEMBER 23

Route into
THE ALPS
September / October 1997

Monte Baldo (6397 ft/1950 m)

VENETO

LOMBARDY

Lake
Garda

km 0   20
mi 0   10   20

SEPTEMBER 19

Peschiera del Garda

242

A SHORT WALK ON ICE
Chapter 1

THE FIRST PALE glimmer of dawn streaked the horizon when I stopped to pull on crampons. Reassured, I paused on the glacier's edge, sitting on granite slabs that still bore scratches from aeons of glacial scouring. A moment's work had crampon straps threaded; ten sharp spikes now adorned each boot, hard metal claws ready for action.

In trepidation, I stepped off solid rock onto a remnant of the Ice Age, conscious that glaciers are not good places for solitary unroped travel. Although a shadow of the glacier it once was, and insignificant compared to mightier glaciers elsewhere in the Alps, the Vedretta di Lares was nonetheless a thrilling place, utterly unlike any environment I'd visited in the Apennines. Glowing faintly in predawn light, the ice river plunged dramatically into hidden depths to the east. To the west it swelled upwards across the broad upper flanks of Carè Alto before cresting like a breaking wave below the mountain's summit. Carè Alto was the first glacial peak I'd reached, and I longed to stand on its summit, but now—with ice underfoot, and who knew what gaping holes under that—I found myself re-evaluating that longing.

Was walking alone up a glacier *really* the right thing to do?

The glacier had looked safely dry from across the valley, free from fresh snow that might hide crevasses. But now that I was upon it I discovered an ambiguous surface, neither bare ice nor old snow. Frost crystals six inches

Looking ahead to Carè Alto, September 26, 1997.

deep coated the glacier, hiding whatever lay beneath, and when I stepped onto them they shattered and splintered like fragile glass, giving way until I found solid footing. The slope directly ahead lacked any suggestive hollows, cracks, or obvious signs that crevasses might lie hidden, but glaciers often hide their secrets well. Mountaineers are always falling into crevasses. Usually it's a sudden and unwelcome surprise.

Tense, but relishing the tension, I moved on. The frisson of adventure, of being on the edge, far removed from help should I need it, was why I was here. Detractors say there is no wilderness left in the Alps. How can there be, they ask, when the Alps have been inhabited for thousands of years, when they have been built upon, civilised, overdeveloped, overrun? It's a valid question, but the answer becomes clear when you step alone onto glacial ice and know with every instinct you possess that you are far beyond civilisation's reach.

This truly was a natural environment where I didn't belong. But, for once, not belonging didn't upset me. This frozen realm could never be home, and it had nothing to do with nurture, everything to do with nature itself.

Unlike a forest, there was nothing here that could sustain or shelter life. It was genuinely inhospitable, genuinely dangerous, and it could only ever be an environment to visit. Unlike the fear felt beneath the Monti della Laga, and far back in the Aspromonte, the fear here didn't feel misplaced. Instead, it seemed justified, even beneficial. The Vedretta di Lares put me firmly in my place, and the personal diminishment—the removal of delusions of my own importance—was curiously and inexplicably empowering.

Tingling with emotion, I paused halfway up the glacier. East now, a rose hue lit the sky, and beneath it ridge after ridge stretched into the distance. From here at 10,000 feet the Alps looked immense, a jumbled mass of soaring rock. It was strangely easy to picture the range's formation, to imagine geological time condensed into mere seconds, as a fragment of the African tectonic plate rammed into the Eurasian plate, as solid rock clashed and buckled, as older rocks were folded over newer rocks, as sedimentary rocks tangled with metamorphic and then igneous, as mighty mountains grew, fell to erosion, grew again. Like the Apennines, the bedrock of the Alps is still rising, an inch or so every twenty-five years—although weathering balances this rise. But, unlike the limestone Apennines, the Alps aren't made from one dominant rock type. What you get here is a complex muddle, a testament to the unceasing powers that churn beneath the earth's ever-shifting crust. The sheer scale of uplifted land in the Alps keeps those incredible forces constantly in mind. To me, Carè Alto wasn't just striking scenery, or a challenging destination to aspire to, but a perfect expression of natural forces beyond our species' control. These forces stirred my emotions, kindling humility and awe, fear and excitement, gratitude and appreciation. There was great power here. It made this place feel as wild as any on Earth.

Alive with every sense, attention razor sharp, I pushed on, considering each step, well aware that the icy crust I was crossing could easily be eggshell-thin, that cavernous voids could lurk directly beneath. Just ahead, horizontal crevasses ran across the glacier's surface, and an icefall hung where an arm of the glacier reached into a side valley. There, unstable seracs loomed ready to fall, and crevasses gaped open; jagged-edged cracks filled with unknowable black depths. My route—a simple dotted line on the map, a cartographer's suggested path—avoided the crevasses and icefall and still looked possible, but my doubts increased.

Sunrise arrived shortly after seven, two hours later than it had back on Serra Dolcedorme in Calabria, revealing how far I—and the year—had travelled. October would be here in only four days, and although summer still reigned it wouldn't be long before the seasons shifted. Once snow buried the Alps the summits would lie beyond my reach, cut off by the avalanche risk—and the journey itself would alter beyond recognition; become slower, colder, harder. Each day of sunshine and warmth was a bonus, an opportunity too good to waste. Half a year earlier, back in my previous life in distant London, sunrises had regularly passed unseen, but now each new day's arrival was an event fully noticed and celebrated. How could I take any of this for granted?

As the sun climbed above the horizon intense pink light spilled across the glacier, transforming my world as completely as winter soon would. Before sunrise, the glacier had been cold and ominous, its massive weight palpable; now, that pressing heaviness was temporarily masked. The glacier glowed like a landscape in an impossible dream. For a while I faced the sun, aware of nothing but the moment. Although the sun lit this spot every morning, it was still a miracle to me. It was an extraordinary kind of ordinary, and the entire population of Europe would be standing here if only they knew.

Carè Alto's 11,362-foot summit was now fully revealed, and I immediately realised that I wouldn't be standing upon it. The wide north face I'd been aiming for had looked easily climbable on the map, but the reality was far steeper, and the band of dark ice stretched across it was clearly iron-hard. Crampons would struggle to bite; a slip would be near impossible to arrest. Wavering, still unable to decide whether to proceed, the decision was made for me when the glacier underfoot suddenly shifted. It dropped just a fraction, and from somewhere below a resonating CRACK rumbled dully. Instinct moved me from the spot in an instant, and without further hesitation I began back down the glacier, stepping with great precision in the marks I'd left on the way up. But there was no regret.

Camp lay far below in the haunts of the living. As always, the return to that softer place from the glacial heights felt akin to rebirth. Greens seemed stronger, flowers brighter, birdsong sweeter, the living earth beneath my feet softer. The Alps offer opposing environments side by side: meadows and forests filled with life directly beside harsh rivers of ice. The dramatic

246

juxtaposition is what makes these mountains special. To not walk upon glaciers would be to miss the best of the Alps. One wouldn't just miss their thrilling Ice Age wildness but also the altered perspective they give. The contrast reveals the truth of the range.

Back at my tent I ate a second breakfast, taking my time, completely at ease in my aloneness, lulled by the wildness around. From a boulder field above camp marmots called. From the south a soothing breeze blew and set meadow grass swaying. Away across the deep Val Rendena the castle-like walls of the Brenta Dolomites gleamed in the sun. A full lifetime spent savouring this one spot would have been too short a time, but other landscapes still lay ahead, and I thrilled at the prospect of visiting them. One thing was now clear: this was no longer the same walk. Everything had changed since leaving Lake Garda: not just the landscape—the sights, scents, and sounds—but the entire character of the journey. Its very personality. The Apennines might have belonged to another life.

Dawn on the Vedretta di Lares glacier, Carè Alto, September 27, 1997.

STEPPING BACK IN TIME
Chapter 2

EIGHT DAYS EARLIER I was in Torbole, relaxing alongside Base Camp, lounging on a padded recliner beside a hotel swimming pool. The only ice in sight was clinking in my glass.

'Well, this is the life,' my mother said, looking up from her book. 'I bet you'll miss this next week.'

'True, it's not so bad.' I agreed. 'I could've done with a few moments like this in the Mezzogiorno!'

But I didn't think I'd miss it. Not the comforts, at least.

For seven days The Walk had been on hold; not forgotten by any means, but distant, someone else's journey. The time off had been needed. A wonderful excess of sleep, food and rest had mended the physical damage inflicted by the searing Val Padana, and the companionship had fulfilled emotional needs I hadn't even been aware of. The togetherness, the talk, the laughter, and the love—it had all been an absolute balm, far more pleasurable than I'd expected. Perhaps I should have been troubled, that someone soon to be alone for an entire winter was enjoying company so much, but being troubled didn't cross my mind—I was having too much fun.

'It's been an amazing week,' I said, really meaning it. 'I'll miss you, for sure. But I have to be honest... I'm ready to get going again. Back to my mountain life.'

In truth, after so much rest, I was more than ready. A week in one place after 1,600 miles of travel had felt strangely unsettling—almost unnatural. My feet and spirit yearned for action, and I even yearned for discomfort again, for how it touched all the senses, for how it made me feel more alive. Not that I could admit *that* to my father.

He looked at me, peering over his newspaper. 'Back to your mountain life? I still think you're mad. But you know that!'

I did know. For a week I'd been sharing my best stories from The Walk, hoping they'd convince him that what I was doing made sense. That it had value. But he remained unconvinced. I still couldn't manage a simple explanation—the words wouldn't come. Everything experienced and learnt couldn't fit into a tidy bundle.

'Perhaps I am mad,' I said, as always taking the easy option: joking, not attempting a serious debate. 'Or perhaps I'm the only sane one, and my sanity merely looks like madness to the insane?'

My father laughed, and shook his head. 'How likely is that—that you understand something everyone else has missed? No, you're mad… and I think you're living in cloud cuckoo land! But we're used to it, and don't worry, we'll keep on doing everything we can to help.'

I knew they would, and I was grateful beyond words. Having parents willing to support an endeavour they didn't understand, or approve of, was a rare thing. Without Base Camp, there would be no resupply parcels, there'd be fewer sponsors, fundraising for the homeless would be less advanced, and my own funds would have been significantly lower. A month earlier, my father had talked the *Daily Express* into paying for the stories I was sending back. There'd been no original agreement for payment—I'd been too scared of losing the opportunity to ask—but my father had negotiated with the paper, threatening to end the reports if reasonable reimbursement wasn't made, and the funds had been won. As a result, my appreciation for Base Camp had grown even stronger.

'I still can't believe you got the *Express* to pay,' I said. 'I'll never take your help for granted.'

Both parents smiled and returned to their reading. It was our last afternoon together, a final few companionable hours. Over the week, we'd done far more than sit beside the pool. There'd been strolls around Torbole, a trip to Venice, a boat cruise up the lake, a drive into the Alps—we'd shared and

Base Camp, Ken and Val, on Monte Baldo above Lake Garda, September 18, 1997.

experienced a great deal. But it was the easy, light-hearted conversation, and the many fits of laughter, that I'd enjoyed most. As adults we got on so well—another thing I couldn't take for granted.

Staring at them discreetly, I thought back to my childhood, and cringed at how much I'd taken for granted. But those days were long gone. Since leaving Melito, my appreciation for my parents had only grown. It didn't matter that they didn't understand The Walk—their love remained unconditional, and their support came without hesitation. I could only hope that if ever I had children I would be a parent even half as good.

That said, the lack of wild nature during childhood felt even more glaring now that I'd had so long to consider it. On previous journeys, I hadn't given much thought to my upbringing, but the intensity of the Apennines had pushed it to the forefront—and the week with my parents, reliving childhood to some degree, had set me examining it more deeply. I'd spent time comparing what I'd found on The Walk to what I'd grown up with in Pinner, searching to understand *why* a timid little boy had willingly swapped the comforts of suburbia for the discomforts of the wild. And the answer had become clear: my return to nature had been inevitable. No matter my nurture, no matter where or how I might have grown up,

I would always be a product of nature. All my senses, bodily functions and instincts had been shaped and fine-tuned by the natural environment over uncountable generations—the science was established. Nature was a powerful force, as I'd experienced first-hand throughout the Apennines, fierce and unrelenting in its work, forever finding ways to reclaim its own. Well, I was nature's own, and I'd been reclaimed—thoroughly. The outcome had been set in stone from the moment I'd first laid eyes on Dartmoor at ten and had sensed my own connection to it. Being called back to nature was the most natural thing in the world.

Sitting beside the hotel pool now, I pushed my theory further. Was it possible that The Walk was a natural reaction against an *un*natural upbringing? A rebellion of sorts? The more I considered it, the more possible it seemed. While my childhood had been sheltered, the journey was exposed—as nature is. While my upbringing had been safe, the journey was risk-filled—again, as nature is. While life in Pinner had been predictable, life on foot was unpredictable, a journey into the unknown, an exercise in embracing chance. The idea that it was a rebellion got me wondering: would I have taken my relationship with nature to such obsessive levels if I'd grown up experiencing it more regularly? Would shorter adventures have been all I needed? Would life be better balanced? Regardless, there was wonderful irony in what my parents had unintentionally achieved, how the safe suburban existence they had so lovingly created had resulted in an adulthood that was the exact opposite.

Tentatively, I tried putting my theory into words. 'It's all your fault,' I began, looking at Base Camp.

'What's that, love?' my mother asked.

My father raised his eyebrows.

'Um… well…' I stammered, and quickly changed tack, losing confidence. In all probability, the only person who would ever truly understand the journey was me—and that was fine. Months earlier, I'd let go of what I'd wanted the Apennines to be, and now I could let go of my need to convince my father.

'I said I had a thought. Perhaps you should stay in Italy and walk with me!'

My mother laughed, and then sighed. 'Oh, I wish we could.'

But they couldn't. They were leaving for England in the morning.

I slept soundly on that last hotel night, savouring the soft hotel bed, not knowing when next I'd sleep in one. But I woke early, and spent a couple of hours re-evaluating my new theories. By departure I had run into several serious flaws. If a return to nature truly was inevitable, why hadn't my three brothers returned as I had? In fact, why hadn't everyone? And if nature truly was where I was *supposed* to be, why was it suddenly so distressingly difficult heading off into it now, leaving Base Camp behind?

Why was it even more painful than leaving Pinner had been?

Why had there been no warning I'd feel this way?

Why were goodbyes so hard?

I stood outside the hotel, facing my parents. Ten Ton was packed and on my shoulders. I was ready to go, but once again didn't want to.

'Good luck, then,' my father said gently, clearly wanting to say more, but struggling to say even that. His eyes were moist too. We were emotional lightweights, the two of us.

'Just go, love,' my mother said tenderly, knowing that a drawn-out farewell was a bad idea for us all.

I tried to speak, but suddenly couldn't. Any attempt would lead to tears. Instead, I produced a twisted grin—more of a grimace, really—accepted a tight hug from my parents, and then turned and strode quickly away.

On my own again, I raged inside. What was wrong with me, dammit? I belonged on The Walk, in nature, and I belonged there by myself, standing on my own two feet, needing no one. But the loneliness suggested otherwise. Confusion reigned. Was it merely a lingering immaturity that I still needed to overcome? Had I simply not grown up yet? Or was I missing something more—something fundamentally important?

From Torbole I caught a bus back to Peschiera Lago Garda, and then began walking. I was thrilled to be underway again, but remained torn, unsettled by the loneliness. Overcoming it took effort—my mind struggled to let go of the companionship left behind—and it wasn't until late afternoon that I managed to suppress its stabbing ache. Ten Ton didn't help. After a week of easy living the load crushed me. With winter approaching the pack was now heavier, stuffed with additional gear and clothing: thermals, extra layers, winter hat and gloves, a warmer coat, a new sleeping bag. The sleeping bag was rated to five Fahrenheit, minus fifteen Celsius, and to boost its warmth I'd also added a waterproof bivvy bag to my load for use inside the tent. The greatest challenge in winter backpacking isn't cold or snow but encroaching dampness, and the waterproof liner would—hopefully —protect my sleeping bag when everything else I owned had succumbed.

Or was winter's greatest challenge going to be loneliness? Would my sleeping bag protect me from that?

Pushing the questions aside I walked on, considering other changes to my gear, listing them to keep loneliness at bay. In place of my trusty old Peapod I now carried a new tent, a squat dome that soon became, simply, the Blob. Capable of standing freely without pegs, it was easy to pitch on frozen ground or deep snow, and unlike the Peapod wouldn't collapse under falling snow. The Blob was supposed to cling to the earth with limpet-like tenacity when the elements raged, which they likely would at some point over the next six months. Although small, it was still vastly more spacious than the Peapod, and with a positive attitude the long dark winter nights shouldn't prove too claustrophobic. When I reached camp that evening I considered some kind of baptismal ceremony to mark the Blob's first use, but a dive-bombing gull beat me to it and performed the act with spectacular accuracy. I couldn't tell if it was a good or bad omen, but I had to laugh; regardless of how I felt about nature, nature was shitting on me all the same.

Upon my feet I wore replacement boots: a second sturdy pair donated by Scarpa. In time the boots would soften up and let me step upon the earth with the gentleness I preferred, but at Lake Garda they were still stiff and heavy. In an attempt to break them in I'd worn them throughout Base Camp's visit, even lounging beside the hotel swimming pool with them on (and receiving some comically puzzled looks for doing so). On the final day I had taken them for a test hike atop Monte Baldo, a mountain directly above Lake Garda. Base Camp and I had ridden the cable car up, but after the week of inactivity I'd declined the return ride and had run down instead, descending 4,000-plus feet at breakneck speed, loving the freedom and exhilaration of gravity-assisted travel without a load on my back.

But I should have known better. The result was skinned toes, blistered heels, and quads that now screamed. Clomping along, feet in pain once again, I cursed myself for the fool I undoubtedly was. More serious-minded adventurers didn't make mistakes like this.

Rounding out the new gear were crampons, a climbing harness, a few carabiners, and some Prusik loops: equipment to help me climb glaciers and reach an Alpine summit or two. I hoped to find fellow mountaineers aiming for high summits who might let me join them on their roped climbs, and a harness was essential for that. Mountaineers are often a generous and welcoming bunch; on previous Alpine journeys the willingness shown by strangers to let me rope up and tag along had led to several fine summits. The biggest Alpine mountains often sport so-called 'tourist' routes, the *via normale* glacier climbs that are little more than steep walks, and an extra body on the rope for these climbs makes little difference. If anything, it adds to safety. As I set off with my ice axe and crampons strapped to Ten Ton, carabiners jangling musically, I felt prepared for the high mountains, but also spectacularly out of place amid the scantily clad sunbathing goddesses draped alongside Lago Garda. Here was I: sixty pounds of food and gear on my back, already sweating from the effort, dreaming of snow and ice; and there were they: at ease in the barest suggestion of clothing. For a moment I paused—the view down here truly wasn't so bad—but then forced myself on, shaking my head wryly at the choices I was making, at the earthly delights that remained beyond my reach.

My route into the Alps led north alongside Lake Garda, and then north-west towards the Adamello mountains. After that, however, some extravagant detours would begin. I wasn't planning the most direct route across the Alps that had ever been taken—far from it. In theory, the Alps could be crossed in less than two weeks, but I was aiming to take two and a half months. My goal was to meander, explore, and seek the wildest corners. As in the Apennines, I had a rough plan in mind, a loose suggestion for a route that I could alter as fancy took me. The plan included the Adamello Brenta and Stelvio national parks, two regions I'd missed on my long Alpine walk three years earlier; a long loop south through the incomparable Dolomites; and then a sweeping tour through the Kitzbühel Alps in Austria. Viewed on a map, my intended route resembled the wanderings of someone completely lost, or who had little interest in reaching Norway, and that was the point. I wasn't entering the Alps to *get* somewhere, but to *be* somewhere. And after all, as I'd learnt months earlier, the shortest distance between two points is a wasted opportunity. I anticipated walking 1,000 miles in the Alps. I just had to make sure I was across the range before the snows grew *too* deep.

The knowledge that snow could fall any day added a dash of uncertainty to my future. During my previous Alpine and Pyrenean journeys winter had arrived in late August, burying both ranges beneath three feet of snow, which made it overdue this year. From now on, at every chance encounter, I asked people if they knew the forecast. Strangers on the trail, shopkeepers and farmers all had better access to weather updates than I.

'Usually, it would be much colder by now,' explained the campground receptionist at Bardolino after my first day's march. 'Colder… and raining. This heat is unusual. But still, this is our last weekend. We close on Monday. For us, summer is *finito*.'

Despite those words it still felt like summer along Lake Garda's palm-fringed shores. Tourists still thronged the villages and amusement parks, topless sunbathers still basked in the frying sun, cars and motorbikes roared along lakeside roads, hundreds of cyclists raced, and out on the shimmering water pleasure boats cruised with engines humming, while optimistic windsurfers idled mournfully, wind absent from their sails. Keen to escape the circus I left the lake behind and weaved uphill through a quieter landscape of vineyards, silver-leafed olive groves, rustic farms, and stone-walled villages. Navigation was straightforward, as it would be for the rest of the journey. The map I carried, like all the maps that followed it, gave a detailed and accurate representation of the land—something I'd never take for granted again. This was walking country—tens of thousands of people came here each summer simply to walk—and the number of paths reflected it. If anything, the challenge now came from choice. There were so many options, and they all had something to offer.

For three days I shared Lake Garda's gentle hillsides with fellow walkers from across the continent: weekenders from Germany, vacationing families from Holland, Italians out for the day. On the second morning I walked for a while with an older couple and their red-headed daughter, a girl about my age whose cheerful laughter helped me forget the load on my back. The girl explained in English that the family were from Rome originally, but now ran a small hotel on Verona's northern edge, chosen for its proximity to these first Alpine mountains.

'We prefer being near mountains,' she explained. 'Somewhere we can walk all year long, even in winter.'

The girl had lots of questions; she'd never met anyone who'd managed to escape work for so long. 'Our walks are fantastic,' she said. 'And so necessary. But they're too short.' She looked at me and laughed. 'So… can I come with you?'

'Of course!' I laughed back. 'But you'll have to help carry my rucksack.'

'It's a deal,' she replied. 'We'll share it, fifty-fifty.'

When we parted a mile later I felt a moment's regret, thinking how fine it would have been if she'd meant it. Solitude was all very well, but there were other options, with obvious benefits that were hard to ignore. Usually, I was too involved with the land, and too weary from crossing it, to have energy available even for thinking about other natural pursuits, for considering the possibility of a girlfriend, a life partner, but the bronzed distractions beside Lago Garda had disrupted my happy detachment. Life was a great deal simpler in the wilds.

On the morning of September 23 I climbed from Lago Garda for the final time, and within two hours entered what was, in all but name, another country entirely. No other change since Melito had been so dramatic or abrupt. In place of palm trees and olive groves I now had forests of fir, pine and larch. In place of noise and bustle I now had quietness and stillness. In place of heat and pollution I now had cool air scented with damp earth and the resin of pine. Chic hotels were replaced with alpine chalets: simpler buildings with log walls and steeply pitched roofs perfectly designed for shedding snow. Flower boxes decorated balconies, and I passed wood sheds filled to the brim with logs neatly split and stacked, ready for the bitter months ahead. Then there were the mountains themselves: bigger and steeper than any I'd seen since the Gran Sasso. And these were just the foothills.

I stopped for the night beside mirror-smooth Lago Ledro, and paid for a patch of earth in an official campsite for what I hoped would be the last time in months. Despite the extra payments from *The Daily Express* and *Spotlight Verlag* magazine, my bank balance was still a concern; the funds coming in did not remotely match the funds going out. Potentially,

I had reserves enough to see me through to April and the top of Denmark, but not if I frittered it away on luxuries like showers or campsites. From now on I'd pay for accommodation only when I truly needed it, when everything I owned was wet or frozen, or when I couldn't stand my own stench any longer.

This last official campsite was a peaceful spot—at least for a while, until a young German couple from Munich pitched their tent a few yards from mine. They were a friendly pair, and didn't mean any harm, but their three-month-old baby girl possessed vocal chords more powerful than any I'd heard all year, surpassing even an opera-singing busker who'd assaulted my eardrums back in Florence. My first night back in the Alps wasn't as quiet or peaceful as I'd expected.

Later that evening, during a temporary lull from the serenade, I grew aware of another out-of-place sound. Rising and falling across the lake, vibrating deeply, was the unmistakable drone of a didgeridoo. Curious, I went off to investigate.

A quarter of a mile around the shore I found the source: a deeply tanned blond-haired man with moon glasses and beaded attire, sitting cross legged on a blanket, blowing into a six-foot-long wooden horn. Guessing he had to be Australian, I attempted a cheerful down-under greeting: 'Crikey, mate! Didn't expect to hear a didge out here!' But my feeble attempt at an Aussie accent confused the man—he didn't understand a word. I soon learnt why. Peter was German, and he'd carved the didgeridoo himself.

'I first heard a didgeridoo when I was a child, and it mesmerized me,' Peter explained in English. 'But I didn't know what made the sound, and I never found out. For years I wondered, and then ten months ago I finally discovered what it was.' Shrugging, as though what he did following the discovery was the most ordinary thing in the world, Peter continued. 'And so I took a large branch, hollowed it out, sanded and varnished it, and taught myself how to play.'

Too impressed to seek further details, I sat quietly as Peter demonstrated all he'd learnt. Using circular breathing he kept the didgeridoo going without break for long minutes, and something about the haunting sound matched the surrounding mountains perfectly. As Peter had said, it was mesmerizing. It stirred the same emotions that wild nature also touched.

'I can also play it like an alpine horn,' Peter eventually said when he took a break. 'Listen.' After taking a deep breath, he pursed his lips against the mouthpiece, paused for a moment, and then blew hard. The resulting explosion of sound was unexpectedly deafening. I actually jumped.

For a moment, the foghorn blast reverberated across Lago Ledro, echoing between mountains; and then, as it slowly faded, it was answered by a penetrating blast of another sort: the baby from Munich, exercising its vocal chords once again.

Ah, I thought, *the gentle musical sounds of the Alps. What would Julie Andrews say?*

The next evening was quieter, a solitary forest camp with a birdsong soundtrack, and the evening after that quieter still. After idyllic miles on narrow trails that weaved into ever-growing mountains, I came upon a remote cabin, used by summer herders but now empty and unlocked. Small but solid, built from stone, and topped with a wood-tiled roof, it was perched in an unbeatable location on a steep slope with a huge view spread below. In the distance a large mountain reared skywards, and at the sight of the gleaming ribbon of glacial ice hung across it I changed my planned route in an instant. I checked my map: the peak was Carè Alto. Clearly I had to head there next.

But not until the morning—the cabin was too palatial to pass by. Inside, a single square room waited. It was scrupulously clean and bright, equipped with simple wooden furniture and bunks, and possessed a promising fireplace. It didn't seem likely that anyone would object if I spent the night—why was it unlocked, after all? Thrilled at the find, I settled into 'The Shepherd's Palace', happily playing house, imagining I wasn't just passing through. I ate dinner out front, feasting on my usual stew while shadows lengthened and Carè Alto's glacier glowed; and later, once the sun fell behind a ridge and a sudden drop in temperature turned exhaled breath into visible clouds, I retreated indoors and set the fire ablaze.

As I sat before the fire, a sense of simplicity, ease, and freedom enveloped me. Here I was, living the life I'd dreamed, utterly unshack-led, the future a blank slate of mountains to climb, valleys to explore and chance encounters to stumble into, with all my physical and mental

A palace for the night, September 24, 1997.

needs well met. The cabin's spartan comforts seemed kingly, surpassing the excessive furnishings of the hotel from my week off, and they were reason enough for the great sense of well-being that filled me. But my contentment went beyond that. It was the thrill of an unbounded future that stirred me most. Comfortable as the cabin was, I had a hard time sleeping. The promise of all that lay ahead danced through my thoughts.

Perfect trails over the next two days led into the Parco Naturale Adamello Brenta and up onto Carè Alto's highest slopes. Being mid-week and post-summer, the trails were fabulously empty, and the mountains felt wilder for it. With each lonely mile a feeling grew that I was Getting Away With Something, or possibly even cheating, being here when everyone else was not. Without the unceasing bustle of summer crowds, immersion into the range came swiftly. Stripped of distractions, the unique spirit of the land—its epic scale and the richness of its contrasting environments—sunk deep. I'd walked across the Alps in high summer during other visits, and knew first-hand how busy certain famous locations could become. I understood why some wilderness connoisseurs dismissed the range. But for what I found now—out of season and away from the big resorts—I saw how this was a mistake. *These* Alps were different from the Alps summer visitors knew; they were lonelier, bigger, wilder. It was almost like stepping back in time, seeing the Alps as they were before the masses discovered them. Although the junk of industrial tourism still befouled mountains elsewhere, in the Adamello I felt far removed from such damage. Genuine wildness wasn't hard to find. It may not have been hundreds of miles wide, but it was most assuredly present. I didn't just see it, I felt it.

I felt the wildness high on Carè Alto, up on its glacier at dawn and in the rugged cirque where I slept. I felt it the day after as I trekked off trail across the grain of the land, weaving around crags, carefully crossing torrents of glacial meltwater, picking a precarious traverse over teetering boulder fields that few travellers likely ever crossed. There was wildness in the remote valley I stumbled into early that afternoon, a secret bowl surrounded by a needled skyline of rock, through which a mountain stream splashed and sang; and although my intention had been to walk many miles more, the bowl was so remote and wild I simply couldn't pass by. For the rest of the day I wallowed in deliberate idleness in a location that bore no sign of my own species. And yet it wasn't unoccupied. Marmots chased each other from boulder to boulder; alpine choughs reeled overhead, jet black against the deep-blue high-altitude sky; chamois crossed the valley below camp, en route from one foraging ground to another, heading nimbly uphill through a maze of rock; and bees and other insects droned, hard at work in the warm summer air. Some people believe they know the Alps. But do they know these Alps?

By the end of the week I reached the Val di Genova, a busier place, but busier for good reason. Curving into the heart of the Parco Naturale Adamello Brenta, the Val di Genova is a trench some 5,000 feet deep. Milky-blue waters rushed along its floor, thick with rock silt scoured by glaciers, and dark forests and ever-steepening precipices rose on both sides towards lofty peaks, 11,673-foot Cima Presanella being the loftiest of all. No landscape I'd visited in almost 2,000 miles had been bigger, and for once the presence of others wasn't a distraction. If anything, the few people added scale. They were so small they made the mountains appear unclimbable.

I took my time trekking up the valley, and paused for a long break where the river cut thunderously through a narrow cleft and exploded into space. It wouldn't do to fall into that! At one time the Val di Genova had been under serious threat. Its powerful waters had developers rubbing their hands with glee; where better for a dam and hydroelectric power plant? Thankfully, sanity prevailed, and now—as part of a legislatively protected area—the valley's future should be assured.

The Adamello Brenta Nature Park was slow in getting started, pretty much mirroring twentieth-century Italian nature conservation. Although first proposed in 1919, the Adamello Brenta wasn't established until 1967, and didn't become fully operational until 1988, just nine years prior to my visit. After a promising start to the century, which led to the formation of Italy's first two national parks in 1922 and 1923 (the Gran Paradiso and Abruzzo national parks), progress slowed and then ground to a halt. Blame Mussolini, blame Fascist policies that had nature working like a machine for human benefit and consumption, blame World War Two, blame a culture of general indifference among an Italian populace that simply didn't notice a land being quietly ravaged, blame local citizens who feared losing access to resources on their doorstep, blame whomever you like, it wasn't until the 1980s that momentum finally returned. It was a little like waiting for buses back home in suburban London; an hour of waiting and then, all of a sudden, three arrive at once. So it was with legislated wild land protection in Italy. In 1987 there were only four national parks: by 1997 the number had risen to twenty, with numerous regional parks and nature reserves also popping up. In less than a decade the percentage of Italy's landscape enjoying official protection rose from three to eleven per cent—clearly good news, not just for Italian nature lovers or visitors from overseas, but most of all for the wild creatures and plants that make the country their home. Although Italy only covers an eightieth of Europe's landmass, a third of the continent's fauna is represented within it, along with half the flora. Given the decades of neglect, the country's industrial surge since World War Two, and the building boom that followed—which took place practically without planning or control—the surviving richness of Italy's wild places is something of a miracle to behold.

I'd reached the Parco Naturale Adamello Brenta at the start of another conservation miracle, this one centred around arguably the greatest living symbol of the mountain wild, *Ursus arctos*—the brown bear. At one time, brown bears roamed the length of the Alps, just as they had in the Apennines, but their clawhold here was even more precarious. By the time of my visit they truly were making their last stand. Extinct elsewhere across the Alps, authorities estimated that only three or four bears survived in the Adamello Brenta, hiding out in the wildest corners. If the odds against encountering one in the Abruzzo had been low, here they were incalculable.

Although bears and people have always coexisted uneasily, attempts were still made as early as the 1920s to protect them. A 1923 law banned winter hunting while bears lay defenceless in hibernation, and in 1936 a complete nationwide hunting ban came into being. Not that it helped. The laws were impossible to enforce, and poaching continued to reduce their numbers. And then there was the factor of space. A bear needs room to breathe and untrammelled space in which to roam, and wildernesses large enough no longer existed in the Alps. So the population shrank, the gene pool diminished, and by the early 1990s the last bears were nearing the end of their lonely lives. When they died, that would be that.

The absolute certainty of extinction finally prompted action. In 1996 the National Institute of Wild Fauna, the INFS, began the uphill task of rebuilding a viable population. To succeed they began developing strategies to keep the bears in the forests, away from people, livestock and crops. They also started an educational campaign to teach the human population not just how to coexist with ursine neighbours but also to see bears as a positive presence—a measurable cultural benefit, valuable for many reasons, not least for tourism. And as for the bears, the aim was to catch brown bears in Slovenia where the population remained relatively healthy, and release them in the Adamello Brenta, beginning with a first round of ten bears in 1999. The bears would roam free, but they'd be carefully monitored and managed.

Of course, at the time I passed through, in September 1997, the actual rewilding lay ahead, but I learnt of it from a shopkeeper in the village of Carisolo, and it was immensely encouraging. And if I could only have known the outcome, that in fifteen years an estimated forty to sixty bears would call this region home, that bears would be successfully mating, that their cubs would be living lives of alpine freedom, then my steps would have been even lighter. Sometimes, when faced with a warming climate, retreating glaciers, and the ever-increasing resource-consuming human population, it can be hard to feel optimistic. But, although we often leave it to the very last minute to do the right thing, there is always hope. The return of bears to Alpine Italy proved it.

At the western end of the Val di Genova I began climbing, feeling like a salmon swimming upstream. As I sweated uphill towards a mountain refuge—the Rifugio Mandron—crowds of mountaineers were heading down, an army in retreat, plastic high-altitude boots clattering over rocks. No one else was going up, which made the mass exodus unsettling; did they know something I didn't? My plan was to camp above the refuge and find a group to join the following morning. I hoped to climb Monte Adamello, a central peak amid a sea of ice. It was for Adamello that I'd carried my climbing gear; its glacial summit would make the dead weight worthwhile. Today was Saturday, and Sunday morning would surely see many groups attempting the region's most popular climb. But why was everyone descending? Finally, I stopped a passing climber, and asked if a storm was due. The answer was no, the forecast was good until Wednesday.

'So why is everyone going down?' I asked.

The climber looked at me strangely. 'Well… the *rifugio* is closed tomorrow. At this time of year it is only open on weekends, and tomorrow is Monday.'

Oops—that explained it. Somehow I'd lost a day. I wouldn't be climbing Adamello after all. Perhaps the crampons and harness really were dead weight.

By the time I reached Rifugio Mandron it was nearly empty; the wardens were battening down the hatches for the week, or possibly even the season, depending upon conditions.

'There's weather coming on Wednesday,' a short, middle-aged, but impressively fit-looking man informed me as he bolted a shutter closed. 'And at this time of year that usually means snow.'

Excited—and nervous—at the prospect that summer now had an end, I set up camp away from the refuge near a small spring. The view from my front door was sensational. The immediate foreground was an intricate plateau of mirror-like tarns, bulging outcrops, and russet-hued grass, and beyond it the mountains of the Adamello rose, dark pyramids of sculptured granite laced with snow and ice. The massive Vedretta del Mandron glacier filled the basin ahead, flowing from 11,000-foot peaks down to a crevassed snout, out of which meltwater roared. As I stared at the glacier, it was obvious to me that it was thawing fast; the broad expanse of exposed, unvegetated rock directly below the snout clearly showed where the glacier had recently extended. But the sight of so much glacial ice still set my pulse racing. The mix-up in days had cost me Adamello's summit—I wasn't going to cross that glacier on my own—but just being here was enough. This wasn't an everyday kind of place, even on this journey.

The location was so stirring that when the time came to move on the next day I couldn't. Instead, after a lazy morning spent basking in warm sunshine like a complacent marmot, I set out on a meandering tour, unweighted by a pack or the restrictions of having a destination. Of their own accord my feet carried me to a lofty perch three miles from camp, a minor summit hanging directly above the Vedretta del Mandron, and I lingered there a long while, savouring the Ice Age arena below. In the crisp mountain air sounds carried far. Every so often I heard the glacier groan like an old man, frequently followed by the sharp rat-a-tat-tat of falling stone. The roar of rushing water was a constant sound, not just coming from mountain streams but also from the glacier's surface and edges. The baking-hot sun and the painful glare of white light belonged to midsummer, not late September. It was no wonder Alpine glaciers were in full retreat.

A couple of hours later I was back at 'Small Spring' camp, and I quickly dismantled it in favour of roomier accommodation. Though the main refuge was now locked and deserted, the winter room was too enticing for a homeless vagrant like myself to resist. The hours that followed were as fine as any I'd ever lived. The sheer pleasure from being alone in such a wild arena was so intense it surged through my body. Revelling in it, I sat outside my own personal Alpine residence, captivated by the sights, sounds and scents, laughing at the knowledge that being here was all down to chance. My original route had me far away on the western side of Adamello, but a postcard of the view now before me, seen by chance in a store window near Lago Ledro, had prompted yet another spur-of-the-moment change of route. Feet stretched out, comfortable in just shorts and T-shirt at 8,000 feet, I was king of my own mountain kingdom. Even in my imagination, the journey hadn't been this good.

Only one concern lurked in the back of my mind: my route the following morning. Aside from heading back the way I'd come, the only realistic escape from the Val di Genova lay to the north over a 9,700-foot notch in

Alpine perfection near Rifugio Mandron, September 29, 1997.

the mountain wall, and the descent from it crossed steep glacial ice. When I scrambled uphill at dawn my stomach fluttered with nerves, reminiscent of those felt before tackling the Hohtürli Pass, and the steel-grey skies overhead felt suitably ominous. I'd noticed before how weather and terrain often seemed to change to match my mood—or did they control it? What had seemed benign and welcoming the day before now felt savage and hostile. Feet skittering off loose stones, legs weak and unsteady, doubt plaguing my thoughts, I climbed to the Passo Maroccaro, and from the top of the pass beheld a landscape as ugly as any I'd ever seen. The cirque below was a forsaken place, strewn with rubble, devoid of life, grey, dark and dead. A dirty glacier stretched through the heart of it, littered with discarded rock and dust, and rising from it were old metal pylons sporting a web of cables and hanging chairs—the machinery of the ski industry. This was another side of the Alps, a place defiled as if by Tolkien's evil Sauron, but an Alps that many people appear to support and enjoy.

The descent wasn't as steep as I'd feared, reminding me yet again that the difficulties we imagine seldom match the realities we eventually face. And yet it was far from easy. My crampons barely bit into the iron-hard ice.

265

If I slipped, ice axe braking would be near impossible—and I'd keep sliding until I crashed into the massive boulders scattered below. It would likely mark the end of the journey. After several half-slips I reached the far edge of the glacier, and although it was menaced by stonefall, the rubble now underfoot made progress marginally less precarious. Complete safety didn't lie far away, but reaching it seemed to take an age. For a half-mile, the journey was an adventure once again.

Finally below the glacier, and breathing more easily, I came upon workers preparing the mountain for the approaching ski season. Bulldozers rumbled backwards and forwards pushing rock into piles, their engines thundering, exhausts spewing. Drills whined like angry hornets; dust filled the air. A hard-hatted worker looked up wide-eyed with surprise as I appeared from above. *Where the hell have you come from?* his expression said, and I understood why. This wasn't an environment for living creatures, and I was beyond glad to leave it behind.

The final sight before reaching greener country below cheered me a little. Sitting alone in the wasteland, far from any road and with little chance of being noticed, sat a large bus-like vehicle with caterpillar tracks. A cardboard sign rested in a window. 'FOR SALE,' it read in hand-scrawled Italian. 'TRANSPORTS 20 PEOPLE. ENQUIRE AT THE RESTAURANT.'

The optimism of it had me laughing for hours.

The Vedretta del Mandron, September 29, 1997.

THE ENDLESS SUMMER
Chapter 3

SEPTEMBER GAVE WAY to October, and for another week summer blazed on. I couldn't believe my luck. Each morning when I unzipped the tent and peered out at yet another cloudless sky I had to pinch myself: *surely this isn't possible*? Admittedly, each dawn came a little later and arrived with a hint of frost, and the slopes were now ochre-hued, not green, but the days warmed quickly and didn't feel autumnal. The sweat upon my back declared high summer, and it was more than I could have hoped for. It felt like an endless summer.

There were minor interruptions—a fleeting snow squall atop Passo Zebrù, some hesitant blobs of sleet beneath the mighty Ortler—but these first signs of winter lasted mere minutes, and soon I was back in shorts and T-shirt, basking in unseasonable warmth. Even Wednesday's incoming weather turned out to be little more than fierce overnight winds, and they troubled me not. I stumbled upon another refuge with a cosy winter room and slept deep and long.

Of course, it won't last,' I told myself each morning. 'It can't possibly. This'll be the last good day.' And I treated each day as though it were, making the most of the freedom summer gives—climbing as high as I could, walking far, camping in exposed locations where winter storms would likely blow me away. At day's end I'd sit back in golden light, soak up the blissful warmth, and repeatedly think: *tomorrow it'll all be over.*

Toasting the Endless Summer at the 'Camp of Serenading Marmots', October 4, 1997.

I'll probably wake to snow. Day after day I thought it, but day after day I woke to sun. And so I began wondering: *perhaps I'm wrong. Perhaps this summer is going to last forever.*

'I can only remember one other autumn as hot and dry as this,' an old man told me. 'And that was when I was a prisoner of war in the Sahara Desert!'

The man was seated on a bench in the town of Bormio, leaning on a stick, watching the world trundle by. He beckoned me over for a chat. Like most old men, and *all* long-distance walkers, he was happy to discuss the weather. 'Usually, the clouds would be thick, the rain hard. But this year?' He threw up his hands as though in exasperation. 'This is not normal.'

Normal or not, I wasn't complaining. Conditions were ideal in every way possible. Even the landscape was ideal. Here, there was no getting lost, no tangled forests, no flies. Life couldn't have been better.

Under clear skies I pushed north into the Stelvio National Park and followed a great loop around it, hardly heading for Norway. Over passes, into valleys, around steep hillsides; onwards I tramped. My weaving route involved some huge climbs, and the physical effort remained immense, but I found nothing but pleasure in it. Working up a sweat in a wild landscape was my life now—it was simply what I did—and I'd fully adjusted. My daily routines were firmly set but hadn't become chores. Striking camp, packing Ten Ton, walking all day, unpacking Ten Ton, pitching camp; it wasn't remotely repetitious. If anything, the simple routines brought pleasure, reminding me how uncluttered my life had become. Each evening saw me land somewhere new; each dawn arrived with unlimited promise. I had space to breathe, space to explore, space to think, space to be myself. I still couldn't take a second of it for granted.

The Stelvio National Park offered uncomplicated walking and endless scope for wild camps. The Stelvio is Italy's fourth-oldest park, established in 1935 by Mussolini's government, and although a strong argument could be made that it was created not with nature preservation in mind but for showy nationalistic pride, the result was still an Alpine region far better preserved than most. Wild valleys, pristine natural environments; these weren't hard to find. Of course, being a national park, there were rules. A sign at the park entrance sported a long list of forbidden activities, so many it seemed that only breathing was allowed—and that only on Tuesdays—but I pushed on anyway, continuing my light-footed approach. For several miles I debated the rights and wrongs of camping wild when local regulations forbade it, but several damaged areas—electricity pylons strung across wild slopes, anchored into the earth by concrete; ski areas cut through forests, destroying natural habitats; wild mountain streams befouled with cow muck—helped make up my mind. No one would ever know I'd passed through.

For 200 miles the terrain was classically Alpine: plunging valleys more than a mile deep, picture-postcard villages filled with wooden chalets, rich meadows of swaying grass, pine-scented forests echoing to birdsong, and above it all soaring mountains capped with snow and ice. Stelvio's glaciers were even more impressive than Adamello's. Long white tongues thrust towards the valleys, icefalls hung cracked and splintered where slopes steepened, and broad upper mountain bowls were draped with hanging glaciers. They shone in the sunlight, smooth like satin sheets. The mountains were the tallest I'd see on the entire journey. Monte Cevedale, the Gran Zebrù and the Ortler all towered over 12,000 feet. The highest mountain

Classic Alpine scenery in the Stelvio, with valley chalets barely visible beneath the glacier-capped Ortler (12,812 feet / 3,905 metres), October 5, 1997.

of all appeared unexpectedly one morning from a remote pass: 13,284-foot Piz Bernina, twenty-five miles away in Switzerland. I'd spent several days exploring the Bernina region during my trans-Alpine walk three years earlier, and the memories flooded back. The famous Biancograt, a knife-edge snow ridge leading to Piz Bernina's summit, still looked truly spectacular.

The view to Piz Bernina was unexpected, but so were the World War One battlements I came upon. They ran along the crest of the Brocchetta di Forcola, a pass that lay twenty-two miles from the Austrian border, although back in 1915 it had marked the border itself. From this strategic high-altitude vantage point Italian artillery had fired north over the Stelvio Pass at Austro-Hungarian encampments, and the Austro-Hungarians had fired back, many of the shells passing over neutral Swiss territory caught in between. The Brocchetta di Forcola marked the western end of the Italian Front, a battle line that stretched across the Stelvio and Adamello mountains towards Lake Garda, and then up through the Dolomites into the Julian Alps. The fighting along it had been as brutal and horrific as anything that took place on the muddy fields of France and Belgium, with an extra element: the elements themselves. Conservative estimates suggest that of the million-plus soldiers who died on the Italian Front 60,000 did so in avalanches, buried beneath obliterating waves of snow. If any location summed up the sheer insanity of war this was it. Only a world gone mad could have devised trench warfare at 10,000 feet in the depths of an Alpine winter.

As I stepped into one of the trenches I couldn't help but shudder. The trench—walled and roofed with concrete and stone—sat five feet deep in bedrock. Slit windows looked out over the killing fields below, and as I peered through them it was easy to picture Italian youths doing the same. For once, the human history lying upon the land, and the blood that had soaked into it, had real impact on me. Other patches of earth I'd crossed had experienced bloodshed too, but here the physical evidence was so stark it was as if the fighting had taken place weeks earlier, not seven decades. Beneath my feet were rusted scraps of metal, shards of wood, a patch of old leather that may once have been a boot. At school, history lessons had been abstract: mere stories about distant events that had nothing to do with me. But at the Brocchetta di Forcola, the past was suddenly the present, and the immediacy and horror of it put a chill on the back of my neck. Only one other place had touched me so powerfully: the Colosseum in Rome. While my fellow tourists had laughed and posed for photos I'd died a little inside at the amphitheatre's lingering echoes of death, at the ghosts of Christians, slaves, gladiators, lions and bears roaring and screaming in fear and pain. I hadn't lingered long, and didn't linger long at the Brocchetta di Forcola either. The evil of it was more than I could take.

Away from the pass the landscape soon worked its magic, dispelling the gloom. Blue skies unsullied by even a single wisp arced overhead, grassy slopes swept upwards, and glaciers gleamed in bright sunlight. A trail took me north towards the Passo dello Stelvio – at 9,045 feet the second-highest paved pass in the Alps—but before reaching it I noticed another possible

World War One trenches at the Brocchetta di Forcola, October 4, 1997.

destination, and on a whim changed direction yet again. The Umbrail Pass and the Swiss border lay a few hundred feet west, and the idea of crossing into another country suddenly appealed. As I approached the border the momentousness of the occasion struck me: I'd almost walked the length of Italy. How far I'd come!

Two uniformed soldiers guarded the Swiss border. To have my passport inspected I lined up on the road behind three cars, feeling thoroughly out of place. The traffic moved swiftly—the soldiers waved the cars through with barely a glance—but when my turn came their focus sharpened. After ordering me to stand to one side, one of the guards disappeared with my passport into a military building. I waited for several minutes. Further cars were casually waved through. Was I that suspicious a traveller? Did no one else come through on foot? To pass the time I tried engaging the second soldier in conversation. I asked if he knew what the weather forecast was, but he shook his head and glared.

The first soldier eventually reappeared, and with a curt 'Okay' returned my passport and gestured me on. From the guard station, I trekked north for two miles, following a path that twisted across grassy slopes just ten yards shy of the Italian border. And then, after only forty-seven minutes in Switzerland, I stepped back casually into Italy across an unguarded border marked only on paper. So much for the journey's second nation!

From the Passo dello Stelvio—the Stilfser Joch in German—I entered territory that some might argue was The Walk's third nation, the semi-autonomous region of the South Tyrol. The region goes by several names, depending upon who you ask—Südtirol to German speakers, Sudtirolo or Alto Adige to those preferring Italian—reflecting its ping-ponging ownership between Italy, Austria and then Italy again. Of course, the natural landscape showed no sign of any duality, but the villages somehow appeared both chaotically and romantically Italian but also efficiently Germanic, not an easy thing to achieve. The language was the biggest giveaway; although place names appeared in both Italian and German, the majority of the people I spoke with preferred German, some quite militantly. At first, not knowing this, I used Italian out of habit. '*Buongiorno*,' I'd say with a smile, but stern-eyed shaking heads quickly clarified that '*Guten tag*' was the correct salutation. My first conversation should have taught me everything I needed to know. When greeting the owner of a food shop I started out in Italian, observed it wasn't being appreciated, attempted German instead, remembered I barely knew any words, and ended up gushing an incomprehensible mix of Italian, German, French, and English melded together. The store owner merely smiled with good-natured patience: she'd evidently encountered the likes of me before. 'Would it be easier if we only spoke English?' she offered with perfect pronunciation, shaming me on the spot.

It was just as well that my next resupply parcel contained a teach-yourself-German book. I clearly needed it.

My weaving route through the Stelvio National Park—sorry, the Nationalpark Stilfser Joch—carried me south into the very heart of the range. My goal was a great amphitheatre of mountains at the head of the Suldental that featured, among other giants, the Gran Zebrù, or the Königspitze in German. Kurt Diemberger, an Austrian mountaineer whose approach to the high places and whose writings I greatly admire, had featured the Königspitze in two of his books, *Summits and Secrets* and *Spirits of the Air*. Brilliantly capturing the essence of the Alps, and the emotions that come from adventuring upon them, Diemberger described two climbs on the Königspitze: a pioneering first ascent of a route that overcame a huge summit cornice, the 'giant meringue', and a solo ascent and descent of a vast ice face, the description of which was vertigo inducing. Through Diemberger's evocative words I felt that I already knew the mountain, and now I was so close I was hungry to see it for myself.

In the heat of late afternoon the ascent up the Suldental from the hamlet of Gomagoi seemed as long as any I'd ever walked, but several hours of sweat finally carried me away from verdant forests and green pastures to a harsher world above. And harsh it was. Instead of the massive glaciers marked on my map the upper valley was now a place of rocks and rubble; ugly, as though destroyed by some huge open-cast mine. As the evening sun slipped behind Königspitze the valley fell into deep shade, becoming desolate as though abandoned by life, sunlight, and even glacial ice. I knew that Alpine glaciers were in rapid retreat, but no place I'd seen brought it home more than here. The sight was disturbing. It altered my perception of what the Alps currently were and hinted at what the entire range might one day become.

Depressed, I flopped to the ground. Above me, the Königspitze was still an impressive sight: an imposing peak with a shrunken glacier at its foot and steep ice slopes climbing to a sharp summit. Although the 'giant meringue' had collapsed since Diemberger's climb decades earlier, it was visibly reforming, and I stared up at it trying to imagine the determination needed to overcome such a precarious obstacle balanced in such a vertical place. As adventures go, my modest little trek suddenly seemed embarrassingly tame.

Eventually, cooling temperatures and a growing desire to have the day's effort done pushed me on, and within minutes I reached the Rifugio Città di Milano, or the Schaubachhütte. Weary beyond measure, hoping to find a winter room, I was delighted to discover the refuge open for business. To hell with the budget: I was due a soft bed and food cooked by someone else, and a little companionship wouldn't go amiss. Refuges weren't even expensive: they were designed for mountain travellers, after all. Numerous writers like Diemberger have written about the hospitable nature of hut wardens, recording how they were often mountaineers themselves, how they understood walkers and climbers and their needs. Hoping to meet just such a warden, I entered the Schaubachhütte, only to find the exact opposite. Working alone in a large room, dressed in black, and violently swabbing the floor, was a stern-faced middle-aged lady. As I stood in the doorway and asked meekly about spending the night she glared at me angrily. Point-blank refusing to converse in Italian, she fired back a torrent of guttural German, and then returned impatiently to her work. Polite persistence on my part had the lady confirm, with some reluctance, that the refuge was open, but the exorbitant price quoted for a night upon a dormitory bunk—given in German Deutschemarks first and only in lire when I pressed—put the option far beyond my means. The rate was equivalent to three weeks' food.

Deflated from discovering that I couldn't even afford a night in a mountain refuge, dispirited by the woman's inhospitality, and still saddened by the sight of so much glacial retreat, I heaved on Ten Ton and trudged on into the evening's fading light. Keen to escape the unwelcoming arena, I slogged uphill for another 2,000 feet, gasping from the altitude, from the steepness, from weary limbs, from uncertainty about where I'd camp. Progress was painfully slow—a hundred steps was all I could manage before each rest—and daylight was all but gone by the time I reached the Madritschjoch, an exposed, wind-blasted pass. I didn't stop for even a second. At 10,246 feet it was the highest low point of the entire journey. By the guiding light of my headlamp I descended carefully on the far side, and at the first suggestion of flat ground made camp, pitching the Blob in darkness. I'd covered twenty-five miles, and climbed over 7,000 feet— rarely had I been so happy to end a day's tramp.

The following day couldn't have been more different: I barely covered twenty steps. Sleeping late, I awoke to a hiss of rain upon the fly, and, peering out, saw fog smothering the slopes, hiding from view everything but the immediate foreground. The sight immensely cheered me. At last, some weather! I took my time over breakfast, and then decided to take my time over the entire day. Why push on at all? It wasn't as if there was anywhere I absolutely *had* to be, and the 'Lonely Glen' camp was a ruggedly attractive spot. Among the greatest pleasures in backpacking are the wild-weather days—days spent holed up in one place. There's pleasure in camping somewhere remote, pleasure in being still, pleasure in creating a tiny cocoon of comfort while the entire environment outside is cold and wet. Time slows; details sink in. Lying quietly, I lost myself within the sound of the rain, a lullaby percussion that I still couldn't take for granted. I watched stems of grass bobbing outside like tiny dancers; I gazed at the fog shifting in eddies about the boulder-strewn slope; and I laughed at myself, long and hard. What kind of adult was I, spending my time watching grass dance and fog swirl? Curled within my sleeping bag I read and ate the hours away, got up to date with the reports I was supposed to be writing, and counted my blessings. An entire day confined to a tent barely six feet long and three high. And not a moment of it dull.

Dawn bought a resumption of normal service: a sky so brilliantly blue you'd swear it had been over-inked. A hard frost silvered the slopes, and dismantling the tent was slow, cold work. But what a delightful place to develop numb hands! A couple of thousand feet higher, the season's first snow coated Monte Cevedale and its glaciers. The white places looked achingly untouched.

With the sun out the frost soon thawed, and I warmed quickly as I paced down the valley to a lake and then climbed towards another pass. With each step I felt more immersed in the land, less connected to the world of people. It reminded me of a similar state of detachment experienced earlier in The Walk, back in the sultry Mezzogiorno—only there it had felt negative. As I followed a twisting path through a delightful rock garden of bilberry, dwarf pine, and sparkling granite, I thought back to early June and Campania, remembering my spiralling descent into loneliness, frustration and anger. There, I'd not only come to feel like an outcast—I had been treated as one. Hotel receptionists had judged me as unworthy and had turned me away. A policeman had accused me of being a vagrant. People had stared at my dirty clothes and their expressions had revealed disgust. It had been hard to take, and also hard to dismiss. Deep down, I'd started to believe that the disgust was deserved, that I wasn't quite good enough for the comforts others took for granted, that I wasn't worthy of the home I'd left behind—that living unwashed and alone beyond society's edge, hiding away in the forest at night, was all I was due. Like the homeless individuals I was walking to raise money for, my self-esteem had taken a battering. I'd felt discarded. Only an escape to the Amalfi Coast had pulled me back to reality.

But here, the feeling of living outside of society was totally different. It was a positive state of being, not negative. Here, the separation from people, homes and ordinary comforts didn't make me feel as though I was going without. Quite the reverse: I felt I had more now than I'd ever had before. Here, I wasn't getting the discomforts I deserved—I was reaping the rewards I'd earned. Clearly, I hadn't been discarded, and I wasn't an outcast. How could I be? What a ridiculous idea—I was here by choice. Looking around, taking in the perfection of the rugged slope, I suddenly felt connected to something bigger than the world of people, something more fundamentally important and far more real. In Campania, I'd felt diminished by my detachment from society. Here I felt elevated by it. How far I'd come!

The detachment stretched to how I felt about other people. Rightly or wrongly, I was starting to imagine that I had little in common with them, even with other hikers. When the weekend arrived, late-season hikers emerged in packs—stout folk with walking sticks and bright-red socks pulled knee high. They stuck exclusively to the lower trails, never venturing into the wild haunts above tree line that I preferred, and they moved impressively slowly. Even with the absurd Ten Ton on my back I pulled level on climbs, and powered swiftly ahead. They made me feel super-fit— not superior by any means, but definitely different, and that added to the feeling of detachment.

At night, the hikers all retreated to the valleys, to their cars and homes, to the commitments and chores of everyday life. One of them, a hassled-looking man in his late forties, spoke wistfully. 'Wish I was doing what you're doing,' he murmured, 'sleeping out.' I wasn't sure what to say, but later wished I'd probed further. Did he *really* wish it?

The feeling of disconnection was especially strong with valley folk. Early one afternoon I reached Coldrano, a small village in a deep, flat valley. After restocking my pantry, I found an unobtrusive corner of the village square, and perched comfortably to watch life unfold. As the well-heeled citizens hurried to and fro I felt very much like an outsider looking in. Even in this prosperous and supposedly relaxed corner of Italy people looked rushed, and even stressed—as well as overdressed, over-styled, and over-clean. Of course, as an unwashed backpacker with time on his hands, my perspective was seriously warped. Plus, I was well aware that I knew little of their lives and shouldn't judge. But the adornments to ordinary life no longer appealed to me. So much of it, seen from my unusual vantage point after months of going without, looked superficial and unnecessary, for show alone, and it clearly all took an immense amount of work. Feeling even more disconnected than usual, I realised that I wouldn't have swapped places for the world. But I recognised the irony. I was fairly certain that Coldrano's residents wouldn't have wanted to swap with me either!

Freedom consumed me as I returned to the forest. There was no way I could compare what I was feeling with homelessness now. And I felt shame that I ever had. As I left the valley behind I smiled as an obvious thought struck. *Of course you feel as though you're living apart from society—you ARE living apart from society. You idiot! How else could you possibly feel?*

The Endless Summer continued, although with a hint of change. Rain hit in the small hours of October 7, lashing the Blob, and I woke disoriented to a bucking tent, for a moment thinking I was back on some rugged British fell. By dawn the squall had passed, but banners of cloud still hung from summits and a great ocean of cloud filled the Val Ultimo below. It was a dramatic sight: a boiling cauldron of cloud pierced by dark, sharp-tipped peaks. At sunrise, a blood-red sky gave way to gold, and by the time the sun burst free of the horizon I'd run through an entire roll of Velvia slide film and was halfway through the next. No sunrise on the journey had been finer.

By late afternoon the valley clouds had spilled upwards, smothering the mountains in a sopping-wet fog and reducing my world to a few square yards of greyness. Beads of moisture soon coated my hair. Clothes were soon dripping wet. Another refuge, the Rifugio Lago Corvo, emerged from the murk late in the afternoon at exactly the hour my desire to keep walking dimmed, and at the sight of its unusual winter room I gleefully settled in. The room was perched above a great drop, its walls almost entirely made of glass, and I named it the 'High-Altitude Conservatory'. Inside, I found a wood stove, a stack of firewood, tables and chairs, and metal-sprung bunks.

Candlelit dinner above the clouds in the 'High-Altitude Conservatory', October 9, 1997.

The mattresses had been removed, but I didn't care. A bed was a bed! And there was no inhospitable warden to turn me away.

Singing, I unpacked, and built a tidy fire in the stove, but the fire was a mistake. In moments, a suffocating cloud of dense black smoke poured from the stove, and soon the fog within the room was denser than the fog outside. It took half an hour with the door flung wide before I could even find the stove to see what the problem was: a pile of old ash blocking the flue, as well as a hidden damper that might not have been open. Fixing these, I tried again, but the result was the same: a Dickensian London smog filling the room. Coughing, I waited outside until the noxious cloud had dispersed, and accepted defeat. On the plus side, at least I'd smell of smoke next time I met someone, not the scent of unwashed vagabond.

Despite the lingering smoky aroma I slept well—until midnight, when sleep was forgotten. An unusual brightness pulled me from my dreams. Sitting up in confusion I peered outside, and any lingering drowsiness vanished in an instant. 'Oh my!' I exclaimed in surprise, and with little conscious thought found myself casting off the sleeping bag, stepping outside, clambering onto a rocky outcrop, and staring in awe at perhaps the most unworldly landscape I'd ever seen.

Hanging in the sky was a dazzling moon, two-thirds full but somehow brighter than any full moon had ever been. Below it lay the fog. It had fallen back into the valley and now filled it like milk in a bowl. Rising above it, far across the valley, were the jagged black silhouettes of the Brenta Dolomites. A brisk wind blew where I stood, but the fog's surface a few hundred feet lower barely stirred. It seemed frozen, so solid that I felt I could easily walk across it. And everything—the fog, the rocks beneath my feet, the star-pricked sky, the very atmosphere itself, even my own hands when I turned them side to side—everything was lit by the moon, transformed as if by alchemy into molten silver. The world had become a thing of pure fantasy, a dream creation beyond imagination, and after returning indoors to grab my warmest clothes I sat and basked in it for unforgettable minutes that stretched into hours.

The journey had delivered many situations beyond ordinary, but none as beyond ordinary as this.

Dawn came with fire in the sky, surpassing the previous day's sunrise for sheer intensity of colour, but soon a monochrome grey ceiling developed, and by the time I set out the fog had risen back from the valley, smothering the view once again. The route I'd planned plunged straight down into the fog; but instead, heeding an instinct I couldn't explain, I set out along a narrow path that curved upwards. The reward came quickly, as it often does when instinct is trusted. Within a third of a mile, and with a wolf howl of delight, I burst free into clear air, and for several hours afterwards walked in a never-never world sandwiched between two layers of cloud: the overcast above, the inversion below. I didn't rush the miles, and paused often. For several hours I was even more detached from the rest of the world than usual—as unshackled as the mountain winds, as free as I'd been at any point during the preceding 2,000 miles.

When the time eventually came to descend, I passed the foggy barrier in seconds. Beneath it all was grey, damp, and dark, the land subdued and melancholy. The village residents were going about their business with heads down, seemingly oppressed by the low clouds overhead. From down here one wouldn't believe that a bright, fairy-tale world existed so close above. If I hadn't seen it myself I probably wouldn't have believed in it either. The hidden otherworldliness of it perfectly symbolised the entire Walk.

Above the clouds and detached from the world, October 10, 1997.

Over the next few days the glacial giants of the Stelvio fell behind and my path led downwards into milder landscapes around the Val d'Adige—the Etschtal in German. The valley was broad and flat bottomed, and it cut through the heart of the region, hemmed in between spectacular walls of limestone. Forests still cloaked the mountains above, but at lower elevations the land was idyllically rural. Small villages nestled amid vineyards and apple orchards. Apple harvesters were hard at work in hot sunshine, sleeves rolled high, plucking great quantities of fruit by hand, filling wooden pallets that tractors pulled away. Twice I benefited from their generosity, gratefully receiving free apples. Astonishingly, in this kingdom of apples —a region responsible for fifty per cent of Italy's entire apple harvest— there wasn't a single apple for purchase in any local stores. Indeed, buying any kind of food down here was a challenge. In the first village the shop had closed at noon—I arrived ten minutes too late. In the second village the shop was closed for the day. 'It's always closed on Thursdays,' a lady told me snootily, with a look that said: *everyone knows that.* And in the third village the shop was closed until the following summer! Finally, I tracked down a few essential supplies in a dusty old store that from appearances hadn't been restocked in several months. It looked like something from the far south—a dash of the Mezzogiorno to keep me on my toes. Still, I bought stove fuel, a few loaves of rock-hard bread, and some chocolate bars that were only revealed as chocolate bars once I brushed away the dust covering them. The food was just about edible, but the stove fuel was practically useless—liquid soap would have burnt more fiercely. For the following week I was forced to sit with a rumbling stomach beside my stove waiting hours each evening for dinner to heat.

Back in shorts and T-shirt, sweating hard on climbs, I revelled in what must surely be the last burst of the Endless Summer. Several times people told me that tomorrow's weather would be '*Brutto*', but it never was. A single passing thunderstorm one afternoon exploded with summer-like intensity, and squalls rattled through at night, but the days stayed mild and the living easy. And yet, the seasons were changing. Each time I peered back towards the Stelvio more fresh snow appeared to have fallen, and upon the trees closer at hand the leaves continued to turn—warmer tones edging out summer's greens. After crossing the Val d'Adige I made camp in a beech wood thrillingly reminiscent of Calabria, except here the leaves shimmered gold not green, and many now lay upon the ground. Crunching through them, kicking them into the air, I played as though I was ten again, as though I were back in Pinner's local woods with my grandfather and three brothers. But the memory from childhood wasn't welcome. It prompted a sudden burst of homesickness, accompanied by a jarringly intense dash of loneliness, reminiscent of how I'd felt leaving Base Camp at Lake Garda. Unsettled, I brushed the loneliness aside, scared of indulging it lest it take a firm hold. Plus, I didn't want it to spoil my fun. I wasn't a child anymore, but that didn't mean I couldn't still play. I was free to kick through leaf litter, free to throw great handfuls of leaves in the air if I wanted, and nothing was going to stop me, least of all loneliness. If someone on a walk like mine couldn't play with nature, who could? Playing was my duty!

The days grew shorter, which began to have an impact. Sunrise now came at 7.30 a.m., and although the ten hours of daylight that followed should have been plenty, I kept running out of it. I didn't finish walking most days until after dark—and finding a pitch by the light of my head-torch wasn't straightforward. The trouble was, I couldn't get myself going at dawn until sunlight hit the tent, and often, when camped in a deep valley or forest, the day was many hours old before that happened. As morning temperatures dropped ever closer to freezing the problem grew worse. The later I started the later I finished, and the later I finished the later I started the next day. Quite how I'd manage during the shorter and icier days of midwinter I couldn't guess. I tried not to think about it.

As I climbed away from the Val d'Adige with the fabled Dolomites in my sights, I encountered another challenge thrown up by the season: hunters. The first encounter nearly made me fly straight from my boots in surprise. One moment I was ambling peacefully along a soft trail through bird-filled woodland, inhaling the rich and heady scents of mulchy decay, and then the next an almighty BANG exploded to the right, shattering the peace. 'HEY!' I gibbered at full volume in English, too rattled to remember to use Italian, 'Don't shoot,' I yelled. 'Walker… coming through.' Curiously, the unseen hunters chose not to reply, but no more shots were fired. From that point on I sang even more often than usual, especially in the woods. I saw several hunters over the next few days, and was probably seen—and heard—by many more. All were men; most were closer to retirement age than youth. One in particular stood out, quite literally. While following a rough track up a tight valley late one evening I glanced upwards at an exposed outcrop, and upon it stood a silhouetted figure, dark and stern, long coat down to his knees, rifle held in his arms. Passing far beneath I shuddered involuntarily, feeling watched and threatened. Of course, I knew I was in little danger, that I personally wasn't being hunted, but the disquieting sensation of fear remained. Having a man with a gun lording it over the valley entirely changed my perception of the place, transformed it from a friendly home into a dark haunt to leave as swiftly as possible. I could only imagine how the valley's permanent residents felt.

The hunt—*la caccia*—is a cherished way of life for many Italians; not just a legal right but a cultural tradition stretching back thousands of years. What, after all, could be more human and natural than heading into the woods for food? But something about it here seemed marginally *un*natural. Perhaps it was the way the hunters didn't look as though they needed extra sustenance from the wild. Or perhaps it was the approach several of them took, standing in groups on the trail looking hopefully into the trees. 'What are you hunting?' I asked one group, and the reply was a shrug of shoulders, and an answer that seemed to embrace every living thing that moved: 'Boar, deer, wild sheep, fox, squirrels, birds.' Or perhaps it was simply that these forests didn't seem big enough to support hunting. This was still a wild place, but it wasn't a vast wild place, and its wildlife was already depleted. However much an essential part of the culture it was, however deeply it connected local hunters with their land, and however responsibly the best hunters hunted, I still couldn't suppress a feeling of dismay. Hunting here had clear impact on the land and on how its inhabitants behaved, and not in a way that added to the natural community's richness. It got me thinking about American conservation pioneer Aldo Leopold's 'Land Ethic', a simply stated but deeply considered observation on approaching the land in an ethical way. 'A thing is right when it tends to preserve the integrity, stability, and beauty of the biotic community,' Leopold wrote in his 1949 book, *A Sand Country Almanac*; 'It is wrong when it tends otherwise.' To me, the hunters I saw were 'tending otherwise'.

Tramping on, my feet carried me ever closer to the Dolomites. I passed the Piramidi di Segonzano, continued up the Val Regnana, cut through the wild and precipitous Catena del Lagorai range. The Piramidi di Segonzano—forty-foot-tall pillars of earth rising above the woods like giant exclamation marks—were an unexpected sight, and an example of the natural variety so enriching my journey. Built from a soft conglomerate of sandy soil and pebbles, they stood tall where erosion-resistant rock caps rested atop them; where no cap sat, the land had washed away. So thin and delicate were many of the pillars that it seemed incredible they could stand at all, but no doubt people had thought that of me too, seeing my skinny legs ticking away beneath the oversized Ten Ton.

After several weeks without a shower I finally succumbed and stopped at a small hotel, the Rifugio Gambaccini. But it wasn't only to wash away grime. England's football team were playing Italy in their final World Cup qualifying match that night, and that was something I had to see. A shopkeeper confirmed that the match was going to be broadcast live on TV, and the Rifugio Gambaccini's hospitable owner confirmed that his TV would be showing it. Sure, I was due a shower, but more than that I was due a break from The Walk.

The Piramidi di Segonzano, October 13, 1997.

It was the perfect break—and not just for the football. Freed for once from the need to sweat uphill, to find and make camp, I relaxed outside until check in, basking lazily for several hours beneath the Endless Summer's blazing sun. Once my room was ready I moved in, took a long shower —a therapeutic treat—and followed it with a pleasure so luxurious and decadent I almost cried from the beauty of it: stretching out on a real bed. Dinner was eaten downstairs, in company with the owner's eleven-year old son, Giovanni, an enthusiastic lad who was the exact opposite of all I'd been at a similar age. While I would have stammered with shyness, he behaved as though he'd known me for years, chattering about football, remote-controlled cars, his stereo sound system, and the music he played on it. For the most part we understood one another perfectly, but there were several moments of confusion. When he asked: 'Do you like smashing pumpkins?' I thought it an odd question, but quickly realised it was probably a Trentino custom, something perhaps the boy thought all people did in the autumn. Fascinated, I tried to find out more, quizzing him on where he smashed them, and why, but my questions only brought confusion— until comprehension lit his eyes, and then laughter consumed him. 'No,' he

285

explained, once he regained control. 'People here don't smash pumpkins. I only wondered if you liked the music of my favourite rock group, the Smashing Pumpkins!'

As the match's start drew near the TV was turned on. By this time the restaurant was so crowded with Italian supporters I could barely see the screen, and so cacophonous with their laughter and singing I could barely hear it. Being the only Englishman amid a crowd of rowdy Italian soccer fans suddenly struck me as precarious. English football hooligans had frequently rampaged across Italy, and the horrific Heysel Stadium tragedy—where charging Liverpool supporters had caused a stampede that left thirty-nine Italian fans dead—was still recent history. Not that the Italian fans here showed any sign of aggression, but how would they react if England won? Happily, I never found out. The restaurant's owner—to much heckling from his boisterous customers—couldn't get the TV tuned to the correct channel. This worked out well for me. Ignoring his country-men, the owner led me upstairs to his private quarters, and it was there in comparative peace that Giovanni and I watched the game. The match was memorable—not for England's unusually competent performance, or for how the final score (tied) sent both teams through to the following year's finals in France, but for Giovanni's exuberant companionship. Bouncing up and down on his chair, screaming at the screen, asking endless ques-tions about the English players, he helped banish The Walk from my mind for several hours. I hadn't realised it needed banishing, but based on how I felt afterwards—curiously renewed—it appeared that it had.

A few days later, back above tree line, alone upon the autumn-burnished slopes of the rugged Catena del Lagorai, the momentous change I'd been anticipating since Lake Garda finally arrived. At first it went unnoticed. I was flying uphill, hypnotised by the rhythm of effort and oblivious to the surrounding environment. In the back of my mind I was aware of dark clouds far behind, where the Brenta Dolomites were at war with the sky, but it took a while before local conditions registered. Eventually, however, I noticed tiny white flecks drifting through the air. What they were I couldn't initially fathom, and I ignored them. But finally it came to me—it was snowing! And here I was, powering uphill in T-shirt and shorts! The higher I climbed the colder the world appeared, with ice upon puddles and frost in the shade, and when finally I paused for a break I discovered that the temperature was right on freezing. I'd felt warm to that point, but now that my brain was aware of the cold my body suddenly felt it. Laughing at my inappropriate attire, I made a quick change into long trousers, hat, gloves, and fleece, and pushed on through gently falling snow.

The flakes were still floating down later that night while I lay in camp. They weren't heavy, and they barely whitened the ground, but as they settled with a soft murmur upon my shelter they clearly announced that six months of sunshine and heat had come to an end. By dawn the snow had ceased and the sky was clear, but a thuggish wind that cut daggers through my layers turned the day's miles into an unwinnable battle, and by evening it was almost too cold to write my diary. My fingers had trouble manipulating the pen. That night, frost furred the inside of the tent, and by the following morning the song of a nearby mountain stream was muffled, locked away beneath ice. The task of packing Ten Ton and dismantling camp took three times longer than normal. The Blob, frozen into unyielding cardboard, wouldn't easily fit into its bag. By the time I'd forced it away sensation was lost from my hands and feet and it took two vigorous miles before it was painfully restored.

Over the next two days the cold intensified. Soon, the once-soft earth became so hard that tent pegs wouldn't penetrate. Small streams froze solid, forming miniature glaciers that stood out bright white against ochre-hued slopes. Wet stretches of trail turned to sheet ice, slowing progress. Bird life became sparse; marmots were heard and seen no more; the scents of the land became harder to detect. Life was suddenly harsher and relaxing became less easy. I relearned the hard way that sweating was a mistake—it led to uncontrollable shivering when I stopped—and I slowed my pace to avoid it. My fingers felt perpetually chilled, even in gloves. The entire environment—previously so familiar—was suddenly less known, if not altered completely. What had been welcoming was now indifferent; what had been comfortable now felt exposed. Everywhere I looked I saw signs of the approaching winter.

The Endless Summer had finally ended, and I gulped at the cold reality that lay ahead.

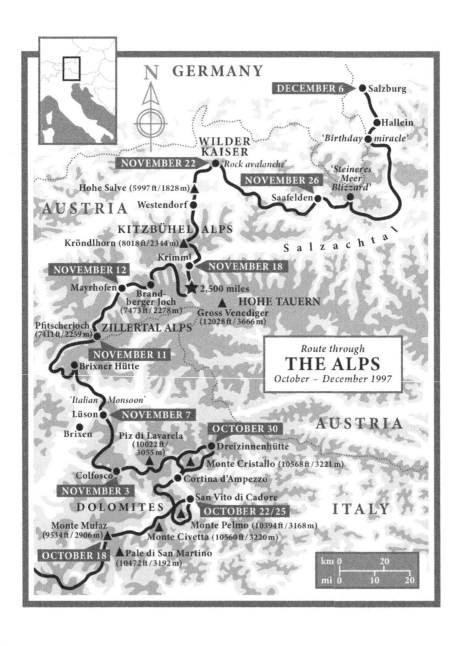

N GERMANY

DECEMBER 6 ● Salzburg

● Hallein

'Birthday ● miracle'

WILDER
KAISER

NOVEMBER 22 ● *Rock avalanche*

'Steineres
Meer
Blizzard'

NOVEMBER 26

Saafelden ●

Hohe Salve (5997 ft / 1828 m) ▲

AUSTRIA Westendorf ●

S a l z a c h t a l

KITZBÜHEL ALPS

Kröndlhorn (8018 ft / 2344 m) ▲

Krimml

NOVEMBER 12

NOVEMBER 18

Mayrhofen ● ★ 2,500 miles

Brand-
berger Joch
(7473 ft / 2278 m)

▲ HOHE TAUERN

Gross Venediger
(12028 ft / 3666 m)

Pfitscherjoch
(7411 ft / 2259 m) ZILLERTAL ALPS

NOVEMBER 11

● Brixner Hütte

Route through

THE ALPS

October – December 1997

'Italian Monsoon'

Lüson ● NOVEMBER 7

Brixen ●

Piz di Lavarela
(10022 ft /
3055 m) ▲

OCTOBER 30

● Dreizinnenhütte

AUSTRIA

▲ Monte Cristallo (10568 ft / 3221 m)

Colfosco ●

● Cortina d'Ampezzo

NOVEMBER 3

● San Vito di Cadore

DOLOMITES ▲ OCTOBER 22/25

ITALY

Monte Mulaz
(9534 ft / 2906 m) ▲ Monte Pelmo (10394 ft / 3168 m)

▲ Monte Civetta (10560 ft / 3220 m)

OCTOBER 18 ▲ Pale di San Martino
(10472 ft / 3192 m)

km 0   20

mi 0   10   20

288

BROTHERS OLD AND NEW
Chapter 4

WHAT DO YOU do when someone tells you they might die next year, next month, or at any moment? What is there to say?

Perhaps you say nothing—and let eyes, and then an embrace, do the talking.

That was my response, and my two companions—Flavio and Graziella —understood. In silence we communicated, and then we turned and stared across the remarkable Dolomites from our summit perch, and for a while no one said anything at all.

I'd climbed into the Dolomites the previous day. For weeks—if not months —their stabbing peaks had been in mind, pulling me on, and now I was here I could scarcely believe I was back. The Dolomites were 'my' mountains, well known from five previous visits; the closest thing to home I had experienced since starting The Walk. Each time I'd left I'd tried fixing the range into my memory, and before each return believed I knew what to expect, but the range always blew my expectations to smithereens. Mere memories can never do justice to the Dolomites.

The Dolomites aren't like the rest of the Alps. Here, the mountains stand isolated from one another, rearing skywards with shocking abruptness.

Down low the land is gentle—there are forests, villages, and rolling meadows, places of life and colour—but all that ends at tree line. Suddenly, rock takes over. There are huge walls and multi-pinnacled peaks, thrusting towers and turrets, shapes that belong in a gothic fantasy. Each peak is an individual, offering its own unique take on what a mountain should be. There's Drei Zinnen with its three huge teeth; Cristallo with its majestic buttresses; Civetta with its immense wall; Pelmo with its castle-like battlements; the Sella group with its lost-world plateau of desert-like desolation; the Tofana group with its russet-hued faces and pyramid-sharp summits; Sassolungo with its gravity-defying steepness; and the queenly Marmolada with its shining ribbon of ice—the list could go on. In the Dolomites, rock comes in so many variations of vertical that just when you think you've seen it all you discover that you've barely scratched the surface.

The steepness of the range is distinctive, but so too is the way the mountains glow. At sunrise and sunset the Dolomites play games with light few other ranges can match. The vast acres of exposed rock don't just reflect sunlight; they consume it, become it, until you'd think the rock was lit from within. The sight of this alone makes the Dolomites worth visiting.

I reached the edge of the range on October 17, and pitched my shelter in an upland valley facing the walls and towers of the Pale di San Martino group. Heavy clouds hung overhead, sliced at by sharp summits, but by sunset the overcast began breaking, and that was all it took. In an instant the walls and towers were ablaze with colour: golden to fiery orange to violet-peach, and you could have picked up my jaw from the grass at my feet. As the show unfolded I ran through two entire films, and didn't notice my hands growing numb. The Dolomites do that: they help you forget everything.

My route into the range led over the 8,592-foot Passo del Mulaz. The ascent was unrelentingly steep and loose, but the scenery robbed it of difficulty or effort. My map showed a summit above the pass that looked reachable, and a refuge just below it, and I made both my goal. Unsurprisingly, given the shape of the land, Dolomite summits aren't the easiest to reach. But one has to try. Anyone who merely looks at these mountains will never know them. Knowledge comes from close acquaintance, from the use of feet and hands. In the Dolomites one definitely has to use hands.

In crisp afternoon light I topped out at Passo del Mulaz and weaved

Evening sunlight on the Pale di San Martino Dolomites, October 17, 1997.

down to the refuge beneath it, the Rifugio Volpi al Mulaz. Staying the night depended upon finding water, not so easily done in this barren high-altitude rock desert, but a streak of old snow a stone's throw from the refuge solved that problem. With water guaranteed I moved on to the building. The main refuge was closed, but it offered the usual winter room, albeit one that was small, dark, and icebox cold; it was warmer outside in the sun. The room's heavy door creaked as I pushed it open, and it was inside that I met Flavio and Graziella, a couple who, in less than twelve hours, would steal and then break my heart.

Flavio and Graziella were bustling around the room amid scattered piles of gear and food. Flavio was tall and dark haired, an outdoorsman if his tan was anything to go by. He wore a beard and an open, welcoming smile—a smile Graziella shared. Pushing back her dark brown hair, which shone brightly in the room's flickering candlelight, Graziella spoke first.

'You look as though you have come a long way,' she observed, hitting the nail on the head with spectacular accuracy.

We made our introductions. Flavio told me he was forty-four, and a climber, photographer and friend to many great Italian mountaineers; Graziella revealed she was a decade younger, and new to the mountains, but she admitted they were getting under her skin. Her English was significantly better than my Italian, and she took on the role of translator, greatly easing communication. They both wondered why I was here, out of normal season: 'It is not usual, a foreigner, alone, at this time of year.' Piece by piece the couple teased my story to the surface, and greeted it with enthusiasm. They opened their pantry, carried up here with much effort, and sliced a fresh baguette for me, spread it with goat's cheese and ham, then handed over a small but precious bottle of water. Their generosity was increased, quite possibly, by appreciation. I suspected they wanted to sleep alone, and although they protested when I told them I'd camp outside I imagined I saw relief. In any case, my tent was warmer than the winter room. It was living up to its name quite spectacularly.

I pitched the Blob in sunlight, marvelling at the surrounding rock towers, and labelled the camp 'Val Perfecto'. Shelter up, I returned to the snow patch to collect extra water for dinner. The snow was glacier-hard, and to break into it I used Excalibur, making several fearsome strikes before I'd chipped enough ice free. Thawing the ice took patience, but the effort was worthwhile. It made this camp—the highest of the entire journey at 8,400 feet—possible.

A little after five I ambled back to the pass to catch the sunset, but my feet, through a will of their own, didn't stop there. Step by step they carried me upwards, along a vague climber's trail that switchbacked across steep ground, and before I knew it I was standing atop Monte Mulaz.

As Dolomite summits go it was a modest affair, but the view raised its stature. Stretching from the astonishing rock pinnacles of the Pale di San Martino to a hundred-mile arc of glacial peaks, it demanded attention. South-west was the Val Padana and my past; had I really crossed that wide space just a month ago? West were the Adamello and Stelvio mountains, my route through them clear. And north lay the Austrian border and my future. It was a thrilling thing to see in a glance what the next few weeks held in store. On a long walk a summit is so much more than a high place to reach. It can offer an overview of an entire story.

As the sun dipped west I remained rooted to the spot. The world spun, shadows lengthened, and the rock beneath my feet began to glow. Soon, the colours that had so entranced me the evening before returned, tinting the world gold, and this time I wasn't just watching the display, I was part of it. On the highest rocks behind me a stone arch had been built, and hanging

On the summit of Monte Mulaz, October 18, 1997.

from it was a brass bell, and to celebrate the moment I almost reached for it—but didn't. There was magic up here that required reverence, not bell ringing; there was something precious that a single thoughtless act could destroy. As day slipped towards night I simply stood in awe, treasuring the moment, and the throbbing silence was sound enough. It wasn't until the final glimmer of daylight faded from the highest peak that I returned to earth and acknowledged my position: alone on an Alpine summit with night almost upon me. With reluctance, I turned downhill.

A little later, when I reached camp in near darkness, Graziella appeared. 'We have made dinner,' she called out. 'Enough for you too.' And she led me back to the refuge. I'd already eaten dinner hours earlier, but extra fuel wasn't something I could refuse, and I was soon glad I hadn't. The meal was a rare treat, and a real feast: a rich meat sauce on pasta; a huge, leafy salad; and red wine filling my plastic mug. But the companionship surpassed it. After so many months alone companionship was always going to have an impact, but I'd never experienced anything like the impact that followed. Something unexpected took place while we ate, talked, and laughed. I could feel it happening to me, and could see it on my companions' faces too. Perhaps it was Graziella and Flavio's natural friendliness, or perhaps it was my own lingering high from the summit, or perhaps it was The Walk itself—the way it always transformed ordinary situations into extraordinary moments—but Flavio and Graziella changed before my eyes from complete strangers into cherished friends I might have known for years. It didn't only show in our talk but through unspoken communication, through simple looks that seemed to hold deeper meaning, through the absolute ease of our being together. It was remarkable, how being with the couple felt as comfortable as being at home. I didn't understand it, or probe it, but the connection and belonging filled me with joy.

Weary eyelids eventually brought the evening to a close, and I retreated to my tent. Graziella came running after me, carrying a pile of rough blankets from the winter room. 'So you won't be cold,' she explained. 'We will see you in the morning then? Five-thirty?' I nodded; yes. I'd offered to show Flavio and Graziella the route up Monte Mulaz. I suspected the morning was going to be memorable.

Sleep felt short—my alarm seemed to ring just seconds after I'd closed my eyes—but rising was easy. Clutching my stove and breakfast I stole across a moonlit landscape to the refuge, and joined my friends in the winter room. Flavio had coffee on the go; Graziella thrust a plate of chocolate cake into my hands. It was the sweetest breakfast I'd eaten since leaving England, and my new friends laughed at my expression of delight. I laughed back, but wished there was something I could give them. My friends had been wonderfully generous. I couldn't imagine I had anything to offer in return.

We set off at six, a full moon overhead, a pale hint of dawn on the eastern horizon. Flavio carried the only pack, choosing to bring to the summit a Thermos of tea and more cake. I walked with just my camera slung over my shoulder and trusty Excalibur in one hand. The silence was intense, the air cold and crisp. Expectancy filled every step, every breath.

Flavio took the lead as we walked in single file, but he kept wandering from the path. Eventually, I took his place. 'This way,' I suggested, and Flavio laughed, shaking his head.

'These are our mountains,' he mocked himself. 'But you are more at home on them!'

'Our English mountain guide,' Graziella added with a laugh as we continued on our way.

Progress wasn't fast, but we reached the summit before sunrise.

Flavio held me back just below the top so that Graziella could stand upon it first. Jubilantly, they took turns ringing the bell, and this time it added to the moment. '*Straordinario!*' Flavio exclaimed as he grinned and looked around, and then—laughing at the cliché—we all shook hands. Sharing the summit somehow made the place even greater.

Dawn came: fire upon summits and rock walls near and far. '*Straordinario!*' Flavio exclaimed again and again. He and I took it in turns naming distant peaks; several he'd climbed, a few I had too. Pulling out tiny but powerful binoculars Flavio studied the view, and after Graziella's turn let me take a look. I turned them north towards Austria, examining my future intently. On my long Alpine walk three years earlier I'd soloed 12,028-foot Grossvenediger, crossing the large glaciers with some trepidation, and through the binoculars I followed the route again. In a few weeks I'd be beneath Grossvenediger once more. I wondered if I could climb it a second time.

We remained on the summit for an hour, drinking Flavio's sweet tea. Our mood was celebratory, but when we turned to descend it suddenly and dramatically changed.

Earnestly, Flavio began sharing what had apparently been on his mind since first we'd met. Through Graziella's translation the story unfolded.

'I lost my brother last year,' Flavio revealed, simply. 'He died, suddenly. A brain haemorrhage. One moment here, the next gone. We were very close. He was older than me by one year, and he died at forty-five.' *Only forty-five*, I thought; *half a life*.

'The same thing happened to my father when I was young,' Flavio continued. 'He died the same way, at a similar age. In his mid forties.' He stopped talking for a moment, looking uncertain. 'I will be forty-five in a few months.'

Silence followed. I couldn't think of a thing to say, so said nothing. But the fondness I'd been feeling for Flavio grew beyond measure. My chest felt tight.

'When you first appeared you reminded me of my brother... in so many ways. And then when you said your name...' Flavio paused again before continuing. 'You have the same energy, the same spirit. You both love the mountains. His name, also, was Andrew.' At that I almost choked, felt my eyes moisten. The emotion of the moment, up here on the

Graziella and Flavio on Monte Mulaz, October 19, 1997.

remarkable glowing summit, was almost too much to bear.

'Perhaps it sounds crazy, but we are all linked together,' Flavio said. 'Every human being: we are all family. Even when we have gone we remain here in spirit. My brother is here on this summit. This I know.'

Reaching forward, I grabbed Flavio by the shoulders, hugged him, and did the same with Graziella.

'*Mio fratello il mio amico*' ('My brother and my friend'), Flavio murmured.

I nodded, and repeated his words, looking him straight in the eyes.

And then, finally, we began our descent.

We walked in silence at first, but the sheer drama of the landscape slowly worked its magic, and by the time we were halfway down we couldn't stay silent any longer. Awe and joy triumphed. The Dolomites do that: they help you forget everything. '*Straordinario!*' Flavio exclaimed, yet again. We all beamed, all three of us on a high.

Too soon we were down, and it was time for me to continue my journey. My new friends kept me company while I dismantled the 'Val Perfecto' camp, shaking their heads at the sight of Ten Ton fully packed.

'You are crazy!' Graziella commented. 'It is not possible what you are doing! I have never met anyone like you.'

Flavio had the last word. He asked me to wait a moment and walked off to the refuge, returning with a parting gift.

'Take this knife. Every time you use it you will remember me.'

Eyes moist again I racked my brain, trying to come up with something I could give in return. But Flavio read my thoughts.

'I have a new brother, and I will know you are in the mountains. You have given me everything.'

We shook hands, embraced a final time, and then I set off. My friends stood side by side watching me go. They looked so small beneath the Pale di San Martino's towers. When I glanced back a final time they waved madly, and then I turned a corner and saw them no more. Suddenly alone again, I felt something tear inside.

For the next four days I walked detached from the real world, climbing around and over my 'straordinario Dolomiti', thinking about life, death, and the whims of fate, taking nothing for granted. Towers soared overhead, rock walls blocked out the sky, clouds swirled, and my nightly dreams paled against each day's incredible reality. At some point, unnoticed, I passed a major milestone—2,200 miles—and The Walk became the longest I'd ever taken. I also noticed that I'd just passed a key date, October 18. This was the date I'd pencilled in for arrival at the North Cape in one year's time, and passing it meant there was less than a year to the end. Step by tiny step, I was crossing the continent.

Once I'd skirted two more improbably steep mountains—Civetta and Pelmo—I jumped aboard a bus and then a train, Venice-bound. In Flavio I'd found a new brother, but I'd soon share the range with an old one. Paul, one of my three brothers, and two years my junior, was flying out for eight days along with Nick, a long-time college friend of his. I'd shared several short backpacking trips with Paul over the years—weekend walks, mostly, and one week-long trek, Paul's longest continuous hike. He was one of the few people I knew who made walking in company better than walking alone. Our shared miles had always brought peals of laughter. Paul was thin like me, but three inches taller, and also loved mountains, although with far more balance than I managed; he had other interests too. Nick was shorter and stockier, and I had no idea whether he liked mountains or not, but if Paul thought he should tag along that was good enough for me. What I knew for certain was that he and Paul were very much alike. They shared a long history, the same sense of humour, and many of the same interests. Both were serious mathematicians, capable of computing abstract concepts far beyond my understanding. Fortunately, they hadn't come for serious scientific conversation but simply to have fun. They set the tone from the start, with humour that bordered on juvenile, which suited me just fine. After a short stay in Venice it was a happy band of three who struck uphill back into the Dolomites.

Neither Paul nor Nick had visited the range before, and I took great pleasure showing it off. The unveiling took place in the village of San Vito di Cadore, where the pale walls of Punta Sorapiss and Monte Antelao leaned over the rooftops, crowding out the sky. Paul and Nick were suitably impressed, but played it cool.

'Hmmm,' Paul observed, twisting his face as though disappointed. 'It's okay, I suppose. But I thought you said there were mountains?'

'Yeah,' Nick offered. 'If you ask me, this all looks a bit, well, flat.'

Laughter accompanied our climb from the valley, and barely ceased over the next eight days. Soon I was laughing in my sleep once again. No other set of miles since Melito had been so light-hearted or fun. Sure, I had enjoyed myself and, sure, I had laughed, but not like this, not to the point where I could barely breathe. Paul and Nick wasted no opportunity to poke fun at one another, at themselves, and especially at me—and soon I was doing the same. Perhaps I'd fallen into the trap of taking the journey too seriously, but my companions pulled me back from the brink. It was a clear reminder that even Mad Mountain Jack could spend too much time alone.

For a week I shared my wandering way of life, and knowing that it would only last a few days I enjoyed it all the more. Ten Ton seemed less heavy, each mile less long, each climb less steep. At the back of my mind I sensed that the interlude was going to make the journey afterwards harder, but I pushed the concern aside. Before starting I'd known there would be lows as well as highs, and I'd known I'd just have to deal with them. Anyone could complete a long walk when happy, when things were going well. But coping with the low points and pushing on regardless was where the true test of character lay.

Sleeping alternately in camp and then in winter rooms, we looped around fortress-like Monte Pelmo. The concave amphitheatre of its east face was a perfect spot for a yodelling contest. Nick went first, Paul second, and I third, but the fun really began when we joined our voices together. The echoes rolled long and loud, reverberating about Pelmo's massive walls for a surprising length of time, and they had an impact. Just as we were preparing to try again, we heard the sound of huge rocks thundering down the mountain.

Nick's eyes widened. 'Whoa! Did we do that?'

'Er... maybe we should stop?' Paul observed, looking nervously up.

A moment's silence followed while we considered things carefully like the mature adults we supposedly were. Then, we all looked at one another, grinned, and in perfect unison gave it everything we had. This time, however, nothing fell.

We laughed again that evening at the friendliness shown to us by a large brown horse. He was grazing close to the hut we'd settled into for the night, and every time we ventured outside he came trotting up. At the first approach Nick stepped forward and patted his head, but this was a mistake. It prompted a certain part of the horse's anatomy to grow to an impressive length.

'Oo-er,' Nick mumbled, backing away carefully.

From then on, every time we peeked outside, the horse cantered forwards, and each time its penis grew.

'Well,' Nick finally said, turning to admonish me. 'You might have warned us. English horses don't behave this way.'

Beneath clear skies I led my companions across the range, detouring to some of my favourite viewpoints. Each day grew a little colder, but worse lay in store. I had a history with Paul of inviting him on walks that provided atrocious weather, such as the week he'd spent with me during my three-month Pyrenean traverse. Before his arrival conditions had been perfect, and I'd promised him more of the same, but once his boots were on the ground sunshine had given way to rain, the rain to sleet, and then to driving snow, and before his visit was over the ground was buried beneath three feet of the white stuff. This time, to cover myself, I'd advised that anything was possible, but I hadn't told him how cold it was going to get. Honestly, I hadn't known.

Snowflakes were spiralling through the air as we descended to the chic resort town of Cortina d'Ampezzo to resupply. Backlit by the sun, the flakes sparkled diamond-bright; they put us in a festive mood, and set us singing a medley of Christmas carols. By afternoon the snow had ceased falling, but not the temperature, which went into freefall. It was as if someone had pulled out some kind of climate plug, draining away all warmth and plunging the mountains into midwinter cold. The suddenness of the change was shocking. One moment we felt warm enough to keep our sleeves rolled, but the next not even gloves could provide sufficient insulation.

Finding water that night was a challenge. The closest stream to camp had turned to impenetrable ice. Overnight the temperature plummeted further; by dawn the walls within our tents were coated with frozen condensation half an inch thick, and our water bottles were solid through to their cores. Paul was startled when he tried to eat one of his apples. It had been transformed into a rock-hard cricket ball. He nearly broke a tooth.

My keyring thermometer—or 'Random Number Generator' as Paul termed it—recorded zero Fahrenheit, close to minus eighteen Celsius. Everything around us was locked in silence, stilled as though dead, frozen as though even time had succumbed to the cold. No birds sang, no creatures stirred. There was just us—three shivering figures emerging from our tents into an indifferent landscape. As we stood outside, the cold seemed to intensify. It was shocking, grasping, heartless. Quite possibly the Random Number Generator wasn't even close. But one thing was absolutely certain: none of us had any desire to hang around.

Never before had I wished to strike camp so swiftly, but never before had it taken so long. Pulling on boots was a challenge. The frozen leather wouldn't bend, and to force the boots on we had to hammer them with our fists, kick hard against the ground with our feet half in them. The laces were also a problem—they'd become stiff as thick wire, too inflexible to tie. It was nigh on impossible to manipulate them while wearing thick gloves, but with gloves off it quickly became impossible to manipulate our fingers.

Nick and Paul testing the ice shortly after leaving the
'Camp of the Creeping Frost', October 29, 1997.

There were other difficulties. With numb fingers it was a struggle to force my sleeping bag into a stuff sack that now seemed several sizes too small. The tent wouldn't roll up with thick ice inside it, and the poles wouldn't spring apart; their joints were locked rigid. Thawing them involved breathing on each joint in turn, and then rubbing hands up and down the metal to generate warmth. Everything was more complicated; everything took three times as long. Before Ten Ton was half packed my feet were numb and my hands hurt so much I wanted to scream.

Alone, I may have quaked at the season ahead, panicked even. Happily, I wasn't alone.

By common consent we opted to spend the next night indoors, and I knew just the place. On the far side of Cristallo, up a forested side valley above the blue-green Lago Landro, sat a one-roomed log cabin; I'd slept in it three summers earlier, and recalled that it had a pot-bellied stove. Arrival —stepping onto the porch through clouds of our own breath, easing shut the door on the frozen world outside—was a moment to cherish. The cabin was surprisingly warm inside, and all being well the stove would make it warmer. Remembering the horrible smog put out by the stove back at the Rifugio Lago Corvo I carefully checked that this stove's damper was open, confirmed that the flue wasn't blocked. Everything looked in order, but still I hesitated before striking a match.

Within minutes, I wished we'd left the stove alone. It was another smoker—it belched sooty clouds no matter what we did with it—and within half an hour we'd transformed the once-warm cabin into a freezer-cold open-windowed barn filled with suffocating black smog.

'And to think,' Nick observed sarcastically, 'I almost booked my holiday in a nice hotel on a Greek island. What a mistake that would have been!'

Unsurprisingly, none of us slept well. Paul and Nick fared the worst. Their sleeping bags were damp from the previous night's condensation, and the cabin's rickety bunks weren't to their liking. Paul tried sleeping on the top bunk, Nick below, but Nick began imagining lice in his bunk. So Nick tried sleeping on top, Paul below, but Paul grew worried that the creaking wooden slats above him were going to snap under Nick's weight. Then, both decided it was so cold they should pitch their tent *inside* the cabin and sleep in that. They got the tent up, with some difficulty in the small space, only to discover it was still awash with ice and water, and mopping it dry led to even colder fingers. Finally, just as they were ready to settle in, they noticed several sharp nail heads piercing the cabin floor—nails that would likely puncture their tent and sleeping pads. So back to the bunks they moved.

I watched their exertions and laughed; it was the best evening's entertainment in a long time.

By dawn, the temperature inside the cabin was ten Fahrenheit, minus twelve Celsius. Outside, the sky was so intensely clear and blue it produced a feeling akin to vertigo. We contemplated the risk of falling into it.

'The colour reminds me of my feet,' I murmured, and the joke wasn't far off the truth. They'd been cold now for two days straight. And winter had barely started.

By the time we escaped the deep, shadowy valley into direct sunlight, ominous mares' tails were rushing across the sky and a sharp wind had picked up; it felt as though a storm was on the way. But in spite of everything, our spirits remained high, and as always in the Dolomites the astonishing scenery so ensnared our collective imagination that we forgot the chill. When the three-toothed monument of a mountain that is Drei Zinnen came into view my companions couldn't play it cool any longer.

'Okay… so it's not *all* flat, then,' Nick begrudgingly admitted.

Paul was more succinct. 'Oh!' was all he managed, which pretty much said it all.

We settled into the winter room of the Dreizinnenhütte, a windowless cave no warmer than the world outside. My suggestion that we camp was outvoted. Paul and Nick took one look at the soft-mattressed bunks and the tall pile of blankets and wouldn't be swayed. It was probably just as well. Once darkness fell the wind strengthened until it was howling across the uplands, rattling the shutters, tearing at the earth's surface, flinging about dust. When I peered outside an hour later, the beam from my head-torch cut into heavy fog and driving snow. The ground outside was soon completely white.

With two camp stoves supplying heat, and a blanket draped over the imperfectly fitted doorway to reduce draughts, we raised the temperature a degree or two above freezing, and after all we'd endured it felt tropical. Sitting on real chairs instead of the ground, eating hot food, drinking tea, laughing with companions, wrapped in blankets like native American chiefs, listening to the raging storm outside, we felt beyond merely comfortable. The ferocity of the weather, the remoteness of the hut, the hard miles leading to it: all these elements combined to create a feeling of unsurpassable pleasure. Our small capsule of comfort surrounded by an environment in turmoil was the height of luxury, existence distilled to perfection. Nick summed it up best when he stated: 'Well, this *is* better than a Greek hotel after all.'

For me, this perfection was painfully sharpened by Paul and Nick's approaching departure. I'd grown used to having them around, grown used to the way they distracted me from my journey, grown used to our shared

Winter whitens the Dolomites, October 31, 1997.

laughter. It wasn't just the jokes; everything seemed easier and better in company—a surprising and troubling revelation for me to admit. Alongside Paul and Nick distances didn't seem so far, the wildest places weren't so intimidating, and decisions felt less committing. For the past week the pressure had been off, and mistakes wouldn't have mattered quite so much. For seven days The Walk had been a less serious game. It was now clear: walking in company and walking alone were two entirely different pursuits. They didn't have anything in common.

The evening passed with cards, laughter, and friendship. But churning beneath the light-hearted optimism that I wore on the surface was a growing panic based on all that lay ahead: the cold reality of winter and the even colder isolation of solitude. Outwardly I may have been laughing, but I was shaking inside. I still had a year to go—a year alone. What had I been thinking to have considered this a good idea? To my surprise, I managed to keep the panic in check during our final miles the next day back to Cortina, but a storm raged inside, fiercer than the storm that had blanketed the Dolomites in snow. Soon every shared minute was precious. When the bus that would whisk them away was delayed my heart skipped with joy. Two more hours of company: nothing in the world was better than that! But time stops for no one, and too soon Paul and Nick were inside their bus, waiting for it to leave, separated from me by an uncrossable chasm of glass, and my breath was suddenly coming in short, ragged gasps.

This felt worse than parting from Base Camp. First Base Camp, then Flavio and Graziella, and now Paul and Nick. It was cumulative; each time the anxiety grew worse.

The wait for actual departure was purgatory. I didn't want them to go —with all my being I wished for a different reality—but knew they had to, and I wanted it over and done with. *Just go now*, I willed the bus through clenched teeth. *Just please… bloody… go.*

Finally, it did. With a cheerful wave and grin my brother and Nick were carried away, and I sat watching as the bus drove down the road in slow motion and disappeared around a corner.

Tougher adventurers would have dealt with the parting with more stoicism. *Edmund Hillary, Roald Amundsen—they would have held it together*, I told myself. But not me; I lost it. I choked and sobbed, my resolve crumbling, my belief in the journey cracking apart and tumbling to the ground in broken shards. *I can't do this anymore*, I screamed inside. *I've had enough!* I wanted out. I wanted people in my life again. I wanted friends, family. Holding my head in my hands, I acknowledged a simple truth: more than anything I wanted to go home.

And what made it worse was knowing I wouldn't.

The following hours were the bleakest of the entire walk to that point. Nothing made sense any longer—especially the journey. It was as though everything I'd known about myself had turned out to be false, as though every decision I'd made had been the wrong one, as though all my fundamental beliefs about life and how to live it had been incorrect. The discovery that I needed other people, that I couldn't stand on my own two feet, turned my world upside down. I'd lost my identity. I wasn't Mad Mountain Jack after all, and never had been. I wasn't the happy-go-lucky wanderer I had wanted and pretended to be. I was a child, small and defenceless, abandoned and alone, and it was worse by far than being lost in the depths of the Aspromonte.

Disoriented, I left Cortina, wandering in a daze through an internal landscape that I couldn't get a grip on, that I had no frame of reference to, seeing little of the external landscape. The world inside was a maze—dark and confusing, threatening and surreal—and I didn't know how to navigate it. I'd committed everything to this single path through life. It was a mistake beyond comprehension. The realisation made me anxious to the point of almost throwing up. My journey *had* to work. If it didn't, what was I left with? A return to my previous life was unthinkable.

I marched in haste for the rest of the day, six hours in total, and they felt like six hundred. Not knowing what else to do I pushed hard, hoping exertion would still my troubled mind. But it wouldn't be still. The snow-covered trail seemed like the delicate surface of a glacier, and I kept breaking through it, plunging into crevasses of anxiety and loneliness. My thoughts spiralled in endless circles—seeking ways out, finding none. When I settled into camp I tried not thinking at all, focusing on camp routines, but I stumbled through them on autopilot, and the negative thoughts continued.

At first I failed to notice the details of the surrounding landscape—the golden larch decked in snow, the thrusting towers of dolomitic rock, the sharp winter air. But slowly they caught my attention, appearing on the periphery, offering a pinch of solace. Sitting bleakly in camp that evening I watched three chamois clatter by, and then a fleet-of-foot fox, and then alpine choughs wheeling overhead—more wildlife than I'd seen throughout Paul and Nick's visit—and at these signs of life a tiny wisp of positivity stirred. By sunset, the journey still felt pointless, my spirit still dashed around like a lost dog, but my eyes were a little less red.

Before daylight the next morning I scrambled to the summit of Piz di Lavarela, more for something to do than for any real desire to reach a summit. Sunrise came, and from 10,023 feet I watched the Dolomites glow. And that was when the recovery truly began. I sat statue-still for two hours in sunlight that was unexpectedly warm, and by the time I returned to camp the snow cover was dripping at the edges, thawing away, exactly like my own icy gloom. Soon, living grass poked through the melting snow, rocks steamed as they dried, and the entire world was suddenly brighter. It was hard to believe the transformation.

Instead of striking camp I chose to stay put and enjoy the warmth:

there'd probably not be another day like it all year. Why waste it moving on? By afternoon, I was back in shorts, pottering about camp barefoot for possibly the last time. As the hours passed I grew increasingly captivated by the landscape and my situation in it, increasingly intoxicated by my future. It seemed unbounded again; a life of freedom, not a jail sentence. I was able to acknowledge a simple truth: here *was* where I wanted to be, not home.

I was who I'd thought after all. I was Mad Jack, and it was a relief to know it. But I was also *more* than I'd thought—a real discovery. I just didn't yet know who or what that 'more' was, and—terrified of plunging back into loneliness—I didn't attempt to find out. I filed it away to examine and explore another time.

For now, the panic was broken, and it was the Dolomites that had done it. They'd won me back, smothering loneliness with wild drama so awe-inspiring I couldn't stay desolate for long. The Dolomites—my *straordinario* Dolomites—so impossibly grand all I could do was sit outside my tent and shake my head in wonder.

The Dolomites do that: they help you forget everything. And wild nature does that too, if one gives it a chance. It can heal more ills than we even have names for.

Winter's first crisis was over.

Evening light striking Monte Cristallo, October 27, 1997.

ADDIO ITALIA, HALLO ÖSTERREICH
Chapter 5

WHEN I STEPPED from Italy into Austria I couldn't see anything of the new country. Actually, I couldn't see much of anything at all.

Snow and fog smothered the landscape, creating a surreal, blank, nothingness. I'd reached the Pfitscherjoch, a lonely mountain pass that marked the Austrian border, and it was an empty no-man's land that the elements had wiped clean of detail. Winds had piled the snow into knee-deep drifts that buried the pass, and fog hid everything else, muffling sounds, limiting vision. But for occasional rocks jutting through it would have been difficult to know which way was up, which was down. Like the glaciers I'd tiptoed onto a month earlier, this was another location where I most assuredly wasn't at home. The Pfitscherjoch was unlike any other place on The Walk, and it was thrilling because of it. The deep, undisturbed snow burying it made it as wild as any location I'd been, an environment where humankind didn't hold sway. It prompted a familiar frisson of doubt —and a hint of fear. But, as on the glaciers, it wasn't a negative Monti della Laga fear. I didn't feel that I was letting myself down by feeling it, or that it was getting in the way. Instead, it felt appropriate, and valuable; like good advice, like a reminder to pay attention. Was I in control, here on the deep snow? I wasn't sure. Was I scared? A little. Did I truly want to be here? Oh goodness yes.

And where exactly did Austria begin?

———

For the previous week the weather had been persistently wet. Dark clouds had hung wall to wall across valleys, mists had drifted through forests, cold rain had fallen—often heavily. Rivers had begun to gush and then roar, rainwater had dripped constantly from pine trees, mushrooms had appeared on the forest floor as though taking over the world, and the mountains themselves had vanished. Forget winter; the Endless Summer had morphed into an Italian Monsoon.

It had been a delight to begin with; the relative warmth of it, the earthy scents unlocked, the half-forgotten pleasure of walking down a muddy trail with boots going squelch-squelch-squelch, the rhythmic percussion of rain on the tent fly. The conditions prompted fond memories of backpacking back home in Britain, but before long the dampness began to penetrate, and soon my entire universe was uncomfortably wet. From its first use back at Lago Garda the Blob had been prone to condensation, generating its own microclimate of dampness. Even in dry air small puddles had formed overnight in its corners, but now the puddles had become ponds. Even worse, the heaviest downpours were penetrating the tent's seams, and the wetness was working into my clothes and gear, seeping into my own skin. The only dry haven was my sleeping bag, kept dry with immense care; the waterproof bivvy bag was most assuredly earning its place on my back. Without it, nights would have been unpleasant indeed.

Mornings were the worst. Pulling on wet socks, damp clothes and still-sodden waterproofs; dismantling and packing away the drenched tent; striding forth under pressing skies into unrelenting rain: it took some getting used to. The zero-Fahrenheit morning with Paul and Nick had been uncomfortable, but these soggy just-above-freezing days were significantly worse. Chilled to the bone, fingers barely working in soaked gloves, I had tried reminding myself how much I'd longed for rain months earlier. But it only partially helped. Uncomfortable was uncomfortable, whatever form it took. Unlike loneliness, it wasn't a state of mind but a measurable physical reality.

To distract myself I began dreaming about spring. I pictured myself crossing Denmark in April, saw sunshine sparkling on the North Sea, imagined glorious warmth washing endless sandy beaches. But then I stopped.

Looking so far ahead was foolish. I wouldn't reach Denmark for five months! And looking ahead was also wrong: I was here on The Walk to be truly *here* on The Walk. I took to singing instead to take my mind off the rain, and began talking to trees and rocks as a distraction. And I spent time trying to convince myself that walking was, in fact, far easier on my own. Long miles passed unnoticed while I compiled a light-hearted list: 'The Top Ten Reasons Why Solo Is Better'. It soon covered all the important basics.

Reason one: if you don't want to get up in the morning you don't have to; solo hikers can do whatever they bloody well want. Two, when you make a major navigational error you can get away with pretending it was the plan all along. Three, you can walk as fast or slow as you like, stop as often as you like, and change direction on a whim whenever you like—the soloist has utter freedom. Four, you can look at the view without someone exclaiming 'Just look at that view!', and focus on how quiet the landscape is without someone shouting 'Isn't it quiet?' Five, you can argue your point of view without fear of contradiction, even if you know you are wrong. Six, every joke you crack will be funny, every observation wise, every song you sing perfectly in tune. Seven, loud explosions of flatulence can be cheered without embarrassment, and even with pride. Eight, you can chatter with inanimate objects, and even with yourself, without your sanity being questioned. Nine, if you happen to walk into a tree because you weren't paying attention there's no one there to mock you. And ten (the most important reason of all), you can consume as much chocolate as you like without ever having to share.

Days passed and the rain continued. My route through the Italian Monsoon took me on a parting loop through the Dolomites, curving beneath the ramparts of the Sella massif and the thrusting Puez-Odle, giving only fleeting glimpses of both. Then I turned north, tramping through a landscape of lower mountains, dark forests and rural valleys: a brief low-altitude respite before the Austrian border. I passed through villages where everyone appeared to be out chopping wood. Entire tree trunks had been delivered; axes were flying, chainsaws roaring. From the temporary shelter of an old wooden barn late one morning I watched an elderly man trying to protect his woodpile from the relentless rain. Using a plastic tarp he'd cover one side of the woodpile, walk around to the other and cover that too. Trouble was, the tarp was too small, and when he

The Italian Monsoon. Wet weather near Brixen, November 8, 1997.

covered the second side he pulled the tarp off the first. Again and again he pulled the tarp backwards and forwards across his woodpile, uncovering different sides in turn, until I couldn't take it any longer. In pity, I splashed out into the deluge, suggested in Italian (not understood), and then by sign language that he create a more compact woodpile, and helped him do it while the rain worked deeper into my clothes.

German had now become the dominant language, and the place names reflected it: Lüsen, Mühlbach, St. Jakob, Pfitscher Tal. The few conversations I had were in German, although calling them 'conversations' overstates their length and complexity. I'd been practising *Deutsch* for weeks, but still only knew a handful of key phrases. Still, what I could say I pronounced well; so well it seemed that people didn't believe I only spoke a little. When a storekeeper in Mühlbach began talking too quickly I held up my hands, and explained with perfect guttural harshness: '*Es tut mir leid… mein Deutsch ist sehr schlecht.*' ('I am sorry… my German is very bad.')

'No it is not…' the storekeeper replied in German, beaming. 'It is *really* good.' And he continued with a torrent of German, not one word of which I understood.

From the village architecture—somehow harsher and less flamboyant than further south—to the less melodic language, to the grim, northern weather, I felt I'd already left Italy. But finally, on November 11, I left it for real.

The day began with a 6 a.m. alarm, the now-familiar drumming sound of rain, and a groping hand that reached from my sleeping bag and reset the alarm for 6.30… *p.m.*. The 'p.m.' was a genuine mistake, but when I realised the error shortly after seven I was tempted to pretend I hadn't noticed it. After all, 'Solo Is Better Reason One' meant I could get away with staying in bed all day if I wanted.

But Austria lay just a few miles ahead.

Awash with emotion, excited and sad at the same time, reliving all that Italy had been, not sure I really wanted to leave, I eventually rose, struck camp, and pushed up my last Italian valley. I soon passed the last Italian village, the last Italian farm, and eventually the last Italian. He was a farmer, red faced and dressed in an ancient raincoat, and he was driving a hilariously small tractor up the paved mountain road. Behind the tractor, attached to it by rope, and facing downhill in the opposite direction, was a large cow. It was fiercely resisting the tractor's tug. The tractor was winning the contest, but only by increments, and only because the cow's scrabbling hooves couldn't quite find purchase on the slick road. So slowly was the tractor moving that I easily pulled level, and then overtook it. The farmer turned to glare at me through the open sides of the cab. '*Bella giornata!*' ('Beautiful day!') I joked, smiling happily, singing in Italian for the very last time.

'*Nein,*' fired back the farmer, grim-faced. '*Es ist verdammt schrecklich.*'

I didn't understand the words, but got the general gist.

Further up the valley, at 5,000 feet, the rain turned to sleet, and within 100 yards to snow. Soon, the green-brown Pfitscher Tal was grey-white, the pine trees heavily decked, the narrow road snow-smothered and untracked. The higher I pushed the deeper the snow lay, until I found myself walking through an environment utterly transformed. This was a softer place, a hushed place; a mountain realm blanketed and somnolent; a stilled world of simplified shapes and exquisite, understated beauty. I grinned at it, laughed aloud. Couldn't help myself. This was more like it: a winter wonderland! Austria here I come.

Only it wasn't as easy as that.

Even six inches of unbroken snow can dramatically reduce progress; the knee-deep snow I encountered practically stopped it. At 7,369 feet the Pfitscherjoch isn't especially high, or hard to reach, or difficult to cross. On the Italian side an unmade road leads to it, switchbacking upwards at an easy grade. There's also a trail taking a more direct route, completing in less than two miles what the road achieves in seven. Although steep, the trail would be simple to follow in midsummer, leading across friendly, grass-covered slopes, but on that November day I couldn't imagine it. As I fought my way upwards, pushing through drifts, each step an achievement, lost in the whiteness of it, wrapped in dense fog, I felt 1,000 miles from summer, and 1,000 more from the human world. It was just me and a snowbound mountain, all signs of my own species obliterated. Summer, other people, and even the journey itself, ceased to exist.

The two-mile climb took most of the morning. It seemed appropriate: I wasn't sure I wanted to leave Italy, and it seemed Italy didn't want to let me go; at least not without a fight. And a fight it was; a long, hard, sweaty fight. By the time the angle eased, and I reached what I guessed was the pass, my thermal shirt was clinging wetly to my back and my hair was plastered flat beneath my hood. From the feel of it I might have just completed a marathon, and a break was long overdue, but in my sweat-soaked state pausing at the wintry pass didn't seem like the smartest idea.

And yet it was hard not to. This was a key moment in the journey—a stage of my life was about to end. I didn't want to rush the passage into Austria. I wanted to mark the border, celebrate walking the length of Italy, set the moment apart. What I desired was a sign from the mountain gods that I had done well. I wanted to be recognised for making it this far, to be granted an award for all I'd achieved. But, of course, I got nothing. Literally, just a great blank nothing. The map showed a private refuge close to the pass, and there was probably some kind of marker at the exact border, but

I couldn't see either. In these conditions I could stand thirty feet from the refuge and not know it. I wasn't even sure I was still on the trail. Nothing was going to happen. Clearly, the mountain gods didn't care.

But then, just as I took a step to move on, it happened—exactly the way it was supposed to. From out of nowhere the gods breathed, the fog stirred, shifted, and suddenly a great rent was torn. Sharp snow peaks came into view, hung with tatters of cloud: the mighty Zillertal Alps. With astonishing speed the clouds shrank before my eyes, making way for a dazzling sun, and within five minutes the fog, falling snow and utter blankness had become a distant memory. The Pfitscherjoch sparkled, magical beyond belief. No reward could have been finer.

The clutter of buildings at the pass was now revealed, as was the border itself, fifty yards to the north. Leaving a trench in the snow I ploughed to it, rejoicing with every step. The border was marked with a four-foot stone pedestal and a large metal sign that read: '*Confine di Stato, Staatsgrenze*' ('State Border'). A smaller sign beside it held a paragraph of text in German and Italian, important entry information no doubt, but I gave it little thought. I was ready. Whispering a heartfelt 'Thank you' at the land I was leaving I stepped from the South Tyrol to the North Tyrol, from Italia to Österreich, and didn't look back.

Within minutes, obliterating fog rolled back in.

Two evenings later I approached my first Austrian town, Mayrhofen. Sheltering beneath steep-sided mountains where several valleys meet, Mayrhofen is a perfectly situated Alpine town, or so I supposed from the map. I approached in twilight, rain tipping down, and couldn't see much of it. The town was below snowline; my clothes squelched as I walked. All I could focus on were the town's bright lights and their shimmering reflections in puddles, and on the idea of finding myself somewhere warm, dry, and indoors to sleep.

A soft orange glow spilled through the leaded windows of a small *Gasthof* near the centre of town. Stepping inside felt like arrival of the best kind, although for a moment it resembled a scene from a Spaghetti Western when the stranger steps into the saloon. The murmur of voices died,

A sudden and temporary parting of the clouds at the Pfitscherjoch, November 11, 1997.

heads turned, and everyone stared, but happily they lost interest within seconds and no one asked me to step outside and draw my Colt .45. Leaving my pack near the door, surrounded by a spreading puddle as water oozed from it, I strode over to the bar. '*Ja*,' the barman confirmed, they had a *Zimmer* free that I could sleep in and, '*Ja*,' I could order a beer. The room cost less than a quarter of the amount I'd been asked to pay for a dormitory bunk back at the unfriendly Schaubachhütte beneath the Königspitze, and the beer—cold, strong and golden—tasted '*sehr sehr gut*'. Forget the Schaubachhütte's welcome; *this* was true Alpine hospitality.

Two bar stools north of my perch sat a grey-haired wisp of a man. He sported a huge chin, a pronounced brow, wiry eyebrows, and intense blue eyes. I can still picture his features clearly because I got to inspect them from close range. The man shunted towards me, changing stools to the one beside mine, and spoke, asking—I guessed—who I was, why I was here, and where the hell I had come from.

The answer should have been easy—a brief explanation of The Walk was the first German I'd learnt—but there was one problem: my stammer. It placed a roadblock in the way.

My stammer hadn't been a problem in Italy, with its beautiful, melodic language. Whatever it is that makes me stammer never comes into play when I sing, and after six months of singing Italian I'd practically forgotten that the affliction even existed. It had been a glorious change. For the first two and a half decades of my life my stammer had been painfully disruptive. As a child, stammering had played a pivotal role in who I was and how I behaved. I was quiet because of it, shy and retiring. I went to immense lengths to avoid talking before groups, to avoid embarrassment, but couldn't always manage it, especially at school. What certain hard-hearted teachers were thinking when they called me up front before an entire class of gleefully expectant kids and asked me to read aloud I'll never understand. Perhaps the teachers needed light entertainment, relief from jobs they hated. But it wasn't entertaining to me. The taunts and ringing laughter left deep scars.

Over the years, I'd developed tricks for dealing with the affliction, but still hadn't completely overcome it, and probably never would. Solitude was one trick; mountain walking another. Out in the wild I could be myself, could fully relax, and most conversations with strangers were brief exchanges that required little more than a passing 'hallo'. The wild wasn't just a place I came to regard as home; it was also where I could escape public humiliation. But there was great irony in that. My long walks across the Alps and Pyrenees, partly taken to avoid public speaking, eventually led to public speaking of an even more prominent kind, to slide show talks given to groups of strangers—people who had heard about my journeys and wanted to know more—and at that I had to laugh. The best trick of all, I eventually discovered, was learning to laugh at myself.

My reply to the grey-haired Austrian in the *Gasthof* ground to a halt when I came to the words '*Zu fuss*' ('by foot'). 'Z' had always been a horrible letter, and the German pronunciation was especially awkward—a mighty cliff that offered no easy route of ascent. To scale it I ceased talking altogether for a moment and began working at the sound silently, another trick I'd developed. Of course, my Austrian companion didn't understand why my words had ceased. Perhaps thinking I was about to impart some wonderful secret, he leaned forward, bringing his face to within inches of mine, but this was a mistake. I'd have warned him to stay back if I could have, really I would, but I was too engaged in the epic struggle to do anything else. Slowly, pressure built, like flood waters deepening behind a dam, like magma rising beneath a volcano, and eventually it had to give. When the 'Z' finally emerged it burst free in a cataclysmic eruption of sound. My poor Austrian companion had little warning. Wide-eyed, he lurched backwards, almost fell off his stool, and spilled half his beer over the counter. Afterwards he looked at me as though he thought I'd played a dirty rotten sort of a trick.

It was a perfect example of why I'd become a solitary wanderer. Feeling my face burning, not knowing where to look, I downed my beer in one gulp and retreated hastily to my room.

SNOWSHOES FOR AUSTRIA
Chapter 6

IN MAYRHOFEN I bought snowshoes to help with the ever-deepening mountain snows. Whether or not they actually helped is still up for debate, but they certainly provided entertainment.

Mayrhofen was a well-tended place, and it perfectly summed up the Austrian Alps. Even in foul weather, with skies scowling and sleet flying, the town looked prosperous and orderly. Chalets, stores and hotels were all spick and span, and balcony flower boxes spilled colour even though it was mid-November. For a town of only 3,600 people Mayrhofen boasted more gift shops, restaurants, galleries and boutiques than you'd think it would need, and far more garish neon signage. If all the neon signs I'd seen throughout the length of Italy were brought together the glow still wouldn't match Mayrhofen's. At the sight of it my first impulse was to scoff, but then I found an outdoor gear shop and in it the snowshoes I needed, and I instantly forgave the town its tourist-pandering gleam.

The snowshoes were basic in design, and because I didn't know better I bought them. They lacked the features that make modern snowshoes such efficient tools for traversing snow: sharp-toothed crampons, a snow-shedding design, reliable bindings that hold the forefoot securely in place but allow the heel to rise free. These snowshoes were simpler and far less functional. Elliptical in shape, they measured twenty inches by ten, and weighed more than I expected. The rim was a metal tube, the bed a lattice

The only photo I took of my snowshoes shows them
strapped to the side of Ten Ton, November 16, 1997.

of leather straps, the bindings wrap-around flaps with a belt-like buckle that locked the entire foot in place. They were far from perfect, as I'd soon discover, but I was thrilled to see them. I couldn't wait to try them out.

I didn't have long to wait. The following day, ten miles east of Mayrhofen and 3,000 feet higher, I was back at snowline. Ahead lay the Brandberger Joch, a 7,473-foot pass on the northern edge of the Zillertal Alps. The approach had been easy, on perfect trails that weaved through scented forests and across pastures that in summer would be dotted with cattle. There were log-walled chalets and farmhouses, and more fellow hikers than I had expected for the time of year: fourteen all told, all locals, all English-speaking. The landscape looked lovingly cared for, the valley farms and upland pastures clean and tidy. Most Tyrolean farms are small family-run affairs, typically featuring ten or so cows, a few pigs, and a dozen or more hens. The cows are taken up to summer pastures in spring, brought down again in autumn, and spend the winters in barns feasting on home-grown hay. Income comes from their milk, and produce like potatoes and corn, but few farmers make a living from farming alone. Many rely on government subsidies and second jobs, working at ski resorts, hotels, or as mountain guides; some turn their summer living rooms into winter bedrooms for visiting skiers. The struggle to make ends meet isn't surprising. The Tyrolean landscape—so verdant in summer, so sparkling in winter, so spectacular to look at—is still a harsh mountain environment where the elements reign unchecked. The life of a Tyrolean farmer may look idyllic, wandering peacefully along behind cattle to a flower-strewn alp, but idyllic takes work. Mountain life isn't meant to be easy; residents and visitors alike have to earn the right to be present.

Labouring hard for my own idyllic mountain life, I climbed from the valley, reached snowline, and climbed on. It wasn't until the snow lay shin deep that I stopped to try out the snowshoes. Chuckling with excitement, I dropped my pack, strapped on the snowshoes, and took my first step. But the result was farcical. Attempting to lift the left snowshoe I discovered that it was pinned beneath the right, and I toppled forwards, landing face first. Brushing myself off, spitting out snow, I looked around with embarrassment in case anyone had seen. For the second attempt I adopted a wider stance. This time I managed ten shuffling steps, and was just about to celebrate when the straps failed and both feet slipped free. Before the third attempt I buckled and re-buckled the bindings, fingers going numb, until I was certain they'd hold. I pulled on Ten Ton and, with Excalibur in hand for balance, began walking, but the pack's extra weight made the wide stance awkward; I sank as deeply into the soft snow as I would have with no snowshoes, and after a single minute the bindings failed yet again. For half an hour more I persevered, determined to make the snowshoes work, and only succeeded when I tied on a spare pair of shoelaces as extra bindings. At last I could make real progress, or so I thought. Progress stalled when I reached steeper ground. A thirty-degree angle turned the snowshoes into skis, and for each step up I slid two down. The end came when I glided ten feet back the way I'd come and landed in a heap, squashed beneath Ten Ton. Shaking my head I climbed on, but with the shoes attached to my pack, not to my feet. *Do real adventurers endure farces like mine?* I wondered.

The long climb that followed through knee-deep snow was an exercise in endurance, and by the time I reached the Brandberger Joch the sun hung low in the sky and my legs were about done. But the effort was worthwhile;

The Brandberger Joch at day's end—a wild place, November 15, 1997.

the hard-earned pass was a thrilling prize. To the south and west the Stubai and Zillertal Alps cut a jagged-toothed skyline, an exciting realm of endless snowy peaks. Saucer-shaped clouds capped the glacial giants, an ominous cloud bank lurked to the west, and a chill wind tested my layers. But I barely noticed the cold—rising elation swamped discomfort. No human-made sound reached my ears; no sign of my own species marred the panorama. Once again, I'd returned to the 'other' Europe, to a land unpeopled and untamed, and the elemental *realness* of it renewed my energy, set my spirit free. When the day's final burst of sunlight pierced the clouds and silvered the flanks of a distant mountain I forgot everything but the moment, and stood in awe, inhabiting a place beyond conscious reckoning. I remained rooted to the spot far longer than was wise.

Darkness fell during the descent. At first I tried the snowshoes again, and they worked for 100 yards, but too soon an increase in angle forced me to remove them. The following hours weren't pleasant. I stumbled ever downwards, tripping over rocks hidden beneath the snowpack, sliding on ice, plunging into trapdoor holes, motoring onwards on a tank drained of gas. When I reached ground flat enough for camp, long after nightfall, I'd passed beyond mere tiredness, beyond discomfort; but as with crossing the Val Padana I had grown further in self-knowledge because of it. I now knew what I could do, had seen how long I could keep going, and I understood that I wasn't as limited as I might once have thought. With the memory of the wild pass still fresh I pitched my home and settled in, and quite possibly no one across the entire sweep of the Alps slept better that night, or dreamed greater dreams of fulfilment.

A new rhythm to the journey developed over the next three weeks. It was slower and more restrained, heavily influenced by the winter-subdued land. Progress became less about what I wanted and more about what conditions would allow. As in Calabria, the natural environment dictated life. Previously, I'd learnt to bend to heat, dryness and tangled forests, but here in Austria it was cold, dampness and snow, and it wasn't bending that was required but complete submission. The Endless Summer was now a distant memory, and life was no longer straightforward but, oddly, as time passed, a sense of ease returned. Progress was slower and harder, camping took more work, chores were more time-consuming, and attention to detail was more critical, but repetition transformed daily tasks into manageable activities, while acclimatisation robbed the cold of its sting. My body and the processes that carried it across the Alps slowly adapted to the new season, and winter, it turned out, wasn't as uncomfortable as I'd feared.

Surviving the season's complications meant developing a new set of coping tricks. One complication was my boots, which froze so rigid each night I couldn't pull them on come dawn. For the first few days I spent time each morning thawing them out over the stove, but this wasted fuel and precious minutes of daylight that would have been better spent walking. Trying a new strategy, I began wrapping the boots in plastic and bringing them into my sleeping bag at night, joining the water bottle already there. They made for lumpy bed companions, but the frozen-boot problem was solved.

Soaked living quarters was another complication. On the coldest nights, when clear skies allowed a billion stars to blaze overhead and all warmth was sucked into the heavens, steam from my cooking and mois-ture from my breath froze inside the tent into thick hoar frost. To remove it each dawn I tried scrunching up the tent and shaking it out, but this only partially worked, and when I re-entered the tent each evening it was like crawling into a dark, damp, ice-encrusted cave. So uninvitingly squalid did my lodging become that I began painstakingly scraping and brushing it out each morning before striking camp. Despite a need for haste, despite feet and hands going numb, I was thorough with my ice removal, sweeping away every last fleck. To further help, I began pitching the inner tent for a few minutes during the day if a sunny spot could be found, and with these tricks I just about stayed ahead of the creeping dampness, although the battle was never completely won.

Surprisingly, I found the nights when temperatures plummeted far below freezing easier to deal with than the warmer nights when they hovered at freezing or just above. The warmer nights led not to ice within the Blob at dawn but a dripping, sopping mess. My ceiling often sagged with condensation, and mopping up wasn't pleasant; ice was far simpler to remove. On the other hand, the warmer nights meant my boots and water bottle wouldn't freeze, which left more room in the sleeping bag for me. The evenings passed more comfortably too. When falling snow spread an insulating blanket upon my home I was free to sit up during the long dark evening hours instead of retreating to the depths of my sleeping bag. And I grew to love the soft flutter of flakes upon my ceiling, loved not having to wear gloves. It was fascinating how thirty-two Fahrenheit had come to feel warm when seventy had once felt cold.

Instead of fighting dampness and cold every night I'd hoped to occa-sionally sleep in winter rooms. Austria offers a network of over a thousand mountain refuges, but of the twelve I reached only one had a winter room that was unlocked. Still, this room was a find. Although hilariously small —I could almost touch all four walls at once—it was clean and bright, with wood-panelled walls, a large window facing down the valley, and two soft bunks. It also had the most efficient wood-burning stove I'd ever encountered. The fire took one match to start, not a single wisp of smoke escaped from it, and within half an hour I was stripped to shorts and T-shirt. Outside, snow was flying; inside, heat reigned. I hung wet gear from hooks, draped the Blob across furniture, and steam soon filled the air.

The room grew so hot and steamy I ended up dubbing it 'The High-Altitude Sauna'. It was like returning to the Mezzogiorno for a night.

A few days later I slept a second night under cover, although this one not so comfortably. Dropping beneath snowline late one afternoon, I walked through penetrating drizzle towards a small village. On its outskirts was a football pitch—muddy and deserted—and beside that a small wooden shelter designed for a handful of spectators. The shelter offered three walls and a roof, plus ample floor space for my tent, and I took up residence without hesitation. The shelter was visible from a road, but not from any buildings. No one turned up to protest. Pleased with my opportunism, I relaxed in contentment, but the night wasn't as comfortable as expected. Cold air blew through gaps in the wooden floor, the surface felt harder and bumpier than any patch of earth I'd ever slept upon, and although I was out of the rain the air was still sodden with humidity. Despite leaving the Blob's entrance open, condensation soon ran down its walls and pooled on the floor, and by midnight even the inside of the bivvy bag felt clammy. I tossed and turned in sleeplessness, feeling cold and foolish. As a trick for coping with winter, the shelter was an abysmal failure.

Fortunately, other coping tricks were more successful. I learnt to keep all straps, laces and zippers free of snow. Over time, snow has a habit of turning into ice, and frozen straps and zippers are a pain to deal with when fingers are already numb. I began pitching the Blob without pegs, anchoring it in place with small mounds of snow. After stamping a flat platform in deep snow, or pushing snow aside when it lay less deep, I built the mounds against the tent's sides, and then compressed them with my boots. It was far easier to remove snow at dawn than pegs frozen into the ground. To further simplify each morning I began half-packing Ten Ton before sleep —the less work I had to do each frigid dawn the less painful each frigid dawn was. I began taking more breaks each day. A five-minute break and snack every hour interrupted the journey less than two or three longer stops. Plus, shorter breaks meant that I stayed warmer, fuel intake was better distributed, and I covered more miles. The further I pushed into Austria the more proficient I became at coping with winter. Just as it was strange how freezing point now felt warm, so too was it odd how living outside in the snow had become almost normal.

In contrast to the ever-sunny Apennines, no two days in Austria were

Coping with winter in the Hohe Tauern, November 17, 1997.

the same. A grey overcast one day gave way to swirling snow the next, to dazzling wall-to-wall sunshine the day after that, and then to finger-numbing fog, to driving sleet and rain, to snow again, and then to penetrating frost. These ever-changing conditions may have increased the journey's difficulties, but they also added great theatrical drama, and I wouldn't have traded them. Predictable was for people living indoors, for people following routines little affected by nature. Unpredictable was far more exciting. What new challenge would conditions bring? What else would I have to do to adapt? Day by day I lived with the tides of the season, not shutting out the elements as I'd done back in suburban London, but surrounded by them. My wandering way of life had never felt more removed from the settled life most people lived. I was free to embrace the discomforts that most people spent their days avoiding. I was free to study what most people barely noticed. A snowstorm might be a minor inconvenience to the average citizen, but to me it became a major event around which my life was forced to revolve. Back during the Endless Summer I'd considered myself fully immersed in the land and its rhythms, but it was nothing to the immersion I experienced in the Austrian Alps.

Nature's rhythms and whims ruled my existence, and because of them I lived in a wilder place. *My* Alps weren't the same as the Alps the locals inhabited, and they were far removed from the range most visitors experienced. As in the Apennines, I wondered if anyone else saw the range as I did.

Of course, this wildness was still a matter of perspective; Austria clearly wasn't an untrammelled land. Roads had been blazed into many high valleys, forests had been clear-cut into ski runs, cables and chairlifts had been strung web-like over uplands, rivers had been penned back behind concrete dams. But these abominations were less troubling than I'd expected. They didn't break my appreciation of the land, or upset me as deeply as I'd imagined they would. It was almost as if the scars didn't fully exist to me, or as if they were nothing more than temporary wounds. I could sense, resting beneath the surface, a land that honestly didn't care, a land that knew such things—like all things—would eventually pass. Deep time would heal all the wounds we'd inflicted. The roads would one day crumble, the ski runs grow back into forests, the pylons fall, the dams crack and collapse, the rivers run wild and free once again, the wildlife live unmolested. Humanity may or may not be around to see it, but the wild would ultimately triumph, and the inevitability of it soothed the sadness and anger I would otherwise have felt. The thousands of miles I'd walked had carried me to a new way of seeing the land, and even the grubby fingerprints left by my own kind's heavy-handed stewardship couldn't bring me back. Marred as they were, the Austrian Alps still filled me with uncontainable joy.

Still, I wondered at how such environmental degradation had been allowed. Although issues like acid rain and warming temperatures were so global in scale they were beyond a local population's ability to combat alone, other issues clearly weren't. Traditionally, Austria's mountain folk had lived lightly upon the land. The smaller villages and hamlets, the mountain chalets built from natural materials like wood and stone, the farmlands that blended into wilder margins—all these existed in sympathy with the land. In places, Austria resembled a near-arcadian paradise where people lived alongside nature, not upon it. But some things—post-war development, the proliferation of ski resorts, the damming of valleys—had spread on an industrial scale, not in sympathy at all. Were so many ski runs truly needed? Was such a vast network of forest roads necessary? Was electricity in such demand that so many wild valleys had to be dammed and lost?

Couldn't more areas have been set apart and left inviolate? Weren't some things worth fighting against? Weren't some things worth fighting *for*?

Austrians elsewhere had proved that the people could fight back. In 1984, when the Danube-Auen wetlands near Vienna faced destruction, a local outcry had screamed 'NO'. Unperturbed by the noise, developers began preparing the region for the dam and power plant they aimed to build, illegally cutting trees, and at that protesters took direct action. People came in their thousands to occupy the wetlands. Many were forcibly and bloodily evicted, and authorities hoped that news of this would dissuade others from joining in. But the reverse occurred. Swiftly, the occupation grew, protests increased, and by the following summer authorities had little choice but to cancel the power plant. As is often the case in Austrian politics it was a ground-up movement that delivered change—change that saved the homes of roughly 5,000 plant, animal, bird and fish species. In 1996, the Danube-Auen became a national park, a priceless and irreplace-able environment 'given to the people of Austria as a present'. But it wasn't a present at all. The people had earned it. And it wasn't even something that could be 'given'—it existed for its own sake. Just as the Alps did, as all natural places did.

Happily for me, long stretches remained relatively free of development. I stole through forests where I felt like the first human visitor ever, wandered above tree line and felt like the last person alive, spent many days and nights in glorious unbroken solitude. Snowfields were marked with nothing but the prints of deer, chamois, and countless smaller mammals; forests rang with birdsong. From close range I watched a woodpecker fiercely drilling a pine trunk, hunting for insects without mercy—the wild drama of untamed life and death visible right there before my eyes. In a sun-filled forest clearing I came upon a magnificent roe deer stag, its antlers held high and proud. For a moment, we locked eyes and stared at one another intently, as if seeing into each other's souls, and I was transported to another place, charged with energy from another time, overcome with emotions so ancient they predated civilisation, with ideas that predated even language. And then the stag turned and leapt away, powerful and alive beyond imagining. Yes, wildness in Austria definitely remained.

My route across the country led from villages to forests to snow-bound upland meadows. I grew to love the variety, appreciated the small

My weaving tracks across the Kitzbühel Alps, November 19, 1997.

settlements as much as the wildest corners. Industrial tourism was hateful, but I'd also hate to see the Alps without people. People belong in nature, not apart from it, and Austria was at its best where people and nature lived side by side.

From the Zillertal Alps I tramped east to the Hohe Tauern, where the snows lay even deeper. Discovering that a return to Grossvenediger's 12,028-foot summit wasn't on the cards I turned north, stravaiging onwards into the Kitzbühel Alps. Every few days I left the tent pitched and explored the mountains with a lighter pack, making no progress towards Norway, but progressing in experience, knowledge and joy for my efforts. The Kitzbühel Alps were perfect for such unfocused detours. They were lower and more rounded than their neighbours, and easier to travel, although their snow-covered forests and ridges were still challenging enough. Hard work—and hapless snowshoeing on occasions where the terrain was less steep—carried me to a handful of modest summits, and from these I gazed far and wide: south to the glaciers of the Hohe Tauern and the distinctive summit of Austria's highest peak, Grossglockner; north to the walls and towers of the limestone Wilder Kaiser range. The finest summit view came one evening from Hohe Salve, a prominent but pint-sized mountain overrun by the machinery of the ski industry. The ascent was yet another spur-of-the-moment addition to the journey, a quick 1,500-foot climb from camp. I'd just set up the Blob, noticed the summit above, reasoned I could reach it before sunset, and dashed upwards like a madman. I won the race with five minutes to spare. My award was alpenglow blazing on the Wilder Kaiser, and clouds filling the valleys far below, and a final explosion of sunlight that painted the clouds and mountains gold. The ski tows vanished, and all I could see was the perfection of the mountain world.

The following morning it wasn't just the ski tows that vanished, but all signs of my own species. First light revealed a perfect temperature inversion: sunlight and relative warmth up where I stood, frigid temperatures and a cloud sea below. I'd experienced similar conditions back in Italy, but this Austrian inversion set harder and lasted longer. Held between the rolling Kitzbühel Alps on one side and the vertical walls of the Wilder Kaiser on the other, the super-chilled valley air had nowhere to escape, and for four spectacular days I wandered alone above the clouds in a world other people might never have touched. The cloud sea persisted when overcast skies rolled in, and shone white as snow when sunshine returned. Sounds from the valley occasionally reached me—a barking dog, church bells, the drone of an engine—but they were distant and muted and only accentuated my glorious detachment. For variety, I dropped into the fog twice, entering a world where frost coated every pine needle and twig, but then burst free above it again, reborn into clarity and fifty-mile views. In conditions like these, winter's discomforts were insignificant.

A shorter-lived but equally memorable treat came my way after the inversion broke. A shift in wind brought snow; flakes soon filled the air. Setting up camp in a wood of bare-limbed beech trees I noticed hundreds, if not thousands, of long cobweb strands hanging straight down. I'd never seen anything like them, and I'd never seen anything like what happened to them. The falling snowflakes were huge, and as they wafted through the forest they caught on the cobwebs, building up layer upon layer. The snowfall ceased after nightfall, and when I took a short walk after dinner I discovered a fairy-tale scene. Lit by torchlight, the snow-decorated cobwebs flashed and sparkled like crystal chandeliers, and when I brushed against them I imagined a sound like tinkling glass. As with fireflies in the southern Apennines, and the nightingale I'd listened to in Basilicata, and the moonlit cloud sea below the 'High-Altitude Conservatory', the cobweb chandeliers were a spectacle of unsurpassable beauty. It was curious how the most miraculous moments had all occurred at night.

The following evening served up another natural spectacle that I'm unlikely to ever forget, but for different reasons. My goal that evening was the Gruttenhütte, a refuge perched beneath the Wilder Kaiser's towering limestone walls, but fate kept me from reaching it. I reached the trail leading to the refuge with daylight starting to fade. A sign suggested that the hut still lay two hours distant—perhaps further given the unbroken snow—but the thought of its winter room kept me moving. But then something, suddenly, made me stop dead. Perhaps it was simple tiredness, or a realisation that I didn't really want to push on in the dark, or perhaps an instinct or premonition, but whatever it was it may have saved my life. Five minutes after I'd halted three chamois clattered across a cliff directly above the path I would have been following. I watched one of them dislodge a small rock, which dislodged a larger rock, which dislodged even more rocks, and soon piano-sized boulders were thundering down: an impressive volume of rock in motion, a veritable avalanche strafing the path I would have been on. Breath held in awe, I stared at the thundering cascade, and I couldn't picture how I'd have emerged unscathed. Later, it was a more thoughtful and appreciative hiker who rested in camp. I could have died on the Hohtürli Pass, and could have died here. Another life had been used up. How many more did I have spare?

———

On November 26 I reached the town of Saalfelden and tracked down a palatial private room for a budget-saving unpalatial sum. After handing over 200 schillings I unfolded myself into luxury, and winter fell away like snow sloughing from spring trees. Although I'd learnt to cope with the season the release I felt upon escaping it revealed a great deal. I'd thought I was living in ease, but clearly hadn't been. The pressures of winter—the unending and unwinnable fight to keep everything dry, the difficulty of travel, the numerous times when my hands and feet had succumbed to the cold, the fact that I was always 'on', never able to fully relax—had worn me down.

The single night indoors felt like a two-week vacation in the Caribbean.

Unpacking, it wasn't long before I'd transformed the once-tidy room into a place of mess and chaos. I pitched the tent to dry, spread out clothes and gear to do the same. Books, notes and maps lay in piles. Food sat scattered. Within minutes, a pungent staleness hung in the air, and the scent lingered even though my body was soon showered and clothes laundered. The following morning when I packed everything away I discovered soggy leaves, pine needles and mud on the floor, and dirty smears on the walls. It took an hour's work before I'd returned the room to an acceptable state. Sure, I could have checked out leaving the mess behind, but I always liked to leave a place as I found it, indoors as well as out.

As usual, the day off had involved chores, but also more mail than normal. From Saalfelden's post office I had collected the latest resupply parcel and also—to my great delight—a huge batch of mail; fourteen items all told. In a few days I'd turn twenty-eight, and once back in my room I tore into the birthday post with excitement. My three brothers had sent English treats: great slabs of chocolate and a bag of butter toffee. A large packet of flavoursome miso soup came from a good friend. Base Camp had sent some much-needed odds and ends to replace bits of kit wearing out, as well as a small birthday cake with a candle on top. This, I decided, would be saved for the birthday itself. The letters and birthday cards had me laughing and exclaiming aloud: a friend with a new baby, another announcing his marriage, another with a thrilling tale of misadventure on a granite rock face in France. There was even good news from the photo library: the missing films from the southern Apennines had been found, in a flower bed in Rome of all places, and the finder, a passing stranger, had forwarded them on! Most moving of all were words of love and pride from my mother, and upon reading them tears suddenly welled. I was an emotional lightweight—I'd known it for years, but on this occasion I battled the tears back. No one, especially Base Camp, would have wanted their correspondence to send me plunging into loneliness.

Extricating myself from bed after a night of exquisite comfort was a time-consuming business, not helped by images on the TV. At exactly the same hour the previous morning I'd summited a nearby mountain, Asitzkopf. The summit view had stretched from Grossglockner on the southern horizon to rock peaks closer at hand, on fire with alpenglow above yet another sea of cloud, but it also included a tall metal post on which a slowly revolving camera was fixed. I'd wondered where the camera's footage appeared, and twenty-four hours later found out: on the Weather Panorama TV station. It was surreal, seeing another Asitzkopf summit view at sunrise—from bed. Although I knew I'd rather be up there in person, I couldn't help but enjoy the view from down here. Seeing it from bed was undeniably more comfortable.

Cloud sea beneath the Wilder Kaiser, November 23, 1997.

TO FINISH IN GOOD STYLE
Chapter 7

THE ALPINE STAGE of The Walk had only one more week to run and, as in the Apennines, I was determined to finish in good style. There'd be a reward for trying, I was certain of it.

Here, instead of following a Crinale-style ridge, I faced the lonely expanse of the Steinernes Meer, a wild mountain plateau of almost 40 square miles perched at 6,000 feet. Steinernes Meer means 'rocky sea', and in summer it is exactly that: a desolate karst landscape where acres upon acres of hard grey limestone sit exposed in endless ribs and cracks. Under snow, and with the assistance of snowshoes, I reckoned its open spaces would grant spectacular passage across the border into Germany and out of the Alps—exactly the stylish finish I wanted.

Ready for the adventure, I left my room in Saalfelden and stepped into a chill, windless morning. Overhead, plain white clouds stretched across the sky; and, in the flat light, surrounding mountains looked like cardboard cut-outs, the forests, ravines and crags upon them like printed images, two-dimensional in their faded shades of grey. Staring hard, I probed what I could see of my route. Above Saalfelden the land rose steeply, first through forested foothills, then up open slopes. From where I stood there was no hint of the plateau beyond the climb. But I could picture its emptiness. As I imagined myself up there, committed and alone, a familiar frisson of doubt returned. It was as unsettling as always, but this time I embraced it—or tried to. An easy finale that didn't stir the emotions wasn't the finale I sought.

Striding out, I followed a road to the valley's edge and then picked up a trail leading into the forest. The trail was one I'd walked three and a half years earlier during my Alpine traverse, but to my surprise nothing along it looked familiar. The previous visit had occurred during high summer, when open glades had been filled with knee-high grass and a mass of wildflowers, but snow now buried the land. I hadn't expected the route to look the same, but I'd thought I'd recognise something. Instead, it was as though I'd never been here. The strangeness of what should have been familiar added to my nerves.

For the first mile the snow underfoot was firm and well-tramped, and I gained altitude easily—although I kept my pace slow, seeking to avoid breaking sweat. But the further I walked the less travelled the trail became, until soon I left all other footprints behind. The unbroken snow only lay six inches deep, but that was deep enough to slow me.

After an hour's toil I paused for fuel: fresh bread, chocolate, a long swig of water. I looked around at the dark forest, noticed flakes lazily drifting down, and heard a gust of wind as it sighed through the pines—a hint of coming change. Over the next hour, the snow grew heavier, the wind strengthened, and by noon the air was filled with a mass of flakes swirling in mesmerizing patterns. The trees soon whitened, making the forest a brighter, softer place. Walking on, I forgot my doubts and saw only the beauty. *This* was why I was here, crossing the Alps in late November. This was the winter wonderland I'd always longed for as a child.

Such conditions had been a dream—an obsession—since childhood. Growing up in London, snow had been rare, and had never lasted long. Some winters had even passed with no snow at all. When I was seven, a decent snowfall finally occurred. It lay unusually deep, perhaps four inches, and it was perfect for snowman building. But, frustratingly, I wasn't allowed outside to play. Suffering a cold, I was kept indoors by my mother, and I watched nose to glass while my brothers laughed and romped. To try cheering me my mother filled a small plastic tub with snow and brought it indoors, and in it I built a three-inch snow midget. But its brutally short lifespan only made things worse. The unfairness left a mark, and from then on I never left snow untouched. From such minor childhood events can a life change direction.

It wasn't just the beauty or novelty of snow that so captivated me as a child, but also its magical transformative powers. Snow was made of magic: this was plain to see. Not only did it utterly transform the landscape, it transformed people too. It reconnected them with nature. I witnessed grown adults playing in ways adults never usually did. I saw serious people discovering that they could laugh. Snow even altered the rules adults imposed, occasionally even meaning no school—the holy grail of childhood. Adulthood may have partially claimed me since, but my appreciation for snow hadn't dimmed. In part it explained why I fell so hard for mountains, for the heavier snows that lay upon them. Snow would always mean 'no school'. It would always represent freedom, and forever invite play. It was a bridge straight back to childhood, and as I saw it that was no bad thing.

Relishing that bridge, truly living my childhood dreams, playing at being an explorer, I continued upwards. A happy hour passed surrounded by snow-laced trees. The moment was as perfect as any previous moment on The Walk, but when I reached the forest's edge at 5,000 feet the magic came to an abrupt end.

Ahead now was open country—in theory. According to my map, a narrowing valley rose 1,000 feet to the plateau, and a trail zigzagged up it, but all I could see was a great white nothing. Since leaving Saalfelden, the morning's high clouds had lowered, and fog now clung tightly to the ground. Looking ahead, I could barely see the trail. Land was indistinguishable from sky. Flakes were falling ever harder, the wind was blowing ever stronger, and my doubts returned. And this time they were harder to embrace.

Intimidated, I walked on, my determination to finish in good style propelling me forward even while my instincts clamoured for staying in the forest. Away from the sheltering trees the snow rapidly deepened, first becoming shin deep, then knee deep. The snow was heavy and wet, too consolidated to push through easily, and I had to lift each foot up and over the surface, and then balance myself carefully, waiting to see how far I'd sink. Occasionally I'd find secure footing; more often I plunged to my knees. It was as though the laws of physics had changed—as though the earth's surface, normally so firm and reliable, had altered its physical properties and had become an unsupportive, leg-swallowing morass. Twice, I sunk

Leaving the forest, November 27, 1997.

into waist-deep snow traps, and had great difficulty getting out. The soft edges caved in as I tried climbing them. When a third snow trap swallowed me to my belly I had to remove Ten Ton and heave it on ahead. For a scary moment, as I battled the crumbling edges, I thought I was truly stuck.

Wallowing on, it was like that familiar nightmare: running hard but getting nowhere fast. So much effort, so little progress. It reminded me of the 100-yard stretch above a tunnel back in Calabria that had taken me an hour to complete, only here it was snow that hindered progress, not brambles. With each passing minute, the wind strengthened, and soon it was blasting across the mountain, shrieking, pushing me sideways, whipping up a maelstrom of white. Stinging spindrift struck my face. It blew into my eyes, up my nose, and even down my neck, despite my cinched hood. I remembered my crossing of the Pfitscherjoch into Austria. Back there, progress had seemed hard, but it was a summer stroll compared to this. There'd been no wind, no falling snow, and the knee-deep snowpack hadn't extended far. Here, I faced an entire plateau of it.

If I even reached the plateau.

At least I wasn't cold. Quite the reverse. Ploughing uphill through deep snow while wearing a huge pack is one of the surest ways to get warm. And I *was* warm—too warm. Sweat was flowing freely. Aware of it, I pictured myself up on the open plateau, assaulted by the full force of the wind. I'd have to take breaks—travel was too strenuous not to—but the wind would attack my wet body without mercy, and at each stop I'd chill in seconds. It would be worse than unpleasant. My doubts edged closer to fear. This wasn't the winter wonderland I'd dreamt of as a child any longer. And it didn't feel like play any longer either. *Well, did you get what you wanted?* I taunted myself. *Are you feeling stirred?*

Moving forward became my entire focus, my one goal in life, but moving forward was soon all but impossible. I came to a steeper stretch, buried beneath an especially deep drift. If the ground had been flat I could have strapped on my snowshoes, but on this forty-five-degree slope I'd only slide backwards. For what seemed like an age I attacked the drift, stepping up, sinking back down—a treadmill to nowhere. As snow cascaded around me I gave it everything I had, burning energy, pouring sweat, until my legs were trembling. *This is madness!* I thought, plunging ever deeper into doubt. I paused, gasping, waited a minute to catch my breath, and then tried again; this time with real anger, but earned the same result. Finally, I came to my senses. This wasn't merely difficult—it was impossible. Pushing on wasn't good style—it was idiocy. I had to accept it. With snow to my waist and visibility at zero and the wind screaming, it wasn't irrational fear of the unknown that turned me back, but reality. The plan had always been to make it across the Alps before the snows grew too deep, but I hadn't quite managed it. Too deep they now were.

Soaked, weary, defeated, I retreated the way I'd come, and the ease of progress mocked me. I knew that I had no choice, but I still felt like a failure. It wasn't supposed to end this way. What about the rewards? Hadn't I earned them?

Safely below the blizzard, I looped east beneath the Steinernes Meer and then turned north up the Salzachtal, the valley of the river Salzach. As I lost altitude, the snow-smothered forests gave way to farmland, and the surface underfoot changed from knee-deep snow to sopping-wet slush and then to no snow at all. But this didn't last: the storm caught up late afternoon and flung stinging ice pellets at the back of my head. Winter was chasing me from the range.

I wasn't finishing in style—I was finishing in defeat.

———

The five days that followed were the most uncomfortable and miserable since Calabria. Stuck in the valley, mostly confined to roads, I splashed through every kind of precipitation: sleet, hail, drizzle, rain, and snow. No waterproofs in the world would have kept it all at bay. One by one my coping tricks failed. Slush soaked through my boots, rain penetrated my coat, condensation flooded the tent. The mornings dawned drab and sodden, the landscape grim in a thousand shades of grey. I woke each dawn to the Blob sagging under heavy wet snow, and the following hours saw the snow disintegrate into slush, and super-saturated clouds press ever harder upon my shoulders, and creeping dampness sink ever deeper into my core. Each night I camped among puddles. Dampness and water filled my dreams, with rivers rushing, dark fog clinging, and endless droplets drip-drip-dripping. My feet were constantly white and wrinkly, every pair of socks I owned were now wet, my fingers never seemed to work as they should, and my gloves soaked up water like sponges. Twice, when following roads, passing vehicles soaked me further, splashing through puddles, hurling miniature tsunamis my way. In villages, residents had their heads down, their shoulders hunched, and their hoods pulled tight. No one returned my greetings; people looked away, sped up, walked on. Was I really that hideous a sight? I felt rough, as though I'd been pummelled by a thousand fists, weary as though I hadn't rested in weeks. The clamminess of my clothes, the dirt clinging to my gear, the stickiness of my unwashed body; it all became increasingly hard to bear. When I caught a glimpse of my face in a store window the reflection was haunting. I'd be twenty-eight in a few days, but I looked eighty-eight.

All I could think about was summer, and warmth, and sunlight. And home. Such thoughts, of course, weren't beneficial. My morale plummeted, and the miles were desperately long.

I even ran low on food. When I reached the small town of Mühlbach early on a Saturday afternoon I found its store already closed for the weekend. Dinner that night was half a mug of leftover miso soup, tasty but not filling, and the following breakfast was my last two toffees. Ravenous and depressed, I gave in and devoured the bite-sized birthday cake I'd been carefully saving. It helped, but not much. At least I still had the lone candle to light when my birthday came.

That Sunday was a long, cold, hungry day. As before, when conditions had been at their most uncomfortable, I began comparing myself with the homeless. Even though I knew it was a fallacious comparison to make, and profoundly unhelpful, I couldn't stop myself. I was living in squalor. Everything I owned was dirty and wet. My shelter was insufficient. My empty stomach churned. And I was adrift and alone—so remote that people were turning away in disgust, and splashing me as they drove by, not even seeing me, treating me as though I were insignificant and worthless. And, once again, I felt worthless because of it.

The only thing that helped was knowing that my grim situation still didn't come close to the desperate situations real homeless individuals experience. My journey from Calabria had revealed a little of what being homeless might be like, but not the complete lack of hope. No matter how unpleasant this was, no matter how miserable I felt, I *was* still here by choice and *could* step away any moment. I wasn't homeless—I was merely a spoiled suburban boy who'd made an extraordinarily foolish choice.

But I'm worse than that, or so a nagging voice told me: *I'm also a fraud.* Supposedly, I was on a mountain walk. A nature walk. That was what I'd told everyone—that was what I'd told myself. Yet here I was, slinking along a paved road through a populated valley. I wasn't only letting others down, I was letting myself down. And I'd let Mad Mountain Jack slip away. As I splashed along the Salzachtal I sunk ever deeper into misery, feeling more like a fool, a fraud and a failure with every sodden step.

I grew unreasonably upset, not with conditions but with how pitifully I was handling them. Hadn't I learnt a single thing? Hadn't I learnt to value the difficult moments for how they made the good moments even better? Hadn't I learnt that discomforts didn't last, that storms always passed? And hadn't I learnt to treasure *all* aspects of wild nature, even rough weather; and *all* aspects of the journey, even the uncomfortable bits? Hadn't I learnt to let go of expectations?

When Monday arrived I retook control, became Mad Mountain Jack once again—determined and resilient, adventurous and optimistic, even if the optimism was forced. I stocked up on fresh food from the most appreciated grocery store I have ever visited, and then, pushing deep weariness aside, turned back for the hills. I bloody well wasn't going to leave the Alps with my tail between my legs. Forget 'bending to nature'; the Alpine stage of The Walk was going to finish on my terms.

Leaving the banks of the swollen Salzach I climbed back into the snow-smothered landscape, gaining altitude steadily along silent forest tracks. The mud and slush of the valley swiftly gave way to deep pillows of fluffier, drier snow, and although temperatures plunged conditions seemed more forgiving. For the final time I donned the snowshoes, but the snow was too feathery to support them; once again they were more hindrance than help. Of the 320 miles I'd covered in Austria fewer than 20 had been by snowshoe. They'd been dead weight most of the way, but I didn't regret owning them. When I reached Salzburg in a few days I'd post them to Base Camp, and in April Base Camp could send them back. Norway's vast spring snowfields would be more consolidated than these newly laid Alpine snows, and I had a hunch that up there the snowshoes would come into their own.

By the time I swapped closed-in forest for wide-open *alm*, winter lay thigh-deep, and it was still falling from the sky. Visibility was minimal. Once again, fog blurred the slopes, and the temperature had fallen to fifteen Fahrenheit, minus nine Celsius. The wisdom of being here, high on an Alp, in biting December cold, in fading afternoon light, with gear and clothes sopping wet, suddenly struck me as questionable—and yet I wasn't about to turn back. Not this time. The landscape was sensationally beautiful, bewitchingly soft and downy, a Christmas card sprung to life, the winter wonderland I'd longed for as a child. And this time it wasn't going to defeat me.

With icy fingers probing at my damp layers, and my coat already stiff as board, I began considering camp. One option was to dig into the two-foot drifts right where I stood, but then I spied a small cabin a little higher, and decided that was more appealing. The cabin was locked, but it offered a covered porch with a dry concrete floor, plus walls on two sides that would keep off the prevailing wind. Although it would likely be as uncomfortably hard to sleep on as the sports shelter, it surely had to be warmer than out on the exposed mountainside.

Reclaiming Mad Mountain Jack, December 3, 1997.

My hands began to go numb the moment I ceased moving. I cursed the week of appalling weather, cursed my wet gloves, cursed my wet... everything. A vision of myself frozen to the spot, encased in a cartoon-like ice cube, flashed before my eyes, and feeling a dash of concern I set to pitching camp with as much speed as I could muster. Speed, unfortunately, wasn't possible. Every part of the tent had frozen—what had been wet that morning in the valley was now glued with ice. I couldn't even free the tent from its bag—it was locked inside and wouldn't budge. Then I had to unstick the inner tent from the outer, and the walls from the groundsheet, and the poles from one another, and the sleeves the poles had to fit through. What normally took three minutes became a thirty-minute epic, and for a while it was touch and go whether I would succeed or not. My fingers almost failed before the tent was up. By the time I'd threaded the final pole and created the last snow anchor my hands and feet were so on fire from cold I wished they would simply drop off.

With shivers racking my body, the temperature plunging further, and

341

panic surging, I hurled all my kit inside and leapt after it head-first. Stripping off my wet clothes was a real test of bravery, but soon I was wrapped in the thermals I kept solely for camp, and cocooned within my bivvy and sleeping bags. Lighting the stove was the final near-insurmountable challenge. My useless fingers could barely hold the matchbox, let alone strike any matches, but somehow pig-headed desperation won the day, and despite spilled matches and a small area of burnt skin the stove finally blazed into life. For the next half-hour I let it burn, using it not to thaw snow and rustle up dinner but for heat alone. As its warmth chased winter from the furthest corners of the tent my shivers faded and blood returned to feet and fingers—and how I shuddered in grateful agony at the return of sensation. Slowly, I was pulled back from the brink. Another close call.

The world outside was locked in deep freeze, but my tiny shelter became a capsule of warmth. Regular bursts from the stove kept the cold at bay. With great care I even managed to partially dry some of my wet clothes and gear. The ability to carve out a nest of security and comfort in such brutal December cold, all needs taken care off, filled me with satisfaction. Civilisation only lay six miles below, but in these conditions it felt like a hundred. I was camping alone in an environment that could kill; the thrill of it increased my comfort further. I slept that night as untroubled as a hibernating bear, and didn't stir the next morning until dawn was many hours past.

It was my birthday, and what a day it was! There was nowhere I had to be, I had a mountain of fresh food to feast upon, a stack of birthday mail to re-read, a good book to lose myself in, and the world outside had never, ever, been more heartbreakingly beautiful. Snow covered everything, smoothing out shapes, forming sensuous flowing curves and sculptured abstract forms no human artist could ever create or match. The clean, sugar-sweet scent of it hung in the air, and the intoxicating silence of winter pulsated. Shifting mists still limited long-distance views, and the light remained flat and white, but there was an otherworldly magic to the snow-softened landscape, and it transported me to an otherworldly level of happiness. If my seven-year-old self could have only known what lay ahead he wouldn't have minded being stuck indoors while his brothers played.

Early afternoon, I dressed in my almost-dry clothes and went for a wander. I carried no pack, followed no itinerary, just roamed light-hearted and free through folds of feather-light snow. Steep ground lay 100 yards above camp, and I repeatedly climbed it, then hurled myself back down, taking great bounding strides and leaps through powdery softness while clouds of it rose about me. I was a grown man, but why shouldn't I play? Others do, and not just children. Flying down the slope I remembered a group of marmots I'd seen during my long Alpine walk. It had been late June, but a large snowfield still clung to the mountain just below camp. Marmots, as usual, were out in the sun; some motionless, keeping a sharp-eyed lookout for danger, but others were playing—no other word could describe it. Again and again they launched themselves onto the snowfield, tobogganing down it on their bellies, before scampering back to the top and doing it again. It was comical to watch, and heartening to witness. I didn't want my own species to be the only one capable of emotion and play, and the marmots proved we aren't. We share our planet with like-minded citizens—more, probably, than we'll ever know.

Buzzing from my own play, I returned to my cabin-porch camp just in time to welcome visitors. Three cross-country skiers arrived, out on a long day's tour. Bemused by what I was doing, shaking their heads at my story, they gave me a small bottle of peppermint schnapps when they left, 'to hold the night's chill at bay', and the spreading warmth each sip provided added greatly to the day's festivities.

The highlight—of both the day and possibly the entire Alpine stage of the journey—came as daylight faded. Stirred by the subtlest suggestion of a breeze, the fog began to shift, break apart, and soon the Salzachtal came into view far below. I stared down at its quilt-work fields and toy-sized cabins, across it at endless hills and mountains, and upwards at the craggy limestone giants rising so fearsomely above camp. Unable to believe my good fortune I grabbed my camera and rushed outside, and the evening became a clear reward for all I'd endured—for all the miles, effort, and discomforts. Even for my failed attempt at crossing the Steinernes Meer. Across the valley the highest summits glowed, while below them the entire landscape was glazed with a piercing cold ethereal light. Layers of silver-blue mist drifted above forests; frost coated every surface, pine needle and branch; virgin snow swept smoothly down the mountain from my feet. No landscape between here and Calabria had been more pristine. Elated, I ran through an entire film, and then ceased rushing, slowing myself with

Ethereal evening above the Salzachtal – a birthday miracle, December 4, 1997.

a single breath, pausing to let the hard-won moment sink deep, stilling myself to reconnect with both the earth and with myself. I'd endured much to be present right here right now. This was what I'd come to Austria for; this was what I'd been seeking; this was why I'd begun The Walk in the first place. This was perfection, wild nature at its best, arranged entirely as nature wanted it, and I grabbed it as tightly as I could.

Lingering long after sunset, I stood knee deep in winter, happy with the choices I'd made. Overhead, the clear sky blushed red, as though it knew it had performed well. There was no doubt about it: *this* was finishing the Alps in style.

I reached the city of Salzburg forty-eight hours later. Under blue skies, Mad Mountain Jack waltzed along the frosted banks of the River Salzach, grinning widely, singing joyfully, unnerving the highly cultured natives.

In Salzburg I planned to take a five-night break before I plunged onwards into the numbing depths of a Central European winter. The forests of the Böhmerwald lay ahead, dark and elemental, as did even fiercer conditions no doubt, and far beyond winter the immense wildernesses of Norway and the Arctic. But with both the Apennines and the Alps won nothing could dent my rekindled optimism. The journey was 2,750 miles old. It had become everything I'd hoped it would become, and far more besides.

I'd begun The Walk wanting to spend time in the wild, wanting a new way of life—wanting to live on my own terms, in freedom and simplicity, with the earth beneath my feet. All this I'd achieved. But I hadn't anticipated finding such a strong, life-affirming sense of purpose. Pacing into Salzburg, moving forward along the Salzach's banks, I realised that moving forward was what my life as Mad Mountain Jack had always been about. Every single thing I'd done from the journey's very first step had been tied to that one major theme. Moving forward had underpinned every thought and action; it explained why every physical and mental challenge had been faced. The challenges may have appeared pointless to others—unnecessary, if not absurd, to put oneself through so much discomfort—but each one took me another step forward. *That* had been the point of them. At sunset every day I had known, deep down, without consciously acknowledging it, that I was further ahead than I had been, that I had made progress; not just in distance on the ground but progress in who I was. I'd moved forward, I'd grown. I'd added another layer of experience, another layer of understanding. I'd expanded my knowledge of myself and the entire world. The idea that I was engaged in a constant state of reaching, a constant state of forward progress, felt profound. It turned the journey into a quest. Not just a quest to cross a continent on foot, or a quest to move closer to the natural world and find belonging within it, but a quest for betterment—a quest each day to become *more*. Until Salzburg, I'd only sensed that purpose. It had been there, but hidden beneath the surface. But now, finally, I understood what that purpose was.

I was walking to move forward—forward in every way possible, and it was a deliberate undertaking, a path I'd chosen for myself. Back in London I'd been standing still, doing time, going nowhere. But for seven months I'd been doing the exact opposite, and it had given life a depth of meaning that had been sorely lacking in the suburbs. Life shone because of it, even if I didn't know where it would ultimately lead.

What was I moving towards? That was the big question.

Would I learn the answer before reaching the North Cape?

There was still so much to find out.

The Alpine stage truly finished when I made a string of phone calls home, letting Base Camp, the charities, and several of my sponsors know I'd successfully crossed the Alps. Everyone offered their congratulations, which caught me completely off-guard. Being congratulated felt wrong; it definitely wasn't deserved. I was doing what I loved, living a dream, arguably a selfish thing, and I didn't need congratulating for that. And I'd never once expected *not* to succeed. Sure, there'd been low points, but none that had genuinely threatened The Walk. And sure, I was walking an unusually long distance—but as I saw it long had never equated to impossible. My walk was something millions of people could do. From the very first day I'd been able to perfectly picture the last. I knew I'd reach the North Cape; knew I'd one day stride across untracked snow to stand on a dark headland at Europe's wild northern edge. I had no doubt at all. Being congratulated for reaching Salzburg prompted a wry smile. It felt a little like being congratulated for getting out of bed. And then I laughed out loud. They all had it wrong—I should be congratulating them! Getting out of bed and heading off to work and the same old routines day after day after day... what they were all doing was far harder.

It was an utterly contented mountain vagabond that settled with a sigh into Salzburg. Great adventures lay ahead, I had no doubt. There'd be new places to discover—new corners of the 'other' wilderness Europe most people missed. There'd be difficulties too, challenges to face, and rewards to earn. But I'd be moving forward, no matter where I was, no matter the discomforts, no matter how challenging or lonely winter became. I'd be moving forward, forever becoming a fraction more than I had been just moments earlier, forever discovering more with each step about the miraculous natural world I inhabited.

The dream still had 4,000 miles to go.

The Walk continues:

A 7,000-Mile Walk of Discovery
into the Heart of Wild Nature

'The newest classic of our outdoor literature'
Foreword by Jim Perrin

On
SACRED
GROUND

ANDREW TERRILL

ACKNOWLEDGEMENTS

FEW OF US walk through life alone. I certainly didn't during my walk across Europe. I may have taken the steps, but I was never unsupported. Without the following people, the journey (and this book) would not have been possible. For everyone who helped, I remain profoundly grateful.

First of all, I feel gratitude beyond measure and expression for my parents, Valerie and Ken—Base Camp. There isn't sufficient space here to describe all their gifts, all the lessons they have taught by word and example, and all their support and love, so let's just say they have gone many thousands of miles beyond parental duty and leave it at that. Of one thing I am absolutely certain: if all parents approached their role as selflessly, compassionately, and thoughtfully as mine, the world would be a far better place.

I am grateful for my three brothers: Philip, Paul, and Stephen, not just for the part they played in a remarkable childhood, but also for the unique qualities each one brings to the world. My brothers continue to inspire me. Because of them I am more than I would ever have been.

I am grateful for my grandparents, Violet and Denis Terrill, and Lilian and Kenneth Hayward, for the unconditional love they gave. I feel special gratitude for 'Grandpa' Hayward for taking my brothers and I 'up the woods' so many times. Short in distance those walks may have been, but they had lasting impact. It was Grandpa who first revealed to me nature's magical side.

I am grateful for Sue Girvan, one of the most selfless individuals I have known. As 'Akela' she made my first camps possible, and as a friend later in life she has demonstrated the power of giving. Generations have benefited from Sue's many gifts, and the world is a more loving place because of her.

When I made the decision to begin my walk without sufficient funds to finish it, several individuals and businesses answered my cry for help. Without that support the journey would have floundered. In alphabetical order, I need to express my sincerest appreciation to: Bridgedale, for donating twenty-four pairs of hiking socks; Color Line, for granting me free ferry passage from Denmark to Norway and from Norway to England; the Cotswold Outdoor store in Shepherd's Bush, London, for offering a generous discount on much-needed backpacking gear; First Ascent, for donating two Therm-a-Rest sleeping pads; Fuji Film, for twice donating 200 rolls of Fuji Velvia slide film, first for my Europe walk and then again for my journey up the Rockies three years later; the National Map Centre for donating many of the maps I needed; Lowe Alpine, for generously donating two rucksacks, two sets of waterproofs, and an entire wardrobe of backpacking clothes;

Paul Brown and Dan Thory from Rex Interstock Photo Library (now Shutterstock), for processing for free all my photos from the journey, cataloguing them, and then forwarding them to media outlets as needed; the late Robert Saunders, a pioneer of lightweight backpacking tents and a genius in the tent-making craft, who twice gave me Jetpacker tents for my long walks; and Steve Roberts from the Scarpa Mountain Boot Company Ltd, for donating three pairs of Manta boots for my walk up Europe, and further pairs for the walks that followed. Although unconnected to this journey, I also owe a great debt to Philip Barnett for funding my 6,000-mile journey up the Rockies through his business, Radical Ltd.

The Walk generated a modest amount of publicity at the time it took place, and I would like to thank all the media outlets that considered it worth covering. I am especially grateful to Ian McMaster and *Spotlight Verlag* magazine, for coming on board as a part sponsor; the editors at the *Daily Express* and the *Express on Sunday*, who helped the journey reach a far larger audience than it might otherwise have reached; and the team at the now-defunct travel website, *TravelDex*, for hosting my online trail reports.

Even though my exploits could never compare with theirs, I received incredible encouragement and support from the staff and volunteers at the Cardinal Hume Centre and The Passage. I remain in awe of the work they do and the dedication with which they do it. They are the ones doing the wonderful thing.

I am grateful to everyone who donated to The Passage and the Cardinal Hume Centre. There are far too many people to list, but their generosity made a real difference to real lives. It remains an absolute inspiration.

My appreciation and thanks go to the many friends and strangers who wrote to me while I was walking. The encouragement made a lasting difference, often boosting my morale when a boost was very much needed.

I am grateful for *all* the people of Europe I met during the journey. A small number of them appear in this manuscript, most do not, but they are all appreciated for how they enriched The Walk. Some of them gave extraordinary assistance and hospitality to a complete stranger in his hour of need—their trust, generosity and friendship will never be forgotten. A few of them—for reasons only known to themselves—added to my adventure by withholding help, by turning me away. I am especially grateful for this, for how it revealed the true power of kindness. These people taught more than they will ever know, and my gratitude for them endures.

I wish to thank the many individuals who have supported my writing over the years, including Geoff Birtles, former editor at *High Mountain Sports* magazine, who took a chance on an unknown writer almost 30 years ago and published my first outdoor feature; and Cameron McNeish and John Manning, former editor and deputy editor of *The Great Outdoors* magazine, who turned me into a writer through years of encouragement. My thanks also goes to Emily Rodway and

Carey Davies, former and current editors at *The Great Outdoors*, for continuing to support and encourage my work. Without their patronage it is likely this book would never have been written.

I wish to thank a true friend, Bryan Palmintier, for patiently loaning his slide scanner far longer than was probably expected. I would also like to thank Danielle Grandquist, Bard Warden, and Victoria Wolf for rescuing me from the web design crevasse I fell into while foolishly travelling solo and unroped.

My gratitude goes to all the individuals who gave up their time to read my manuscript and provide feedback, including Jillian Lloyd and John Henzell, and especially my incredible beta readers: Mike Dano, Kate Gilliver, Ingrid Marshall, John Manning, and Doug Skiba. They went far deeper than I could have hoped, and bravely and honestly voiced their criticisms. Without their suggestions my story would still meander like a hiker lost in fog, and would occasionally make as little sense as every single Calabrian map I ever held.

I am beyond grateful to my editor, Alex Roddie, who didn't just fix the many grammatical errors in my manuscript but also suggested ways to significantly improve the story. For years I had a hard time believing that the praise authors heap upon their editors could be deserved, but now I finally get it. I am in debt to Alex for his astonishing attention to detail, his insightful observations, and above all for his clear vision. A great editor can take a manuscript to the next level, and that is exactly what Alex did.

I am grateful to Liz Jones, who proofed the final manuscript with extraordinary attention to detail. Talk about eagle-eyed! I wish Italian cartographers could have called upon Liz before I'd used their maps. I'd have been lost far less often.

Last but definitely not least, I am grateful for my three partners-in-life: my wife, Joan, and my two children, Riley and Naomi. My walks into wild nature led to a level of happiness and fulfillment I once imagined was impossible elsewhere, but Joan, Riley and Naomi have proved that my imagination was seriously flawed. Riley and Naomi are extraordinary human beings, more compassionate and aware than I was at even twice their age. They have shown me more about life than I have taught them, and astonish me, inspire me, and bring joy to me every single day. Joan does all that too, and more. She makes the darkest winter nights bright; life's most confusing fogs clear; the rockiest summits reachable; and the most mundane of life's trails the most meaningful to follow. She is one of those rare people that others flock to for the way being near her lifts one to a calmer, happier place. Her extraordinary patience during the decades-long writing of this book says everything that needs to be said. As Mad Mountain Jack I merely *thought* life was complete, but with Joan by my side I *know* life is. No lonely mountain vagabond could ever dream up a more perfect partner.

—Andrew Terrill, Golden, Colorado, March 2021.

A PLEA FOR THE HOMELESS

MY WALK across Europe raised awareness and funds for The Passage and the Cardinal Hume Centre. Both charities are still at work, taking care of the immediate needs of individuals and families who no longer have homes, and providing a passage for them back into society. Both charities still need support.

During my walk, many of the physical hardships I experienced set me imagining what it might be like to live beyond society's edge. More significantly, I also experienced a brief glimpse of the mental disintegration that can occur when one is looked at with disgust and is treated like dirt. Even though I had chosen my situation, my self-esteem and mental health still took a hit. The speed with which I began doubting my self-worth still shocks me.

I hope that the story of my walk did more than entertain. I hope you were also moved. Out of respect for the work it took to write, I hope you will put aside five minutes to go on a short journey—a journey of empathy to the far side of a chasm that I hope you will never experience for real.

So please, go and sit outside right now, or imagine yourself outside—and try to imagine having no inside to retreat to. Imagine that the home you currently have, and all your possessions, and the income and supports that make it all possible, and the people you rely on have all been snatched away by events beyond your control. Imagine not knowing where to turn for help, or where to look for shelter. Imagine not having easy access to water, not knowing when next you'll eat. Imagine rain soaking into your clothes, and wind cutting through to your core, and grime covering your body. Imagine people passing by (looking so warm, well-fed, well-dressed, and comfortable). Imagine them looking at you with swift sideways glances, but then turning away in either discomfort or disapproval, their minds made up, ignoring you as though you don't exist. Imagine how that makes you feel: how small, discarded, and worthless. Imagine lying down to sleep not knowing if your few possessions will be there when you wake; imagine walking all night simply to stay alive. Imagine living in constant fear for your safety, and in a constant state of despair, or perhaps even worse, in a state of numb, uncaring acceptance. Imagine your health—physical and mental—rapidly failing. Imagine that you can't even imagine a life indoors any longer. That life is for other people. Not for you.

Are you imagining it?

But then imagine someone stepping forward to help.

Below are details of the two charities I walked for. I hope you are in a position to help. Truly, no amount is too small.

THE PASSAGE

The Passage has been working with street homeless people in Central London for over forty years, providing resources which encourage, inspire and challenge them to transform their lives. We start by making contact with people on the street through outreach work. Our resource centre provides a warm welcome each day offering basic services of showers, clean clothes, and food and drink, followed by advice and help with a whole range of issues including mental health, substance misuse, physical healthcare, finding housing, employment and claiming welfare rights. We provide supportive hostels and follow-on support once people move into self-contained accommodation to avoid loneliness and isolation and the risk of repeat homelessness. We help over 3,000 individuals each year.

passage.org.uk/homelesswalk/

THE CARDINAL HUME CENTRE

Everyone should have a full life, but poverty at a young age can steal that potential. Too often poverty and homelessness in early life are repeated and compounded into later life. The Cardinal Hume Centre has been supporting people out of poverty and homelessness since 1986. Our approach is to build a relationship with each individual, to recognise everyone is different and often face complex and interrelated challenges. We proudly stick to the ethos of our founder, Cardinal Basil Hume. We provide a place of welcome, sanctuary and support to everyone who comes to the Centre. In any year we support more than 1,500 people with critical practical advice and support, our foodbank, access to our family area, and our hostel for young people.

cardinalhumecentre.org.uk/the-earth-beneath-my-feet

ABOUT THE PUBLISHER

ENCHANTED ROCK PRESS, LLC, is an independent book publishing imprint founded to celebrate the remarkable, fragile and enchanted planet we call home. Supported by publishing professionals, our mission is to share experiences that transport readers into the wild. We want to inspire people to step outdoors into our planet's enchanted places, and we want to do it in a way that encourages a thoughtful, joyful, and above all respectful approach.

As a small publisher, we face an uphill task (appropriately, given our mountain-themed subject matter) to reach a broader audience. If you have enjoyed this book, please tell other readers about it, and *please* consider leaving a review on Amazon, Goodreads.com, or elsewhere. Your review will make all the difference in the world. Thank you.

AUTHOR'S BIOGRAPHY

ANDREW TERRILL grew up in Pinner, suburban London, far removed from mountains and wild places. He didn't step onto a mountain until he was fifteen, but after that there was no going back. In the three and a half decades since, travelling on foot into wild nature has been a central part of his life. After completing several ultra-long walks, he settled in Colorado, where he now lives with his wife and two children. Open country lies just steps from his front door, and rarely a day passes without him visiting it. A regular contributor to *The Great Outdoors* magazine over the past two decades, *The Earth Beneath My Feet* is his debut book. He has plans for further long walks.

Learn more at **andrewterrill.com**.

Made in the USA
Coppell, TX
03 December 2022

87680163R00218